Women in War Films

Women in War Films

From Helpless Heroine to G.I. Jane

Ralph Donald
Karen MacDonald

ROWMAN & LITTLEFIELD
Lanham • Boulder • New York • Toronto • Plymouth, UK

Published by Rowman & Littlefield
4501 Forbes Boulevard, Suite 200, Lanham, Maryland 20706
www.rowman.com

Unit A, Whitacre Mews, 26-34 Stannary Street, London SE11 4AB

British Library Cataloguing in Publication Information Available

Library of Congress Cataloging-in-Publication Data
The hardback edition of this book was previously catalogued by the Library of Congress as follows:

Donald, Ralph.
Women in war films : from helpless heroine to G.I. Jane / Ralph R. Donald, Karen MacDonald.
pages cm
Includes bibliographical references and index.
Includes filmography.
1. War films—History and criticism. 2. Women in motion pictures. 3. Sex role in motion pictures. I.
MacDonald, Karen, 1947– II. Title.
PN1995.9.W3D635 2014
791.43'6522—dc23
2013048582

ISBN 978-1-4422-3446-8 (cloth : alk. paper)
ISBN 978-1-4422-7563-8 (pbk. : alk. paper)
ISBN 978-1-4422-3447-5 (ebook : alk. paper)

Printed in the United States of America

Contents

Chapter One

Introduction

Most war films, especially the more intense combat films, focus on men fighting their wars. Anthropologists tell us that from the earliest times, men did the hunting and fighting, leaving women to do the really hard work back at the cave. Hollywood, a bastion of male power, has traditionally made sure that war films clearly show combat to be a man's job, unsuitable for women, due to the female's nurturing and nonbelligerent nature. To change this established order threatens to revise gender identities developed over centuries of social construction. Judith Hicks Stiehm wrote in 1981: "Were women to enter combat, men would lose a crucial identity—warrior. This is the only role now exclusively theirs, the one that is as male-defining as child-bearing is female defining" (296).

Susan Jeffords quotes William Broyles, Vietnam veteran and former editor of *Newsweek*, who adds more:

> War is an initiation into the power of life and death. Women touch that power at the moment of birth; men on the edge of death. . . . [War is] for men at some terrible level the closest thing to what childbirth is for women: the initiation into the power of life and death. Following this logic, men who don't go to war now have a sort of nostalgic longing for something they missed, some classic male experience, the way some women who didn't have children worry they missed something basic about being a woman. (1990, 203)

In 1989, both Jeffords and Eric Leed asserted that war, as a gendering activity, is one of the few remaining "male experiences" in our society. Until 2013, even the increasingly androgynous American armed forces' liberalizing of rules and regulations regarding sexual equality has stopped short of absolute parity in many combat assignments. Female casualty lists in Iraq and Afghanistan notwithstanding, the United States' paternalistic culture seems to stop short of equality when deciding whether to order women into harm's way. Even the 2013 announcement by the Defense Department that women will be allowed to fight on the front lines next to the men falls short of total equality because (1) this new liberalization will take as much as ten years to percolate through the commands to all levels and in all combat specialties and (2) women are only allowed the opportunity to "qualify" for combat assignments.

In the history of American war films, when women do fight, Hollywood often displays it as an aberration. For example, in the 1943 war/fantasy film, *A Guy Named Joe*, Irene Dunne flies a dangerous bombing mission against the Japanese, but does so without official permission, and only with guardian angel pilot Spencer Tracy to assist her with the manlier, tactical aspects of flying a bombing run. Or in occupied countries films such as *This Land Is Mine* (1943) and *Edge of Darkness* (1943), Maureen O'Hara and Ann Sheridan stand up bravely against the Nazis, but only as civilians resisting an occupying force, not as uniformed soldiers. In more recent years, roles such as Meg Ryan's in *Courage under Fire* (1996) and Demi Moore's in *G.I. Jane* (1997) have pushed back against traditional gender restraints in war films. However, as major plot impediments to these heroines' success in their quests, these films' screenplays constantly remind audiences about their femininity and the overt and covert gender discrimination they encounter in American military culture. Although science fiction war films often place women on the battlefield and even promote them to positions of command, these roles exist in a future that has not yet fully materialized.

Like Homer, when he placed Menelaus's errant wife, Helen, right in the middle of *The Iliad*, Hollywood has often included women in war films to provide a "love interest," or in Homer's case, to explain one of the chief reasons that men fight each other. Including women in their war film screenplays is simplistically explained as an old Hollywood formula for box office: providing their heroes with heroines to attract and distract and/or to add some more sex appeal to a film. Trailers promoted these women as afterthoughts to the combat scenes, reminding audiences that besides watching the fighting men kill the enemy, they will learn about "the women who loved them." Critics and historians usually conclude that producers have added the women to expand the appeal of a war film to potential female audience members and/or to titillate the male audience with primitive, archetypal emotions about the male defending the female from invading marauders.

A writer on the Helium website with the nom de plume of Charlotte Starlet notes, "The representation of women across all media tends to focus on the following: beauty, size/physique, sexuality, emotional (as opposed to intellectual) dealings and relationships (as opposed to independence/freedom)." Laura Mulvey, regarded as one of the most prominent feminist film critics, is famously quoted as saying, 'narrative fiction film created images of women used for the gratification of men.'" In "Television and Gender Roles," Daniel Chandler (n.d.) concurs: "Viewers are frequently invited to identify with male characters and to objectify females. This has been called 'the male gaze.' This mode of viewing . . . is an invisible and largely unquestioned bias—the masculine perspective is the 'norm.' Girls learn from most TV that it is a man's world, and learn to displace their own perspective."

Although Annette Kuhn credits feminism with spurring improvements in the social construction of sexuality, she adds that even in the "second wave" of feminism in the 1960s, images of women can still be "criticized by feminists on the grounds that they objectify women—that is to say legitimate and constitute social support for an ideological construction of women as objects, in particular as objects of evaluation in terms of socially predefined visible criteria of beauty and attractiveness" (5–6).

But there are many other reasons besides objectification for women to appear in war films. And in war films, the roles that women really play are often more complex and certainly more varied. This book discusses what those roles might be, and what past and present treatments of women in war films explicate and inform audiences about our culture. The movies discussed within these pages were written and produced either by Americans or by other English-speaking producers. All films mentioned received major distribution to audiences in the United States.

A RELATIONAL CONSTRUCT

Before proceeding with our discussion of female roles in war films, we will devote a few paragraphs, as we did in our 2011 book, *Reel Men at War: Masculinity and the American War Film*, to men's socially constructed and perceived differences between the sexes, because how men in war view women becomes a key motivator for both their behaviors and that of "the women who loved them."

Of all the military's initiatory customs and practices, probably the most significant is the physical and symbolic separation of neophyte soldiers from the world of women. But Americans begin to establish this separation long before boys reach puberty. Michael Kimmel (1987) writes that gender is a relational construct, providing males with the opposite sex as a basis of negative comparison and a clearly drawn, inferior role model. Jo Freeman and Nancy Henley (1994) note that nonverbal communication differences in women and men reinforce the inferior role model concept. Women are socialized to project deference to the male by using more restrained, subtle gestures that communicate a deferential subservience. The male is socialized to use more obvious gestures, often using their hands to exhibit confidence and power.

Practically from the time an American boy child is old enough to understand English, he hears that "Big boys don't cry: Only girls do," or other discriminatory behavioral prohibitions, such as "Don't play with dolls: Dolls are for girls," and "That scraped knee doesn't really hurt a little man like you, does it?" In various ways, boys are shown multiple examples of the so-called inferior, flawed, incomplete variety of human being they must avoid at all costs becoming: a female. By the time most boys reach manhood, having experienced so much negative comparison with girls, it's not surprising that they have become convinced that females must somehow be grossly inferior to males—at least with respect to traditionally male activities and behaviors, such as making war. And by systematically excluding females from their sports teams, clubs, the "old-boy" network in business, top government positions, and from combat roles in the military (at least until quite recently), a self-fulfilling set of male role definitions has become firmly imbedded in American history and culture. And needless to say, in Hollywood, a patriarchy if there ever was one, nearly every film is written and produced from the paternalistic perspective, as if there is no other possible point of view on the planet.

This mind-set is easily seen in the behaviors of young men's instructors in military basic training. At the outset of training, recruits are not automatically given the status of soldiers. This distinction they must earn. Initially, they are labeled everything from "maggots" to "boots," "trainees," or "young people"—never full-fledged Marines, soldiers, sailors, or airmen. Significantly, recruits are not even initially permitted the status of full-fledged males. Often derisively called "girls" or "ladies" by their drill instructors, recruits must earn their manhood by successfully completing their training. Failure to achieve the benchmarks of their training is labeled as a weakness, associated with the female, asserting the importance of measuring up to the standards that society demands of a male. In *The D.I.* (1957), when drill instructor Sgt. Moore (Jack Webb) reports to his company commander that a certain recruit continuously "fouls up" in his training, the captain insists that harsh treatment will shape up this recruit. Webb is hesitant to push the youngster too far too fast, but the commander orders immediate action: Otherwise he threatens to personally assist Webb in "cutting the lace off his panties." Obviously, the company commander buys into the notion that weakness or inability to perform in the male is due to his overinvestment in female attributes and behaviors.

Making this notion even more plausible is the fact that the female brain produces more oxytocin than the male brain. Oxytocin is the neurochemical which promotes nurturing behaviors, thus creating female attributes and behaviors associated with caregiving (Hanson and Mendius 2009, 36). And caretaking is the antithesis to the bellicose, antisocial, warrior-like behaviors the company commander is intent on instilling in his recruits.

Monica Henry (2006) reminds us that gender roles and societal expectations begin long before adulthood:

> Women and men are socialized from childhood on to adopt specific gender roles—man as warrior, woman as caretaker. These gendered roles, strongly influenced by cultural expectations, are reflected in both film and novel. In so doing, they are presented as "natural" and thus reinforced. Femininity is often associated with such traits as emotionality, prudence, cooperativeness, compliance, affection, gentleness, sympathy, dependence, support and nurturing. In contrast, masculinity tends to be linked with rationality, power, strength, competitiveness, ruthlessness, aggression, assertiveness, independence, risk-taking behavior, courageousness and adventurousness. Based on these cultural stereotypes, in both film and novels, male characters are predominantly depicted as being more dominant, violent and powerful than their female counterparts. (2)

EQUATING HOMOSEXUALS TO WOMEN, OR "FAILED MEN"

When a drill instructor (DI) tires of using the female comparative as the undesired mode of behavior, another way to denigrate a recruit's manhood is to implicitly or explicitly imply that the soldier is a homosexual. Again the notion is the same as in *The D.I.*, that anything less than full-on manliness is too feminine for males in the service. And in the military, a quick shorthand for too feminine—and therefore a failure as a man—is to label a man as a homosexual. Just to begin the process of making his training goals clear to recruits, in *Full Metal Jacket* (1987), when a young man announces that he hails from Texas, the D.I. (R. Lee Ermey) retorts with this verbal assault:

D.I.: Holy dog shit! Texas! Only steers and queers come from Texas, Private "Cowboy," and you don't much look like a steer to me, so that kinda narrows it down. Do you suck dicks?

Cowboy: Sir, no sir!

D.I.: Are you a peter pumper?

Cowboy: Sir, no sir!

D.I.: I bet you're the kinda guy who would fuck a person in the ass and not even have the goddamn common courtesy to give him a reach-around! I'll be watchin' you. (*Full Metal Jacket*, 1987)

In Air Force basic training, one of your authors heard the same speech from a training instructor, directed at a basic trainee from California. Instead of "steers and queers," he substituted "fruits and nuts" to construct his metaphor.

Similarly, in *Jarhead* (2005), an equally odious and verbally abusive D.I., Sgt. Fitch (Scott MacDonald), insultingly introduces himself to Pvt. Anthony Swofford (Jake Gyllenhaal):

Fitch: Are you eyeballin' me with those baby blues? *(then he shouts)* Are you?

Swofford: *(also shouting, as is required)* Sir, no sir!

Fitch: Are you in love with me, Swofford?

Swofford: Sir, no sir!

Fitch: Oh, you don't think I look good in my uniform, Swofford?

Swofford: Sir, the drill instructor looks fabulous in his uniform, sir!

Fitch: So you're gay then, and you love me, huh?

Swofford: Sir, I'm not gay, sir!

Fitch: Do you have a girlfriend, Swofford?

Swofford: Sir, yes sir!

Fitch: Guess again, motherfucker. Jody's bangin' her right now ["Jody" is a nickname for men who do not serve in the military, but instead stay home and poach GI's wives and girlfriends]. Get on your face and give me 25 for every time she gets fucked this month. Down on your face!

Swofford: *(in a voice over, as he does his push-ups on the floor)* It was shortly after meeting Drill Instructor Fitch that I realized that joining the Marine Corps might have been a bad decision. (*Jarhead*, 2005)

WHAT WOMEN CAN ACCOMPLISH, COMPARED TO MEN

We find culturally defined differences and limitations for women reflected by Hollywood screenplays. At one point in her seminal book on this subject, *The World War II Combat Film: Anatomy of a Genre*, Jeanine Basinger compares the genre of the women's film to the genre of the war film to demonstrate that men have an automatic advantage in war. Significantly absent, Basinger writes, from most women's films is their ability to set aside petty jealousies and rivalries and work together to achieve a common goal. In contrast, in wartime, Basinger asserts, men can set aside their own wants and needs for the good of the group, or "team," as they have done so many times in athletic contests. Perhaps athletics in their youth give men an experiential advantage when they work closely together in combat (1986, 224).

> Traditionally, a woman's film is passive and the male active. No matter where a woman goes, she takes her restrictive condition of femininity with her. . . . She is acted upon, and even if she . . . takes some kind of action, she has generally been forced into it. . . . From genre to genre, from Brooklyn to Bombay, from cave days to now, she is trapped in the sense that social limitations restrict her life. Her problem is external (society presses down on her and limits her) and internal (she must figure out what she can do about it). (1986, 225)

To sum up these restrictions on women as found in not only war films but in other genres, Basinger writes: "Women tend to be depicted as imprisoned by their emotions, rather than liberated by their actions. Men can set aside their feelings to get the job done, but women are much more complicated, and their emotions can color the outcome of an action, for good or not" (1986, 226).

WOMEN'S ROLES AS SEEN BY HASKELL AND TASKER

Molly Haskell, chronicling the evolution of the treatment of women in the movies in her groundbreaking 1973 book on women in the movies, *From Reverence to Rape*, characterized the best women's roles of the 1960s through the 1970s as "whores, quasi-whores, jilted mistresses, emotional cripples, drunks, daffy ingénues, Lolitas, kooks, sex-starved spinsters, psychotics, icebergs, zombies and ball-breakers. That's what little girls of the '60s and '70s are made of" (327). Women play as many roles in such movies as they do in life. But in genre films such as war pictures, women often are more narrowly drawn because they must serve the needs of the bellicose narrative.

Yvonne Tasker theorizes two recurrent tropes for women in war and labels them as either an auxiliary or a provocative presence (2011, 9). What she means by the term *auxiliary* relates to women's place in most war scenarios, in supporting rather than leading roles. Tasker reminds us that in modern times, World War I spawned the need for women's auxiliary services, which grew in involvement and corresponding hazards for women during World War II. In *Battle of Britain* (1969), demonstrating the downside of women donning uniforms during the Blitz, is Section Officer Maggie Harvey (Susannah York), who encounters a row of blanket-covered bodies of fellow WAAF (Women's Auxiliary Air Force) personnel killed in a German bombing raid on their airfield.

Tasker reminds us that the presence of women provokes significantly different behavior among men, compared to how they would act in an all-male environment. In war films, women may be aspiring soldiers representing competition with males for dominance or distinction in this formerly all-boys club. If they're only present in men's thoughts and in flashbacks (especially during war films of the 1950s), women may be the mothers, wives, and sweethearts back home. Women in men's midst while they're trying to wage war could represent a strange, alien presence that affects male decision making and behavior. Regardless of circumstance, Tasker writes, in the worlds and minds of men, women become provocateurs (12–13).

KOMISAR'S ROLES

Lucy Komisar writes that in most war films, men relegate women to three basic roles. The first she describes as the Madonna: mothers, sisters, daughters, or girlfriends that men put on a pedestal to revere and respect. The purity of heart and behavior of most of these pedestal dwellers put them almost into the realm of the idealized. The second role is much more ambiguous: women variously assigned roles as chattel to acquire and use legally in marriage, or illegally via assault and rape. Some of those categorized as chattel possess the qualities of the Madonna, while others do not. Komisar's third category refers to either "loose" women or prostitutes, who provide temporary satisfaction while the men are away from home (1976, 202–3).

In each of these three categories, Komisar asserts that women remain "the other," a separate and clearly unequal entity that men in war films clearly find distracting to the bellicose task at hand. Yet the men find these women a useful and attractive commodity to think, dream, make plans about or have on hand for what a soldier in *Casualties of War* (1989) defined as "portable R and R." But to fully explicate a more complete typology of women's roles in war films, we must expand significantly on Komisar's list and discuss additional varieties.

HAWKSIAN WOMEN

Another role is a variation on Komisar's second, the chattel type. But depending on the screenplay, this kind of woman can possess aspects of the other two categories as well. This variety of female actor found mostly in war, Western, and adventure films is sometimes referred to in film theory and criticism as the "Hawksian Woman." Classic American directors such as Howard Hawks and John Ford posited obliquely in many of their films that men simply cannot do their jobs efficiently if women are present, or worse yet, *involved* in the undertaking, because men are so easily distracted.

(McBride 1982, 96) As crafted on the screen by Hawks, Ford, and many other writers and directors, these women do not relate to other women nearly as well as they do to men. They're more comfortable in the company of men, and sometimes have backstories (sexual, criminal, or otherwise) that they're not proud of, marking a Hawksian woman a mild to serious threat to any totally "respectable" woman. These independent, self-assured Hawksian women can dish it out with the men, and most of them can take it, too, and it truly irks them when more traditional Madonnas—whom they sometimes look down upon—shun them.

THE GI JANE ROLE

In the latter twentieth century and continuing today, the feminist movement has created more equality and opportunity for women. One of the products of equality in the U.S. Armed Forces is another category of women in war films. In the last decade especially, a more bellicose, aggressive, and some say more "manly" woman has made her appearance in war films. Similar in many respects to the Hawksian woman, she may be more comfortable in a world of male warriors, but she is unlike the majority of Hawks's females, who are mostly noncombatants who are content to kibitz and moralize with the men about what's going on but leave the actual fighting to the menfolk. Instead, either by circumstance or design, a GI Jane actually becomes a participant in a war. Call her a "Rambette" (a female Rambo), as some writers quipped about reluctant warrior Sigourney Weaver when the Vietnam War allegory *Aliens* (1986) was released and again when the TV series *Xena, Warrior Princess* premiered, or, more recently, by the character names we encounter in war pictures and science fiction war films such as *G.I. Jane* (1997), *Aliens* (1986), *Enemy at the Gates* (2001), *Cross of Iron* (1976), *Serenity* (2005), *Courage under Fire* (1996), *The Lucky Ones* (2008), *Starship Troopers* (1997), *Wing Commander* (1999), and *The Guns of Navarone* (1961).

THE SPY

In addition to GI Janes who stand and fight as soldiers, another role for a woman who is an active participant in war is the spy, also called a Mata Hari. Some are what might be called professional spies, such as the famous World War I intelligence agent for Germany, Mata Hari. Other women are thrust into the spy business because their occupation, language, or other skills or relationships put them in a unique position to gather intelligence or even actively engage in sabotage, assassination, and other warlike activities. Such roles are extremely varied. When discussing the female combatant, we will also examine the role of female resistance fighters in occupied countries. We will find that the behavior of these resistance fighters often includes combinations of espionage and fighting.

NURSES AND DOCTORS

In addition, since directors such as D. W. Griffith produced war films as far back as during World War I, there has existed yet another female role, distinct because of her occupation, that appears frequently in films in the war genre. One can refer to her generically as a member of an auxiliary unit, but more frequently as a nurse, doctor, or other aid worker. Women have served as camp followers as long as groups of men have been fighting each other. However, many camp followers could fall under the heading of loose women or prostitutes rather than as angels of mercy such as nurses. Filmmakers often use nurses as convenient love interests in their war films, since they're at hand. In some instances, screenplays have permitted women to bend or break nurses' nonfraternization rules with soldiers. Some, then, are sexually involved with the fighting men they nurse back to health, and some are not, simply portrayed as selfless, pristine Madonnas, aiding the American war effort in as ladylike a manner as practical under the circumstances. Occasionally women are permitted the role of doctors, but unlike male doctors, women physicians in war films are rarely treated with the same godlike respect.

In all cases, as we document, interpret, and analyze the roles of women in war films, we will continually touch on three intertwined objectives. The first is to chronicle the evolution of female roles from the earliest motion pictures about war to modern-day war films, including movies that are a mixture of significant war content and other genres. The second is to discuss both the sociology and psychology of the sexes as war and gender intersect. Finally, we will interpret the messages that women's presence in and near the manly world of war tell audiences about how men coexist with, use, and marginalize "the other."

Chapter Two

Mothers, Daughters, Sisters, and Girlfriends

The Madonnas

As discussed in chapter 1, the Madonna role consists of the mothers, daughters, sisters, and girlfriends whom men in war films protect, revere, respect (mostly), and objectify.

As Western culture was transitioning from the Victorian era, the invention of the motion picture permitted stories, heretofore restricted to the novel or the stage, to be acted out in the silent film. Harry Benshoff and Sean Griffin (2009) describe this post-Victorian Madonna thusly:

> She was childlike, and frequently associated with innocence, purity and the need to be protected. She was often put on a pedestal and worshiped by the men in her life, namely her father and her brothers. When she got to a certain age, she would be married off to a suitable young man. . . . The young woman would then become a wife and mother. (218)

Susan Jeffords (1995) refers to the "traditional depiction of the feminine character" in war films as "passive, fearful, manipulable, submissive," hardly a position of strength, and thus easy to control (428). In war films made shortly after the birth of the medium of film, this was the Madonna's restrictive role. In most of these filmed melodramas, men resolved the screenwriters' plot objectives and rescued women from the clutches of evil antagonists. Lillian Gish's character, first called "The Girl," and later identified as Marie, in D. W. Griffith's World War I film, *Hearts of the World* (1918) was a silent era Madonna prototype. But before that, in 1915, Griffith's *The Birth of a Nation* demonstrated that for the most part, women in Griffith's melodramas would be as restricted as they were in Victorian times. In *Birth,* Elsie and Flora, played by Lillian Gish and Mae Marsh, were relegated to keeping home and hearth like good little Madonnas and to serve as the love interests of the male members of the cast as they come and go, doing all the important things in the film. Males went out to fight for the South during the Civil War and then returned to do battle all over again defending their homes, their honor, and their womenfolk against Yankee carpetbaggers, scallywags, and freed blacks.

In the second half of *The Birth of a Nation*, basically an ill-considered homage to the post–Civil War Ku Klux Klan, there are great threats to the womenfolk. In the climax, representing the Klan, the principal male characters rescue the women in typical Griffith fashion at the last second, saving them from rape and possible murder in the hands of Black militiamen. Besides locking themselves in a room to hide from the invaders, the only initiative these Madonnas seem to take is to consider whether a bullet to the head might be preferable to a fate worse than death.

GRIFFITH'S WWI MADONNA

In *Hearts of the World,* Marie's sole interest before World War I starts is purely romantic: to capture the love of neighbor and American expatriate Douglas (Robert Harron), who lives with his parents in Marie's little French village. As a teenager, she prays for divine assistance in winning Douglas's heart, and as the years pass, according to a title card, "Time brings to the Girl interest in fashions and other little nets to catch love, after the manner of the world." Although Douglas has career interests to pursue, Marie's sole purpose in life appears to be snaring Douglas and becoming his wife.

Douglas certainly notices Marie and returns her romantic interest. He writes her poetry, and in one interesting scene, DWG shows the audience in close-up how he admires her ankles, which is all that is exposed under the Victorian-style long skirts of the time.

However, not all women in *Hearts of the World* are of the category we will occasionally refer to in this book as "helpless Madonnas." Lillian's sister, Dorothy Gish, plays the role of "The Little Disturber," a Gypsy girl who wanders into the village, providing Marie a little competition for Douglas. The audience is given little backstory about The Little Disturber, but the audience watches her earn her living as a street entertainer. Whether or not this Gypsy augments her income as a prostitute or a thief—or both—is impossible to tell, but in terms of this book's stated female roles, The Little Disturber should at least be categorized as chattel. From the start, we see that The Little Disturber is quite different from the passive Marie, who seems incapable, either by nature or nurture or both, to do anything at all for herself until much later in the film. The Little Disturber, on the other hand, seems capable of taking care of herself, while Marie is supported by her parents, in the manner of a child, as described above by Henshoff and Griffin.

Unlike the demure Marie, The Little Disturber is also quite sexually liberated for the era. This is another reason modern audiences may suspect that she is experienced in love and romance. The Little Disturber doesn't waste much time boldly making a pass for Douglas, who rebuffs her. That doesn't faze her, as she continues to follow him around the town in the manner today we would describe as a stalker. Contrast this to Marie, who passively waits, batting her eyelashes, hoping Douglas will make the first move.

On one of the occasions when The Little Disturber romantically accosts Douglas, Marie is nearby and observes the part of their interaction that wrongly appears as if Douglas accepts her advances. But typical of the helpless Madonna, Marie simply shuffles away in tears. Instead of standing up for herself and doing anything about a rival trying to seduce her boyfriend, Marie sits at home, impotent, waiting and fretting. Douglas, still true blue, goes to great lengths to convince Marie that The Little Disturber means nothing to him, vowing his love for Marie, "forever and ever." As if to prove his affection, he proposes and she quickly accepts. They are betrothed.

Meanwhile, a German spy named Von Strohm (George Siegmann) appears, posing as a tourist, surreptitiously mapping out the town for what DWG implies is Germany's malice aforethought, their planned future aggression toward France. (Interestingly, silent film director and actor Erich von Stroheim plays a minor role as a German soldier in this film, and likely his colleague Griffith used a variation on von Stroheim's name to create the villain character Von Strohm). While engaged in his military reconnoitering, the German spots Marie and is attracted to her, making bold but clumsy advances. True to both Marie's faithful affection for Douglas and her distaste for Germans (after all, this is a propaganda film), Marie, in the first sign of any backbone in this picture, makes it known to the spy that she rejects his suit.

Then comes the war, upending Douglas and Marie's wedding plans, as Douglas enlists in the French Army. Marie waves a wet hankie as her fiancé marches off to battle, and true to the role of the helpless Madonna, tearfully packs away her wedding things in her hope chest until Douglas comes home.

The war devastates the village. Apparently, during Von Strohm's intelligence gathering before the war, he determined that this village is of some kind of strategic importance. Thus the Germans make the possession of the village a priority. Many French civilians are killed in the German assault, including Douglas's and Marie's parents. In the battle for the town, Douglas is wounded. Marie, finally doing something, uses ripped pieces of her wedding dress for bandages for the wounded. However, the sight of all this devastation is traumatic for Marie's delicate sensibilities, and she ends up wandering about in the rubble, half-dazed. This is when she happens upon the wounded Douglas, lying apparently lifeless. This causes Marie—never much of a coper to begin with—to turn nearly catatonic, but The Little Disturber—now her friend and ally in this time of war—nurses her back to health. After witnessing friends and family die at the hands of the Germans, Marie exhibits posttraumatic stress disorder (PTSD) symptoms. When she finds Douglas and thinks he is dead, she reflects the freeze response inherent in the fight, flight, freeze symptoms of PTSD.

Finally, the French are driven back and the Germans occupy the town.

In *Hearts of the World* and many other "occupied countries"-themed war films produced with propaganda in mind, there is a constant threat of rape, mistreatment, and even murder against women. Of course, such threats are acted out or implied only by the enemy. Nearly universally, the occupying army is portrayed as dismissive of the local townspeople, considering them inferior creatures. Having conquered them, the enemy shows these defeated people no respect or consideration of their human rights. Especially in these scenarios, the enemy considers women not as Madonnas, but as chattel: part of the spoils of war. It is thus with the invading Huns of this war epic. Actually, it is the same formula and treatment of women that DWG had used throughout his career. Usually, his films end with male heroes rescuing women about to be ravaged by some beastly stereotypical villain, twirling his moustache in gleeful anticipation. DWG virtually invented this scenario in countless earlier short silent films in which the villain ties the heroine to the proverbial railroad tracks, and the hero must rescue her before the train turns her into kibble.

FRENCH WOMEN UNDER GERMAN OCCUPATION

After the Germans take over the town, The Little Disturber is forced to work as a bar wench in the inn, distastefully and somewhat belligerently serving beer and wine to the enemy. The Germans force Marie, now recovered from her shell shock, into service as a slave laborer in the fields. But Marie—ever the faint heart—is not up to lifting bales and performing other field laborers' tasks. This enrages a big, burly German sergeant, who savagely whips and beats her. Once again, The Little Disturber comes to the rescue, hiding Marie in a room above the inn while she recovers from her beating. Unfortunately, Von Strohm is also back in town and spots Marie at the inn. As DWG's title card narrates, "He takes advantage of the opportunities war offers scoundrels of all races and ages." Drunk, Von Strohm makes foul comments and physical advances. Ever the victim, all Marie can manage is to cower against a wall, sniveling in fear. Marie's feelings of helplessness related to the earlier traumas are triggered and she is paralyzed into the freeze response again, unable to take action. Making it clear that now he plans to rape her, Von Strohm chases Marie around the tables at the inn. At the last minute, Von Strohm's superiors arrive at the inn and order him to accompany them. Finally showing some initiative, Marie takes the opportunity to escape the inn. In doing so, she joyfully encounters Douglas, now recovered from his wounds. He is wearing a German uniform so he can reconnoiter around the village in advance of a planned French counterattack.

Later, although this French attack is underway, it seems that the German sergeant and Von Strohm have nothing better to do than to pursue Marie, who they don't know is also hiding Douglas at the inn. But the sergeant discovers Douglas, and as they scuffle, Marie shows a little backbone, picks up a knife and stabs the sergeant in the back. Of course, she does even this weakly, and the sergeant, although wounded and staggering, is still able to fight. Fortunately, Marie's attack allows Douglas time to grab a pistol and finish him off.

Von Strohm returns to the inn, ignoring the French attack, still lusting after Marie. Discovering the sergeant's body, with the help of some of his soldiers, the German tries to break down a door behind which Marie and Douglas are hiding. Instead of coming up with ideas about how to defend themselves or escape, Marie chooses this moment to pester Douglas, insisting that if the Germans break down the door, Douglas must shoot her, thus avoiding the proverbial "fate worse than death" that awaits her in Von Strohm's hands. He reluctantly agrees. Thus Griffith rehashes the climactic sequence of *Birth of a Nation* in which the same threat-followed-by-last-minute-rescue scenario plays out. But, interestingly, rather than being rescued by men, a young woman saves the day. The Little Disturber uses a hand grenade she had stolen earlier to kill Von Strohm and the other Germans, saving Marie and Douglas. Later, the French retake the village, concluding the story, after which all protagonists presumably live happily ever after.

WINGS AND *HELL'S ANGELS*

Two other significant World War I films made before the 1930s included the first film to win an Oscar for Best Picture, William Wellman's *Wings* (1927), and Howard Hughes's *Hell's Angels* (1930). We will discuss *Wings* in this chapter, because once again there are two women, one a Madonna and the other, not quite a Madonna, who can be categorized either as chattel or a camp follower. Like Marie and The Little Disturber, one woman in *Wings* is totally passive, only inadvertently contributing to misunderstandings and anger between the two male protagonists, while the other is the opposite, an enterprising young woman. We will hold off discussion of *Hell's Angels* until chapter 4 on prostitutes and camp followers, because the only substantial female character in this film, Helen (Jean Harlow) can best be described as a trampy camp follower.

In *Wings*, our Madonna character's name is Sylvia (Jobyna Ralston), a young woman who is the love interest of both male protagonists, Jack (Buddy Rogers) and David (Richard Arlen). Sylvia, however, loves David, but is such a coward that she can't muster the courage to tell Jack that his constant attentions are a waste of time. In this sense, she's even less of an assertive person than Marie in *Hearts of the World.* Sylvia prepares a locket with her picture inside to give to David before he leaves for the war. Unfortunately, Jack visits her and spots the locket. He mistakenly believes that Sylvia has prepared it for him, and thanks her profusely. He vows that he will carry it into battle, keeping Sylvia on the pedestal of his adoration. Sylvia can't bear to correct Jack (heaven forbid she contradict a *man*), and lets him keep the locket as he departs. Later, when David is killed, she will chastely mourn his passing.

The other female character is Mary (Clara Bow), the spunky girl who lives next door to Jack, who is hopelessly in love with him. Just to be around Jack, Mary will even put up with his constant talk about his adoration of Sylvia. Actually, Jack is pretty much of an idiot about it, not able to see the obvious affection Mary has for him. Unlike Sylvia, who will spend the entire picture at home, pining away for David like a dutiful Madonna, Mary decides to become a camp follower so she can stay close to Jack. Mary enlists in the Women's Motor Corps (WMC), a uniformed auxiliary service that preceded the not-yet-created Women's Army Corps. WMC volunteers served both on the home front and near the front lines in France, driving and even servicing supply and medical vehicles, freeing up U.S. Army males for combat.

Serving in the WMC in France, Mary actually comes under fire, as a German Gotha bomber drops bombs on an Allied position. But then Jack and other American fighter pilots arrive on the scene and attack the bomber, shooting it down. A soldier tells Mary that the plane that downed the Gotha is called the "Shooting Star," and that the pilot is a famous ace. Mary recognizes the "Shooting Star" as the name Jack gave his racing jalopy back home and puts two and two together. Mary finds out that Jack's unit is nearby, but before she can visit him, Jack gets leave and goes to Paris. Mary follows. In Paris, she finally catches up with him, but Jack is in a dance hall, stone drunk, and doesn't recognize her, especially as he's not seeing straight and she's dressed in her WMC uniform. When she finds him, Jack is more interested in the French floozie who's drinking with him. With the help of another French woman who works there, Mary loses the uniform, dressing up alluringly in a skimpy dance hall outfit, and wrests Jack away from the French woman. Boldly, she takes Jack to a hotel room to have him all to herself, but Jack is too drunk to understand anything, and just passes out on the bed. It appears to the audience that if Jack were not dead drunk and passed out, Mary might have surrendered her virtue to him, if only to assure that no other women would win his love. But this was not to be: Jack is out cold for the present. Marie leaves him on the bed and walks behind a dressing screen to change out of the dance hall dress and back into her uniform. She thinks that perhaps when Jack wakes up, the two can still spend some time together.

But fate intervenes. A major war offensive has begun and all flyers' leaves, including Jack's, are cancelled. Military Police (MPs), informed of Jack's whereabouts by a well-meaning friend, invade Mary's hotel room to get him. Unfortunately for Mary, she is totally naked behind the dressing screen when the MPs burst in! The MPs assume that Mary and Jack have just made love, so Mary is arrested. Later, the WMC sends Mary home. Apparently, in the WMC there's a morals clause that prohibits their volunteers from bedding down with American servicemen, although their double standard appears to permit the men to fraternize all they want with French floozies. Amazingly, Jack, still drunk, never does realize who was with him in the hotel room that night.

Shortly before David's ironic death in combat, Jack discovers the truth about Sylvia's locket. This causes a temporary rift in the men's friendship. Later, after David's death, sadly gathering up his possessions to send home to his parents, Jack discovers Sylvia's love letters to David and realizes that it is David whom Sylvia has loved this entire time. When Jack returns home, David laid to rest, Jack encounters Mary and the two talk the night away. Romance is finally happening for this couple, as Jack realizes what a wonderful young woman she is. They see a shooting star, and Jack asks, "You know what you can do when you see a shooting star?" he asks. Mary replies, "You can kiss the girl you love," and he does.

FLYBOYS

Another classic World War I Madonna appears much later in film history, in *Flyboys*, released in 2006. This is a semi-historical re-creation of the exploits of an actual group of Americans who enlisted in the French Flying Service before the entrance of the United States into the war. When Lucienne (Jennifer Decker) is introduced, the audience as well as the protagonist at first assume that she is a prostitute, because American flyer Blaine Rawlings (James Franco) meets her in a French bordello. Blaine has survived a plane crash and awakes with only a few superficial wounds. As he regains consciousness and looks around the parlor, he notes that he is surrounded by women slouching around seductively in their underwear. He concludes correctly that he is in a bordello, being tended to by the beautiful but fully clothed Lucienne. The other pilot who crashed along with Blaine enters the room, having just enjoyed an assignation with one of the prostitutes, so when Lucienne guides Blaine to a nearby bedroom, he has every expectation that he is about to get lucky. This only increases when she tries to make him understand that he should remove his pants. She speaks no English and he, surprisingly for a flyer wearing the French uniform, doesn't speak French. But, as it turns out, the reason Lucienne needs Blaine to remove his pants is because he has minor wounds from the plane crash on his leg, and she needs access to his leg to clean and bandage it. Blaine's first meeting with Lucienne ends when his flying colleague enters to inform him that their ride back to the aerodrome has arrived and they must leave.

Later, still smitten, Blaine returns to the bordello, asking the madam for Lucienne. That's when he finds out she's not a prostitute: She just happened to be visiting the bordello to barter with the madam with her farm produce when Blaine was brought in, unconscious. Instead, he learns that she lives on a farm outside of town. Blaine, a cowboy and rancher before the war, hires a horse and rides out to her farm, where he meets Lucienne's deceased brother's children, whom she cares for. Communication remains difficult between the two, at least for now, but a romance ensues. On another visit, he lands his plane in one of Lucienne's fields, and takes her for her first ride in an airplane. Little by little, he learns some French and she learns a lot of English so they can carry on a conversation.

Unlike a Madonna who lives back home, away from the fighting, Blaine's Madonna and the children live uncomfortably close to the front. Later in the film, the Germans advance and Blaine realizes that Lucienne and the children may be in danger, isolated on the farm. Rough-looking German soldiers are pictured rampaging across the area, and it takes very little imagination to assume that director Tony Bill was creating a scene suggesting that rape or murder could be in store if Lucienne doesn't flee. Blaine comes to the rescue, again landing his plane on Lucienne's field. He evacuates the children, but doesn't have room in his aircraft for Lucienne on this first trip. Then the Germans arrive and break into Lucienne's house, looting whatever they can find. As one German gulps down a bottle of milk, Lucienne, who's been hiding inside, makes a break for it. Outside, she hides from the Germans until Blaine returns for her. He almost succeeds in his rescue completely, but Lucienne is wounded by German gunfire just as his plane takes off. Fortunately, Lucienne recovers, but she and the children are now refugees and must sit out the war somewhere other than on her farm.

This story is loosely based on true stories of a group of American volunteer flyers, and so, at the end, narration titles tell us what happened to each pilot after the armistice is signed. We learn that after the war, Blaine searched for Lucienne and the children, but never found them. He returned to the U.S. alone and later became a successful rancher. No record exists of what happened to his Madonna.

Lucienne symbolizes the role of the Madonna, a heroic young woman caring for her brother's children, cultivating flowers as a hobby and running a farm in the midst of a war. Perhaps there might have been a more physical side of Blaine's and Lucienne's relationship if the Germans hadn't intervened, but all we are shown in one short scene is a romantic kiss in her kitchen. Totally in love with Lucienne, Blaine would have sacrificed his life to save her from the Germans. This Madonna was the symbol of all that he was fighting for, all that he was dedicated to protect.

MADONNAS DOING THEIR BIT

Changes came at the end of the 1930s, and especially after Pearl Harbor, as women's images changed from pre–World War II mainstream media representations as girlfriends, wives, daughters, and mothers to new kinds of women, the kinds who were needed to help win a war. Advertising media, egged on by the federal government, began to portray Madonnas with smudges on their faces, hair wrapped up in kerchiefs with wrenches in their hands, serving as defense plant workers. Also, in posters and ads across the country, Madonnas began to appear in the uniforms of female auxiliary services and as military nurses, roles the government needed them to play while their men were away, fighting the war. This wasn't to last for long—just the length of World War II—but while it did, the first seeds of what was to blossom as women's liberation a generation later were planted. Andi Zeisler (2008) characterizes this wartime era in *Feminism and Pop Culture*:

> They were supposed to be sassy, spunky pinch hitters in the workplace, according to that iconic Rosie the Riveter image that beckoned from OWI [Office of War Information] posters. But these images changed once the war was over and the boys came home. The media forces that had hurried women into factories were now herding them back into the home to make room for men. (28)

Thomas Doherty (1993) also reminds us that the women whom American soldiers left at home in World War II crossed over into their men's exclusive world to lend a hand and do their bit, substituting for their men to aid the war effort. Feature films, documentaries, and newsreels of the1940s praised "Rosie the Riveter" types and other women who temporarily dispensed with their assigned homemaker roles in American society and worked at the defense plants and other manly occupations. Wartime U.S. Office of War Information (OWI) publicity called these women "home front warriors," despite the fact that this hyperbole "tightened the jaws of combat veterans. Forthright home front warriors had the decency to blush at the equivalence" (165). In many films, especially those made during World War II, filmmakers made it clear that the Madonnas whom American soldiers left behind on their pedestals worshipped their brave men in uniform.

Since You Went Away

As described by Doherty, in the OWI-characterized "unconquerable fortress" of an American home in 1943, David O. Selznick painstakingly sets the opening scene in the Oscar-winning *Since You Went Away* (1944):

> An establishing shot frames a window containing a blue star banner, the sign that a family member is serving in uniform. A dissolve then initiates entry into the interior of the home. [Director John] Cromwell's camera glides over the exposed mementos of the living room. Backed with lilting musical cues, the uninterrupted shot tracks laterally from detail to detail:
>
> 1. A creased and indented leather chair, palpably empty of the household patriarch
> 2. A bulldog at the feet of the chair, awaiting the master
> 3. A military parcel ("Rush," reads the label, "Military Raincoats")
> 4. A day calendar (showing the date: Tuesday, January 12)
> 5. A crumpled War Department telegram ordering Capt. Timothy Hilton to report for duty at Camp Claiborne, Louisiana. In the foreground lies a set of car keys, monogrammed "T.H." (a possession only an American male off to war would relinquish)
> 6. A plaque with a tiny mounted fish and the legend "Caught by Anne and Tim Hilton on Their Wedding Trip, August 23, 1925")
> 7. Two bronzed baby shoes
> 8. A portrait showing the three females left behind, wife (Claudette Colbert) and two young daughters (Jennifer Jones and Shirley Temple)
> 9. The blue star banner, viewed now from the interior, while through the window a car pulls into frame, in the rain, to park in front of the house.
>
> Claudette Colbert then enters the manless fortress to begin a year without her husband. (169–70)

In this highly cinematic scene, director Cromwell not only sets the opening picture for this home front melodrama, but clearly delineates the roles that men and women were expected to play in World War II America: Men are the kings of their castle, but as the rulers of their domain, they must occasionally don their armor, pick up their swords and venture forth to protect their domain against enemies. Women are left to raise the drawbridge, maintain hearth and home, care for the children, supply whatever small artifacts from home as the men may request they subsequently send along, take up as many duties of the man as they can manage while he's gone, and wait, patiently, lovingly and loyally, in the manner of the family Schnauzer, for the master's return.

Thanks to Margaret Buell Wilder's book and her own screenplay adaptation, Colbert's main character, Anne, is allowed a significant character arc during the course of the picture. At first, Anne doesn't have much time to sit around feeling sorry for herself, because she's too busy comforting her two teenage daughters, who already miss their father, Tim, a lot. Next, with the family's income dropping from her husband's substantial prewar salary as an advertising executive to an Army major's pay allotment, Anne must lay off the family retainer who did all the cooking and cleaning, tackle the family finances, and make the decision to take in a lodger for extra income. Finally, at the end of this first horrific day as a single mother and head of the household, she closes the door to the master bedroom and for the first time, faces two empty twin beds. Anne dives into Tim's bed and allows herself a good cry.

We are given the impression that Tim pretty much ran the household, paid all the bills from his substantial salary and left Anne, who has a cook/housekeeper to lighten the load, to mothering tasks only. As the girls are grown and almost ready to leave the nest, this has left Anne with considerable time on her hands, which she probably spent before the war in social and volunteer activities.

True to the book and to producer David O. Selznick's vision for this wartime classic, Anne's daughters are also prototypical young Madonnas. Jennifer Jones is angelic as Jane, the elder daughter, who, after graduating from high school, decides to forego college for the duration to serve the war effort as a nurse's aide in a veteran's hospital. Shirley Temple is Jane's younger sister, Bridget, nicknamed "Brig," who's still in high school. The delightful Brig serves by volunteering for every war effort committee appropriate for youngsters, such as rolling bandages or collecting for scrap drives. Brig, with some help from Jane, also uses her Madonna persona to charm the bile out of their curmudgeonly lodger, Col. Smollett (Monty Wooley).

One thing *Since You Went Away* teaches us about Madonnas is that such mild-mannered women can't be pushed to anger without good reason. However, Anne has just such a reason in a woman she refers to as a friend, Emily Hawkins (Agnes Moorehead). Emily is a wealthy divorcée who pretentiously exudes an air of upper crust, has no charity in her heart, and scandalously flirts with anything in pants. Emily is a hoarder and purchases extravagant (for wartime) delicacies on the black market, which the wartime Office of War Information–approved screenplay takes great care to condemn. How these two women ever became friends in the first place is one of the few weaknesses of the plot, because the odious Emily is in every way the polar opposite of Anne. Emily drops by the house to cluck and shake her head and pontificate about Jane's decision to be a nurse's aide, implying that giving sponge baths and touching wounded limbs is beneath a young woman of good breeding. This infuriates Anne, Brig, Jane, Col. Smollett and their friend, Naval officer Tony Willett (Joseph Cotton), who happens to also be visiting.

Emily: Hello, Jane. What's this I hear about you working at the hospital?

Jane: I'm a nurse's aide.

Emily: A nurse's aide? Oh! What a revolting idea for an unmarried girl of your age. Well, our whole code of living seems to be completely ignored these days, and possibly it's none of my business—

Tony: *(interrupting)* You're quite right, Mrs. Hawkins. It is none of your business.

Emily: I must say, Lieutenant, or Commander, or whatever you are, the Navy hasn't improved your manners any.

Anne: Please, Tony. Please, Emily. It's the Colonel's birthday, and we're trying to have a party.

Emily: I'm sorry. I meant no offense to you, Jane. I simply feel that well-brought up young girls shouldn't be permitted to have such intimate contact with all sorts of—

Jane: *(interrupting)* All sorts of boys who've lost their arms and legs? They're young too, lots of them. But they weren't too young for that, Mrs. Hawkins, and I don't think breeding entered into it, either.

Colonel Smollett: Bravo, Jane.

Emily: I don't care to debate it with you, Jane. But surely there are women more suited to such—

Jane: *(interrupting)* That's just it. There aren't women more suited. And women who might help, like you, Mrs. Hawkins, think you're doing your part if you attend a canteen dance for your own pleasure.

Anne: You're tired, honey. Why don't you go upstairs?

Jane: Yes, Mother. But there are just one or two more things I want to say.

Bridget: Come on, darling. She's not worth it.

Jane: We're not V-girls! We're simply helping with the wreckage. (*laughs sarcastically*) All right, Brig, let's go play with our dolls! Don't worry, Mrs. Hawkins. Please don't worry if our precious well-bred hands come in contact with those mangled bodies. We'll survive! Even if they don't! (*runs upstairs with Brig*)

Emily: Anne Hilton! What on earth has happened that you would permit a child of yours to talk that way without so much as . . .

Anne: (*interrupting*) Without so much as what? Thank heaven my child has the courage to say to you what should have been said long ago. And let me add that I'm ashamed. Ashamed that I've put up with you, that I've even known you.

Emily: Well! From now on, you needn't know me. Don't you think for a minute you have me fooled, Anne Hilton. I've not forgotten how you felt about your husband joining up. And may I ask just what other noble sacrifices you've made to give you the privilege of being so self-righteous?

Anne: I'm afraid that's just it, Emily. I haven't really made any sacrifices. Oh, I haven't hoarded and cheated and done all the other selfish, unpatriotic things that you've done. But as far as making sacrifices, I'm afraid we're two of a kind. And the realization of it doesn't make me very proud or happy. (*Since You Went Away*, 1944)

Realizing that her daughters have found ways to aid in the war effort and that she has done nothing besides keep the house running, Anne is guilt ridden. She has managed to find ways to make ends meet and run the house, which in and of itself has shot her character arc upward. But the argument with Emily makes her realize that this achievement isn't enough when there's a war on. She decides to also find a method of national service: For the first time since she married, Anne will leave home and venture outside to work, laboring for the duration at a defense plant. While working at this factory, we are again reminded of Anne's Madonna status, as she has a conversation with an immigrant woman from Russia (Alla Nazimova). She complements Anne, saying that when she left the Soviet Union to come to the United States, "You are what I thought America was." This is a Madonna who has grown far beyond helpless or do-nothing, like Sylvia in *Wings*.

Anne also must deal, as so many households did during the war, with an ominous telegram from the War Department. Her message was to inform her that husband Tim is missing in action. At first, there is the normal amount of denial, but over time, everyone in the family begins to accept the possibility that Tim might never be coming home. Lifelong bachelor and old family friend Tony Willett (Joseph Cotton) visits again to console Anne, who once upon a time chose Tim's proposal of marriage over his. Although Tony's suave, attractive presence at a time when Anne's resolve is at its weakest constitutes great temptation, Anne remains faithful and steadfast in her hope that Tim is still alive. Tony, still in love with Anne, remains a gentleman who will always be a friend to this Madonna, but no more.

Anne's virtue and patience are rewarded in the final scene, when she receives a cablegram from Tim, telling her that he's alive and well, and on his way home on leave to spend a joyous Christmas with his beloved family. Tim will find a significantly different Madonna when he returns: a woman whose character arc has soared to great heights while he's been gone.

Mrs. Miniver and *The Best Years of Our Lives*

A film such as Best Picture Academy Award winner *Mrs. Miniver* (1942), although portraying an English—not American—family enduring the German blitz, was immensely popular—and heavily promoted—in the United States by not only MGM but by the Roosevelt administration. In this six-Oscar performance, the Minivers are shown to be a quiet, affluent, middle-class family leading a humdrum but cheery life, concerned only with flower festivals and village gossip. Finally the war rudely intervenes, and Mr. Miniver (Walter Pidgeon), who must be considered too old to enlist or has some undisclosed medical condition, nonetheless volunteers himself and the family's pleasure boat to help evacuate Allied soldiers from the British disaster at Dunkirk. During the course of the picture, domestic goddess Kay Miniver (Greer Garson) matures far beyond the everyday concerns of a housewife. Soon the war, most immediately in the form of a downed German flyer, parachutes into her backyard, and she encounters the face of the enemy—in the form of a wild-eyed Nazi (Helmut Dantine)—firsthand. Kay's son Vin (Richard Ney), a dashing young Royal Air Force officer, now risks his life flying Spitfires and shooting down Nazi bombers overhead, but ironically, it is not Vin, but his lovely new bride Carol (Teresa Wright), a young Madonna, who later is killed in a German air attack.

Monica Henry defines the role of the 1940s Madonna in films such as *Mrs. Miniver* and *The Best Years of Our Lives* (1946) as an exercise in goodness:

> These films exemplify women who support the war effort by keeping the home fires burning, faithfully waiting for their men to return, and acting as caregivers when the soldier comes home. These "good women" are held up as models to emulate, and women are made to feel inferior or guilty if they are unable to meet these standards. . . . The message for women in this movie [*Best Years*] is very clear—be a "good" girl and take care of your man. (2006, 5)

In a film that takes place just following the end of World War II, William Wyler's Best Picture Oscar–winning *The Best Years of Our Lives* (1946), the women who lovingly greet two of the three male protagonists upon their return from fighting in World War II are a prototypical Madonna mother and daughter plus a Madonna "girl next door." Myrna Loy and Teresa Wright, as wife Milly and daughter Peggy, who excitedly greet Sergeant Al Stephenson (Fredric March) when he returns home from the war, are among Hollywood's clearest Madonna prototypes. Later, Al suffers from posttraumatic stress and depression and self-medicates with alcohol as he tries to adjust to his old life and job at a bank. Madonna Milly steps in and mothers him back to his old self.

Peggy, as Al's dutiful daughter, gives good advice and hope to her father's young army acquaintance, pilot Fred Derry (Dana Andrews), whose lowlife wife Marie (Virginia Mayo), whom Fred met and married much too quickly during the war, had betrayed him multiple times while he was away. Peggy is attracted to Fred, and can't stand what Marie has done to him. Fred remains faithful to Marie and will do no more than have a drink with Peggy, but it's obvious that he is attracted. And it doesn't take long for Fred to realize that Marie is a no-good, especially compared to the likes of Peggy. Fred gets back his old soda jerk job at the drugstore, but gets into a fight with a "Jody" draft-dodger who criticizes everything Fred fought for. He is fired.

Later, Fred confronts Marie about her infidelities, and she tries—without any evidence—to defend herself by accusing Fred of the same thing:

Marie: What do you think I was doing all those years?

Fred: I don't know, babe, but I can guess.

Marie: Go ahead. Guess your head off. I could do some guessing myself. What were you up to in London and Paris and all those places? I've given you every chance to make something of yourself. I gave up my own job when you asked me. I gave up the best years of my life, and what have you done? You flopped! Couldn't even hold that job at the drugstore. So I'm going back to work for myself and that means I'm gonna live for myself, too. And in case you don't understand English, I'm gonna get a divorce. What have you got to say to that?

Fred: *(disgusted)* Don't keep Cliff [her latest boyfriend] waiting.

Marie: What are you gonna do?

Fred: I'm going away.

Marie: Where?

Fred: As far away from Boone City as I can get.

Marie: That's a good idea. You'll get a good job someplace else. There are drugstores everywhere. (*The Best Years of Our Lives*, 1946)

Audiences also infer that after the end of the movie's story, Peggy and Fred, who remain attracted to one another, are likely to become involved.

When real-life disabled veteran Harold Russell, playing a more traumatized version of himself named Homer Parrish, comes home without his arms and full of self-pity, it's his saintly childhood sweetheart Wilma (Cathy O'Donnell), literally the girl next door, who patiently loves him through his difficult adjustment. The despondent Russell first rejects Wilma, unwilling to believe that she could still love an armless man. He discusses his problem with fellow veterans Fred and Al:

Homer: I didn't see much of the war. . . . I was stationed in a repair shop below decks. Oh, I was in plenty of battles, but I never saw a Jap or heard a shell coming at me. When we were sunk, all I know is there was a lot of fire and explosions. And I was ordered topsides and overboard. And I was burned. When I came to, I was on a cruiser. My hands were off. After that, I had it easy. . . . That's what I said. They took care of me fine. They trained me to use these things (gesturing to the twin hooks attached to his forearms). I can dial telephones, I can drive a car, I can even put nickels in the jukebox. I'm all right, but . . . well, you see, I've got a girl. (*The Best Years of Our Lives*, 1946)

Later, Fred and Al discuss Homer's problem:

Fred: You gotta hand it to the Navy; they sure trained that kid how to use those hooks.

Al: *(wisely)* They couldn't train him to put his arms around his girl, or to stroke her hair. (*The Best Years of Our Lives*, 1946)

But Wilma is a younger version of Al's Madonna wife, Milly, and shows Homer that her love for him is far greater than his disability. After Homer has tried to get Wilma to abandon him, she finally decides to lovingly confront him:

Wilma: Tell me the truth, Homer. Do you want me to forget about you?

Homer: I want you to be free, Wilma, to live your own life. I don't want you tied down forever just because you've got a kind heart.

Wilma: Oh, Homer! Why can't you ever understand the way things really are, the way I really feel? I keep trying to tell you.

Homer: But, but you don't know, Wilma. You don't know what it'd be like to have to live with me. To have to face this . . .

(*He holds up his hooks.*)

Homer: every day, every night.

Wilma But I can only find out by trying. And if it turns out I haven't courage enough, we'll soon know it.

(*Homer has asked Wilma into his bedroom to see what happens as he prepares for bed. After removing his hooks and harness, he "wiggles" into his pajama top.*)

Homer: I'm lucky. I have my elbows. Some of the boys don't. But I can't button them up.

Wilma: I'll do that, Homer.

Homer: This is when I know I'm helpless. My hands are down there on the bed. I can't put them on again without calling to somebody for help. I can't smoke a cigarette or read a book. If that door should blow shut, I can't open it and get out of this room. I'm as dependent as a baby that doesn't know how to get anything except to cry for it. Well, now you know, Wilma. Now you have an idea of what it is. I guess you don't know what to say. It's all right. Go on home. Go away like your family said.

Wilma: [*She kneels in front of him*] I know what to say, Homer. I love you and I'm never going to leave you . . . never. [*She kisses him.*] (*The Best Years of Our Lives*, 1946)

Hawks's *Air Force*

In chapter 5, we will discuss one of the prototype Hawksian women in Howard Hawks's World War II classic, *Air Force* (1943). Here we mention one Madonna and—if we properly interpret her character's unstated backstory—one Hawksian woman-turned-Madonna wife and mother who each have small but significant roles at the start of this classic war film. The first Madonna, played by Dorothy Peterson, is referred to in credits only as "Chester's Mother." Chester (Ray Montgomery) is the newest and youngest member of the crew of the B-17 bomber the *Mary Ann*, the wide-eyed youth through whom screenwriter Dudley Nichols (nominated for an Oscar for *Air Force*'s screenplay) introduces the audience to most of the other principal characters and a number of war propaganda talking points. Unfortunately, in the plot conventions of war films, this young, innocent boy might as well walk around with a bull's-eye on his back, because youths like this along with soldiers who talk about the fact that they're "short" and due to rotate home soon are usually the first to die. It's almost a war film cliché, like the doomed crewmen in *Star Trek* who wear red uniforms.

Chester shows his age and lack of experience (in real life—but not in this carefully crafted propaganda film—he would be razzed unmercifully by his comrades about Mommy showing up to wish him good-bye) by asking his captain, Michael "Irish" Quincannon (John Ridgely) if he would step over to the edge of the tarmac before they leave to meet his mother, who has come down to the airfield to see him off. With great feeling, she asks Quincannon to take good care of her son. The captain, ever the team player, points out that Chester, the radio operator, "will be taking care of me. That's the way the crew of a bomber functions. I wouldn't worry." "I won't," she replies. In her emotional state, Chester's Mother has forgotten that she has brought a package to give to him. Chester reminds her not to worry, while she, trying bravely not to cry, hugs him hard and says, "Good-bye, son," and kisses him full on the lips. If there was ever a classic gray-haired, sweet mother stereotype, Mrs. Chester sat for the painting.

The other Madonna in *Air Force*, Quincannon's wife, Mary (Ann Doran), arrives late, just in time to say good-bye to her husband. Fearing she wasn't going to make it, Quincannon is ready to give up hope when he hears her shout his nickname, "Irish!" She couldn't bring their baby, because it's past his bedtime, but Mary brings a toy pilot on a little chain as a memento and "this," as she wraps her arms around him and gives him a great big kiss. Later, Quincannon would hang the toy in the cockpit of the *Mary Ann* as a reminder of the Madonna and child he's fighting for. Giving a hint that she liked to be and probably used to be "one of the boys," Mary asks, "Oh, Darling, couldn't I stow away?" Quincannon jokingly reminds her that this is against regulations. He promises that when he returns from this flight (from the San Francisco Bay area to Hawaii), he'll take leave and they'll finally have their long-delayed honeymoon. They discuss how often he's been gone on flying missions, and he says that at least Mary won't have time to get bored with him. "Oh, I'll never get bored with you, Irish," she replies. "It's been fun, every minute of it . . . good fun! I'll be waiting." Another big kiss, and Quincannon bids her good-bye, saying, "So long, kid." As other Madonnas, Mary has completely devoted her life to Quincannon and made him the center of her world.

Unfortunately, Quincannon and Chester are the two members of the *Mary Ann*'s crew who are killed in combat during this epic story.

WOMEN POWS

There is yet another variation on the role portrayed by the Madonna to consider: A number of war films through the years, especially those set during the war in the Pacific in World War II, dramatize the unthinkable conditions female prisoners of war had to endure. During World War II, American war propaganda posters and motion pictures that featured women POWs featured some rapacious Japanese soldier casting lustful eyes on American women under their power. The more angelic and Madonna-like that screenwriters made the women, the more the threat to their honor and the more cringingly suspenseful the situation. In films we'll discuss later in chapter 8, filmmakers created suspense with the threat of American nurses falling into the hands of beastly Japanese. In films about this subject made after World War II, the plots centered mostly on the terrible conditions in Japanese camps and how the suffering women worked to survive while caring for each other. Such a film is *Three Came Home* (1950).

In this prison camp film, a woman, her husband, and child are caught up in the Japanese occupation of Borneo at the start of the war. Based on the memoirs of Agnes Newton Keith, the film is essentially true. In this film, as in many other characters she played during the war, Claudette Colbert plays a variety of Madonna. She is Agnes, who is trying to survive war under the cruel thumb of her family's captors, the Japanese. Married to an English diplomat, at first Agnes, her husband, and young son are allowed to stay in their homes, but later all are rounded up, put into two concentration camps and subjected to brutal treatment at the hands of the enemy. At one point, transferring their prisoners from home to the prison camp, sneering, abusive Japanese soldiers won't help Agnes heft a heavy suitcase. Pregnant, she later has a miscarriage.

In the camps, men are separated from the women and children, and for long, agonizing periods of time, Agnes hears nothing about her husband, Harry (Patric Knowles). As a good Madonna, Agnes tries to care for her young son and assist some of the other women in her prison camp dormitory. Finally comes word that Harry is alive, and is proposing a secret meeting that night. But this is a very dangerous thing to do, requiring both Agnes and Harry to virtually break out of their respective prison enclosures and meet in the jungle. Up until now, Agnes has been an obedient prisoner. Pondering the situation, she decides to become less obedient, and sets off for the rendezvous. Managing to escape from her dorm and creeping along outside of the wire fence surrounding the women's enclosure, Agnes is so frightened she has a panic attack. Coincidentally, a Japanese officer chooses this moment to inspect the women's dormitory, and Agnes has to hurry back, barely making it to the dorm and into her bed in time.

Later in the film, Agnes has grown in courage and become a leader among the women prisoners. In one scene, Agnes is alone, away from the other women, doing laundry when a Japanese soldier assaults her, attempting rape. She somehow fights him off and he runs away. Agnes, less passive than initially, decides to report the incident. The Japanese call her a liar, and insist that she sign a paper stating that she lied about the attempted assault. But Agnes is smart enough to know that if she signs, she will be shot for falsely accusing a Japanese soldier of a dishonorable act. She refuses to sign and is severely beaten. Finally, a reasonably sympathetic Japanese officer intervenes, and the incident is swept under the rug.

As in some of these Madonna films, Agnes is allowed some amount of character arc. At the start of the film, despite her achievement as the author of a novel, she does not appear to be very resourceful or to be able to think independently of her husband. Other women in similar circumstances in the film appear to have the same limitations. As befits the era, these women are codependent in their relationship with their husbands and cannot make decisions on their own without the approval of their husbands. But Agnes and some of the other women secretly disobey some of the orders of their Japanese jailers, and Agnes thankfully tries to stand up for herself when she is assaulted.

Later, after the Hiroshima bomb is dropped, the Japanese become less abusive and finally abandon the prison camp. Agnes, her son, and Harry all survive and are reunited.

Sands of Iwo Jima: A Madonna from New Zealand

There are two women characters of note in the John Wayne classic, *Sands of Iwo Jima* (1949). One of these women is another Madonna like Peggy from *The Best Years of Our Lives,* and the other is a tragic fallen woman whom we will discuss in chapter 4.

Pfc. Peter Conway (John Agar) comes from a long line of Marines, son of a famous father, an officer of legendary toughness. However, Conway is full of resentment bordering on hate for his father, who considered his son too soft. Instead, it is implied that his father would prefer a son in the mold of Conway's platoon sergeant, John M. Stryker:

Conway:I embarrassed my father. I wasn't tough enough for him—too soft. "No guts" was the phrase he used. Now Stryker: He's the type of man my father wanted me to be . . . yeah. I bet [his father and Stryker] got along just fine together. Both of them with ramrods strapped on their backs. (*Sands of Iwo Jima*, 1949)

Much of the conflict not dealing with the enemy, the Japanese, in this film is between Conway and Stryker. Conway is an educated humanist who appreciates literature, music, the finer things in life—basically a complete rebellion against all of his father's likes and values. Later in the film, however, Conway sees the importance of Stryker's no-nonsense, tough guy approach to self-discipline in the conduct of war. But before Conway sheds all of his son-father rebellion, he will come into conflict with Stryker many times.

On liberty in Wellington, New Zealand, Conway meets his Madonna in a serviceman's canteen. Allison approaches him, as hostesses are supposed to do, to ask Conway if he'd like to dance. For a moment cranky after another run-in with Stryker, when he turns and lays eyes on Allison (Adele Mara) he is immediately smitten with a thunderbolt. Mood suddenly changing, Conway flashes that famously toothy John Agar grin. As they dance, a sailor tries to cut in, and Conway, both competitive around sailors (as many Marines are) and furious with the idea of someone cutting in on his time with Allison, barks, "Shove off, Mac" and the frightened sailor complies.

When the music changes from a slow dance to a fast swing number, Conway asks Allison, "What would you say if I suggested we go outside for some fresh air?" She replies, "I'd say I'm not supposed to leave the club with servicemen, but to you I'd say 'yes.'" Allison is also smitten, and this is how the romance begins.

The two exchange life stories the rest of the evening, and when he must catch the train back to camp, Conway asks if he can see her on his next liberty. She enthusiastically agrees and they conclude the evening with their first chaste kiss. Subsequently, every chance he gets, Conway spends all his off-duty time with Allison. Later, to a buddy, Conway asks if he believes in love at first sight, and says he plans to marry Allison. His buddy quips, sarcastically, "You'll feel better in the morning."

But Allison's Madonna hook is set, and Conway proposes. They have a military wedding, exiting the chapel surrounded by his buddies. The men's wedding present to Conway is a boxed set of baby booties, a portent of things to come. Although the young couple has only forty-four hours of liberty for their honeymoon, that was enough. Allison becomes pregnant, but out of consideration for Conway, who was heading into battle, she keeps the good news to herself.

Now Allison becomes the focus of Conway's life: She becomes the Madonna he fights to protect and his hope for the future. However, ironically, his infatuation with her nearly gets him killed. His battalion fights in the battle for Tarawa, and then is transferred to Hawaii to take on replacements and train for their next job, the invasion of Iwo Jima. During mail call, Conway receives a letter from Allison saying that she's been pregnant, but didn't want him to worry about it. She informs him that he is the proud father of a baby boy. Conway is delighted. Later, in a training exercise in which the men practice tossing grenades, one clumsy replacement's live grenade tumbles backward toward a group of Marines rather than forward onto the grenade range. Stryker sees the danger, and shouts at the men to run and duck to avoid the explosion. Moony-eyed, rereading his letter from Allison, Conway just stands there, next to the spot where the grenade landed. Stryker tackles him, knocking him to the ground, saving his life. Stryker, slightly wounded from grenade shrapnel, is furious with Conway: "When will you wake up? You wanna see her again, keep your mind on your work!" This becomes a turning point for Conway, who realizes that without Stryker's help, his Madonna would be a widow and his child fatherless. From then on, Conway quickly develops into the prototypical Marine, even into a leader. When Stryker is killed on Iwo Jima, it is Conway who channels the sergeant as he growls, using Stryker's favorite euphemism for action: "All right, saddle up! Let's get back in the war!"

OLD-SCHOOL DUTIFUL WIVES

Women playing similar roles to Mary, Wilma, and Allison can be found in *Flying Leathernecks* (1951), *Thirty Seconds over Tokyo* (1944), *Air Force*, and *Destination Tokyo* (1943). The wives in *Flying Leathernecks* and *Thirty Seconds over Tokyo* are happy and content with their wifely pursuits while their pilot husbands are deployed overseas.

In *Flying Leathernecks*, Col. Daniel X. Kirby's (John Wayne) wife, Joan (Janis Carter)—unlike Sgt. Stryker's impatient and dissatisfied ex-wife—is both experienced and delighted to greet her warrior upon his return. A cab pulls up and Dan exits, having just returned from fighting in the Pacific. He spots a letter to him that Joan has set out for the postman, and picks it up as he turns the key in the lock and enters. Joan, in a dressing gown with slightly disheveled hair, grins in delight, but says, softly, "I could divorce you for this, coming home without notice . . . a girl's entitled to know in time (she runs a hand through her hair) to have her hair done." Dan just gives her one of those big John Wayne grins and says, "You look pretty good to me," and they kiss enthusiastically and hold each other. Next they head for the bedroom of their young son, Tommy, to awaken him. He's delighted to see his father, even though he calls him "Major" at first. Dan replies that he's been promoted to lieutenant colonel, but still thinks "colonel" is a little too formal. Like a good Madonna mother, Joan suggests that Tommy greet his father with a kiss, but Dan, all John Wayne man all the time, who calls the boy by the nickname "Boot," insists Tommy is too old to be kissing men. Instead, they roughhouse on the bed and wrestle like baby bears, while Joan sits on the bed looking on, contentedly grinning.

Playing the perfect wife, Joan never has uttered a complaint about having to be a single mother while Dan's been away at war. Still, Dan, surveying his precocious son, asks, "Was it rough, baby?" Joan just smiles and replies, as if to say she had the easy part of the separation, "Look who's talking . . . the guy from Guadalcanal." The real fighting with the Japanese during the battle of Guadalcanal, part of the Solomon Islands, which are key to the defense of Australia, was intense, and Marine aviator casualties alone during the six months of fighting totaled 147 killed and 127 wounded.

Next, Joan tells Tommy it's time to go back to sleep, but the boy is too excited and wants to stall as children always want to do at bedtime. He insists he's hungry and asks for some cocoa. Dan says that he'd like some, too, and Joan could bring Tommy's to him in bed. Tommy grins and says, "Your orders have been countermanded." But Joan firmly replies, "Not even a four-star general outranks me in this house." A Madonna, yes: a doormat, no. Tommy remains in bed, but Joan finally relents and says, "I'll bring you a cup." Her orders *were* countermanded, but she doesn't mind. Tommy will take a little while getting back to sleep, though, because Dan has brought him a souvenir, a Samurai sword. As Dan exits the room, Tommy stops waving the sword around long enough to jump off the bed and into Dan's arms for a big hug. That's when Tommy softens and says, "Welcome home, 'Dad.'"

Later that evening, alone in the kitchen in their breakfast nook, Tommy now asleep, Joan finally gets around to asking how long Dan's visit is going to be this time:

Joan: I've been building myself up to ask the sixty-four-dollar question. How long?

Dan: *(grinning and teasing her)* How long what?

Joan: *(realizing he's toying with her)* Answer me, or I'll dent your head!

Dan: You're going to have me along for a long time. I have a [naval air] station job at Goleta [near Santa Barbara, CA].

Joan: *(delighted in having Dan home from the dangers of war for a change, she breaks into a big smile)* A station job? Oh, what a beautiful sound! *(gleaming, she sits on his lap and puts her arms around his neck)* And Goleta? Beautiful, hot, dirty little town. *(she hugs him)* We'll probably live on the wrong side of the tracks. Darling, I'll never complain about Goleta again.

Dan: You're not the complaining type. *(romance suddenly on his mind and a gleam in his eye)* Are we all buttoned up?

Joan: Cat's out; doors locked. *(she flicks off the light on the wall behind Dan)* All secure, sir.

Dan stands, Joan cradled in his arms. He carries her off to the bedroom, grateful that this Madonna is his.

Joan, another prototype Madonna like Mary Quincannon, is delighted to have her man at home, but has no illusions about what the future holds for a combat pilot. She knows that after a time, her Marine will tire of duty at a training base and that this ambitious officer will hunger to test his ideas about Marine fighter-bombers performing close air support for ground forces. So later, ensconced in Goleta, Dan gets the orders he's asked for and now has the tough task of telling Joan. But, as usual, he underestimates her. Dan comes home, walks in the front door and finds her in the dining room, repainting his name and lieutenant colonel rank on his travel bags.

Dan: *(joking)* There's a strange man in the house. Anybody want to kiss him?

Joan: *(smiling)* Um hmm.

Dan: *(He comes into the dining room and kisses her; then Dan sees what she's up to.)* What goes?

Joan: Oh, I'm putting "lieutenant colonel" on all your gear, so you won't lose it while you're traveling.

Dan: *(realizing she already knows about his transfer)* You know more than you've been officially told.

Joan: Spies should concentrate on wives. They always know what's going on on any base.

Dan: I've been finding it hard to tell . . .

Joan: *(interrupting)* . . . that you turned down Washington to get a squadron? That shouldn't be hard to tell me.

Dan: Well, I . . .

Joan: *(interrupting again, but this time with a stiff upper lip.)* . . . It's as simple as this: They wanted the best, and the best is Colonel Kirby. I understand.

(Dan kisses her cheek, but only the audience sees sadness on her face. She hides that expression from him as best she can.)

Dan: *(humorously and affectionately)* No wonder those beautiful gals on those tropic isles couldn't tempt me.

Joan: I've seen pictures of those isles and the gals. Are you telling me you love me?

Dan: Right.

Joan: Then why don't you just say it?

Dan: *(softly but emphatically)* I *love* you. *(they kiss)* Glad I didn't marry one of those "burst into tears" dames.

Joan: *(on the verge of tears)* What good are tears? *(She rises and begins to exit)* Excuse me.

(Off camera, she encounters Tommy, who enters the house and approaches his father.)

Tommy: Hey, Dad, Mom's crying. When I asked, she said, "Take a walk."

Dan: Then we better take a walk, kid.

(Father and son exit by the kitchen door, hand-in-hand. But before he exits, Dan hesitates, wondering if instead he should go find Joan and comfort her. But then Tommy calls out, "Come on, Colonel," and he exits.) (*Flying Leathernecks*, 1951)

Dan was probably right to spend some time with his son and leave Joan to have a good cry. He instinctively knows, also, not to discuss or analyze this relationship too closely with her. She knows her husband well and won't criticize him for following his career, even if it takes him into harm's way rather than to a posh assignment behind a desk in Washington. This is the kind of Madonna who will keep the home fires burning, like Anne in *Since You Went Away*, and hope and pray that Dan returns alive and unharmed to her when the war is over. Eventually, having proved his fighter tactic theories and suffering from a broken shoulder, Dan is transferred home, his war over. For Dan and Joan, if not for all the Marine families in this film, there will be a happy ending.

Joan signifies more than another Madonna: She is the embodiment of the role Hollywood tried to create as the ideal housewife for 1951 and the postwar era. When television arrived, it continued picturing the socially correct housewife embodied in actresses such as Donna Reed and Barbara Billingsley's June Cleaver characters. But unfortunately, what Joan, Donna, and Barbara embodied in perfect Madonna behaviors, they lacked in any evident self-actualization. These wives and mothers lived exclusively for their husbands and families, never seeming to take the time to live for themselves. Dan and Joan had the type of marriage that was common in that time, in which the husband, as the sole breadwinner, dominated the decision making in the marriage. If wives, the majority of whom during this era did not work outside the home, had any power at all, it was in a "senior-junior" manner, in which the wife had input but the husband had the final say.

So in *Leathernecks*, as if he's a bachelor, footloose and fancy-free, Dan makes his decision to go back for another combat tour before going home to face Joan. He never considered a family discussion with Joan about his choice of a Washington job vs. commanding a squadron of fighters in deadly battle against the Japanese. Dan probably knew that if he brought it up, Joan would have an opinion, a wife's kind of an opinion, and he'd either have to knuckle under or ignore it. Dan chooses the age-old practice of not asking for her input, doing what he wants and taking the heat for it afterward. Considering that there was a war on, one could chalk up Joan's quiet acceptance of Dan's choice to patriotism, as if she really believes that Dan and his fighter tactics are critically needed for the war effort. But being married ourselves, your authors believe that a substantial amount of couples would still have exchanged words—heated or otherwise—about such an important, life-or-death decision.

In the twenty-first century, few middle-class couples can afford to survive solely on the husband's salary. Thus, among many couples, a more equal partnership structure has emerged as women have become equal or even higher wage earners than their husbands.

Act of Valor

Although we don't see 1950s-style Madonna wives very often in the twenty-first century, they do exist occasionally in modern films. An example is found in the Navy SEAL antiterrorist war film, *Act of Valor* (2012). Alisa Marshall plays the unnamed wife of Lt. Roarke, a SEAL team leader. She knows that every time Roarke takes off on a mission, he could be killed. But like Joan, until Roarke leaves the house, she keeps up a brave exterior. But when the door closes, she loses it, crying, slowly collapsing on the floor, cradling her head in her hands. On this mission, her instincts were correct: At a critical point, Roarke is faced with a no-win scenario: a hand grenade tossed among three of his men. With no time to escape, Roarke sacrifices himself for his men, falling on the grenade. At the funeral, as his grateful men pin their SEAL badges on his coffin, her tears flow, but she manages to send her husband into eternity with dignity.

Thirty Seconds over Tokyo

In *Thirty Seconds over Tokyo*, Lt. Ted Lawson's wife, Ellen (Phyllis Thaxter), is a relative newcomer to a Madonna wife pedestal. She's a war bride, and newly pregnant when Ted leaves her to pursue a top-secret mission, which she later would discover was the Jimmy Doolittle raid on Tokyo. Although she's half a world away, Ellen is constantly on Ted's mind, both as the Madonna on whom he focuses his postwar plans, but also as the reason he has ventured out to do battle. At one point, another pilot, Bob Gray (Robert Mitchum), asks Ted if he's OK about bombing the Japanese homeland. Thoughtfully, Ted replies that he doesn't really want to kill anyone, not even the Japanese, but if it's a choice between them bombing Tokyo and an enemy pilot dropping bombs on Ellen, he willingly will fly bombing missions without any misgivings. Then, after the daring Tokyo raid, when Ted loses a leg in the crash of his bomber, his first thought is of his Madonna, how they used to enjoy dancing together. He wonders whether she'll be repulsed by a one-legged husband. Charmingly, Ellen, now eight months pregnant, is equally worried that when Ted sees her for the first time since his return, he will be repulsed by her figure, or lack of one. Of course, when they finally meet, love is blind and all they can see is each other.

Destination Tokyo

Like Hawks's *Air Force*, the World War II film, *Destination Tokyo* (1943) begins with the crew's departure from the San Francisco Bay area, but this time, it's the submarine *Copperfin* on a highly dangerous, secret mission. And unlike Irish Quincannon in *Air Force*, Capt. Cassidy (Cary Grant) can't say good-bye to his wife in person, because his family is out in Oklahoma City. And, because it's Christmas Eve, he can't get through to his wife by phone to bid them glad tidings because the long distance lines are clogged with holiday phone callers. So he'll have to express his love via U.S. Mail. In the captain's cabin, the audience sees him writing the letter with pictures of his wife, young son Michael, and daughter Debbie in a triple frame behind him. It reads:

> Cassidy: Sweetheart, we're shoving off ahead of schedule. Something urgent. I tried to telephone you and the children to wish you a merry Christmas, and to tell you I'm now wearing three stripes on my sleeve, and some embarrassingly shiny scrambled eggs on my cap. I hope you like the nylon stockings, Darling. Don't ask me how I got them. Tell Michael I couldn't find a toy submarine. Tell him it's the war: He'll understand. There's even a shortage of teddy bears, but I found one for Debbie. I hope her chicken pox didn't leave any marks on that sweet face. I've got the same good crew and a few new men from sub school . . .

(He pauses, looks at her picture, and changes the subject to something more romantic.)

Cassidy: If we were together tonight, Darling . . .

(But his reverie is interrupted when the mail orderly arrives, and he must seal his envelope and give the sailor the letter, so it can be mailed before they cast off.) (Destination Tokyo, 1943)

As the film concludes, after a somewhat unbelievable adventure, the sub is returning from its perilous mission, soon to dock in San Francisco. Crewmen are on deck, glad to see a U.S. port of call, and the audience hears many sailors give voice to their thoughts about what they're going to do or see when they get liberty. For example, the cook (Alan Hale) looks forward to liberty at home with his Madonna, so for a change, she can do the cooking for him. Capt. Cassidy, too, daydreams aloud about hearth and home, but assumes that the Madonna of his reverie is still back home in Oklahoma. As he gazes at the dock, he catches a glimpse of a woman and two small children. To Lt. Raymond (John Ridgely), Cassidy says that he thought he saw his wife and children on the dock. "I couldn't be that lucky," he complains. "Look again," Raymond says. "Navy wives have a way of knowing when their men are coming home, Captain." Cassidy looks through his binoculars, and, sure enough, it's his Madonna and children, smiling and waving. "You're right," the captain says, smiling, "I couldn't be *that* lucky, but I *am*."

SAVING PRIVATE RYAN

A modern war movie that nonetheless hails back to the 1940s in tone is *Saving Private Ryan* (1998). Mrs. Ryan (Amanda Boxer), a mother on a pedestal—ostensibly a widow—is seen only briefly near the start of the picture. As it turns out, Mrs. Ryan's needs are as much the purpose of the exercise as finding her youngest son. After the Pentagon discovers that Mrs. Ryan has recently lost three of her four sons in the war, they are determined that Mrs. Ryan's last surviving son be removed from harm's way and returned to his mother. In a wordless and particularly poignant scene during which she is about to be notified of her three sons' deaths, all we see of the mother is her back and part of her profile as she dutifully washes dishes in the kitchen of her Iowa farmhouse. She watches a car approaching the farm, and starts to act both concerned and curious as she realizes that it is an Army vehicle. She dries her hands and heads to the front door—now concerned—to see who is arriving—and why. When a grim-faced officer and a local minister get out of the car and head for her front door, she instinctively knows that at least one of her sons has been killed, and she drops to the floor and faints.

She does not yet know that in a few terrible days she has lost three of her boys.

Having invested the audience with the importance of saving the last of the four Ryan boys for this tragic-heroic mother, the rest of the movie deals with the adventures of the squad of men sent into the D-day-plus-two Normandy farmland to find her son. However, as the principal motivator of the entire picture, Mrs. Ryan is often discussed both positively and negatively among the men assigned to find Ryan, as they complain and argue about the justice in sending more soldiers into harm's way to rescue just one. As one soldier says, "I have a mother, too." But Mrs. Ryan, as the pathetic, suffering Madonna grieving for her lost children, takes precedence.

PLATOON'S MADONNA

Although most of the females in *Platoon* (1986) are chattel, there is one invisible Madonna who in a way harkens back to Mrs. Ryan. Much of the narration in *Platoon* is in the form of letters from protagonist Chris Taylor (Charlie Sheen), an Army infantryman serving in a rifle platoon in the jungles of Vietnam, to his "Grandma." Chris has parents he could write to, but his relationship with them is evidently far from ideal, and he knows he can't express his feelings to them. So instead he writes to his loving and presumably doting Grandma to explain the terrible place he's in, and how big a mistake he made in volunteering for combat duty in Vietnam. At one point, he asks Grandma not to tell his parents, because presumably only she would understand. To gain such trust, Grandma—never seen or heard in the film—must be a Madonna, a loving, understanding older woman of the Greatest Generation in the mode of a modern Mrs. Ryan who will listen, understand, and if she were close enough, would stroke his cheek and whisper, "There, there, Chris. Things will be all right."

MADONNAS OF *THE BIG RED ONE*

Throughout this book, we will discuss different roles portrayed by female characters in Sam Fuller's epic war classic, *The Big Red One* (1980). Here we will discuss his Madonnas. Sicilian women similar in age to Mrs. Ryan are living in Sicily during World War II, women who have probably already lost most of their sons in disastrous Italian campaigns all around the Mediterranean. Now a new indignity: These women have been rounded up by the Germans and forced under gunpoint to pretend to work with rakes and hoes on make-believe crops on a hillside. The purpose of this pretend farming is to camouflage a hidden tank that is raining artillery shells on Allied forces fighting their way up the island of Sicily. When reconnaissance aircraft fly over, the tank backs up into a bombed-out house, and all that is seen or photographed is an idyllic setting of farmer women working in a field.

Meanwhile, a U.S. Army infantry squad, the protagonists of *The Big Red One,* are assigned the job of locating the German gun and, if possible, taking it out. They have no luck until they meet a young boy named Matteo (Matteo Zofoli) who has a problem of his own. His mother has been killed in the fighting, and the boy is dragging her body around behind him in a hand cart trying to get her a proper burial. The GIs ask the boy if he knows where the German gun is located, and he insists that he can lead them straight to it. But the boy has a price: First Sarge (Lee Marvin), the squad leader, must promise to get the boy's sainted mama buried in a proper casket with six brass handles. This must be a wonderful mama for a boy to go to such lengths. Perhaps in life she was another Madonna. She surely was to Matteo. Sarge agrees, and the boy, who refuses to leave his mother's decomposing body, drags her along in the hand cart as they head out for the German gun. The soldiers must wear kerchiefs over their noses and mouths to bear the body's growing stench, thanks to the hot Sicilian sun.

When Matteo leads them to the gun, the squad assaults the German position, killing all the Germans except one soldier who was guarding the Sicilian women. He is wounded and still alive. The women, demonstrating that they are, after all, the Sicilian version of Madonnas, do the rest, dispatching the German with gusto with their rakes and hoes. Then, in gratitude for their deliverance (Madonnas rescued again), the women cook a feast for the squad. For the first time in weeks, the men feel human. When the squad moves on, the women agree to provide a new home for the orphan Matteo. "A little mothering is good, but this beats 'em all," says Zab (Robert Carradine), the official narrator of the film and the stand-in for real life World War II G.I., writer/director Sam Fuller. As for Matteo and his mother, the U.S. general is so pleased about destroying the German gun that he provides a silk-lined casket with six brass handles and a first-class burial in a cemetery.

We will briefly discuss one other woman from *The Big Red One* who could very well fill the Madonna role. The squad has just foiled a German ambush around a burned-out tank when a man and woman on a motorcycle and sidecar race out onto the battlefield. The man driving the motorcycle is dying of a gunshot wound, presumably the result of stealing it from the Germans. The young woman is in labor and about to deliver her baby, so it's up to the squad to help her. A squad member, Johnson, has had some medical training, so of course the Army made him a rifleman. But in this emergency, the Sarge promotes Johnson to "doctor" and orders him to help deliver the baby. In a field littered with the junk of war and dead Germans, there is no decent place to do the job, so the Sarge tells Johnson to move his "maternity hospital" inside the tank.

Once inside, Johnson realizes that nothing is sterile, including his hands. Sarge improvises, finding yet another use for G.I.-issued condoms that was never imagined by the Army. The first use the audience was shown at the beginning of the film was to keep rifle barrels dry and free of salt water during amphibious landings. At any rate, Johnson covers his fingers with condoms and starts to work on the girl. Now in transition and close to delivery, the girl is hysterical and screaming with pain. Johnson turns to the Sarge, who's assisting, and asks him, "How do you say 'push' in French? Sarge responds, "*poussez*." So Johnson yells to the girl, "pussy," "pussy," "pussy!" Sarge corrects Johnson's pronunciation, and they both shout "poussez" at the terrified girl. She finally understands, pushes hard and the baby is born. Assuming this young Madonna-in-training and her child survive the war, they will have quite a story to tell about her son's birthday.

1950S MADONNAS

When one places a woman on a pedestal, there are two inherent dangers: the woman can fall from it, or a man might find the height unscalable. Basinger writes in *The Star Machine* (2007) that although Hollywood producers, writers, and directors of the 1940s over-glamorized their female stars, they always made sure that they were within reach. Since it was important to create and maintain Madonnas for men to worship as the objccts of their sacrifices in the war, it was vital to cast the right kind of women, "wholesome and fresh-looking." They included, Basinger writes, "Donna Reed, Jeanne Crain, Phyllis Thaxter, Teresa Wright and Lorraine Day" (482). In addition, MGM took Ella Geisman from the Bronx to create a slightly imperfect, but nonetheless desirable Madonna to compete with the likes of Reed and Wright, and renamed her June Allyson.

THE PERFECT MADONNA?

There is always danger in proclaiming one actress the greatest or most perfect Madonna of them all, but it's author's choice: June Allyson played the role exquisitely with all-American Van Johnson in *Two Girls and A Sailor* (1947) and *High Barbaree* (1947), for bomber pilot Jimmy Stewart in *Strategic Air Command* (1955), and fighter/test pilot Alan Ladd in *The McConnell Story* (1955). Allyson also played a Madonna nurse—the everywoman's polar opposite of M*A*S*H's promiscuous "Hot Lips" Houlihan—at first resisting the unsavory advances of womanizing doctor Humphrey Bogart in a Korean MASH unit in *Battle Circus* (1953) and then civilizing him. Of course, they fall in love, and Allyson's character will someday get what she wants on her terms: marriage.

Basinger describes Allyson as perfect but imperfect, because of her raspy voice and less than Veronica Lake face, but many males in 1950s audiences thought these flaws just added to her attractiveness. Basinger writes that Allyson was every man's perfect wife, "the loyal, steadfast homebody, always loving, always supportive, always keeping the home fires burning while wearing a reasonable little outfit. Allyson was fun, too, but she adapted to her husband's wants" (2007, 487).

Basinger also explains that a Madonna wife must be pretty flexible, a good sport like the wives in *Leathernecks*, *Air Force*, and *Destination Tokyo*. In the baseball picture *The Stratton Story* (1949), June Allyson fills in as catcher so her husband can practice pitching. She holds her husband's coat as a faithful swing band groupie wife in *The Glenn Miller Story* (1954) and later keeps a stiff upper lip as the sorrowful war widow when Miller's plane crashes. While her husband risks his life to test jet fighters in *The McConnell Story* (1955), this June Cleaver prototype waits patiently in a spotless frock, apron, hose, and heels in their home and cooks dinner—keeping an ear out for the sound of crashes (Basinger 2007, 487).

MADONNAS OF THE MODERN CINEMA

American war films of all eras—not just those made during and immediately following World War II—include the occasional homage to the classic Madonna. For example, a more recent Madonna is found in the film, *We Were Soldiers* (2002). In this Vietnam War story, Madeleine Stowe plays Julie, the mother of five and wife to Lt. Col. Hal Moore (Mel Gibson). While her husband, commander of one of the U.S. Army's first air cavalry units, is fighting a pitched battle against ten-to-one enemy odds in the Ia Drang Valley in Vietnam's Central Highlands, Julie Moore holds down the fort back in officers' housing at Fort Benning, Georgia. Shown in this film to be a marvelous mom as well as a devoted wife, Julie is no helpless Madonna. She is very active outside the home, organizing and helping the officers' wives of her husband's battalion. Among the tasks she performs, she conducts meetings with the other Madonnas to discuss homemaking problems and solutions on base, such as the best supermarkets, laundries, and other things necessary to run their homes.

But first, she's a Madonna of the home, responsible for raising her five kids. As Hal, a Catholic, recites bedtime prayers with the children, Julie stands in the doorway, smiling. When one young child, Cecile, isn't reciting her Hail Marys, Hal asks her why. Cecile announces that she wants to be a "Nethodist," like her mother, so instead of reciting memorized prayers she can make up her own. Julie, still observing, stifles a laugh. Later, children asleep, Hal and Julie are in their own bed, talking. Joking around, Hal begins to wrestle with Julie, tickling her. Finally an embrace as he says, "When I pray, whatever I want, I thank God for you."

In a few scenes, we see Hal working hard on his books and notes after everyone (he thinks) is asleep. He knows and studies the battles in which the Vietnamese have beaten the French, slaughtering them and driving the European invader from their country. Now, after a change of name for his battalion, they have become the First Battalion of the Seventh Air Cavalry, essentially Custer's old outfit. Hal, as an avid student of military history, desperately wants his battalion to avoid Custer's fate. He studies the tactics and tendencies of the enemy late into the night. But while he labors, we see Julie standing in the shadows behind him, concerned, worried, supportive.

In the early morning of the day that Hal and his battalion leave for the war, Julie, in bed, plays possum as he kisses her cheek. To avoid a teary scene, and channeling Joan in *Leathernecks*, she pretends to sleep until she hears the click of the front door latch. Lying in bed for a few moments, she changes her mind and rushes down the front steps of their house in her nightgown. She looks for him but she's too late. A fast walker, he's already out of sight. So she just whispers one last "I love you."

Later, Julie's courage is sorely tested when the men of Moore's Seventh Air Cavalry begin their fighting and dying in Vietnam. The Army—amazingly—has not thought to provide any proper means to notify families about all these new American casualties. Seeing taxi drivers deliver telegrams containing death notices from the Defense Department to other officers' wives, the resourceful Madonna springs into action. She and another officer's wife bravely assume the grim duty of more sensitively delivering the terrible news to these new widows, ordering the taxi driver to deliver all future Defense Department telegrams directly to her.

Director Randall Wallace cuts back and forth from the savage battle in Vietnam to this battle of feelings and sorrow on the home front. On one occasion, in the middle of a battle, a North Vietnamese soldier makes a futile bayonet charge into the American enclosure and is headed right for Hal before he is shot and killed. Later, examining the soldier's personal papers, Hal discovers a picture of the man's wife—his Madonna—who bears an uncanny resemblance to Julie, a reminder that for soldiers, Madonnas are universal.

Monica Henry (2006) comments that possibly with the exception of a few films like *Since You Went Away* produced decades ago,

> the emotional, physical and financial sacrifices of these women have been long ignored in war films, as they have been deemed unimportant or uninteresting. What does a woman responsible for running the household, taking care of the children and perhaps holding down a job while going through extreme emotional trauma have to do with war? Everything. The very fact that the Vietnam

film, *We Were Soldiers*, devotes a significant amount of time to showing the relationships between soldiers and their wives, home-front activities of military wives and the impact that the fear and loss of life has on the women suggests that their contribution and role in the overall war effort is beginning to be acknowledged by the public. At least part of their story is finally being told and viewers are forced to think about the continuing costs of war beyond the immediate ones on the battlefield. (6)

Courage under Fire

There are many other examples from war films of the Madonna who holds down the home fort while the husband is deployed in harm's way. In *Courage under Fire*, Mrs. Meredith Serling (Regina Taylor), channels Julie Moore as the wife to whom her husband, Lt. Col. Nathaniel Serling (Denzel Washington), returns, but he doesn't come home uninjured. Instead of feeling relief when Serling returns from fighting in Operation Desert Storm in Iraq, Meredith realizes that her husband, although not suffering from wounds, is nonetheless psychologically damaged. The major difference between the returns of Serling and Hal Moore is that Moore returns a celebrated hero, while Serling comes back to a posting at the Pentagon under a cloud, because through no fault of his own, he ordered friendly fire that killed one of his own tank crews. Serling, out of harm's way and working at a staff job at the Pentagon, suffers terribly from survivor guilt over the incident, made worse since the Pentagon seems intent on giving him a medal and sweeping the whole unfortunate occurrence under the rug. As many PTSD sufferers do, he attempts to drown his troubles in alcohol. But his personal troubles have to stand in line for his attention because he must also investigate varying and somewhat conflicting reports about a nominee for a posthumous Medal of Honor, Karen Walden, the first female candidate for this, the United States' highest military decoration. (We will discuss the Walden character in depth in chapter 6.) The pressure on Serling to certify Walden for the medal is tremendous, coming from politicians trying to make style points with the public, from his boss, the general, who wants the investigation finished quickly with no controversy, and from a reporter who has discovered part of the cover up of his friendly fire incident. All this makes coming to terms with Serling's own problems more stressful.

On one occasion, while sitting at the dinner table with his family, Serling once again relives the incident in his mind, and although he's home and safe and many months have passed since he was in Iraq, he still can't block out images of the destroyed tank and his friends who burned to death. He is suffering flashbacks in which these memories repeatedly return to haunt him. Flashbacks are like movies of the trauma that Serling experienced. They seem extremely real to Serling as he deals with his PTSD. Meredith, sitting across the table, watching him suffer, knows she's powerless to help. She will stand by, supportive as she can be, caring for his children while he bravely fights his demons. Making matters worse, when he talks to her about it, his unwillingness to do so as an Army officer (who must always sound confident to both his men and his superiors) and his male pride keep him from admitting his helplessness in this matter. Instead, at least when he discusses it with Meredith, Serling stonewalls her, saying that he can handle the situation, when implicitly both he and Meredith know he can't. He must travel to interview witnesses for his investigation, and his departure turns into more of a separation from Meredith and his family. Serling and his Madonna both hope that when he returns, he will have found some way to live with what happened.

At one point in the investigation, Serling is back in Washington for one day. He drives his rental car to within a half block of his house, but doesn't go in. He's not whole yet, and nothing has changed. He just sits in the car and watches his kids play in his front yard. Always a vigilant mother, Meredith spots him, walks over to the car and sits in the passenger's seat.

Meredith: Are you back?

(No answer from Serling.)

Meredith: You know, it took me a long time to learn how to be an Army wife without totally obliterating myself, but I did it. So it wouldn't be a hardship if my husband wasn't in the Army anymore. You don't have to figure it out . . . [referring to the incident in Iraq]. You just have to admit that you can't. You have to want to be here with us, that's all. We'll be here . . . *for a while.* Now go away. If you're not going to stay, I don't want the kids to see you. (*Courage under Fire*, 1996)

Meredith is reasonably patient, but she needs to deliver some tough love—a kick to the seat of the pants, perhaps—to urge Serling to continue working on his problem. So she tells him she's not going to wait forever for her husband to either solve his problems or get some help to solve them. She has both the welfare of her children and herself to consider. This entire speech was delivered calmly—not emotionally—but lovingly.

Ironically, in solving the mystery surrounding the Medal of Honor recipient, Serling finally comes to grips with his problems. After the medal ceremony, Serling pins his own Silver Star medal on Capt. Walden's grave, travels to visit the family of his friend, the tank commander who was killed in the incident, and be truthful about how the man really died. Serling also rejects alcohol and comes to grips with his past. Meredith patiently waits like service wives of previous generations have done, delivering no further ultimata, and finally is rewarded when her husband sorts out his feelings and decides to get on with his life.

This soldier tacitly realizes that his Madonna and children should be the focus of his life, and that his constant rehashing of his mistakes in combat draws him farther away from them. Symbolizing both love and forgiveness, Meredith's Madonna figure shines like a beacon in Serling's bleak worldview, and the beacon finally leads him home. As to Serling's future, it may be bumpier than Hollywood screenwriters characterize it. Serling has made some excellent first steps, but he is not entirely cured. Using alcohol as a way to drown his memories may be behind him, but not every trace of memory. Former Army captain Luis Montalvan (2011) writes, "PTSD is a dwelling disorder; it makes a person psychologically incapable of moving beyond the trauma of his or her past" (87). A person who suffers from PTSD will always have the triggers of the trauma. If they receive the mental health counseling they need, they can learn coping skills to deal effectively with these triggers as they arise in their lives.

Impatient Madonnas

Not all Madonnas are as patient, loving, and helpful as Meredith, as they help their men cope with PTSD. Briefly mentioned in Capt. Willard's (Martin Sheen) voice-over in the opening scenes of *Apocalypse Now* (1979) is a woman by audience inference we believe to be a long-suffering Madonna he left back in the States. Awakening in a boozy haze in a shoddy hotel room in Saigon, Willard gradually comes to and realizes where he is:

> **Willard:** Saigon . . . shit. I'm still only in Saigon. . . . Every time I think I'm gonna wake up back in the jungle. When I was home after my first tour, it was worse. I'd wake up and there'd be nothing. I hardly said a word to my wife until I said "yes" to a divorce. When I was here, I wanted to be there; when I was there, all I could think of was getting back into the jungle.

Willard is not by any means alone in his PTSD. Soldiers often feel disoriented when they come home, as if they don't fit in their old lives. Culture shock between life in war zones and life at home make adjustment difficult if not impossible, as in the case of Capt. Willard.

In her article "Friendly Civilians," Jeffords notes that before Willard leaves his hotel room on his epic journey to assassinate Col. Kurtz (Marlon Brando), he goes through a transformation: He must separate himself completely from the civilizing influences of wife, home, and family. Those values that the Madonna represented had no relevance to Willard when he was in-country. Jeffords comments:

With his cigarette still hanging from his lips, he burns a hole in the center of [his family picture], destroying his wife's image. Willard thereby severs his last ties to home and to the woman who does not understand his "mission." Before he goes deep into the Vietnam jungle in search of his prey . . . Willard must cut himself off from his past, from his emotions, from his familial values. On the perilous trip upriver to Kurtz's camp, those who refuse to abandon those values, those who cling to their past, will die. (Jeffords, 1995, 429)

As with Capt. Willard's wife, in *Sands of Iwo Jima* (1949), the estranged wife of Sgt. Stryker (John Wayne) remains unseen. She is only referred to in conversations between Stryker and his close friend, Pfc. Charlie Bass (James Brown). Backstory indicates that Stryker's wife divorced him before the movie's timeline began. Her absence, along with his separation from his young son, weighs heavily on Stryker's mind. Every time he earns a liberty, the otherwise gung ho, by-the-book sergeant gets falling-down drunk. Apparently Stryker was a Master Sergeant, but had lost stripes over his alcohol problem. Both Stryker and Willard realize that they weren't good husbands and state that they don't blame their long-suffering Madonnas for divorcing them. Actually, Stryker's story thirty years earlier is not that unlike Willard, who manages to forget about his empty life for a time by devoting himself to his work, but between assassinations, he goes off the wagon and onto a bender. Likewise, Stryker's days are occupied with preparing his troops for combat, but some nights, especially when he gets liberty, loneliness overcomes him, and he tries to drown his sorrows in a bottle. Unlike his character in *Flying Leathernecks*, John Wayne's Sgt. Stryker was never able to find a satisfactory balance between his life in the macho world of Marines and any regular maintenance of a family life. Both Stryker and Willard have lost their Madonnas. In Stryker's case, perhaps that's why there is fatalism about his character that both endears him to the audience and foreshadows his death, as if, sooner or later, fate will demand payment for his sins. And Wayne's Stryker is probably the best role of his career, nominated for an Oscar. (Admittedly, Wayne received an Oscar for simply playing a slapstick version of his cowboy stereotype in *True Grit*, but his Stryker character is by far his best work as an actor.) In *Apocalypse Now*, Willard's fatalism is a little harder to find: He certainly has the instinct to survive, but the way he places himself in harm's way without much thought about the consequences convinces audiences that he isn't that concerned with death.

The Hurt Locker

If we jump to a film made in 2008, we find that nothing much has changed about the allure of danger that Willard found in his job as an assassin, and the lack of satisfaction he felt back home, despite the undoubted best efforts of his Madonna. Willard won't talk to his wife about his missions, both because they were classified and because, since he is an assassin, he can't speak about the unspeakable. This is not the case in the Academy Award–winning *The Hurt Locker* when Sergeant First Class William James (Jeremy Renner) returns home from his assignment as a bomb squad leader in Iraq. Very similar to Willard's problem, James has developed an addiction to the adrenaline-filled excitement he feels when he pits his technical bomb diffusing knowledge against the deadly creativity of the Iraqi terrorists, hell-bent on killing as many GIs and civilians as they can.

Nothing else, not his son, his long-suffering Madonna, home, or anything, makes James's heart race or gives him any pleasure. To begin with, James also has a strange spousal relationship with his ex-wife, Connie (Evangeline Lilly). In a conversation with the second in command of his squad, Sgt. Sanborn (Anthony Mackie), he explains that he and Connie are divorced, but when he's home, they live together as if they were still married. The audience assumes that she does this for the sake of their infant son and to keep a roof over her head.

Sanborn: (*looking at a photo from Will's box*) Who's that?

James: That's my son. He's a tough little bastard. Nothing like me.

Sanborn: You mean to tell me you're married?

James: Well, you know, I had a girlfriend and, uh, she got pregnant. So we got married, we got divorced. Or, you know, I thought we got divorced. I mean, she's still living in the house and she says we're still together, so I . . . I don't know. Wha-what does that make her? I don't know. . . .

Sanborn: Dumb . . . for still being with your ass. (*laughs*)

James: (*kicks at Sanborn*) Hey! She ain't fucking dumb, all right? She's just loyal. She's just loyal, that's all.

Later, in a drunken scene with his squad, Sanborn pulls out a box of James's keepsakes, which he keeps under his bunk. James explains, "This box is full of stuff that almost killed me." Mostly this box is full of detonating devices, which are keepsakes from James's many duels with death while working on the bomb squad. But then Sanborn holds up a wedding ring on a chain. James tells him that his marriage, too, almost killed him.

When he's at home, no matter how hard James tries to settle in to living as a sometime spouse and father of a baby son, all he can think about is getting back into the war. We see him at the supermarket, trying to choose between breakfast cereals, while he surely is comparing this choice to bomb defusing, choosing whether to snip the red or blue trip wires on an IED. Finally, he picks a box of cereal at random and sighs. The differences in culture between Iraq and the United States are so vast that the overconsumption symbolized by the American supermarket and the numerous choices of cereals are also too overwhelming to James. He had left a third world culture in which life is hard and the people live in extreme poverty and sometimes starve. He may feel occasional anger at the vast differences he has experienced.

Next, he's mucking out dead leaves from his rain gutter. Before long, he's making the case to Connie for returning to Iraq for another tour by telling the undemonstrative, old-fashioned, passive Madonna about a terrorist bombing that killed a number of children in a town square, connecting the incident to the fact that the Army needs more bomb technicians. James is trying to connect with her motherly instincts to lamely try to persuade her that he's needed, but Connie impassively—and perhaps resignedly—silently continues slicing carrots with a reconciled look, as if this means he's definitely headed back for another tour. But unlike Dan and Joan in *Flying Leathernecks*, Connie has no way to relate to what James is saying, and feels even more powerless than Joan about decision making. This is probably one reason why they are divorced. Their interpersonal communication remains roadblocked.

This is not because James hates Connie or his son. Back in Iraq, he develops a fatherly relationship with a twelve-year-old Iraqi boy, and back at home, he seems delighted to play with his own one-year-old son, but even the child's favorite toy, a jack-in-the-box, reminds James of a bomb that may go off unexpectedly. We learn in his speech to his son that his addiction to adrenaline and his feeling that he is estranged from this world back home trump his affection for his wife and son, and the danger will soon draw him back into the combat zone. The boy giggles when the jack-in-the-box pops open:

James: You love playing with that. You love playing with all your stuffed animals. You love your Mommy, your Daddy. You love your pajamas. You love everything, don't ya? Yeah. But you know what, buddy? As you get older . . . some of the things you love might not seem so special anymore. Like your jack-in-the-box. Maybe you'll realize it's just a piece of tin and a stuffed animal. And the older you get, the fewer things you really love. And by the time you get to my age, maybe it's only one or two things. With me, I think it's one.

In the very next scene, we realize that James has volunteered to return to Iraq and to his dangerous occupation. We see James exiting a transport plane. In the next scene, James is once again dressed in his bomb-diffusing armor,

walking down the center of an Iraqi street like a Western gunfighter, prepared once again to do the only thing left in his life that he loves. What's left
for James's patient, loving Madonna? Considering how dangerous James's
job is, perhaps Connie will end up with a GI life insurance check. Or having
lost patience with James's incurable adrenaline addiction, Connie might go
the way of Willard's wife and complete the rest of her divorce by taking his
son and moving away.

Navy SEALs

The clear separation of the "men's club" of military men from the world of
women is also seen in *Navy SEALs* (1990), often described as the film with
the highest testosterone count since the *Rambo* movies. These super-com-
mandos exist in a world in which only three basic scenarios occur: (a) Their
team is dispatched into war zones on suicidally dangerous missions, (b) they
train and plan for more suicidally dangerous missions, (c) when back home
on leave between suicidally dangerous missions, they drink, womanize, and
carry on like Vikings celebrating the sacking of a town.

In one sequence, Chief Petty Officer Billy Graham (Dennis Haysbert),
known simply as "Chief," a highly respected member of the team, has nonetheless made what his buddies consider a serious error in judgment: He's
getting married in the morning to his Madonna, Jolene, known as "Jo" (S.
Epatha Merkerson). Too taken aback by this tragedy to complete his jeep ride
to the church where the ceremony is about to begin, one SEAL leaps out of
the vehicle and plunges off a bridge and into a river. Later, as the bride walks
down the aisle, the SEAL team's electronic pagers begin beeping at once,
which means that they have been summoned back to their base for an emergency mission. Without blinking an eye, the Chief leaves his Madonna—in
shock—literally at the altar, as he and the other SEALs make a run for their
cars. "I know this is bad timing," Chief says to Jo. "With you guys," she
replies, "it's always bad timing." All Chief can say is, "I'll call you when I
can," and runs out of the church to catch up with the team. "Saved by the
beeper," one SEAL quips.

Later, after they return from their mission, Chief Graham and his impatient fiancée discuss rescheduling the wedding. Throughout the conversation
there is one thing that is implicit: Although Chief sincerely loves Jo and
wants to marry her, when they marry, Jo knows that she must stoically and
patiently accept "the whole package," which means that her husband's fraternity of warriors will always come first in his life. Before all else and everyone, Chief Graham is a SEAL, a valued, high-status member of an elite male
fraternity. As his wife, Jo must resign herself to the role of "the little woman," someone to whom her man will come home to when duties and other
unofficial male bonding rituals (drinking, pranks, partying, etc.) permit.

Nonetheless, Jo is ready to make these sacrifices for Chief's sake: "I know all that. If anybody knows that, I do. It's part of the package. I'm in it for the long haul. I love you, Billy."

Sadly, Chief Graham, one of the nicest and most mature men in the SEAL unit, is killed on a mission, and Jo is left to join his mother at the cemetery to mourn her fiancé's passing.

There are more impatient Madonnas to discuss in chapter 3, "Women as Chattel." Deciding whether to discuss these impatient wives in this chapter or the next is a difficult choice, but because their husbands lack the proper respect for these Madonnas and treat them more like property, we'll talk about them in the next chapter.

Chapter Three

Women as Chattel

Chattel (n.): Movable property. As we noted at the end of chapter 2, we often find that there is less than a sharp dividing line in war films between the Madonna and the second of Komisar's roles for women, chattel. Following the male hegemonic pattern, it often is men who draw the lines for their Madonnas. Women are treated and objectified as if they were men's possessions rather than coequals, and in war, where the rules and ethics of civilization often are not enforced, men treat women as they please. Sometimes, character development and plot reversals topple women from their pedestals, and they fall from Madonna status all the way to Komisar's third type, women as whores (or at best a woman of loose or "situational" character).

In post–World War II America, Hollywood's portrayals of Madonnas who toppled from that pedestal still had to accommodate the old Production Code. This severely limited what they could show and how much "wickedness" women would be allowed to display in this genre of films. In the 1950s, few women were even allowed to fall all the way from Madonna to unfaithful spouse, for example. Most fell safely into code-safe roles such as the creative tightrope act created for the female protagonist in Dick Powell's Korean War film, *The Hunters* (1958).

THE HUNTERS

The roller-coaster ride from marital fidelity and back again begins when fighter pilot Maj. Cleve Saville (Robert Mitchum) meets a drunken Lt. Carl Abbott (Lee Philips) in an officer's club at Kyoto Air Base in Japan. It's the night before Saville is to be transported to Korea to join a fighter squadron flying F-86 Sabre Jets against the Red Chinese. Coincidentally, Abbott is a member of Saville's squadron. Saville tries to help the near comatose Abbott keep his appointment with "a girl" in a nearby restaurant, only to discover that the "girl" is Abbott's beautiful wife, Christine (May Britt). "Chris," as she is called thereafter, has dropped everything back home and dutifully followed her husband as far as Japan so she can be as close as she can. But instead of enriching their relationship, her presence in Japan has inadvertently made it worse. Abbott's alcoholism stems from the problem he has with his flying: He considers himself a coward because every time he takes off on a mission, he's petrified with fear. Also, Abbott has flown thirty missions but still hasn't shot down a single enemy aircraft, so his confidence problem extends to his assessment of his abilities as a combat pilot. Making matters worse for Abbott, his new colleague, Cleve Saville, is a heroic character, an ace from World War II who has shot down many enemy planes. Among his fellow flyers, Saville's nickname is "The Iceman," because he has the ability to go about his lethal task while displaying little to no emotion. Abbott is immediately convinced that he cannot measure up to Saville in virtually any manly category. Whenever Abbott gets leave to go to Japan—which in this story is amazingly often compared to, say, an infantry officer—Chris's presence reminds him only of these perceived shortcomings. Because he has not shot down a plane—probably in part due to the paralyzing fear he feels in the cockpit—Abbott considers himself unworthy of his wife's devotion. When on leave, much to Chris's distress, he spends more time in Kyoto bars than with her. Although neglected, Chris continues to play her part as Abbott's "property," his mobile camp follower, loyal and supportive, apparently willing to wait patiently until Abbott snaps out of it—that is, until she meets the suave Cleve Saville.

Weeks after their initial meeting, Saville is again in Kyoto and has a chance meeting with Chris. Saville, highly attracted to Chris, takes her to lunch, and they end up making a splendid day of it, enjoying Japanese tourist attractions. Later as the conversation inevitably turns to her husband, Chris explains her frustration. She seems unable to help Abbott, but still clings to the hope that eventually, if he survives the war, their relationship can return to its happy, prewar status. Chris's attraction to Saville is obvious, and when he takes her home, they experience their long-awaited first kiss. But that's as far as she's willing to go. "I'm off balance," she protests, torn between her attraction to Saville and guilt over her feelings for a man other than her husband. "Don't push me too hard—please." Although it's apparent by the way he acts and talks that through the years, he has had many brief affairs, this time Saville backs off, and even promises to include Abbott in his flight, in the hope that this assignment, considered an honor because of Saville's status among his fellow pilots, will make Abbott "feel closer to what he thinks he should be." As Saville gallantly turns to leave, Chris apologizes to Saville and asks him to forgive her, implying that she's being unfair to him. "Forgive you?" Saville reacts honestly: "I'm in love with you." The plot definitely thickens at this point. Will Saville continue to be a white knight, championing the lady, even if it means helping Abbott become the man she married? It's hard for the audience to see through unspoken motives and Robert Mitchum's phlegmatic exterior. Is Saville going through the motions of gallantry, perhaps leaving the fortunes of war to decide which man—the husband or the suitor—survives? Perhaps that's the secret to Saville's "Ice Man" demeanor: a fatalistic attitude about life and death in love and war. Certainly, if Abbott is killed, Saville has a clear path to take over possession of Abbott's chattel.

Abbott's new assignment as Saville's wingman doesn't start well. Being a wingman in a fighter squadron means that Abbott's job is to fly beside and a little behind Saville, guarding his "six" (six o'clock: directly behind him) while the more experienced pilot engages enemy planes. Instead of helping Abbott, however, seeing how an ace does it has the opposite effect, and as he watches, he feels even more inadequate compared to Saville, who is quickly becoming a jet ace. The drinking continues.

The next time Saville is in Kyoto, he again calls on Chris, and they have another idyllic day together. Toppling a bit from her pedestal, she admits that she wishes their romance "should have happened before I knew Carl. Now it's out of time, out of place." She is willing to see Saville, even to go out on "dates," but there is where Chris has drawn her curious line of fidelity, and she won't cross it: She won't let Saville possess her. Smitten, Saville protests, taking a flyer on the fighter pilot's "here today, a smoking hole in the ground tomorrow" motto:

Saville: The time's always now; the place is always here.

Chris: But not like this.

Saville: Is there any other way?

Chris: *(sadly)* I don't know . . .

Saville: *(hopefully)* Would you give him up?

Chris: No.

Saville: But you said yourself, your life is running out to nowhere. So is mine, to nowhere, to nothing.

Chris: I can't desert Carl.

Saville: Well, then, what's left for us, except . . . *(implying in a 1950s movie way that all that's left for them is illicit sex)*

Chris: *(resigned, interrupting)* All right, Cleve. If it will mean anything to you at all. *(She actually moves toward him, ready to reluctantly submit.)*

Saville: *(frustrated, remembering he's both an officer and a gentleman)* No. You're right: It is out of time, out of place. *(He begins to gather his coat and hat, and heads for the door.)*

Chris: Cleve, will you . . .

Saville: *(understanding what she's about to ask, and interrupting her)* You know, a woman is a strange and wonderful thing. I'll give you odds that you were going to ask me to look after Carl.

(Chris wordlessly smiles and hugs him chastely.)

Saville: *(cont'd.)* I'll look after him, Chris. I'll look after him. *(Saville exits and as the door closes, Chris cries.)* (*The Hunters*, 1958)

Now Saville is even more conflicted. His code appears to be that of knightly chivalry. There are themes here from the Arthur-Guinevere-Lancelot triangle. As Lancelot, he is sworn to protect the one man who stands between him and happiness. But Abbott turns out to be hard to protect. More and more frustrated with his perceived lack of manliness, Abbott becomes more desperate to do something heroic, to prove himself to Chris, even if he dies trying. He asks Saville if they come into contact with the skillful Chinese jet ace "K. C. Jones" in their upcoming missions, that he be allowed to lead the attack, with Saville pulling back and becoming his wingman. But Saville is brutally honest with Abbott and refuses to alter their arrangement, explaining that Abbott probably couldn't handle someone as capable as K. C. Jones. Left unsaid is that Saville has promised Chris to look out for Abbott, and so he would not intentionally put the less proficient pilot into a mismatch battle to the death with the skillful Chinese pilot.

But as luck and screenwriter's irony would have it, soon afterward, Saville and Abbott come up against a larger force of Chinese MiGs, led by ace K. C. Jones. In the ensuing wild dogfight, Jones shoots down Abbott's F-86. Although badly wounded, Abbott still manages to eject. Saville, of course, shoots down K. C. Jones, and then begins searching for Abbott. Seeing that Abbott's parachute—and the lieutenant—are hung up in a tree and that he appears to be injured, Saville, true to his promise to Chris, intentionally crash-lands his fighter and rushes to help him. Another pilot in Saville's flight, Lt. Pell (Robert Wagner), supports Saville's actions from the air, strafing North Korean soldiers who are out to capture or kill Saville and Abbott. But in doing so, Pell's plane takes a hit from antiaircraft fire and is also shot down. Together, Saville and Pell rescue the wounded Abbott, and in a trek of many days through enemy-held territory, and at a risk of their own lives, bring Abbott safely through to Allied lines.

Later, as both Saville and Abbott recover from their wounds in an Allied hospital in Kyoto, Chris visits both men. Abbott is being flown back to the United States for more treatment. The experience seems to have changed the lieutenant, and he promises that if Chris goes with him, he'll give up the alcohol and his thoughtless ways and they can try to recapture the love they once shared. Chris, ever the camp follower, agrees to return home with Abbott and later bids good-bye to Saville, thanking him. It's clear in this scene that Chris and Saville will always love each other, but both of them know their 1950s socially determined duty: Chris—property of Abbott—to marital fidelity, and Saville to honor, loneliness, and his beloved Air Force.

Benshoff and Griffin (2009) explain that not only war movies but most genre films served the cause of hegemonic masculinity that created the notion of women as chattel in the first place:

> Most Hollywood genre films of the 1930s, both pre- and post-Code, were still centered on men [with the exception of women's films, of course] and tended to simplify female characters into basic types drawn from the virgin-whore dichotomy. The Western also dealt predominantly with male adventure, and women's roles were reduced to either the saloon girl (itself a long-time Hollywood euphemism for prostitute), or the good daughter of the rancher, or perhaps a virginal schoolteacher. In the horror film or the action-adventure movie, women were primarily helpless victims waiting to be carried off by monsters or marauding madmen, so that they might be saved by patriarchal heroes. (228)

World War II and postwar women were somewhat more liberated, this thanks to women's gains made as more active participants in the war effort. As adjuncts to male warriors at or near combat zones, females were allowed to transcend the restrictive role of the post-Victorian child-woman we encountered in Griffith's *Birth of a Nation* and *Hearts of the World*. But during the 1950s, as demonstrated by Chris's powerlessness in *The Hunters*, women were still allowed few roles to play. After the Code fell and the 1960s culture of drugs, sex, and rock 'n' roll gave women many new options, the daughters of Rosie the Riveter came to their majority, giving birth to the women's liberation movement.

Depending on the era the screenplay was written, a Madonna might be tempted to step down from the pedestal but might choose to do nothing about it. In *Since You Went Away*, Anne was often tempted to infidelity by the handsome, debonair Tony, but remained faithful, even when her husband was listed as missing in action. Because *The Hunters* was produced fifteen years later, a Madonna goes to the brink of unfaithfulness, but at least technically (although not biblically) remains faithful to her marriage vows. If *The Hunters* had been made in the twenty-first century, the story might have been quite different. But just a half dozen years later in *The Americanization of Emily* (1964), and two decades later in *Coming Home* (1978), Madonnas who have tired of their restrictive roles as chattel are ready and willing to step down from their pedestals. We will discuss these two films later in this chapter.

THE WIVES OF *CASABLANCA*

Before them, we must discuss *Casablanca*, in which Rick catches a young Madonna tipping dangerously over the edge of her pedestal, trying to make a decision about whether she should be unfaithful to her husband in return for realizing their goal to reach the United States. These two young people (Annina and Jan Brandel, played by Joy Page and Helmut Dantine) are a married couple from Bulgaria, where "things are very bad." (This is odd casting for Dantine, who distinguished himself during the war playing wild-eyed Nazis in films such as *Mrs. Miniver* and *Edge of Darkness*.) Annina and Jan don't have the money for the standard bribe to obtain exit visas to Lisbon (and on to their goal, America). They have spent more of their money than anticipated just getting as far as Casablanca. Jan has been reduced to gambling in Rick's casino in the vain hope of winning the needed money. Police Prefect Major Renault, the original sleazy politician with a particular eye for young ladies, has a side business in which he seduces young, pretty chattel like Annina in return for safe passage out of Casablanca. Renault has privately propositioned Annina, stating that if she agrees to sleep with him once, the bribe amount will be waived and they can fly on to Lisbon and America. Annina, a true Madonna, is desperate. She sees that Jan is losing in the casino, so she asks Rick, as a man of the world, what he thinks about her going through with Renault's proposed bargain:

Annina: Oh, monsieur, you are a man. If someone loved you very much, so that your happiness was the only thing that she wanted in the world, but she did a bad thing to make certain of it, could you forgive her?

Rick: *(heartsick over his own romantic problems)* Nobody ever loved me that much.

Annina: And he never knew, and the girl kept this bad thing locked in her heart? That would be all right, wouldn't it?

Rick: You want my advice?

Annina: Oh, yes, please.

Rick: Go back to Bulgaria. (*Casablanca*, 1943)

Rick Blaine has a reputation as a man "who sticks my neck out for nobody" to live up to, so he can't just plainly tell Annina what he intends to do. He rises from the table, leaving Annina dejected, and heads for his casino. There, he spots Jan, frustrated, losing what little money he has left on the roulette wheel. He approaches Jan, and advises him firmly to bet all the money he has on one number. He gives his roulette croupier Emil (Marcel Dalio) the high sign, and as the ball spins, Emil secretly pushes a button under the table and Jan wins a great deal of money. Then Rick advises him to let his winnings ride on the same number for the next spin of the wheel. Jan does so, and not so amazingly, wins again. Rick tells Jan to cash in his winnings and leave. Jan and Annina have their exit visa bribe money, and the Madonna's virtue is saved. When a grateful Annina realizes what Rick has done, she throws her arms around him in thanks. But Rick takes her hand and points her toward her husband.

Then, of course, there is the love of Rick's life, Ilsa Lund. When they met in Paris, Ilsa and Rick become lovers. But they are forced to flee Paris because the Germans are about to occupy the French capital. With a price on Rick's head, he and Ilsa and piano player Sam must catch a train to somewhere in unoccupied France. But as the rain at the station provides the perfect mise-en-scène, Rick receives a note from Ilsa: "Richard, I cannot go with you or ever see you again. You must not ask why. Just believe that I love you. Go, my darling, and God bless you. —Ilsa." Given the facts at his disposal and knowing little about Ilsa's backstory, Rick jumps to the conclusion that Ilsa was afraid of the life of a refugee, or that she was hesitant to follow through on the proposal of marriage he had made earlier in the day. Regardless, although all one can see on his face is bitterness, Rick's heart is broken.

Only later, in Casablanca, does Rick discover that before they met, Ilsa was married to Czech freedom fighter and underground resistance leader Victor Laszlo (Paul Henreid), whom she believed had been killed by the Germans. But Ilsa had just discovered the day she and Rick were to leave Paris that Victor was still alive, ill, and in need of her help. So instead of being a faithless fiancée, Ilsa was actually a faithful Madonna.

Later, the situation is much different when they again encounter each other in this North African city. Ilsa is traveling with Victor, and the two are desperately trying to avoid capture by the Germans and get from Casablanca to Lisbon and on to America, where Victor will try to raise money and other support for Europe's anti-Nazi resistance movements. Unfortunately, Casablanca is currently in the hands of the Vichy French, collaborators with the

Germans. Initially, a drunken Rick meets privately with Ilsa, but it doesn't go well, and Rick insults her, comparing her to a prostitute:

Rick: Why did you have to come to Casablanca? There are other places.

Ilsa: I wouldn't have come if I'd known that you were here. Believe me Rick, it's true I didn't know . . .

Rick: It's funny about your voice, how it hasn't changed. I can still hear it. "Richard, dear, I'll go with you anyplace. We'll get on a train together and never stop—"

Ilsa: Don't, Rick! I can understand how you feel.

Rick: *(scoffs)* You understand how I feel. How long was it we had, honey?

Ilsa: *(on the verge of tears)* I didn't count the days.

Rick: Well, I did. Every one of 'em. Mostly I remember the last one. The wow finish. A guy standing on a station platform in the rain with a comical look in his face because his insides have been kicked out.

Ilsa: Can I tell you a story, Rick?

Rick: Has it got a wow finish?

Ilsa: I don't know the finish yet.

Rick: Well, go on. Tell it—maybe one will come to you as you go along.

Ilsa: It's about a girl who had just come to Paris from her home in Oslo. At the house of some friends, she met a man about whom she'd heard her whole life. A very great and courageous man. He opened up for her a whole beautiful world full of knowledge and thoughts and ideals. Everything she knew or ever became was because of him. And she looked up to him and worshipped him . . . with a feeling she supposed was love.

Rick: *(bitterly)* Yes, it's very pretty. I heard a story once—as a matter of fact, I've heard a lot of stories in my time. They went along with the sound of a tinny piano playing in the parlor downstairs. "Mister, I met a man once when I was a kid," it always began. *(laughs)*

Rick: Well, I guess neither one of our stories is very funny. Tell me, who was it you left me for? Was it Laszlo, or were there others in between or . . . aren't you the kind that tells?

(Ilsa tearfully and silently leaves Rick's cafe. Rick's face falls in his hands sadly, knowing that he's said all the wrong things.) (*Casablanca*, 1943)

Later, Rick finds out the truth about Ilsa and realizes that when she wrote that "dear John" note to him, she was only being faithful to the husband she had just discovered was still alive. Now Rick admires her again. Plus, she serves the cause of freedom as Victor's muse and helpmate. But Ilsa is still deeply in love with Rick, and can't help herself: She begins to topple from the pedestal. Rick has two stolen letters of transit that can be used to get Laszlo to Lisbon, and he tells her that he'll make it happen for Victor. He also lies to her, saying that he and Ilsa will send Victor safely on his way and then these two can live happily ever after. At this point, she's willing to leave Victor for Rick, but only if Victor is free to do his work, which she has always known is her husband's first priority. However, Rick has known all along that if he and Ilsa did this dishonorable thing, it would haunt them forever. And despite appearances, Rick is an honorable man. When the time comes, at the airport, in classic Hollywood fashion, and using the best dialogue Oscar-winning screenwriters Julius and Philip Epstein can write, Rick puts things right and sends Ilsa along with Victor on the plane to Lisbon. He explains it to the confused and conflicted Ilsa this way:

Rick: Inside of us, we both know you belong with Victor. You're part of his work, the thing that keeps him going. If that plane leaves the ground and you're not with him, you'll regret it. Maybe not today. Maybe not tomorrow, but soon and for the rest of your life.

Ilsa: But what about us?

Rick: We'll always have Paris. We didn't have, we, we lost it until you came to Casablanca. We got it back last night.

Ilsa: When I said I would never leave you.

Rick: And you never will. But I've got a job to do, too. Where I'm going, you can't follow. What I've got to do, you can't be any part of. Ilsa, I'm no good at being noble, but it doesn't take much to see that the problems of three little people don't amount to a hill of beans in this crazy world. Someday you'll understand that.

(Ilsa lowers her head and begins to cry.)

Rick: Now, now . . .

(Rick gently places his hand under her chin and raises it so their eyes meet.)

Rick: Here's looking at you kid. (*Casablanca*, 1943)

GIVING UP THE PEDESTAL

In *The Americanization of Emily*, the title character, Emily Barham (Julie Andrews), an Englishwoman living in London during World War II, has already lost a husband, a brother, and her father to the war. Emily's story reveals a somewhat gradual process of stepping down from the Madonna's pedestal. Instead of wringing her hands and keeping the votive candles burning next to a photo of her deceased husband, Emily first volunteers to drive ambulances. Reading to wounded men and occasionally providing sexual favors to now-healed soldiers on their last night of leave before going back to the war, the pedestal crumbles. Lately, while chauffeuring high-ranking Allied officers around London, Emily meets an American naval officer, Charlie Madison (James Garner), a "dog robber" (personal aide) to a high-ranking American admiral (Melvyn Douglas) intimately involved in naval D-Day planning. Charlie sets "the best table in the European Theater of Operations" for his admiral, providing food and drink that regular British people haven't seen in years, due to severe war rationing. Charlie seems to be doing quite well in romancing the other female British drivers, due partly to his charm, but also because of his "treasure trove" of dresses and other clothes, perfumes, and liquors that he stores in his hotel room. Considering the privations the British are suffering for the war effort, Emily finds this kind of extravagance appalling. As she drives Charlie around London, pursuing his objective of keeping his admiral and other senior officer friends "well housed, well fed and well loved," Emily somewhat hypocritically vents her disgust for the entire "immoral" process.

Later, after Charlie has heard enough of what he considers to be Emily's "holier than thou" criticism of Americans, he remarks, "You're something of a prig, Miss Barham." Truly shocked that he thinks so, Emily says, "I don't mean to be." This begins a period of introspection and growth in Emily's character arc. She wonders if this brash American is right, and whether she is repulsed by or attracted to him. Back at the female drivers' dorm, Emily asks Sheila, her friend, if she comes off as a prig. She replies:

Sheila: Oh, lord, yes, luv. You've been shattering all of us with your virtue ever since you've joined this motor pool.

Emily: Bloody *that* awful?

Sheila: Bloody virgin goddess herself.

Emily: The fact is I'm anything but! I'm grotesquely sentimental and fall in love at the drop of a hat. That's why I gave up hospital driving . . . all those men, moaning in the back of the ambulance . . . especially the lot from Africa. I used to read to them in my off hours. And when they were healed and being sent back to the front, they'd come looking for me to spend their last nights of leave with them. Little hotel rooms, bed and breakfast for a guinea. I paid the guinea myself more often than not. But I couldn't say "no" to them, could I? I'd just lost my husband at Tobruk, and I was overwhelmed with tenderness for all dying men. As I say, I'm grotesquely sentimental. (*The Americanization of Emily*, 1964)

Sheila is dying her hair blonde (at Charlie's behest) and getting herself ready to serve as an escort for a general at one of Charlie's admiral's dinner parties that night. Provided with everything from silk underwear to a cocktail dress, and looking forward to great food and booze, Sheila encourages Emily to attend as well. But Emily has already turned down Charlie's invitation.

Emily: But it all ends up in somebody's bed, doesn't it?

Sheila: *(exasperated)* Well, look who's talking, and after that lurid confession that you've just made.

Emily: *(contrite)* Sorry. I *am* a prig at that. (*The Americanization of Emily*, 1964)

Emily decides that being chattel obtained to decorate an admiral's table isn't the worst way to spend an evening in wartime London. So she decides to attend Charlie's party, and ends up having a good time. Emily still considers Charlie "a complete rascal," but is growing more attracted to the dashing officer at each encounter. Rather than being a hero who might go off to war and get himself killed, Charlie appears to her to be the reverse, describing himself as a "practicing coward." Having lost all the heroic men in her life to the war, Emily finds a ray of hope in Charlie's somewhat craven attitude. However, Charlie isn't completely chicken-hearted. We learn that he was once a heroic volunteer, a Marine who fought bravely at Guadalcanal. But then, he explains, he realized " that a man could get killed" out there. So, thanks to his prior night manager hospitality work in a hotel in Washington and his Pentagon connections, Charlie gets transferred from the Marines to the Navy and much safer work with the admiral, as far away from the shooting as a man in uniform can get.

After his duties at the party are done and everyone has left, Charlie enters his hotel room, only to find Emily sitting on his bed, waiting for him. They kiss and the affair begins. Having tagged Emily as the kind of woman who swoons for heroes, Charlie asks her why she's attracted to him. After all, he's the antithesis of the manly, heroic figure:

Charlie: "I'm yellow, honey. Clear through."

Emily: That's your most attractive quality. Oh, I've had it with heroes. Every man I've loved has died in this war. You'll never get caught in the shooting. That's one thing I'm sure of. You can't imagine how attractive that makes you to me. (*The Americanization of Emily*, 1964)

Having deserted the pedestal, Emily decides that the shortest path away from male hegemony in wartime is to wade into the deep end of the pool and at least enjoy the carnal delights normally reserved for fighting men. But in this instance, she also falls in love, and as the film goes on, Charlie proposes marriage. Ironically, in a clever Paddy Chayefsky–penned comic twist, Charlie ends up an accidental and reluctant hero on Omaha Beach on D-Day, but Emily still loves him despite it. Regardless, no more pedestal for this ex-Madonna.

Flight of the Intruder

Another ex-Madonna is featured in the Vietnam War film, *Flight of the Intruder* (1991). Once the wife of a dashing naval aviator, Callie Joy (Rosanna Arquette) is now his widow and single mother to his daughter. Callie has found a way to be useful to the war effort as an adjunct, providing assistance services for other bereaved widows who, like Callie, followed their men across the ocean like good camp followers to Subic Bay Naval Air Station in the Philippines. There, as in Kyoto during the Korean War, wives of pilots can get to see their husbands more often than infantry officers can.

A-6 Intruder Pilot Jake Grafton (Brad Johnson) has just lost his copilot and bombardier and flies from his aircraft carrier to Subic for liberty, but also to comfort his late copilot's wife. Jake just misses the widow, as she has just left for the United States, but he meets Callie, who's boxing up some things in the woman's apartment. Later, Jake meets Callie again at a bar she frequents, and soon they share a bed. Like Emily, Callie has moved on from the role of the grieving war widow. Far removed from the pedestal, Callie remains attracted by naval aviators—and perhaps the life of an aviator's spouse—and Jake is a handsome, charming fellow. The next morning, Callie introduces Jake to her daughter.

When Jake gets his next liberty, he spends it with Callie. One idyllic day on the beach with Callie and her daughter, Jake asks, "I don't want to complicate things, but if you wouldn't mind, I'd like to write to you." She says she would like this very much. He asks her if getting involved with another naval aviator doesn't bring up bad memories. She says no, but "Maybe I want to remember." This underdeveloped "B-plot" does not give the audience enough time to see how this relationship develops.

Coming Home

In a much better Vietnam War era picture, *Coming Home*, the conflict is half a world away in Southeast Asia, and the Madonna type—at least at the start—this time, of all the unlikely actresses, is Jane Fonda. This antiwar activist actress plays Sally Hyde, who begins the film as the wimpy, obedient helpless Madonna/chattel wife of a Marine captain, Bob (Bruce Dern). Bob is a dominating, patronizing husband who treats Sally far more like a daughter than an equal. Sally, whose character arc is going to take off like a rocket later on, begins as straight-laced and squared away as a Marine's wife could possibly be. Bob is the "commanding officer" in every minute phase of her life. There is no sense at all of the patriarchal but relatively shared life of the couple in *Flying Leathernecks*. You get the sense that at home, Sally is not in command of the house the way Joan was. The audience can see that Bob's arrogance and condescension often irritate Sally, but she does nothing about it . . . for now. When Bob is ordered to Vietnam for a year's tour of duty, Sally must find something to do with her time. Like Emily and Anne before her, Sally decides to volunteer at a hospital. She chooses to work in a Los Angeles Veteran's Administration hospital that cares for disabled soldiers. There she meets a paraplegic veteran, Luke Martin (Jon Voight). Again, like Emily, at first Sally dislikes Luke, especially when the veteran makes disparaging remarks about the war and the government. But little by little, Sally begins to care for Luke and even understand and agree with his left-wing politics. Soon, thanks in part to Sally's efforts, Luke is rehabilitated enough for release. Down Sally comes from the pedestal, symbolized for her growing sympathy for the antiwar movement, curling her hair when Bob likes it straight and buying a funky used Porsche. Sally pulls away from the role as chattel and from the domination of her husband. In a huge act of rebellion for a woman modeling a 1940s/1950s housewife, Sally changes her hairstyle, dress, and attitude from the way Bob liked it to how *she* prefers.

Just before Luke's release, Sally's relationship with Luke had turned to love, and they have an affair. And while making love with Luke, Sally, who was a virgin before marrying Bob, has her first orgasm. This is significant. Bob, apparently, was in charge of lovemaking in addition to every other phase of his chattel wife's life, and was concerned only with his own orgasm. But Luke treats Sally like an equal in bed and makes sure she is satisfied.

Later, Bob returns from Vietnam a broken man, suffering mightily from posttraumatic stress disorder (PTSD). Off balance, he is even more shocked to see—and listen to—Sally, who has become a totally different person, someone he cannot control in any way. But Bob has also changed: He is no longer the confident, gung ho Marine who left a year ago for Vietnam, longing for adventure, glory, and personal advancement. Having witnessed—and perhaps participated in—the cruelty men inflict on their fellow humans, Bob is practically psychotic and grows more suicidal the longer he is back home. What he has seen in the war is horrific, and the only thing that kept him relatively sane was the image of his life back home with his never-changing Madonna, his Sally, always predictable, totally controllable, always his exclusive possession. To make matters worse, Luke and Sally have engaged in some antiwar protests while Bob was gone, and the Marine Corps wants to know if Bob—in a classic case of guilt by association—has become a "security risk." So in addition to his mental health, his career is also ruined. Destroyed by war guilt and his marriage and career ruined, Bob loses his grasp on reality. Bob's reality, in the form of the old Sally, might have been able to nurse Bob back to mental health. Or, perhaps, because Bob would not allow Sally any individualism or self-actualization, if he came back and Sally had remained unchanged, she would not have the skills to help him. As it was, after dealing with Luke and the other wounded veterans, Sally might actually have been able to help, but as changed as her work at the hospital made her, she probably could not reconnect with Bob enough to do anything for him. As it was, Bob is just too far gone. After a few scary incidents, including threatening Sally and Luke with a gun, Bob commits ritual suicide. Dressed in his best Marine uniform, he walks out to the nearby beach and strips away his uniform, symbolic of his repentance for his war crimes in Vietnam. Next, to complete his absolution, he walks out into the ocean to drown, symbolically asking that his sins be washed away.

Hanover Street

Although we will revisit permanently unfaithful wives again in chapter 4, it seems appropriate here to discuss one more Madonna who topples from the pedestal all the way to unfaithfulness but then, plagued with guilt, repents and returns to faithfulness. In this film, unlike *The Hunters*, the Madonna is completely unfaithful and sleeps with another man, this time also a pilot. And unlike *Coming Home*, there is no satisfactory or reasonable excuse for this wife's unfaithfulness: no controlling, condescending, unloving husband who treats his wife like chattel or gives his wife any excuse to cast aside her wedding vows. Instead, the World War II love melodrama *Hanover Street*

(1979) uses every romantic trick in the book including John Barry's exquisitely romantic score and skillful acting to try to turn a sordid affair into a passionate love triangle. But for those who truly value their marriage vows and all that they mean, *Hanover Street* is still about cheating.

Margaret (Lesley-Anne Down), wife of Paul Sellinger (Christopher Plummer), Oxford professor-turned trainer of spies for England's MI-6 branch, also serves the war effort as a nurse's aide in a military hospital. On a street corner in London, she meets David Halloran (Harrison Ford), a dashing young American bomber pilot. He's immediately smitten with Margaret and pursues her intently, despite learning later that she's married. At first, as a bomber pilot might say, she's a "target of opportunity," chattel to be possessed while he can, before he is either killed in a bombing run over Germany or rotated back home to the United States. On the other hand, Margaret looks at Halloran with intrigue, perhaps with a longing in her life for something extraordinary, even risky (ironically, we later learn that Margaret's husband has that same longing). Margaret and Halloran sleep together and, surprisingly for both, also fall in love. What makes this worse, and provides Margaret with no small amount of guilt, is that her husband Paul loves her intently and is completely devoted to her and their delightful daughter. When she sees Paul and their daughter together at home, Margaret hates herself for what she has done. But Halloran's charm and magnetism, plus apparently the sex they share, draw her back to him again.

In one scene, in bed with Halloran, Margaret shares with him her life with Paul and her great guilt for what she's doing by having an affair:

> **Margaret:** He was the only man I'd ever known. I never thought I lacked anything . . . it's just that I wasn't sure if this was it . . . if this was everything . . . maybe that's why I went with you that first day at the bus stop. It's so damned unfair: I try so hard to forget you, I really do . . . which is the same as thinking of you all the time. I don't want to hurt anybody. I don't want to do anything wrong. Sometimes I sit across the dinner table from him and watch him, and I want him so desperately to do something or say something that I can hate. But he never does. I've hurt him so much. It makes me hate myself and wish I never met you. But when I'm with you, it's so strong and I never want to let you go. Why don't things work out the way they're supposed to? (*Hanover Street*, 1979)

Oddly, despite her infidelity, the audience still cares about Margaret, if for no other reason than she has the good taste to feel so damn guilty. Probably what Margaret and Paul need is some old-fashioned marriage counseling. Since they both seem to feel that they are missing something in their lives and in their marriage, they should start communicating how they feel about what is missing and reach out to each other for that much-needed excitement. If they were able to learn effective coping and communication skills within the context of their marriage, perhaps their shared need to risk everything to "feel extraordinary" would not be necessary.

Not feeling at all extraordinary, over on the other side of London at MI-6, Paul yearns for the kind of something a man finds risky and adventurous. But unlike Margaret, he'd never contemplate being unfaithful. Paul is tired of just training spies for dangerous and exciting exploits in Nazi-occupied France. For once in his life, he'd like to be a hero and do the heroic stuff himself. Unlike Bob, the husband in *Coming Home*, the more the audience gets to know about Paul, the more we see how intelligent, kind, and loving he is to Margaret and their daughter, and how much we grow to dislike Margaret for her infidelity.

Although Margaret gives her husband no hint that she's been unfaithful, Paul still feels inadequate as a man, having not been tested in the war like all his intelligence agents. He feels unworthy of his safe life in England and the possession of a beautiful, charming wife. So instead of assigning one of the agents he has trained for another dangerous spy mission to France, Paul decides to do the job himself. Before he leaves, Paul calls Margaret, who's working on her volunteer job at the hospital:

Paul: I love you, Margaret. . . . I know I'm not that special.

Margaret: What are you talking about? Of course, you're special.

Paul: Oh, no, I'm not. We both know it. It's just my curse to be so damned ordinary. I . . . do so want to be dashing. . . . It's not that I don't want to be, but I can't blame you for finding me so unexciting. *(Margaret is paged, and must ring off.)* I love you. *(Hanover Street, 1979)*

Paul never suspects that as fate (and the screenplay) would have it, the pilot who will be assigned to drop him into France is his wife's secret lover. Halloran's plane is shot down, and only Halloran and Paul manage to parachute to safety. For various reasons, including Paul's sprained ankle, the two complete the spy mission together.

During the mission, the following conversation between Paul and Halloran typifies Paul's male angst about what he perceives as his role as a non-heroic bystander. He tries to explain to Halloran why he decided to go on this mission himself:

Paul: All my life, no matter what I did, I've always been the same thing: pleasant. I'm pleasant. I was a teacher; that's a pleasant profession. I'm rather pleasant-looking, if I do say so myself. If anyone was asked to describe me, they'd say I'm . . . pleasant. Now, I never minded it that much before, except now . . . it's beginning to hurt! More than I thought anything could hurt.

Halloran: I don't know what you mean.

Paul: Well, take a good look at yourself, and you'll see a hero.

Halloran: That's a lotta crap. I don't want to be one.

Paul: Even if you don't want to be one, you are. You can't help it. You're the one who's ice skating on the lake when the little boy falls into the freezing water, and you save him. I'm the one who gives you my coat to wrap him in. When it's all over, you're on the front page of all the newspapers, saying it was really nothing . . . and I have a wet coat. (*Hanover Street*, 1979)

From their casual conversations during their mission, Halloran has deduced that Paul is Margaret's husband. Paul doesn't know about the affair and suspects nothing. It is again ironic that in the climax of the film, Halloran ends up heroically saving the life of his wounded rival, assuring that Paul will live to return to his wife. Again, Paul, wounded, plays second fiddle to a hero, but, in the end, it is he who collects the prize commodity: Margaret. During the time that Halloran and Sellinger's plane was listed as missing, Margaret is smitten with even more guilt, believing that perhaps she has lost both of her men, and that it is divine punishment for her sins that caused it. But during the time the two men are missing, Margaret also realizes how much she really loves her husband. So in the climax, meeting with Halloran in the hospital where Paul is recuperating, Halloran tells Margaret how much he admires Paul, and that he knows she must remain with him. Then she tells Halloran once again that she loves him, but resolutely turns and walks away, a tear falling down her cheek, as she heads for her husband's room.

The Battle of Britain

Women who seize opportunities to jump down from the pedestal and serve in the war near their men have helped substantially in the evolution of the roles of women in war. These steps, even though they were at first only in auxiliary service roles, made possible the role of G.I. Jane just a few generations later. We will examine that role in chapter 6.

While jumping from the pedestal to serve, it's not necessary, like Sally or Margaret, to be unfaithful to a husband. *The Battle of Britain* (1969) is a good example. British Women's Auxiliary Air Force (WAAF) section officer Maggie Harvey (Susannah York) tells her husband Colin (again Christopher Plummer, this time as a heroic R.A.F. squadron leader), that she's " not cut out to wave a wet hankie in a sooty [train] station." By this she means that although Colin prefers that his wife serve him as a housewife Madonna, subserviently waiting on her pedestal at their cottage door, Maggie believes that it's more important for her to serve her country in its time of need. This seems to be the sole bone of contention between the two, as Colin, a staunch traditionalist when it comes to male-female roles, stands firmly opposed to the wartime mobilization of women in their country's service. His wife's participation in what he believes should be a man's war is repugnant to Colin. Furthermore, when he learns that his next assignment is to train recruits far up north in Scotland while Maggie is stationed directly in harm's way in the outh of England, he fears for her safety, but he also is concerned about how rarely they will be able to see each other. Colin asks her repeatedly to request a posting in Scotland, but she either refuses or delays applying for the transfer. Maggie has what to her is a very important—and exciting— job, working in RAF air operations. Working to organize Britain's air defenses during this desperate battle is the most exciting thing she's ever done in her life, and her husband insists that she become his portable chattel and give it all up to follow her man. She doesn't want to give up her job for some lesser post up in Scotland. Even when Colin's squadron is reposted farther south, she still won't ask for a transfer to be closer to him. Maggie has risen in officer's rank and responsibility and is stubborn about not relinquishing it. Then one day, a new officer is posted to Maggie's group, a former fighter pilot whose face was terribly disfigured with burns when his Hurricane caught fire. Thanks to Guy Hamilton's fine directing, audiences see in Maggie's face the realization that something like this could just as soon happen to Colin. Ironically, the next day, Colin, too, is shot down in flames. Although he parachutes from his Spitfire, he also suffers major burns. In telling Maggie about Colin's injuries, her commander says he will arrange to have her posted in a position of responsibility nearby Colin's hospital, so she can be close to him while he undergoes plastic reconstructive surgery. This time Maggie agrees. But the change in posting means that Maggie, instead of just being reduced to be her husband's chattel, will still be able to continue her service with the RAF as well as her role as a wife.

Sink the Bismarck!

With a job similar to Maggie's service in the RAF, Women's Royal Naval Service (WRNS or Wrens) officer Anne Davis (Dana Wynter) has found an important way to serve Britain during World War II. In *Sink the Bismarck!* (1960), she has just been posted as the assistant (read secretary) to Capt. Jonathan Shepherd (Kenneth More), director of naval operations (DNO), at the Admiralty in London. Initially, Shepherd, who has lost his wife to a bomb blast during the Blitz, is standoffish and formal with everyone in the department, especially Anne. She appears to have no status in his eyes. He refers to male officers by their rank and last name, but he calls Second Officer Anne Davis "Miss Davis." Anne's role seems to be nothing more than a naval service commodity: She appears to be at the Admiralty simply to do Shepherd's bidding, but not to have an identity or much of a job description. This B-plot of this otherwise historically accurate film about the sinking of a dangerous German battleship is emotional: Because of his wife's death, Shepherd has decided that for the duration, he will stuff all emotions under a thick veneer of duty. Of course, all Shepherd is doing is internalizing his emotions rather than dealing effectively with them. Nonetheless, this pleases the First Sea Lord, who wants a DNO "as cold as a witch's heart . . . with an enormous brain."

However, as time goes on, Shepherd begins to appreciate Anne's intelligence, organization, and highly efficient work in his service. Since Shepherd is trying to be all masculine in this difficult job, Anne decides that he needs help in employing the feminine side of his personality. She takes on the role of Shepherd's conscience. For example, when he chooses to reinforce the home fleet to aid them against the German battleship *Bismarck*, she reminds him that this action strips convoys of their only protection against German U-boat attacks, and that some of those convoy ships are troop ships. So advised, Shepherd glibly replies, "That's the risk we'll have to take." "We?" Anne retorts.

Later we discover that like Emily, Anne's fiancé was killed in the war. She tells Shepherd that her man was killed at Dunkirk. She uses this opening to tell Shepherd that she thinks it helps to talk about personal things, but Shepherd disagrees: "I don't think it helps at all. Getting emotional about things is a peacetime luxury. In wartime, it's much too painful." The pall of emotionless behavior is how Shepherd tries to cope with the loss of his wife and his constant worry about his son, serving as an aerial gunner on the carrier *Arc Royal* in the Mediterranean. Later, when he orders the *Arc Royal* to steam up to the North Sea and join the fight against the *Bismarck*, Anne once again reminds him that his son serves on the carrier. Knowing looks are exchanged.

Under Shepherd's organization, as a number of British warships close in on the German battleship, Shepherd receives word that his son's plane is overdue and the young man is listed as missing in action. This is when Shepherd's philosophy breaks down, and he tells Anne about his wife's death in the Blitz: "I didn't think it was possible to feel such pain," he says. Later, after being notified that his son has been rescued, Shepherd walks into his office, shuts the door, and has a good cry. Anne witnesses this but gives the proud man his space.

Anne turns down an assignment that would have insured a promotion and a trip to America so she can remain at the Admiralty and work with Shepherd. Little by little, Shepherd comes to admire Anne as a person and even as a woman worth pursuing. As they struggle together to coordinate the British Navy's all-out attack against the *Bismarck*, their relationship deepens. At the end, the *Bismarck* sunk, Shepherd, whose character arc has turned him into more of a complete person, and Anne, who has been promoted from his "assistant" to his friend, become a couple, walking down a London street to have a meal together.

"MALE CALL" CHATTEL

Jeanine Basinger writes that one of the staples in combat films are "mail call" scenes, in which young soldiers write and receive letters from home, from girlfriends or family (1986, 50, 63). In *Guadalcanal Diary* (1943), actor Richard Jaeckel plays a Marine whose nickname is "Chicken" (as in "young-ster," or "spring chicken": not meaning "cowardly"). On the troop ship trans-porting them to Guadalcanal, another Marine notices that Chicken, in his bunk, is busy writing a letter. The older man assumes the letter is to Chick-en's girlfriend, and he asks about her. Embarrassed by the fact that the letter is actually addressed to his mother, Chicken lies and describes his nonexis-tent girlfriend as someone "who gives me no back-talk." Even in 1943, Chicken understands that to be considered an equal by his fellow Marines, he thinks that he must have previously established sexual and interpersonal dominance over a female. That his closest relationship is with his mother, instead of a girlfriend, is an indication that he has not yet become a man. In the world of men, when they brag to their buddies about their relationships with women, possessing and controlling females as chattel—as if women were their personal property—is a socially constructed descriptor of male potency.

Far from their women back home, the thoughts of males in combat zones often drift to sex. So stories of controlling and possessing sexually submis-sive chattel command the men's attention. In *Destination Tokyo*, for exam-ple, a self-styled lothario nicknamed "Wolf" (John Garfield) entrances his submarine shipmates with highly exaggerated tales of his exploits with wom-en. In these stories, women are objectified as sex objects, existing completely as "targets" for Wolf's seductive operations. But the audience knows that Wolf is a legend mostly in his own mind. While he narrates stories about his amazing sexual conquests, on the screen the audience sees flashbacks of the *real* happenings he describes, in which Wolf strikes out much more often than he "scores." The men probably have some inkling of this, but don't care. Hearing Wolf's stories about conquests and his chattel women transports them from the world of war to a much more pleasant undertaking.

In *Platoon* (1986), the wallet pictures he carries around characterize Pvt. Gardner (Bob Orwig) as clearly understanding the roles of women as Madonna and chattel/sex object. He offers fellow private Chris Taylor (Charlie Sheen) a look at a treasured picture of his girlfriend, presumably his fiancée, that he keeps in his wallet. "She's the one for me," he claims, as if the girlfriend is his true and only Madonna. But Taylor flips the wallet picture over to the next in Gardner's wallet, a sexy pinup of every 1960s male's favorite chattel and fantasy girlfriend, Raquel Welch. Amused, Taylor sees that Gardner may be settling for the attainable girlfriend while in his fantasy life maintaining wild thoughts of possessing the pinup.

ANOTHER PINUP AS CHATTEL

The World War I aviation epic, *The Blue Max* (1966) features another famous 1960s pinup, Ursula Andress. Andress plays Countess Kaeti von Klugermann, clearly the chattel possession (read trophy wife) of her much older husband, General Count von Klugermann (James Mason). As von Klugermann's young, voluptuous wife, Kaeti is ceremonially the general's spouse, but she feels free to have affairs with whoever suits her fancy, providing she keeps her improprieties suitably discreet. The general very well may do the same, although it's unclear whether or not his nighttime game playing with a noblewoman involves sex or something else. As a decoration for his arm at parties and official functions, Kaeti services the general's ego, but after hours, when the field marshal is off at odd hours playing games, Kaeti has affairs with dashing young flyers, including the general's nephew, Willy von Klugermann (Jeremy Kemp). Later, her affair with another pilot, Lt. Bruno Stachel (George Peppard), devolves into a less-than-discreet series of assignations, and threatens to become a public embarrassment. Stachel rejects her and Kaeti becomes enraged. She has an item of blackmail on Stachel, which she reports to the chief of the General Staff. When General Count von Klugermann finds out that thanks to Kaeti, Stachel, whom he has spent a great deal of time and effort to publicize as a great proletarian war hero, is about to be disgraced, he arranges for Stachel to fly a new but flawed prototype monoplane in a public exhibition. Knowing the plane is unsafe, he tells Stachel to really put the plane through its paces. Then the general calmly watches as the aircraft disintegrates in midair and crashes, killing the young pilot but covering up his wife's indiscretions. The general sternly orders the sobbing Kaeti to dry her tears, say nothing and once again assume her decorative place on his arm. Kaeti has learned that along with the perks, being mere chattel has its limitations.

There is no clearer definition of women as chattel than the commodification of women in the form of these popular pinups. In the 1960s, chattel women in popular culture, such as Raquel Welch and Ursula Andress, were choice pinups for male fantasies of possession and sexual dominance. But they weren't the first: The 1940s had their pinups, too.

FILM ACTRESS CHATTEL PINUPS OF THE 1940S

If the likes of June Allyson and Donna Reed were set aside to be the purest of Madonnas, Hollywood typecast and promoted a number of its actresses as the official sex object chattel of World War II. The number one sex object, the most pinned-up pinup of them all was Betty Grable, pictured most famously from the rear in net stockings to display those gorgeous Grable "gams" (legs). Along with Rita Hayworth, posing for that famous picture of her on a bed in a slinky nightgown, GIs of the greatest generation also pinned up photos of Veronica Lake, Dorothy Lamour, and Hedy Lamarr. Each GI had his favorite beautiful chattel girl tacked to the wall. Grable was a star for 20th Century Fox Studios, but when Paramount made the Oscar-winning *Stalag 17* (1953), Grable ended up playing a part, albeit only in a photo. The film featured a slobbering slob of a POW nicknamed "Animal" (Robert Strauss, nominated for an Oscar for his role), who moaned on for half the movie about his undying love for this super-pinup. Animal becomes nearly suicidal when he learns that Grable has married bandleader Harry James.

It is made clear that in the 1940s, these pinup girls were the stuff of male fantasies of possession and sexual utility when, in *Patton* (1970), the general inspects an enlisted men's barracks. There he spots a poster of a pinup girl, but before he removes it with his riding crop, he gives the pinup a good, long salacious look. Then he smacks the picture with his riding crop, knocking it off the wall, while gruffly announcing to the troops, "This is a barracks: It's not a bordello."

CHATTEL AS THE PRIZE IN *THE WAR LOVER*

In *The War Lover* (1961), B-17 bomber pilot Buzz Rickson (Steve McQueen) considers Englishwoman Daphne (Shirley Anne Field), the girlfriend of his co-pilot Lt. Ed "Bo" Boland (Robert Wagner), as mere chattel, an animal to be hunted, not a woman: just a prize to be won. Egged on by Buzz, and confident that Daphne is in love with him, Bo eventually sinks to Buzz's level and joins the competition.

Buzz Rickson really hates women. Later in the film, we learn that he was orphaned early on, so some of his animosity toward the opposite sex may be due to his relationship—or lack of one—with his mother. Rickson likes to manipulate women to his advantage, and plays various sadistic games at their expense. On one occasion, while on a pass from the southern English air base where they are stationed, Rickson and his aircrew are drinking together in a pub. Just for cruel pleasure, Rickson tries to make a romantic match between a young bomber crewman called "Junior" (Michael Crawford), whom he assumes is still a virgin, with a plump, shy English barmaid (Louise Dunne). When Rickson practically pushes the virgin and the chattel together, Junior is terribly embarrassed and the reluctant barmaid is in tears, humiliated. To make matters worse, other young bomber crewmen in the bar join in. Fortunately for all, a German air raid interrupts the incident.

After this, everyone except Rickson and Lt. Max Brindt (Bill Edwards) flee the bar, heading for bomb shelters. Although Max is very nervous about staying while an air raid is going on, he stays, on sort of a dare, to prove his courage to Rickson. Drinking together, Rickson lowers his guard and tells Max about his first drink and other firsts:

Rickson: I had my first drink when I was 13 and on the road. One night I got terribly hungry. I went up to a farm house to get something to eat. A woman invited me in. She wasn't bad looking, either, except that she was old enough to be my mother. She kept me there 72 hours *(he smiles in reverie)* Man, did I learn a thing or two . . . the boy who came to dinner. . . . That's how I got my schooling, Max, the hard way. Not like Boland and Lynch [his aircraft's navigator]. All they know about life . . . *(a bomb explodes nearby and Max flinches, throwing himself against a wall for added safety. Rickson just toasts the destruction.)* . . . is what's in books. (*The War Lover*, 1961)

Rickson accumulates an ever-growing list of female conquests, but seems incapable of any lasting relationship. All these women are to him are targets, like the ones he bombs on his combat missions. He attacks, conquers and moves on to his next conquest. To advertise his sexual prowess, Rickson hangs a gallery of photos of women, presumably his sexual victories, on the bulletin board of his barracks room. When he decides to go out on the town, he closes his eyes and points at the board to randomly decide which female will be the lucky recipient of his attention that evening. During one mail call, however, the audience can see Rickson's frustration with the process he's created. When he gets no mail and Bo gets three letters, including one from Daphne, Buzz declares that he should mimeograph a letter and send it to his twenty-five girlfriends in the States so he'd get regular mail and not be forgotten. Since he doesn't write them and treats women as his chattel, portable and disposable, he builds no relationships and no woman cares enough about him to write.

When he is introduced to Daphne, Rickson gives her the impression that he enjoys being a bomber pilot. She asks him if that's the case and he says, "I like my work. . . . Lady, I belong to the most destructive group of men the world has ever known." Apparently, Buzz thinks that this line might be a turn-on for Daphne, but later, in discussions with Bo, she explains that like some of the other women we have discussed in this chapter, she was once attracted to a man like that, who was killed in the war, fighting in North Africa. But she also considers this kind of "dangerous" man attractive to the bad side of her character. Now Daphne does all she can to reject those kinds of feelings.

Explaining why to him their bombing missions and his search and acquire missions with women are related, Rickson, the bomber's commander, has nicknamed his plane "the body." A cartoon of a near-naked woman is painted on the nose of the plane. Apparently only with "the body" is Rickson capable of any kind of true and lasting affection. Especially during the climactic final bombing mission, Rickson talks affectionately to "the body" while he flies on, urging this woman, over which he has achieved total dominance and heretofore has received faithfulness in return, to once again keep him in the air and get him safely home.

Rickson dislikes his navigator, Lt. Marty Lynch (Gary Cockrell), and makes a request to his commander that Lynch be removed from his aircrew. This is because, like Bo, Lynch dislikes some of Rickson's off-duty interpersonal cruelties. For example, Lynch is the one who breaks up the unkind teasing Rickson instigates that has terribly embarrassed young Junior and the barmaid. Bo is furious with Rickson for getting rid of Lynch, who coincidentally is killed in a flak explosion on his very next mission, navigating in another bomber. In the middle of their argument, Rickson brings up Daphne, saying maybe it's time he goes after her. This is to change the subject, assert his status as alpha male on board their bomber and satisfy his own ego that Daphne, like every other chattel woman he's ever pursued, can be seduced and conquered. Rickson says this in the form of a challenge. This is when we learn a few things about Bo as well. Although he obviously cares for Daphne, Bo doesn't mind using Daphne as the "bet" in a male-on-male wager. Bo had told Lynch earlier that "Seven missions to go and I'm on my way home," meaning that when his twenty-five-mission tour is completed, he'll be leaving Daphne behind as he heads back to the States. On one occasion, when Bo and Daphne are having a frank exchange of opinions, she says, "Oh, be honest: All you wanted was a war girl." No matter what, Daphne is a commodity to possess when Bo finds it convenient. At least for now, marriage is not in the cards.

On a date to the Paris Club in London, the official bar of displaced Allied soldiers of various nationalities, Daphne jokes to Bo that she's thankful for the French, the Polish, the Danes and so on, but especially for American "lend lease," and gets serious for a moment and adds, "even if it is a short-term lease." Having followed Daphne and Bo to the Paris Club, to see if he can win the bet, Rickson initiates maneuvers designed to steal Daphne from

Bo. While Bo is off getting Daphne a drink, Rickson says to her, "You sure have put roses in Boland's cheeks." Rickson announces that shortly, when Bo rotates back home, he'll be remaining in England, and plans to sign on for another twenty-five-mission tour, flying his bomber until the war is over. Because both men seem to consider Daphne as chattel, Rickson says he wants to be next in line with her. Besides being mildly disgusted by the bawdy multiple-partner imagery that this metaphor suggests, she rejects him for a more thoughtful reason. Daphne has grown beyond men like Rickson, whom she considers "dangerous," and appreciates Bo's charming, educated humanism, if not undying love. In the future, with or without Bo, Daphne will seek out Bo's kind of man, not a Rickson. But Rickson overhears Bo telling a cabbie the address of her apartment and follows Daphne there to make his play in a better arena. Bo has left for the base and when Rickson knocks, Daphne decides to be polite and let him in, even though she's already changed into a dressing gown that looks designed for bodice-ripping. Rickson even points out that he likes what she's wearing. But no effort at being charming and seductive works on Daphne. Finally, hoping to appeal to Daphne's dangerous side, Rickson tries a half-hearted attempt at rape, but is not successful either. Now furious, Daphne insults him by asserting that Rickson "can't make love: you can only make hate!" Rickson leaves, upset by his failure to score.

The next day, on their last mission together, crushed by his lack of success with Daphne, Rickson overcompensates by attempting a spectacular feat of piloting "the body." The bomber is badly damaged in a raid deep into Germany, and good sense suggests that the aircrew bail out over the English Channel before the plane, which is down to two of its four engines and is losing altitude, goes down. But Rickson, trying to bring his "body" home, insists on succeeding with the airplane what he could not do with Daphne. All the crewmembers, including Bo, safely parachute to safety, except Rickson, who stays at the controls. Unfortunately, the bomber is too badly damaged to respond to even Rickson's expert piloting and it crashes into the Dover cliffs.

At the ambiguous conclusion of the film, although Bo and Daphne are shown back together again, walking together across a lawn in Cambridge, no words are exchanged to convince the audience that Bo has changed his mind and now wants to possess Daphne for longer than his last leave before heading home to America.

MEMPHIS BELLE

Of course, not all World War II bomber crewmembers who chase English women with sex in mind are depicted to be as neurotic as Rickson. Some are just young American men, who, as the British said of them during the war, are "oversexed, overpaid, and over here." In the feature film rendition of *Memphis Belle* (1990), there is a sequence in a huge hangar on the Air Corps base full of American GIs dancing to swing band music and drinking with English girls. The majority of these young men have one thing on their minds and one definition of these girls: chattel to acquire and seduce by whatever means possible. Of course, the women know this, too, but they're young, willing, and able. For example, young *Memphis Belle* crewman Richard "Rascal" Moore (Sean Austin) sits at a table, using a tired old pitch on a girl named Faith (Jane Horrocks), who acts like she's heard his pitch a hundred times before: "We may be going to Germany tomorrow, and my short, young life may be snuffed out in an instant. I volunteered because I thought it would be fun. I never thought I could (strategic pause and a sniff for effect). . . . Oh, Faith, when I think I may never see the stars again, listen to good music or talk to a beautiful girl like you." Faith looks positively bored with his act. Rascal leaves their table to get himself and Faith some drinks. As he does so, he confides in a fellow crewman Danny (Eric Stoltz), "She's crazy about me! She's going to jump on me any second!" However, when Rascal returns with the drinks, Faith is gone, dancing with another crewman whom Rascal has earlier nicknamed "Virgil the Virgin" (Reed Diamond). Virgil doesn't know anything about seduction techniques, and spends his one-on-one time with Faith explaining his plans to open up hamburger franchises in the U.S after the war. This kind of "line" is really different than anything Faith has ever heard before, and besides, because of food rationing in England, she hasn't had any meat in months. Off camera, she suggests they go somewhere private.

Later, Virgil and Faith end up in the only private place nearby, the cockpit of the *Memphis Belle*. As it turns out, Virgil really *is* a virgin, and is quite clumsy and awkward as he attempts to engage in foreplay and make love to Faith. Finally, Faith realizes that he's inexperienced and asks, "You've never done this before, have you?" "Why?" he replies, "Am I doing something wrong?" Her womanly instincts aroused by Virgil's innocence, Faith takes out her chewing gum, smiles and sweetly says, "No." Charitably, she pulls him down on top of her as the scene ends.

BACK TO BATAAN

In *Back to Bataan* (1945), apparent turncoat Filipino women who serve as Japanese allies are not safe from the threat of sexual assault. His armies having occupied the Philippines, leering Japanese General Homma (Leonard Strong) talks to a female double agent, Dalisay Delgado (Fely Franquelli), whom he believes is a Philippine collaborator. He seems to consider her both chattel to dispose of as he wishes and fair game for sexual advances. He and Dalisay discuss the next propaganda campaign in which she will be Japan's spokesperson to her people, and she becomes more and more uncomfortable as Homma undresses her with his eyes and fiddles with a dagger that reflects the light on his desk across her face and body. Thirty years later, there might have been a scene in which Homma does more than caress her body with his dagger reflection, but in 1945, Hollywood's Production Code was firmly in place, and molestation and rape were not shown on-screen. Later, Dalisay shows her true colors as a patriot and double agent, and she openly joins up with a company of Philippine resistance fighters.

This isn't to say that Americans have never been portrayed as occupiers who try to have their way with indigenous females. It's just that such scenes don't occur in 1940s pictures, when films about the war were made for only positive American propaganda. In these films, only the enemy treated women like chattel in the lands they occupied. After the war, more reality was allowed. By the time the HBO miniseries *Band of Brothers* was produced in 2001, in the episode "Why We Fight," two American GIs, are looting (another 1940s American no-no) a German farmer's hen house for eggs and whatever else they could find to eat. There they encounter a *zoftig fraulein* whom one soldier tries to bribe with cigarettes and chocolate for her affections. The other soldier tells him to back off, but he forcefully tells his buddy to make himself scarce. His advance against her virtue is off-camera, but quickly we see him exiting the barn where this takes place, rubbing his jaw where she socked him. The difference, of course, between the Americans and the Nazis is that when she hit the American GI, his attempts stopped. In most propaganda films about occupied countries, an enemy soldier's advance would not stop with "no" or with the woman successfully fighting back. In the same episode, back at headquarters, Capt. Speirs (Matthew Settle) enters what he thinks are his sleeping quarters (he'd been moved), only to find his company clerk naked in bed with a pretty blonde German girl. All Speirs wanted was to retrieve some "finders keepers" contraband silver serving pieces he had stolen and was about to mail home, so he gathers up his spoils of war and exits, leaving the clerk and the girl smiling and giggling. An egalitarian officer, Speirs apparently allows enlisted men to collect and possess female chattel.

Similarly, one woman appears at the beginning of the World War II combat comedy-drama *Kelly's Heroes* (1970), who, like the giggling German girl in *Band of Brothers*, seems to have no problem being the chattel of American Sgt. Oddball (Donald Sutherland). Oddball is negotiating with Pvt. Kelly (Clint Eastwood) for the use of his small squadron of tanks for an off-the-books raid across German lines to rob a bank. When an agreement is made, Kelly notices that behind Oddball, lounging seductively on a pile of hay, is a beautiful French girl, apparently Oddball's possession, who doubt-less will feature prominently in his next negotiation.

MERE BODIES TO POSSESS

Down the millennia, rape and pillage have traditionally been a common soldier's spoils of war. In ancient times, commanders looked the other way when their men looted the enemy's towns and raped women, considering these fringe benefits, part of a soldier's expected compensation. There are many instances in war films in which women who under normal circum-stances would be considered Madonnas are regarded as mere chattel by com-batants, are objectified as bodies to be raped, discarded, and sometimes mur-dered. For example, as late as the 1960s, the years pictured in the films *Platoon* and *Casualties of War*, American soldiers consider young Vietna-mese girls as subhuman "gooks" and thus spoils of war. These men have no trouble rationalizing rape and even murder when it comes to such chattel. In *Platoon*, Chris Taylor (Charlie Sheen) steps in to prevent his fellow soldiers from gang-raping two little Vietnamese girls. Irritated that Chris has re-minded them of how far they have fallen from grace, one soldier retorts, "Are you a homosexual, Taylor?" Another argues, "She's just a fuckin' Dink!" Chris responds by shouting, "She's a fuckin' human being, man! Fuck you!" Another reminds Chris that he has not yet learned the rule of the jungle in Vietnam, spits on Chris and says, "You're still a fuckin' 'cherry,' pal . . . you don't belong in the 'Nam, man. It's not your place at all." Implicit then, is that men who find themselves in combat in war zones are permitted to leave their ethics and civilized behavior stateside. In a war zone, even in the twen-tieth century, men do what men at war have allowed themselves to do since the days of the Neanderthal: conquer a foe, pillage the village, and rape the women.

The incident in *Casualties of War* between Sgt. Meserve (Sean Penn) and Cpl. Eriksson (Michael J. Fox) is even more intense, because Meserve and his men, alone and on a long-range reconnaissance patrol, kidnap a young, pretty Vietnamese girl for "some portable R-and-R" (read gang rape) and later murder her. Meserve also knows that all his men must take part in the rape. That way, after they rape, murder, and dispose of the girl's body, none of the five men will dare report the crime to military authorities. So when Pfc. Eriksson objects to everything and will not participate, Meserve and Cpl. Clark (Don Harvey) attempt to shame him into compliance with typical schoolyard attacks against his manhood:

Meserve: What's the matter? Don't you like girls? Haven't you got a pair? Is that your problem?

Cpl. Clark: Maybe he's queer.

Meserve: *(repeating himself)* Are you a faggot? Is that your goddam problem?

(Eriksson looks over and makes eye contact with another soldier, who also objected to the rape, but when confronted by Meserve, backs down.)

Meserve: *(watching Eriksson look at Diaz)* Oh, wait a minute! Maybe he *is* a queer. *(laughingly)* Maybe Eriksson's a homosexual *(Meserve pretends to perform fellatio on his rifle barrel).* We got us *two* "girls" on our patrol.

Later, Meserve again insists that Eriksson participate in the rape. But Eriksson continues to refuse.

Meserve: Maybe when I'm done in there (with the girl), I'm gonna come after you. Maybe when I'm done humping her, I'm gonna come hump you! (*Casualties of War*, 1989)

Later in the film, Meserve kills the Vietnamese girl. When the operation is over, Eriksson turns the men in to authorities who are at first reluctant to arrest and prosecute them. Later, when Eriksson persists with his accusations, he testifies against the men in a court-martial. They are convicted, but these events remain with Eriksson, who suffers from PTSD when he returns to the United States.

PLATOON

In *Platoon*, even older women are considered chattel and if not attractive for sexual assault, are at least disposable. At one point, in a scene with themes similar to the occurrences during the *My Lai* massacre, the soldiers herd the Vietnamese villagers into the middle of town to question them about the Viet Cong supplies they found hidden there. When they rough up one man, an old woman shouts in protest at Sgt. Barnes (Tom Berenger) and won't be quiet. Barnes, furious that earlier in the day three of his men were killed, silences the woman by shooting her. She falls to the ground like a rag doll. Next he grabs more chattel, a little girl this time, and threatens to shoot her in the head unless the villagers tell him what he wants to know about the Viet Cong. Just in the nick of time, Sgt. Elias (Willem Dafoe) arrives on the scene and prevents any more murders. Elias was just in time, too, because the men, equally incensed by the deaths of their buddies, were urging Barnes to give the order to "waste" everyone in the village.

In Vietnam, in part because U.S. soldiers could not tell the difference between the people they are supposed to protect and the Viet Cong, and partly because many Vietnamese made it clear that they didn't want the Americans in their country in the first place, Americans extended the same racist, "gook" characterization of Asians as a subhuman species to all indigenous people, combatant or otherwise. Soldiers who would likely never consider raping or killing Caucasian women back in the United States rationalized their actions by discounting the humanity of all Asians, especially their females. Somehow, calling these women "gooks," "zipperheads," "slants," or "dinks" reduces them to a category of worthless chattel who merit no respect or human consideration.

EDGE OF DARKNESS

Women commodified down to the level of the spoils of war populates many war films of all eras, not just those in the 1960s and 1970s in Asia. And it has often been used in American propaganda films to differentiate between the lack of morality of the enemy versus the relative virtuousness of American fighting men. For example, in *Edge of Darkness* (1943), the German commandant, Captain Hauptmann Koenig (Helmut Dantine), in charge of the garrison occupying a Norwegian town, is frustrated in his attempts to clearly identify the leadership of the local resistance. Up until now, he has forbidden his soldiers from engaging in their usual Nazi invader practices, such as looting the town, molesting or raping the women at will. But Koenig tells an aide that he has decided to let his men "act as they usually do," which includes pillaging and raping, which he hopes will cause resistance leaders to reveal themselves. Koenig arrogantly assumes that if he can identify the resistance leaders, he will have no trouble defeating them. Having no respect for local Norwegian women except as chattel to use as he wishes, a German soldier attacks and rapes beautiful Karen Stensgard (Ann Sheridan), daughter of a respected physician in the town. This causes the desired effect, as Karen's father seeks out the German responsible and shoots him. However, Koenig's strategy backfires. Although the resistance leaders are identified and are about to be executed, the entire citizenry of the town rises up against their oppressors, killing every single German in the garrison.

EXPECTED CARNAGE

In films of different decades, rape and murder are shown as the inevitable—and predictable—outcome of a successful enemy raid. As the Vietnam war film, *The Siege of Firebase Gloria* (1989) begins, Sgt. Maj. Bill Hafner (R. Lee Ermey) narrates as his squad encounters evidence of the Viet Cong's murder, rape, and destruction in a Vietnamese village that had been friendly to the Americans. As his men view the bodies of women who were raped and murdered, Ermey's voice-over informs us that rumors of a ceasefire during the upcoming Tet holiday are obviously mistaken. In a similar scene in *Lawrence of Arabia* (1962), T. E. Lawrence (Peter O'Toole), leading his Arab army against the retreating Turks, encounters a village in which everyone had been killed, including women brutally raped and murdered by the retreating Turks. Something snaps in Lawrence, and the normally moderate officer orders his men to speed up their pursuit of these remnants of the Turkish Army and to show them no quarter. Similarly, in the World War II drama, *China* (1943), when David Jones (Alan Ladd), discovers that rogue Japanese soldiers have killed most of a family of a peaceful Chinese farmers—including a baby—and are inside the farmhouse raping the mother, the heretofore noncommittal American snaps. This heinous act is Jones's personal Pearl Harbor. He enters the farmhouse and, although the Japanese offenders beg for mercy, he machineguns them all.

CROSS OF IRON

Sam Peckinpah's filmic rendition of a World War II German Götterdämmerung, *Cross of Iron*, features a war-weary, disillusioned squad of Germans fighting and trying to survive on the Russian front during World War II. At one point, the squad is on a long range reconnaissance patrol led by Sergeant Steiner (James Coburn) when it comes across a farmhouse occupied by a squad of female Russian soldiers. The Germans take the women prisoner. Only Steiner's moral compass forbids the squad from raping and probably killing the women. Before the squad's attack, one of the women was outside, taking a bath in a rain barrel. A filthy, smiling German joins the naked Russian woman inside the barrel, but Steiner makes him get out and take the buxom bather into the farmhouse with the rest of the women.

Next, a particularly odious German soldier—the only true Nazi in the film—along with another of Steiner's men, the youngest and most inexperienced in the squad, are assigned by Steiner to stand guard over the captured women in the farmhouse. When Steiner is elsewhere, the Nazi flirts with one of these females, but she defiantly spits at him. Determined to establish dominance and to rape this female chattel, the Nazi leaves the young soldier to guard all the women in the farmhouse, saying, "I'm going to be busy for a while," and drags the defiant Russian woman to a nearby barn. There, the Nazi forces her to perform fellatio on him.

Meanwhile, in the farmhouse, one of the Russian women seductively approaches the young soldier, smiles and offers him wine. But when he drinks it, she stabs him with a knife. Even as the young man falls, mortally wounded, the woman cries. Even in war, she knows that killing a trusting boy—German or not—is wrong. Later, when Steiner finds him, he's still alive. He pleads with Steiner, saying, "Don't hurt the girl."

In the barn, although she begins to perform fellatio on the Nazi, the defiant Russian has other plans: The woman bites his penis. Enraged and in pain, the Nazi kills her, but he is bleeding and badly injured and cannot walk. Sgt. Steiner discovers the Nazi with the dead Russian woman. He is so disgusted with the Nazi's actions, both for leaving the young soldier alone with the women and for the attempted rape, he orders all the Russian women into the barn and leaves the Nazi to his fate with the women. Always the pragmatist in this film, Steiner glares at the women's commander and says, "We're even," and as the scene ends, the women surrounding the Nazi close in on him with some variety of savage revenge in mind.

COERCION INSTEAD OF RAPE

In other films, women are not physically attacked and forcibly raped by the enemy, but nonetheless are coerced into providing sexual favors. In *Five Graves to Cairo* (1943), hotel maid Mouche (Anne Baxter) must offer her bedroom to a German officer in return for his help in rescuing her wounded brother from a Nazi concentration camp. Later Mouche learns that the German actually had no intention of helping her and had lied about his inquiries into her brother's situation so that he could take advantage of her.

In writing about the difference between what she called "the angel and the whore," Susan Jeffords uses imagery illustrated by the loose women/chattel in *Apocalypse Now*. She describes the surreal sequence in which sultry *Playboy* playmates descend from a helicopter and then dance erotically before hundreds of sex-starved, drug- and alcohol-enhanced soldiers on a stage jutting out of the jungle by a river. The stage itself is surreal, surrounded by phallic columns "that appear alternately and indeterminably to be missiles and lipstick" (Jeffords 1995, 430) but could more simply be described as erect penises. If a woman is back at home, it seems, she signifies "the world" these soldiers have left behind, a world that to an in-country soldier may seem more unreal than the Vietnam in which they find themselves. But if a woman is in Vietnam, she seems to become chattel, and part of the surreal world of violence, rape, and pillage that is director Francis Ford Coppola's Southeast Asian nightmare.

In the next chapter, we will investigate more of the roles played by chattel women as prostitutes, "loose" and unfaithful women, and camp followers.

Chapter Four

Women as Prostitutes, "Loose Women," Camp Followers, and the Unfaithful

PROSTITUTES

In the past as well as today, war has caused many women to turn to prostitution. Kamala Sarup of Amnesty International writes about a present-day situation in countries plagued with civil wars:

> Millions of women are involved in prostitution for survival on the streets. As a sad illustration of further social decay, there are about a million women who have turned to prostitution due to the war-caused breakdown of social structures and traditional security mechanisms in the World. Thus, many women see the streets and prostitution as a way to freedom from conflict. (Sarup 2004.)

Especially in war zones, or in other locations affected by a war, many women find that there is simply no other way to survive. Some, either as helpless victims of wartime rapes or human trafficking or out of desperation or ignorance, feel they have no choice but to turn to the streets. Although there is little evidence that early silent films or even films of the 1930s broached the subject of prostitution in war zones, later filmmakers have certainly addressed the subject. In some films we will examine, prostitutes are clearly professionals whose work in the oldest profession dates back before the war, while others have the profession thrust upon them, so to speak, by circumstance. The best example of this is not an American film, but it is worth discussing. It's Lina Wertmuller's classic, *Seven Beauties* (1975), which takes place before and during World War II. Big brother Pasqualino (Giancarlo Giannini) has seven unattractive sisters who are sarcastically referred to locally as his "beauties." When one sister is seduced into prostitution by a local hoodlum, Pasqualino murders him. Convicted of the crime, he manages to be transferred to a psychiatric facility. From there, he gets the chance to join the Italian Army rather than remain an asylum inmate, and he does so. After many wartime adventures, including having to prostitute himself to a ghoulish female commander in a nightmarish German prison camp, Pasqualino returns to find that all of his seven sisters, his own mother and the virginal young girl he hoped he would return to and marry have all become prostitutes.

Hamburger Hill

It is rare in war films for prostitutes to speak many lines of dialogue. The more combat scenes play a part in the movie, the more any prostitutes who are featured are relegated to the role of sexual/recreational chattel, mere silent sex objects. *Hamburger Hill* (1987) is an exception. Before being helicoptered north for their apocalyptic battle in the A Shau Valley, young American Army soldiers are the enthusiastic and often drunken clients of a houseful of Vietnamese prostitutes. It is made clear in dialogue that the Mama San (read "madam") in charge (Kieu Chinh) has her girls engaging in what they euphemistically call "boom boom" on an equal-opportunity basis. The girls' favors are available to anyone, including the Americans, soldiers of the Army of Vietnam (ARVN), and the Viet Cong, whoever has the price. But this Mama San does have a few criticisms of the current business climate: Both she and her girls freely disparage the American Military Police (MPs), who don't pay, but still expect sexual favors in return for turning a blind eye toward their semi-illegal enterprise.

In a scene at the beginning of the picture, Sgt. Adam Frantz (Dylan McDermott) and Sfc. Dennis Worchester, old friends serving on their second Vietnam tours, are sharing a large hot tub while two hookers, clad only in towels, stand outside the tub for the present to massage the sergeants' upper bodies. Soon the hookers will remove their towels and join the men in the hot tub. As she rubs his shoulders in a hot tub, one hooker (not credited) agrees with Mama San about the MPs and also tells Platoon Sgt. Worchester (Steven Weber), either as part of an ongoing joke or perhaps repeating a real proposal, that she's ready, willing, and enthusiastic to retire from her current trade and move with him to the United States.

Hooker: No like MPs. We love grunts.

Worchester: We're first class mud rollers.

Hooker: You likee massage? Take me back to the world. [translated, this means "Marry me so I can go back to America with you as a military dependent."]

Frantz: To the big PX [post exchange], eh?

Hooker: Fucking-A! [GI slang for "you bet!"]

(They joke about the hookers' Viet Cong clients.)

Worchester: Oh, man, they all have little dicks.

Frantz: Same-same Marvin the ARVN.

(Then one hooker makes a mistake in political correctness.)

Hooker 1: Marvin is useless. He is tired fighting your fucking war.

Worchester: *(a little drunk and upset about her comment)* My fucking war? My fucking war? You say, *my* fucking war?

Frantz: *(interrupting to calm the drunken* Worchester *down, and putting his arm around his buddy's neck for a moment to focus his thoughts)* Hey, hey, come on now. It's our fucking war, right?

[This reminds Worchester that the Americans are, indeed, Vietnam's invaders and instigators.]

Hooker 1: I no bullshit you: GI like to fight. Vietnamese just want short time . . .

Frantz: *(interrupting)* PX privileges.

Hooker 1: *(As she slips off her towel and slides into the hot tub and cuddles into* Worchester's *arms.)* There it is.

Hooker 2: *(hopefully)* GI never leave. No question.

[This appears to upset Worchester a little: this idea that if they never leave, the war will go on forever.]

Frantz: *(to Worchester)* As you were, now, as you were . . . *(Frantz lightly grasps Worchester's hair and points his friend's head down toward Hooker 1's breast)* Question is, how many of us have to boom

boom before those mean little bastards from the North show up? Now that's the question.

Worchester: *(drunkenly)* Yahoo! *(The boom boom commences in earnest as the scene ends).* (*Hamburger Hill*, 1987)

Full Metal Jacket

Similarly, in *Full Metal Jacket* (1987), the economics of prostitution take center stage, but the chattel in question has very little to say during the price-haggling stage. Only later does she interject a concern. A squad of Marines in Vietnam encounters an ARVN soldier (Tan Hung Francione) whose sideline is as a pimp, approaching the Marines on a Moped scooter with a hooker (Leanne Hong) riding behind him. The ARVN soldier hopes to strike a deal for his hooker's services with Pvt. Joker (Matthew Modine) and perhaps the entire squad of Marines. The rest of this typical GI vs. pimp conversation centers on price negotiations and subsequently whether an African American member of the squad is too well-endowed for the young lady's delicate sensitivities.

Cowboy [Arliss Howard]: *(checking out the shapely hooker)* Mornin', little schoolgirl! *(the men laugh)* I'm a little schoolboy, too. *(Addressing the ARVN pimp)* Whatcha got there, chief?

ARVN: Do you wan' number one fuckee? *(The men feign amazement and laugh.)*

Cowboy: *(mocking ARVN's accent)* Hey, any 'of you boys wan' numbah one [the best] fuckee?

Hand Job [Marcus D'Amico]: Hey, I'm so horny, I can't even get a piece 'of hand!

ARVN: Suckee, fuckee, she give you everything you want. Long time.

Cowboy: *(sarcastically)* Everything you want, ay! How much there, chief?

ARVN: Fifteen dollars each.

(The men make boos and catcalls at this apparently higher than market price, and the haggling begins.)

Joker (Matthew Modine): Noooo. Number ten [the worst].

Cowboy: *(mocking ARVN's accent again)* Fifteen dollar boo-koo money. Five dollar each.

ARVN: *(frustrated, but used to bargaining with GIs)* Come on! She love you good. Boom boom long time. Ten dolla.

Cowboy: Five dollars.

ARVN: No. Ten dolla.

Cowboy: 'Be glad to trade you some ARVN rifles. Never been fired and only dropped once. *(The men laugh and hoot at this insult to the Army of Vietnam.)*

ARVN: *(ignoring the insult)* OK. Five dolla. You give me.

(Swiftly, Eight Ball [Dorian Harewood], an African American, approaches the woman, his five dollars in hand.)

Eight Ball: OK. Let's get mounted!

(Hooker takes one look at Eight Ball and has a short but pointed conversation in Vietnamese with her pimp. It is obvious that she objects to something.)

Eight Ball: Somethin' wrong there, chief?

ARVN: Says no boom boom with soul brother.

Eight Ball: Motherfucker!

ARVN: Says soul brother too *beaucoup*, too *beaucoup*.

Cowboy: *(laughing and hooting along with the others)* What he's trying to tell you is that you black boys pack too much meat!

ARVN: *(extending his hands two feet apart, he repeats)* Too *beaucoup*, too *beaucoup*.

Eight Ball: *(now laughing as well).* Shit. This baby-san looks like she can suck the chrome off a trailer hitch.

ARVN: *(extending his hands two feet apart again, he again repeats)* Too *beaucoup*, too *beaucoup*.

Eight Ball: *(politely tapping the hooker on the shoulder).* Excuse me, ma'am. *(he whips out his penis to show her the actual size, as his buddies hoot and holler)* What we have here, little yellow sister, is a magnificent specimen of pure Alabama black snake *(at the critical moment, director Stanley Kubrick cuts to a more modest reverse angle shot over Eight Ball's shoulder as the hooker stares closely. The pimp averts his eyes.)* But it ain't too goddam *beaucoup. (Appreciative and no longer worried, the hooker, experienced in such matters, agrees.)*

Hooker: OK, OK.

(What remains is for the men to decide the order of events. The biggest and meanest Marine, Animal Mother (Adam Baldwin) insists on going first. All are used to giving in to Animal Mother to keep the peace in the squad.)

Animal Mother: *(joking)* Hey, hey: I won't be long. I'll skip the foreplay. *(Full Metal Jacket, 1987)*

Earlier in the film, Joker and another Marine, Rafterman, sit at an outside table of a café in Da Nang. They begin flirtations and negotiations with another hooker, only to end up mugged for Rafterman's camera by her pimp.

Nearly identical Vietnamese hooker characters are found in other Vietnam War films. As well, there is a minor character named Lolita (Charito Luna) in an awful B-movie about guerilla fighters in the Philippines during World War II called *The Steel Claw* (1961), about a mission to rescue an American general held prisoner by the Japanese. Along the way, Capt. John Larsen (George Montgomery) encounters Lolita, who started "entertaining men" when her mother died and the GI with whom she was living left her.

Catch-22

In *Catch-22* (1970), Italian hookers, like the prostitutes in *Hamburger Hill*, are enthusiastic about being transported to the United States as war brides. They also have a very "live and let live" attitude about surviving wars, as evidenced by the philosophy of the old man (Marcel Dalio) who appears to preside in some way over the whorehouse. He certainly is the alpha male of this establishment, and is served and catered to by all the women. Capt. Nately's (Art Garfunkel) girlfriend, with whom he is infatuated, works as a prostitute, but Nately is uncomfortable with what she does for a living. Nately plans on doing the "right thing" by the woman all his friends call "Nately's whore" when the war is over, and take her and her little sister back with him to America. Nately doesn't mind consulting a prostitute, but he draws the moral line at profiting from their labors, placing him in philosophical disagreement with the old man.

Nately: *(to the old man)* Don't you have any principles?

Old man: Of course not!

Nately: No morality?

Old man: I'm a very moral man, and Italy is a very moral country. That's why we will certainly come out on top again if we succeed in being defeated.

Nately: You talk like a madman.

Old man: But I live like a sane one. I was a fascist when Mussolini was on top. Now that he has been deposed, I am anti-fascist. When the Germans were here, I was fanatically pro-German. Now I'm fanatically pro-American. You'll find no more loyal partisan in all of Italy than myself.

Nately: You're a shameful opportunist! What you don't understand is that it's better to die on your feet than to live on your knees.

Old man: You have it backwards. It's better to live on your feet than to die on your knees. I know.

Nately: How do you know?

Old man: Because I am 107 years old. How old are you?

Nately: I'll be 20 in January.

Old man: If you live. (*Catch-22*, 1970)

The Big Red One

The Big Red One: The Reconstruction (2005), differs from the original *The Big Red One* (1980), because it includes a number of added scenes sloppily chopped out of the original theatrical release by United Artists. These added scenes include events in the film that take place shortly before and after the Battle of the Bulge that suggest that the Belgian prostitutes whom the squad encounters probably were involved in prostitution long before the war. Certainly their current employer, Madame Marbaise (Marthe Villalonga), is highly experienced and world weary. The soldiers of the first squad meet these ladies because Pvt. Zab (Robert Carradine) has received word from home that his mother sold his first novel to Hollywood for the princely sum of $15,000 (Zab is the character representing writer/director Sam Fuller, whose actual wartime reminiscences form the stories told in *The Big Red One.*) Perhaps because Zab is not sure about the odds that he and his buddies will all survive the war, he decides he will use $1,000 of the money to throw the squad a party right now. For the purpose of custom ordering the right prostitutes, Zab asks the men what's "the damndest things you ever wanted to do to a girl." Sitting together in the forest, propped up against trees, deep in erotic imagination, at first no GI says anything. Then Pvt. Kaiser (Perry Lang), back from medical leave after being wounded earlier in the movie during the aforementioned "poussez" scene, has one idea. He announces, "I want a big, *zaftig* girl . . . and stick her plump butt against an ice cold window," he chuckles, "and just hold her there." Zab asks, "Whatcha going to do with a frozen butt?" "Thaw it out," Kaiser replies and laughs. "It may take a while." The men all laugh in appreciation. Then a German artillery attack forces them all to take cover. When it's over, the men learn that Kaiser has been killed.

Later, at the party, in memory of Kaiser, Zab finds a *zaftig* girl and makes sure her fanny is cool, and Pvt. Johnson (Kelly Ward) pinch hits for their late comrade. The rest of the men enjoy their prostitutes, who provide them with skillful dance partners as well as bed-mates. When the soldiers have retired to bedrooms with their prostitutes, cultured Madame Marbaise plays Chopin for the squad's equally world-weary Sarge (Lee Marvin), but soon all good things must come to an end. After the party, the men are transported to Bastogne, surprised to find that instead of the war rapidly drawing to a close, the reported German bulge in the battle line in that sector has turned out to be a full offensive. After surviving that nightmare, the bedraggled soldiers find themselves back at the whorehouse, grateful to be alive. Madame Marbaise, still grateful for the $1,000, is glad to see her American patrons again and serves the exhausted soldiers a meal. The men sit around a large table in the kitchen, eating, when Madame suddenly becomes upset. A strange soldier, not from their squad, but wearing army fatigues, is eating with them. Suddenly, Madame grabs a .45 and shoots him. He's a German infiltrator, specially assigned to behind-the-lines sabotage during the Battle of the Bulge. She explains to the Sarge that she could tell he was German by the (implied sloppy) way he was eating. Although by this it's obvious she and her girls have also spent considerable time entertaining Germans, it is also abundantly clear whose side Madame is on.

The Dirty Dozen and an Imitation

There are both English and German prostitutes in the World War II film *The Dirty Dozen*, but if there is a hierarchy of hookers, in this film the German girls have the edge in looks and class. Although they provide quite similar social company and sexual services, the two groups of women seem to come from quite different worlds. Again, Lee Marvin, this time playing an officer, Major Reisman, is training a dozen army prisoners, convicted of crimes earning them sentences from twenty years hard labor to hanging, for what is probably a suicide mission. In return, the convicts have a chance to distinguish themselves and thereby earn their freedom. They will be parachuted behind German lines near a chateau in France that houses a number of German general officers with orders to kill them all. It is thought that as D-Day approaches, disposing of all these generals may disrupt the German chain of command.

The dozen convicts have trained long and hard, and are finally shaping up into a capable, cohesive unit—with the exception of Pvt. Maggott (Telly Savalas), who remains a dangerously unbalanced homicidal maniac who has a particular hate for prostitutes. The murder for which he was convicted and sentenced to death involved cutting the throat of a prostitute.

Since the dozen's mission will occur any day now, the major decides that the men deserve some "R and R" (rest and recreation). However, he knows that if he gives passes to London to these men, few, if any of them will return. So instead, Reisman has his MPs round up a truck full of common London streetwalkers whom they deliver to the men's barracks in their compound. Some food, alcohol, and the prostitutes will essentially comprise the "last meal" for most of the dozen, who will soon die on the mission. The men are scruffy, dirty, and unshaven and just stare at the hookers for a minute or so. The hookers would have been happier if the men were cleaned up, but they are pros and soon are about their business. The men make quite a party out of it. Maggott, who for the safety of the prostitutes, needs to be kept far away, has been assigned guard duty in a tower high above the compound, and therefore is excluded from the revels. He spends the evening shouting insults and Bible verses in Maj. Reisman's—and the prostitutes'—general direction.

Later, the mission underway, we meet the German prostitutes in the chateau. This spacious mansion, which has been turned into an entertainment center for German generals and other high-ranking officers, is stocked with classy food, liquor, and equally high-class prostitutes, apparently imported from Germany. The women appear to have been selected for their youth and beauty, and are wearing beautiful gowns. The generals eat and drink and flirt with the women, who occasionally slip away to accompany their generals upstairs to the bedrooms.

Meanwhile, Reisman and the dozen have been parachute dropped nearby and have infiltrated the grounds and the building. One of the prostitutes comes upstairs looking for her assigned general and enters his room. Unfortunately, she encounters Maggott, who grabs her, and after brandishing a knife to frighten her and make her scream, sadistically slits her throat. Hearing the woman scream, at first the generals downstairs are startled, but decide that one assignation upstairs has simply gotten a little out of hand. Having no concern for the screaming prostitute, they just laugh, and one officer makes a lewd comment in German which causes the other officers more laughter. The audience now realizes how little the generals care about the welfare of these women. But when Maggott comes out into the upstairs hallway and opens fire with an automatic weapon and is shot, the mission's surprise element is lost. All the officer guests and prostitutes are swiftly ushered into the basement of the chateau to hide until help, in the form of German troops stationed nearby, arrive. In the meantime, Maj. Reisman and the dozen manage to kill all the generals and prostitutes from outside with a combination of hand grenades and cans of gasoline. Nearly all the Americans also lose their lives.

In disposing of the generals, it is obvious that the Americans are equally unconcerned with the welfare of the prostitutes, who along with the generals, die horribly.

In another World War II film, the same *Dirty Dozen* framework is used (one might say "borrowed"), but instead of male army convicts, four women are recruited for a special mission. The B-film in question, *The Hustler Squadron* (1976), is a cheaply made send-up of the *Dirty Dozen*, and features among the four women only one real prostitute. The story's protagonist is another maverick major (John Ericson) who recruits four women to pose as prostitutes and infiltrate an island resort in the Japanese-held Philippines. Like the resort target in *The Dirty Dozen*, this facility, a hotel, is being used as a luxury brothel for high-ranking Japanese generals and admirals. Once on the island, the four women's mission is to infiltrate the prostitutes working in the resort, attract these senior officers for sex, and when they have them alone in their bedrooms, assassinate them. The plan calls for a Filipino partisan commando raid led by the major to follow up the assassinations. This is how the women would be evacuated. Like the Dirty Dozen, the women are given some army commando training so they have the skills to effectively kill their targets and get out alive.

One of the four is indeed a prostitute, on the run from the mob after witnessing a murder. With a contract out on her life, this woman is offered money and a new identity if she will join the group. Another is a Filipino woman who was raped by the Japanese, and therefore has a score to settle. Another, a sexual adventuress, is already a convicted murderer, who looks forward to sex as much as she does having a temporary license to kill. The fourth, a nurse, volunteers because she is supposed to die soon of an undisclosed movie illness, and says she wants to join the team "to save lives."

At one point, imitating the story line of *The Dirty Dozen*, a general, the major's boss, decides to cancel the operation because one of his staff officers convinces him that no woman can overpower a man and kill him. So the major arranges a raid in which the women assault a male officers' barracks and subdue and hogtie a number of them. The amused general relents, and the mission is on again.

During the mission, three of the women succeed in killing their target generals, and a fourth, an admiral, is killed later in the commando raid. Ironically, only one of the four "prostitutes" makes it out alive, the nurse suffering from the fatal disease.

An Oscar for a Prostitute

Donna Reed won an Oscar in 1953 for portraying a prostitute in the World War II film, *From Here to Eternity*, in part because of her fine acting but also because her role was so different than the Madonnas the former farm girl from Iowa was accustomed to portray, such as the angelic military nurse in *They Were Expendable* (1945) or George Bailey's saintly wife in *It's a Wonderful Life* (1946).

Called euphemistically a "recreation club girl," Alma "Lorene" Burke acknowledges that her role at the New Congress Club—read servicemen's bordello in post-1950s language—is a little higher class than a streetwalker, or as she puts it, "about two steps up from the pavement." In 1953, the Motion Picture Code prohibited any mention of prostitution. It was up to clever screenwriters and directors to suggest what Reed's character really did for a living. Lorene's club girl occupation is simply the best euphemism for a prostitute that Oscar-winning screenwriter Daniel Taradash could manage to get past Hollywood's censors. Unlike the other women, Reed plays her club girl attractively but frostily, as if she were a sophisticate. When the soldier she will eventually fall in love with, Pvt. Robert E. Lee Prewitt (Montgomery Clift), is introduced to some of the girls in the club, he looks across the room and is immediately smitten with Alma, whose reputation among the girls is that she thinks she's higher class than the rest. One of the girls, Annette, who's introducing Prewitt around, sees he's attracted to Alma, and sarcastically says, "Don't tell me *the princess* is your style." Unlike the other girls, Alma adopts a patrician air, sits away from the other girls, somewhat aloof and up a few steps, and does not approach the men. She seems to talk only to servicemen courageous enough to approach her. This is in contrast to other girls, including one who leaves the man she's dancing with to literally throw her arms seductively around Prewitt's neck. But Prewitt has eyes only for Alma, pries the other girl from around his neck, and the soldier with whom she is dancing retrieves her.

The unhappy Alma hates her job, and like many prostitutes, just goes through the motions, until Prewitt introduces himself. She is immediately charmed by the soldier, and says, "Aren't you a strange one?" Perhaps it's his hard-headedness and his Southern notions of honor that initially attract her, or perhaps it's Montgomery Clift's good looks. Despite her standoffishness, Alma feels hollow and dissatisfied. She needs a real relationship, someone with whom she can lower her guard with and speak honestly. She chooses Prewitt. She tells him that she grew up in a small town in Oregon, where she dated the richest boy in town for three years. But when it was time for him to settle down, he "married a girl suitable for his position." Jilted and disgraced, Alma left town for Portland. There she learned from a girl just back from the islands that in Hawaii, at a club like the New Congress, a girl "could make a lot of money: So I caught the first boat." Alma had planned to go home in a year, this time "with a stocking full of money, and I'll be set for life."

Although she cares for him, Alma won't settle for a permanent relationship with a career soldier. To Alma, the status of a soldier's wife is no better than that of the waitress she was back in Oregon, and that's just not good enough. She hopes someday to go back home a lady, hopefully a lady of means, and marry a rich man. To Alma, despite her affection for him, Prewitt was never in the cards.

Alma: I—I won't marry you because I don't want to be the wife of a soldier.

Prewitt: Well, that . . . would be about the best I could ever do for you.

Alma: Because nobody's going to stop me from my plan. Nobody, nothing. Because I want to be proper!

Prewitt: *(somewhat confused)* Proper . . .

Alma: Yes, proper! In another year I'll have enough money saved. Then I'm going to go back to my hometown in Oregon, and I'm going to build a house for my mother and myself, and join the country club and take up golf. Then I'll meet the proper man with the proper position, to make a proper wife, and can run a proper home and raise proper children. And I'll be *happy* because when you're *proper* you're *safe*! (*From Here to Eternity*, 1953)

She makes this last speech harshly, through gritted teeth, as if her return to her hometown in Oregon as a well-off woman is solely to prove to everyone in town, including the boy who jilted her—and to herself—that she's really good enough.

But in *From Here to Eternity*, the Pearl Harbor attack changes a great many plans, one of them Alma's. Prewitt has been absent without leave, because of his revenge killing of a man named "Fatso" Judson (Ernest Borgnine) who was responsible for the death of his friend and fellow soldier,

Angelo (Frank Sinatra). Alma has been hiding Prewitt at her apartment since the incident, but because of the Japanese attack, Prewitt, a faithful soldier, insists on rejoining his company for the upcoming fight. However, Prewitt is mistakenly shot by jumpy sentries as he tries to sneak back onto base.

At the end of the picture, as Karen Holmes (Deborah Kerr) and Alma are standing at the rail of an ocean liner that is leaving Hawaii for the mainland, we are party to their conversation. Karen, perhaps because she hopes someday to see her lover, Milton Warden (Burt Lancaster) again, hopes she'll return to Hawaii. Alma says she never will. She makes up a story that Prewitt was a bomber pilot who was killed trying to take off during the Pearl Harbor attack. We can see in her eyes and in her speech that she truly loved him. However, Alma is sailing back to the mainland a year earlier than necessary to save the money she wanted. So perhaps, encouraged by Prewitt's tenacity and sense of purpose, Alma has given up her spiteful plans for a triumphant return to Oregon, and will search for some new role in life that includes neither the country club set nor the bordello.

Stryker's Salvation

In the last chapter, discussing *Sands of Iwo Jima,* we already mentioned Conway's romance with his New Zealand Madonna. But in this chapter, there is another variation on the prostitute. This woman turns out to be a reluctant hooker trying to survive so she can support her baby. Sgt. Stryker (John Wayne) is only a three-striper instead of a master sergeant because he has been reduced in rank for drunkenness while on liberty. The reason Stryker intentionally sets out to get drunk whenever he's off duty is because he has lost his own Madonna, Mary, and someone also important to him, his young son, when she divorced him. Stryker admits in letters to his son and in conversations with Pfc. Charlie Bass (James Brown), his best friend, that he was a bad husband and father, and Mary was right to divorce him. A good friend, Bass follows Stryker when he's on liberty in hopes of keeping him from being arrested again when he gets too drunk.

This time, in Hawaii, Stryker is able to elude Bass, and has planted himself on a bar stool, boozing it up again. Off another barstool comes another Mary (Julie Bishop) with a come-on for Stryker. At first, he is resistant, intent on drinking, and when she offers him her place as a better place to drink, he declines. But when he learns her name is Mary, he softens, and the two head for her small apartment. As it turns out, she's broke, so he gives her the money for a bottle to share. She leaves him at her place to go to a nearby store to get the bottle, and while she's gone, Stryker discovers that Mary has a one-year-old son in the bedroom. When she returns with the bottle, she's also bought baby food. When Stryker asks about the baby's father, Mary replies, "Gone. There are a lot tougher ways of making a living than going to war." Touched, Stryker drops a thick wad of cash in the baby's crib and announces to the child, "So long, Mac," and heads for the door. Feeling she should provide something in return for all the money Stryker has left for them, Mary says, "Wait." "You can't spend it on a coral reef," Stryker replies. Mary smiles and says, "You're a very good man." He jokes, smiling, as he leaves, "You'd get odds on that in the Marine Corps." The audience gets the sense that if Stryker isn't killed at the end of the picture, that when he returned to Hawaii he would look Mary up, as perhaps his chance to try again.

Waiting outside Mary's apartment house is faithful Charlie Bass, expecting to have to carry Stryker back to the base. He seems surprised that Stryker is still relatively sober. Stryker kids Bass on his ability to track his every move:

Stryker: You've gotta lotta bloodhound in you, Charlie. But you can call off the dogs, 'cause I'm about five years smarter than I was a half hour ago, and if you ever catch me feelin' sorry for myself, you got my permission to belt me right in the nose.

Bass: *(grins happily)* Buy you a drink!

Stryker: Lock 'n' load, boy, lock 'n' load. (*Sands of Iwo Jima*, 1949)

The Night of the Generals

As both portable and, sadly, disposable chattel, prostitutes in wartime have often been victims of man's basest instincts, including, in the case of the film *The Night of the Generals* (1967), murder. In many cases, policemen, understaffed and overworked, put solving the murders of prostitutes at a very low priority. But not all policemen consider prostitutes as unworthy of justice and due process. In this film, during World War II, a prostitute is brutally murdered in her apartment in Nazi-occupied Warsaw. A fearful witness, peeking through a crack in the door, sees only one thing to report to authorities: the murderer was wearing the distinctive uniform of a German Army general. The German military police detective in charge of the case, Maj. Grau (Omar Sharif), realizes that because a general is implicated, he has caught a political hot potato. But to his credit, Grau does not relent in carrying out his investigation. He begins by ascertaining that only three German generals were in Warsaw that night. Grau makes himself none too popular by questioning all three generals. These officers can't understand why Grau is so tenacious. After all, a prostitute—especially a Polish prostitute—is to them utterly disposable chattel, nothing to be concerned about. One of the generals has, himself, ordered the killing of thousands of innocent Polish Jews, and considers the whole case especially ridiculous. But Maj. Grau is a true police-man and a detective, and vows to continue his investigation, even if it results in the arrest of a general officer.

Because of Grau's irritating persistence, the generals see to it that the pesky policeman is transferred from Warsaw to Paris and promoted, where, two years later, the fortunes of war result in all three generals being once again in the same city. Lt. Col. Grau is intrigued that he has all three suspects in one city again. Then the actual murderer, Gen. Tanz (Peter O'Toole), butchers yet another prostitute, and this time frames his chauffer, Kurt Hoff-man (Tom Courtenay), who witnessed the murder, for the crime. The power-ful general allows Hoffman to desert in return for his silence. Hoffman, although a decorated army hero, hates the war and is eager to survive it, so he accepts Tanz's offer and flees.

Grau is on the case of this new murder, and is able to recognize the hand of the Warsaw killer in the butchering of the French prostitute. But this time, Grau is able to eliminate the other two generals, so he is confident that Tanz is the murderer. But all this takes place during a time in 1944 when one of the failed assassination attempts against Adolf Hitler takes place. When Grau confronts Tanz, the general shoots him. In the confusion about rounding up the Führer's assassination plot conspirators, Tanz tells the Gestapo that Grau was in on it, so Grau's murder is covered up.

But during the Paris investigation, Grau made a valuable friend in Paris. Aware that Interpol Inspector Morand (Philippe Noiret) is involved with the French Resistance, Grau, not a Nazi, does not report on his brother police-man. Inspector Morand picks up Grau's investigation and stores it away for after the war.

Twenty years later, when another prostitute is murdered in Hamburg, Morand closes in on Tanz. With Interpol's wide reach, Morand stumbles onto the trail of the only witness to the second murder, the chauffer Hoffman, and learns the truth. When Morand confronts Tanz with his crimes, the former general commits suicide.

Forced Prostitution

There is yet another role for women as a disposable, portable commodity that has received little attention in narrative war films: forced prostitution. Both the Nazis and the Japanese, after conquering other countries, forced indige-nous women into becoming sex slaves, usually for use as "comfort women" as the Japanese called their Korean and Chinese victims. Sometimes in war film scripts, a woman fears that a fate like this will befall her, or simply that she will be raped, as in the highly awarded television miniseries, *Holocaust*, in which a girl in a concentration camp is raped by Nazi soldiers. In her case, the shock of the attack causes her to fall into a catatonic state, and the Nazis execute the poor woman as a "mental defective."

LOOSE WOMEN AND CAMP FOLLOWERS

As discussed earlier, due to the production code, films produced during World War II mostly avoided outright mention of prostitutes, but there were plenty of loose women—professional and otherwise—to be found. Such a female is barfly Yvonne (Madeline LeBeau) in *Casablanca* (1943), whose affections seem to bounce back and forth among nightclub proprietor Rick Blaine (Humphrey Bogart), who has rejected her, and various Frenchmen. Finally she crosses over to the dark side, taking up with a German officer. But on this night, when Yvonne (whose affections could have "constituted an entire second front," according to Maj. Renault [Claude Rains]), becomes too drunk and vulnerable, Rick orders his bartender Sascha (Leonid Kinskey) to take her home in a taxi. Before Sascha leaves, Rick hastens to add, "and come right back!" Sascha, realizing his employer won't give him his chance to perhaps take advantage of the sultry Yvonne while she is in a compromised position, reluctantly sighs and says, "Yes, boss."

Sleeping with the Enemy

Later films about World War II, such as the miniseries *Band of Brothers* (2001) and *A Bridge Too Far* (1977), took a few minutes to dramatize the fates of local female collaborators like *Casablanca*'s Yvonne, such as those in Holland who had sex with German soldiers occupying their country. After the Allies retook towns in Holland, the Dutch Resistance executed male collaborators. Women who slept with Germans were dragged into town squares, their dresses ripped off and their hair shaved. Then they were banished from their towns and shunned by the people. In one scene in the "Replacements" episode of *Band of Brothers*, during Operation Market Garden, women are kissing every American GI in the Einhoven town square as they wildly celebrate their liberation (actually, Operation Market Garden later failed, and after the Allies were forced to retreat, towns like Einhoven were retaken by the Germans). One particular Dutch woman is furiously kissing an American soldier, as if she would be willing to make love to him right then and there. But the soldier is ordered elsewhere, and the woman looks on for a moment, deciding if she should follow him. But Dutch Resistance members swoop in and grab her by each arm and haul her off to the town square, where, sobbing, she suffers the fate of other female collaborators. Other Dutch women watch her with disgust as she receives her punishment. The crowd chants something (probably insulting) in Dutch over and over. One American soldier asks the head of the Resistance, "What did they do?" referring to the women being abused in the square. He replies, "They slept with the Germans. They are lucky. The men who collaborated are being shot." The next day, as the Americans move on up a road to the next Dutch town, a female collaborator, stripped to her slip and her head shaven, is standing by the side of the road holding a baby. No words are said, but an American charitably gives her a box of C-rations.

Another female collaborator is found in *The Big Red One: The Reconstruction* (2005). At least, this Frenchwoman is a collaborator inasmuch as when we meet her she is giving German Sergeant Schroeder (Siegfried Rauch) a massage. To her credit, being a masseuse is her job, but many other French refused to work in any capacity for the German occupiers. The con-versation between the two begins when Schroeder compliments her on how well she speaks German. She replies, "Since 1940, everybody in Paris speaks good German." But this in itself is something some French, always protec-tive about their language, might find unpatriotic. Additionally in the conver-sation, we learn that her husband, a French soldier who wouldn't surrender, was killed when the Germans took Paris. The tenor of the conversation communicates that she continues giving massages to anyone, even Germans, because a woman still has to make a living. It's almost as if she blames her husband for dying, leaving her to support herself. After the war, as in Ein-hoven, such "friends" of the Germans—especially those who learn to speak fluent German—might have to explain themselves when the French Resis-tance retakes Paris.

Hell's Angels

We introduced the World War I picture, *Hell's Angels,* in chapter 2, but this chapter is the correct place to discuss the role played by Jean Harlow's character, Helen. Even in the 1930s, there's only one word that comes to mind to describe Helen: a tramp. Directed by Howard Hughes, *Hell's Angels* tells the story of two English brothers, Roy and Monte Rutledge (James Hall and Ben Lyon). Roy Rutledge can only be described as a "boy scout," the epitome of truth, right, courage, and British determination. Sadly, his brother Monte is just the opposite: lazy, self-centered, irresponsible, and ambition-less, unless it's about pursuing a good time. Roy is blind to his brother's lack of character and personal motivation, and loves and forgives him anyway. This is a pattern for Roy, who is unwaveringly faithful to Monte, his friends, his country, and, unfortunately, to Helen.

Helen is a spoiled rich girl who has much more in common with Monte than Roy: She's selfish, reckless, thoughtless, and committed only to a he-donistic lifestyle. What Roy sees in Helen is her good looks, and he brain-lessly assumes that she has good character to match. But this is far from the case. Roy falls for her in a big way, although it's obvious to everyone but

Roy that Helen considers him only another tiresome suitor. When Roy introduces Monte to Helen, he's proud of his girl, and wants Monte to like her,
too. Unfortunately, when Roy is not around, Helen easily seduces Monte,
who can't resist a good time or an easy woman, even if she's his brother's
girlfriend. Monte knows it's wrong to sleep with Roy's girl, but he doesn't
have the character to resist.

When World War I breaks out, the patriotic Roy immediately enlists in
the Royal Flying Corps. More by mistake than due to love of country, Monte
decides to enlist as well, and joins his brother at the front to do combat with
the Germans. Meanwhile, excited about the opportunities and freedom a war
like this gives to women, Helen signs up to serve in an adjunct role as a
military canteen hostess and follows the British troops to France. This is not
out of any sense of patriotism, we later learn. Instead, Helen simply wants to
get away from conventional morality and her family's house, where she has
bristled under the thumb of straight-laced, moral relatives. She finally gets
what she's always wanted: her own apartment where she can seduce men
with no one around to stop her or remind her of the proprieties.

Roy discovers that Helen is in France and approaches her in the canteen,
determined to continue his pursuit. But at the canteen, Roy learns that he has
plenty of competition, and he literally has to get in line to talk to her. She
flirts with another officer from the infantry who proposes marriage, but Hel-
en makes it clear that she doesn't want to settle down with anyone. On
another occasion, Roy catches Helen necking with another soldier. Disap-
proving, Roy wants to take her home. "Home?" she replies. "Who wants to
go home? I'm having a marvelous time, or was until you came in." Roy
foolishly replies that she's his girl. "You fool!" she replies. "I wouldn't
belong to you if you were the last man on earth. You're nothing to me,
nothing. . . . I never had any fun with you. You and your high ideas. You're
too 'good' to live! You make me sick!"

Roy remains hopelessly in love with Helen, but Helen considers herself a
citizen of the world and doesn't plan on any post-Victorian concept of a
Madonna role in her future. Roy's problem is that he initially put Helen on a
pedestal as if she were a Madonna. To Roy, Helen's a Madonna, despite
abundant evidence to the contrary. Unfortunately, Helen is like Monte,
whose self-indulgent philosophy says it all: "Never love a woman. Just make
love to her."

Mary Jane Who?

References to untold numbers of female sweethearts of doubtful virtue are
discussed in many war films, but one of the more memorable names for the
generic slutty girlfriend back home is courtesy of the colorful vocabulary of
Gy. Sgt. Hartman (R. Lee Ermey), the doomed drill instructor in *Full Metal*

Jacket: "Mary Jane Rotten-crotch." In military culture, men perceive their women back home are either too naive or too concerned with themselves and their petty problems to understand how terrible war can be for those at the front. Further, many women in war films are characterized as particularly susceptible to temptation while their men are away fighting. In film after film, the "Dear John" letters speak of such terrible loneliness that can only be assuaged by their new boyfriends, on hand back in the States to offer comfort and happiness. There is even a particular kind of odious, honor-bereft male creature who lurks around at home, ready to offer this comfort and happiness. For some reason, military men have generically named this dishonorable character "Jody." To a GI, Jody represents men who romance away their women while they're deployed, fighting for their country. In World War II, Jody could be a draft dodger, a 4-F (physically unable to serve), someone who works in some war-essential industry and thus is not draft eligible, or perhaps simply a lawbreaker with too many convictions on his record to qualify for military service. In modern post-draft days, Jody can be simply a man back home who does not enlist and serve, and is thus available and quite willing to step in to tempt a soldier's woman to unfaithfulness.

Nonetheless, fantasies of wild sexual adventures when soldiers finally escape the hell of war and return to the "World" (the United States) are a constant companion of these young men. Typical is the statement of *Full Metal Jacket*'s Pvt. Joker (Matthew Modine) in voice-over at the conclusion of the film:

> **Joker:** My thoughts drift back to erect nipple wet dreams about Mary Jane Rotten Crotch and the great homecoming fuck fantasy. I am so happy that I'm alive, in one piece, and short *[soon to be sent home as his tour in Vietnam ends]*. I'm in a world of shit, yet I am alive, and I am not afraid. (*Full Metal Jacket*, 1987)

As Joker makes this statement and the young men march along, they begin singing what amounts to the anthem of their doomed generation, the theme from the Mickey Mouse Club.

UNFAITHFUL WIVES

There are a great many unfaithful wives in these films, especially those produced after 1950. Interestingly, screenwriters seem to provide some of these women with justifying motivation for their behavior. Even Marie Derry, flyer Fred's unfaithful wife in *The Best Years of Our Lives*, who apparently never was faithful to her husband, has an excuse. In dialogue we learn that Fred married Marie, whom he barely knew, after a brief, whirlwind romance, right before he shipped out for the war. Why? Probably on a whim, or also with expectations that if Fred was killed, Marie would inherit his GI life insurance. Plus, while he was overseas, much of Fred's pay was sent to Marie as an allotment, so Marie, who also has a job, could live an upscale life with plenty of extra money. A party girl, Marie simply declined to act like a married woman and continued her previous wanton behaviors while Fred was overseas. After the war, when Fred musters out of the Air Corps, he and Marie finally get to know each other. Fred is no longer the dashing pilot Marie married. Now he's out of uniform and just a drug store soda jerk, and not a very good one at that. Add to this disillusion the fact that Marie probably never did possess the character to be a faithful wife to anyone. She liked it best when she had Fred's pay allotment and no husband hanging around, expecting her to quit her job, become domesticated and help him cope with his PTSD nighttime flashbacks to the horrors of war. But Marie wants nothing to do with the behavioral restraints of marriage: She tells Fred she will divorce him. Monica Henry (2006) describes Marie as "materialistic, vain, promiscuous, impatient with Fred's nightmares and his difficulty in adjusting to civilian life. (As mentioned in chapter 2,) the film ends with Wilma, Millie and Peggy all supposedly happy in their relationships while Marie is presumably destined for a life filled with nightclubs and meaningless relationships" (5). Fortunately for Fred, after his divorce, the Madonna Peggy Stephenson (Teresa Wright), fellow veteran Al's daughter, is ready to catch him when he falls and perhaps become a permanent part of his future.

From Here to Unfaithfulness

Introduced earlier in this chapter when discussing Alma/Lorena the prostitute, there is another woman with another set of problems in *From Here to Eternity*. Capt. Dana Holmes's (Philip Ober) love for and fidelity to his wife, Karen (Deborah Kerr), seem to have never existed. To Holmes, Karen was just his chattel. Neglected and unloved, Karen has also had multiple affairs. It doesn't take long for the audience to understand why Karen doesn't love her husband and is open to an affair with Sgt. Milton Warden, who runs her husband's Army company at Schofield Barracks, Hawaii. Although he's highly attracted to her, Warden knows through scuttlebutt that Karen has slept with some other soldiers. At some level, this bothers him, but testosterone is pumping, and he continues to pursue this attractive woman. He faces twenty years in Leavenworth Disciplinary Barracks (prison), the penalty for any enlisted man caught having an affair with an officer's wife. But the two are falling in love, so against both of their better judgments, they begin an illicit affair. Eventually, after *From Here to Eternity*'s famous love scene on the beach, Warden's emotions and jealousy seep out of his granite exterior. He tells her that he knows about all the men she slept with when she and her husband were stationed sometime earlier at Fort Bliss. This turns into a full-blown argument, and each gather up their clothes to go their separate ways. But before that happens, a frustrated Karen explains to Warden what it took to turn her into an unfaithful wife:

> **Karen:** Come back here, Sergeant. I'll tell you the story; you can take it back to the barracks with you. I'd only been married to Dana two years when I found out he was cheating. And by that time I was pregnant. I thought I had something to hope for. I was almost happy the night the pains began. I remember Dana was going to an officers' conference. I told him to get home early, to bring the doctor with him. And maybe he would have . . . if his "conference" hadn't been with a hat-check girl! He was drunk when he came in at 5 AM. I was lying on the floor. I begged him to go for the doctor, but he fell on the couch and passed out. The baby was born about an hour later. Of course it was dead. It was a boy. . . . But they worked over me at the hospital, they fixed me up fine, they even took my appendix out—they threw that in free.
>
> **Warden:** Karen . . .
>
> **Karen:** And one more thing: no more children. Sure I went out with men after that. And if I'd ever found one that . . .
>
> **Warden:** Karen, listen to me, listen.
>
> **Karen:** I know. Until I met you I didn't think it was possible either. (*From Here to Eternity*, 1953)

Touched by her tragedy, his jealousy erased, Warden understands and holds her tenderly as the scene ends.

Later in their relationship, Warden and Karen tire of sneaking around, always afraid of being discovered. Karen has come up with a plan for them to be together. Although Warden, a sergeant, despises all officers, Karen persuades him to apply for a commission. If he's approved, the new officer would be transferred to the mainland, far away from her husband's command. Then Karen would get a divorce, go back to the States and the two could be together.

First, Karen's husband, Dana, a lazy, odious fellow to begin with, is drummed out of the Army for cruelly persecuting Prewitt for refusing to join his company boxing team. Prewitt did not want to fight in the ring again because he once accidentally blinded a sparring partner. With Dana out of the picture, Karen optimistically meets with Warden to discuss their future. But although their agreement for Warden to apply for a commission was weeks earlier, Warden confesses that he never put in his request. "If I tried to become an officer, I'd be putting on an act. Please don't ask me why." This is when Karen realizes the why of it: "Because you're married to the army," she tells him. To Karen, this would be as bad as competing for Dana's affections with other women. Karen and Warden decide to split up. The next day, with the Japanese attack, Karen also knows that Warden will single-mindedly and to her exclusion pursue his first love and obligation, his job as first sergeant of his company.

On the way home beside coincidental fellow passenger Alma, headed for the States on board an ocean liner, Karen will have to decide whether to follow her cashiered husband into a new and perhaps better life. But the audience really hopes that instead, after the war, Karen will return to Hawaii and try again for a relationship with Warden.

Dear John Letter Number One

Without a doubt, the most famous "Dear John" letter in American film history—much less war film history—comes from Ilsa Lund (Ingrid Bergman) to Rick Blaine (Humphrey Bogart) in *Casablanca.* The scene on the rainy train platform as soldier of fortune Blaine reads Ilsa's farewell note is unforgettable. As the rain, like Rick's suppressed tears, blurs the words on the paper, he crumples the note and tosses it away. But Ilsa, too, has a reason for her apparent unfaithfulness: She has discovered that her husband, Victor Laszlo (Paul Henreid), whom she had believed was killed by the Nazis before she met Rick, is actually alive and in desperate need of her help. So in a way, by rejecting Rick, Ilsa was actually being faithful to her husband.

A Mental Safe House in the Midst of War

In *The Thin Red Line* (1998), as the battle for Guadalcanal rages around Pvt. Bell (Ben Chaplin), we learn the story of his life with his Madonna (Miranda Otto). The tale begins when a buddy asks Bell, who was an officer before the war, how he ended up a private in a rifle platoon. He explains that his love for his wife was the cause, which later would prove highly ironic:

> **Bell:** 'Cause of my wife. I was in the Corps of Engineers. We've never been separated before, not even for a night. I took it for four months, and then I quit. Resigned. They sent me back to the States, told me I'd never get another commission. They said they'd see to it I got drafted, and for sure be in the infantry. (*The Thin Red Line*, 1998)

As he and his fellow infantrymen prepare to disembark at Guadalcanal, Bell thinks about death, and if he is killed, he vows to his wife "to wait for you there, on the other side of the dark waters." Director Terrence Malick, whose film was nominated for seven Oscars, cuts back and forth between the troop disembarkation and an intimate scene between Bell and his wife sometime in the past. Later, marching through the jungle, Bell, always the poet, praises God for his many creations, including "the contented heart," which ironically he attributes to his faithful Madonna waiting at home. In this daydream, they are at home, just holding each other in utter contentment.

Later in the film, scouting out Japanese positions somewhere farther up a grassy hill, Bell tells his men to stay concealed in the high grass while he crawls up the hill alone. As he slithers through the grass, Bell again flashes back to the same memorable day together, as he and his wife caress. Then Malick cuts to a seashore scene, as she wades sensuously in knee-deep surf in a calf-length dress, as Bell watches with admiration. Her voice-over says, "Come out where I am." Then Bell is back on Guadalcanal in the grass, smoking out gun emplacements and mapping the strategy he will suggest to his commander when they assault these positions the next day.

That night, Bell's reminiscence continues. This time he and his wife are in their bedroom, making love. His voice-over says, "We. We together. One being. We flow together like water till I can't tell you from me. I drink you. Now, now." The scene shifts from the bedroom to his wife naked in the bathtub as he strokes her hair. Then back to the jungle.

Later, after the assault the next day, Bell worries that the savagery he has witnessed and participated in will change him into a man not worthy of his Madonna. "My Dear Wife," he writes, "You get something twisted out of your insides with all this blood, filth and noise. I want to stay changeless for you, and come back to you the man I was before." Malick cuts from the jungle again to a shot of Bell's wife in a nightgown, curled up in a ball on a bed. Next she's looking over the sea and then swinging on a swing. Bell's voice-over says, "Love. Where does it come from? Who lit this flame in us?" Then more scenes of war as Bell says, "A war can put it out. . . . I was a prisoner. . . . You set me free."

Then, the objective taken, Bell's outfit is getting some well-needed rest in the rear, eating hot food and receiving the GI's delight, mail. Unfortunately for Bell, the letter he receives from his wife is not at all delightful. It's her "Dear John" letter:

Marty: Dear Jack, I've met an Air Force captain. I've fallen in love with him. I want a divorce to marry him. *(We cut from her standing outside a house as an officer approaches her, and then to Bell, reading the letter, nauseated and wobbly-legged, supporting himself against a truck.)* I know you can say "no," but I'm asking you anyway, out of the memory of what we had together. Forgive me. I just got too lonely, Jack. *(Bell goes from sick to grinning in disbelief and irony.)* We'll meet again someday. People who've been as close as we've been always meet again. I have no right to speak to you this way. I can't stop myself. A habit so strong. Oh, my friend! All those shining years! Help me leave you.

(Bell wanders around the camp aimlessly, lost). (The Thin Red Line,
1998)

Bell has lost his anchor with his home and his reality, what Vietnam veterans
generically called "the world." Bell anchored himself and his sanity in this
savage, unreal island by flashing away and back to his wonderful, "content"
relationship with his wife. There he had everything he needed. But a "Dear
John" letter has changed all that because an unfaithful wife got "too lonely."

The Lucky Ones?

There is no "Dear John" letter when Pat Cheever (Holly Hagan) gives her
husband, Fred (Tim Robbins), the bad news in the Gulf War film, *The Lucky
Ones* (2008). She does it in person. Pat's husband, Fred Cheever, was a
sergeant deployed in Iraq when a Porta Potty fell off a forklift and his back
was injured. Cheever considered the injury good luck, because he was offered and accepted a medical discharge and escaped the bloody insurgency in
Iraq otherwise unhurt. This film begins with Cheever cheerfully anticipating
returning home to his wife and son, getting his old job back and resuming his
former content life in suburban St. Louis. But, as he is about to find out, in
his marriage, apparently all the contentment was one-sided.

First, Fred and his two GI traveling companions, Colee and T. K., are
stranded in New York due to airline flight cancellations. So they combine to
rent a car and drive to St. Louis. When they arrive at Fred's home in an
upscale suburban housing development, no one is home. Shortly Pat drives
up. After an awkward hug hello, and with Colee and T. K. sitting in another
room, Pat drops the bomb on Fred. She has been advised by friends to wait to
tell him for a week or a month, but everything seems to be about how she
feels, and Pat just can't wait to give Fred the bad news. Pat tells him that she
needs a divorce, that she has moved on, she has a new job and "I'm finally
happy." Totally shocked, Fred asks, "You weren't before?" She replies that
she really doesn't know. Apparently, Pat has never communicated her feelings of unhappiness and lack of fulfillment with her husband.

To answer his unasked question, Pat assures Fred that she's not seeing
anyone else: There is no Jody in the picture. She instead says that she's
happier without him. "I want to be alone. I know this seems harsh, but I'm
happy being alone . . . without you." As an audience, there is much more we
want to know about their relationship. For example, as their only son, Scott
(Mark Young), readies himself for college, one wonders if Fred and Pat
married because she became pregnant, and now that Mark is leaving home
for Stanford University, Pat wants to free herself of Fred and experience the
life she might have had if she didn't become pregnant at too young an age
and wasn't forced, by the couple's sense of Midwest propriety, to "do the

right thing" and marry. Or was life with Fred not happy and fulfilling? Was he absorbed with his job and neglectful all these years? We hear no evidence of a lack of love with his affectionate-sounding phone calls to Pat before he arrived home, or in his gleeful anticipation of their reunion.

All told, this was a pretty dreadful homecoming for Fred. To make matters worse, later, when a friend spots Fred in a restaurant, he finds out that the business he planned to return to has been horribly mismanaged while he was gone, and is about to go bankrupt and close its doors. So on top of everything else, he has no job. To make matters even more stressful, son Scott tells his father that he needs another $20,000 to pay for the family's share of Stanford's expensive tuition. Fred realizes that there's nothing for him in St. Louis, so he plans to visit his brother in Salt Lake City to see if there's some work for him there. This allows the film's three-friend cross-country trek to continue. Eventually Fred decides to sacrifice himself by reenlisting in the Army and going back to Iraq. Although lump sum payments do not happen under these circumstances, in this film, Fred's instant reenlistment bonus money provides Scott with the $20,000 in time for the payment deadline. In effect, Fred, who loves his son very much, ends up putting himself in great danger just so his son can attend the college of his choice. This does not sound like an uncaring husband and father.

What is Pat's problem, then? In terms of the story line, the audience is left to wonder. Perhaps there are just some people who are never completely content, never satisfied, who keep looking for something—they don't know what—that they think will make them truly happy.

Jarhead's Many Wayward Women

If there is one scene in war films that hits home most disturbingly about a GI's unfaithful wife or sweetheart, a woman who has totally shunned the pedestal, it may be found in *Jarhead* (2005). After the usual basic training sequences, the action—or in this film, the lack of it—takes place during operations Desert Shield and Desert Storm.

One wife's method of notifying her husband that their marriage is over and that she is having an affair with another man is just downright cruel, regardless of her stated reasons. She sends her husband what appears to be a present: a videocassette of the Vietnam War movie, *The Deer Hunter* (1978). Delighted that she sent him this gift, the Marine happily gathers his buddies around him in the company's day room TV to play the videocassette. But a few seconds into the movie, recorded over the film they thought they would be watching, is home-recorded video of his wife fornicating enthusiastically with a Jody, their next door neighbor. Reacting to this sadistic version of a Dear John letter, the Marine goes ballistic and has to be restrained. But after his buddies rush him out of the room, we see a close-up of the wife on the screen, admitting essentially how this is her sadistic way to extract her revenge for her husband's own lack of faithfulness.

In *Jarhead*, so many young Marines receive "Dear John" letters that the men create a bulletin board on which they angrily post pictures of their unfaithful girlfriends and wives, along with angry captions. In contrast, in the World War II era, if there were any pinups shared publicly with their fellow soldiers, they were not "real" girls: As discussed earlier, they were the likenesses of Betty Grable, Jane Russell, and Rita Hayworth, Hollywood chattel for lonely GIs to daydream about. Then and now, a soldier would show a buddy a treasured picture of wife or girlfriend, carefully stored among the few items he carries on his person. But such a soldier would not post a picture of a faithful wife/girl for the camp to ogle. In this film, then, there are two kinds of pictures, and, therefore, two female roles. Pictures of loving and faithful Madonnas are carried next to their hearts or in their helmets as reminders to gaze at in anxious times, while photos of the second kind, the unfaithful, those fit only to throw darts at, are posted on a GI wall of shame.

Comments from Marines posted along with the pictures illustrate the various feelings of these jilted men: "I loved her," says one; "Looks sweet; all bitch," says another. A third says, "Stay away from her: She'll take all your money." A horribly sad one reads, "She was my fiancé: Now she's with my brother." Another proclaims, "I loved her so much. She took my kid and disappeared."

The film's protagonist, LCpl. Anthony Swofford (Jake Gyllenhaal) begins with a stereotypical relationship with his stateside girlfriend. She begins the picture as his sexy Madonna and ardent lover. From boot camp onward, Swofford carries with him a sexy picture of Kristina (Brianne Davis) in a suggestive pose. She wears just panties and a Marine T-shirt, symbolizing that she's branded chattel of a certain Marine. During the long weeks of tedium before Desert Storm begins, Swofford uses the picture to masturbate in the latrine.

However, as time goes on, Kristina shares in a letter that she's met a male "friend." Swofford doesn't know what to think, so on his next transcontinental phone call, he inarticulately tries to find the words to learn more about him. Kristina maintains, "He's just a friend." But to Swofford, he's probably a Jody. Of course, it doesn't help Swofford's morale much that their platoon NCO, SSgt. Sykes (Jamie Foxx), keeps drumming into the men's heads, "Jody's bangin' her right now." Swofford's last letter from Kristina ends, ominously, with "I'll always love you." But does that mean what it literally says, or is it a recitation of Dolly Parton's lyrics for the song of the same name, which reads like a final good-bye? Swofford does not find out conclusively until he returns from his overseas deployment and visits Kristina at home. This is when he finally learns that Kristina is no longer his girlfriend.

OTHER FAITHLESS WOMEN

In a fictional future war, the Dear John pattern is much less sadistic than in *Jarhead*, but the resultant "kiss-off" recording is no less distressing, especially when it's also shown to a trooper's buddies. In the futuristic war film, *Starship Troopers* (1997), infantryman Johnny Rico (Casper Van Dien) receives a Dear John on a compact videodisc. Thinking it's a regular "letter" from his girlfriend, Carmen (Denise Richards), a pilot in fleet service, he plays the disc recording on a machine in the barracks, and his buddies gather around to ogle his beautiful girlfriend. Unfortunately, Carmen informs Johnny that she's decided she will become a career officer in the Federal Service instead of eventually resigning so that the two can marry. At the end of the message, she asks Johnny to remain her friend. A buddy tells Johnny, "Funny how they always wanna be friends after they rip your guts out."

   In all eras, these Dear John letters often show up during a lull in the fighting, during a time generally reserved for good times: mail call. In the Vietnam War film, *Hamburger Hill*, in between assaults, the men receive food and mail from home. One soldier receives a cassette tape from his girlfriend, full of words of encouragement and praise from both her and his family. The men all listen as the tape is played, each taking comfort from any sounds from "the world," far away from the bloodshed and insanity of their present circumstances. But Pvt. Bienstock (Tommy Swerdlow) isn't as fortunate. He sits, reads a letter from his girl, and appears to be in shock. Finally, one of his buddies asks if he's OK.

> **Bienstock:** *(shaken, in shock)* It's from my girlfriend. Says she's not gonna w-write me anymore. Friends at college told her it was immoral . . . to write to me. *(He assumes an even more blank, shocked look. All he can do is utter little words over and over.)* Oh . . . oh. (*Hamburger Hill*, 1987)

A buddy, Pvt. Languilli (Anthony Barrile), comes over to Bienstock, sits down next to him and puts his arm around him for comfort and support. It is the custom of the African American troops in their platoon, when faced with worse tragedy—such as the death of a buddy—to touch fists on the top and bottom and to repeat the phrase, "It don't mean nothin'" until their soldierly sense of stoic fatalism returns. Here, Languilli and Bienstock—who are white—imitate their African American brothers, but in a tacit manner. They just touch fists: No words pass between them. Then Bienstock just lays his head against Languilli's chest and repeats, "Oh . . . oh."

   Capt. Paul Eddington (Kirk Douglas) is executive officer of a Navy cruiser in the World War II film, *In Harm's Way* (1965), but is close to losing his job. Eddington spends most of his time drinking away his troubles and visiting prostitutes. Most of his dysfunctional behavior is caused by the memory of his deceased but unfaithful wife. At the outset of the film, we see a scene in which his wife, Liz (Barbara Bouchet) is cheating on Eddington with a Marine officer. But that morning, Liz is among the many civilians killed during the Japanese attack on Pearl Harbor. Retrieving her belongings from the morgue, Eddington, furious because he is made aware once again of his wife's unfaithfulness, becomes unstable. He enters a bar, and when a friendly Marine officer offers him a drink, Eddington becomes enraged and attacks him.

Later in the film, Eddington becomes attracted to a young woman, Annalee (Jill Haworth), but in his mind she also is not "faithful" to him. A Navy nurse, she is engaged to another man, but although a girlfriend cautions her against becoming involved with this unstable officer, she is strangely attracted to the danger she senses in him. Inexperienced, Annalee flirts with and teases Eddington, and the old anger within him wells up. Something inside him snaps and he forcibly rapes her. Later, in despair and pregnant, Annalee kills herself. To redeem himself, Eddington flies a "one-way" reconnaissance mission and is killed. Like Rickson in *The War Lover*, Eddington tries to drown his failures with women by doing heroic, manly acts.

In the next chapter, we examine the roles played by Hawksian women in war films.

Chapter Five

The Hawksian Woman

In *Navy SEALs*, most of the men see women as mere sex objects, but the one SEAL who'd rather drown than attend the chief's wedding sees women as much more problematical. He seems to be a firm believer in the Hawksian view we discussed in chapter 1 that women complicate a man's life and make it more difficult to concentrate on what's important to men. In *Navy SEALs*, they define a man's job in two parts: their exciting, dangerous and deadly job followed by partying heartily afterward. An anonymous review of Naomi Wise's (1996) seminal article about the Hawksian Woman in the online *Flamethrower Magazine* says it this way:

> Women in most adventure films only exist to serve the male hero; as something to rescue, leave behind, pine after, or be occasionally annoyed with. However, the "Hawksian woman" is consequential, self-assured, and even at times superior to the hero. . . . They are often saloon singers or something similar, but never depicted as "cheap." They dictate the terms of their romantic relationships. While the men are professionally skilled, the women are "professional human beings." (*Flamethrower Magazine*, 2010)

In virtually all the genre pictures Howard Hawks directed or produced, there is one overriding misogynist theme: The closed-off fraternity of men performing the efficient, professional conduct of their jobs only functions efficiently when the distracting influences of women are minimized. By introducing such counterproductive elements as a woman's *feelings* or a kind of female logic that minimizes the value of dangerous, futile, and risky behaviors, successfully doing a man's job becomes much more complicated.

Novelist and Hawks collaborator Leigh Brackett provides her take on Hawks's ideas about women in his films:

Conventional heroines bore him; he can't have fun with them. As Naomi Wise puts it, they often take over and push the whole plot. More than once [during Brackett's screenwriting collaborations with Hawks], I've argued with Hawks that the girl was getting too pushy, and couldn't we let the poor boob of a hero [e.g., John Wayne in *Rio Bravo*] make just one decision by himself? I was always overruled, and I guess Hawks always knew what he was doing, because it came out right at the end. (Brackett 1977, 195)

It's interesting to note how Brackett came to work with Hawks in the first place. Although the majority of her publications were as a science fiction novelist, Brackett was recruited to assist Hawks as a screenwriting collaborator for two reasons: He liked a tough-sounding novel she wrote *(No Good from a Corpse)* and he didn't know "Leigh" was a woman until he met her. Legend has it that Hawks asked his secretary to summon "this guy Brackett" to work with William Faulkner on the screenplay for *The Big Sleep* (1946). Hawks told film author, critic, and film/TV producer Richard Schickel, "Leigh, I thought, was a man's name, and in walked this fresh-looking girl who wrote like a man." Brackett was herself probably what Hawks would have considered a prototypical Hawksian woman. Thus began a writing collaboration that included many of Hawks's westerns and spanned many years.

In Hawks's films, war pictures and otherwise, many of the secondary B-plot problems that complicate heroes' completing their tasks and quests are caused by women. For example, in *Air Force* (1943), the officers of the bomber *Mary Ann*, who are as gung ho and full of esprit de corps as humanly possible, are out to deliver payback to the Japanese for their attack on Pearl Harbor. But even these single-minded gents become temporarily distracted from their quest because of a misunderstanding over a woman. For some time during this film, these dedicated fighting men lose their sense of solidarity and purpose because of a falling-out over a feisty Hawksian female.

The help Humphrey Bogart's character lends to anti-Axis agents in *To Have and Have Not* (1944) becomes complicated when he must simultaneously juggle a romantic relationship with sultry Lauren Bacall, whom he has nicknamed "Slim." He must try to keep one step ahead of Gestapo-like Vichy French agents while sidestepping Slim's jealousy for a big-eyed but helpless Madonna, a French woman who's making eyes at him. The woman, Helene (Dolores Moran), a far cry from the Hawksian ideal, uses feminine tricks to play up to Bogart's ego, and comes on to him by slipping into a "helpless female" role that she has learned can assist her in conning men into doing her bidding. Watching her go into her act, the independent and resourceful Slim, who would never stoop to such tactics, scoffs sarcastically at Helene's gambit.

In *Only Angels Have Wings* (1939), Cary Grant's task of running a ragtag, military-style outfit that flies the mail over dangerous South American mountain passes becomes even more difficult when a new, fascinating woman (Jean Arthur) comes into his life, followed immediately by his old flame. This becomes another Hawksian juggling act that Grant's character doesn't have time for. Both John Wayne (Sheriff John T. Chance) and Dean Martin's character, Dude, had been efficiently doing their lawman jobs for a long time in *Rio Bravo* (1959), but in this story, Chance becomes preoccupied with an alluring but somewhat neurotic woman of doubtful repute (Angie Dickinson), who is newly arrived at the dance hall and saloon. In the depths of depression, thanks to a woman, a completely defeated Dude tries to drown his memories of a lost love in a bottle of red eye.

Naomi Wise writes that *Rio Bravo* and *Red River* (1948) are two good examples from the western genre of how both the men and the women in all of Hawks's films benefit and learn from each others' natures (Wise 1996, 112). Wayne's character, Sheriff Chance, seems particularly unused to conducting conversations with women, as if he's never come across a woman before. When he is attracted to one, such as Angie Dickinson's character, nicknamed "Feathers" (remember that Hawksian women often are given nicknames), Chance turns into a tongue-tied schoolboy with a crush: totally unable to communicate in a coherent fashion, although talking incessantly isn't a problem for Feathers. During their many exchanges, however, Feathers manages to—if ever so slightly—feminize Chance, while a bit of Chance's Wayne-like masculinity also rubs off on Feathers. In the fight against the film's antagonists, Feathers bravely assists Chance. Then, Wise writes, "Chance is transformed. He discovers his own emotions and his need for help, and in that discovery he comes to maturity as a human being in a world where two sexes exist as equals" (113).

In an article with the eye-catching title of "That's Not Brave, That's Just Stupid," Barbara Bernstein argues that men often engage in dumb, dangerous behaviors just because they are convinced that it is their job to do it, or because a man thinks he's honor bound to see a task through to what could be a disastrous or deadly completion because it's *his job* (Bernstein 1977, 343). This is because *men are what they do*, and to not do their jobs—or to walk away from the job before it's done—is to be unprofessional, which is synonymous with unmanly. Enter the Hawksian woman, whose female point of view provides a contrast in reasoning to a man's, which states, in sum, the title of Bernstein's article: "That's not brave, that's just stupid." For a sex that prides itself on logic over emotion, this point of view drives men crazy.

The best example of Hawksian female interference with "what a man's gotta do" is found in *Red River*. Wayne's classic cattle drive boss, Thomas Dunson, could have been shot by his adopted son, Matt Garth (Montgomery Clift), because of any number of conflicts between the two men. These conflicts—unspoken in typical male manner by Dunson and Garth—are held up for the two men's close examination by tough, no nonsense Tess (Joanne Dru), a woman of doubtful repute whom they encounter on their cattle drive.

Instead, Tess helps feminize the situation by fostering communication on the feelings level with Dunson and Matt, men of few words, and makes them realize that as adoptive father and son, despite their differences of opinion, they still love each other. So, in the climax of the film, when the two men meet at dawn to solve their differences by shooting each other, Tess's intervention saves the day. Brandishing a six-gun (temporarily adopting a more traditionally male role to make her point), Tess breaks up the climactic gun and fistfight between Dunson and Matt:

> **Tess:** Stop it. Stop it. Stop makin' a holy—Stop it, I said. I'm mad, good and mad. And who wouldn't be? You, Dunson, pretendin' you're gonna kill him. Why, it's the last thing in the world you . . . stay still. *(waving the pistol)* I'm mad, I told ya. And you, Matthew Garth, gettin' your face all beat up and all bloody. You oughta see how, you oughta see how silly you look, like, like somethin' the cat dragged—*stay still!* What a fool I've been, expectin' trouble for days when, when anybody with half a mind would know you two love each other. (*Red River*, 1948)

Usually in Hawks's films, men left to their own devices will solve their problems in some manly way, often with guns or other weapons. In *Red River*, the interjection of Tess along with her distracting female feelings and insistence on discussing things becomes an alternative to gunplay or settling the fight by beating on each other with their fists.

Hawks was a versatile director, and produced and directed films in almost every genre. So even in the outdoors comedy, *Man's Favorite Sport?* (1964), we find Rock Hudson competing in a fishing competition while Paula Prentiss's well-meaning help puts Rock behind the eight ball with, in turn, his boss, his non-Hawksian fiancée, the organizers of the event, and—amazingly—a bear. In Hawks's worldview, no matter what job a man's gotta do, one, two, or (in this case) three women will find ways to louse it up.

Film scholars have often identified Hawks by name with this particular female role. However, Hawks was not the only director to include Hawksian characters and situations in his films. For example, Hawks's more famous contemporary, John Ford, is no less a member of the he-man woman hater club. Ford's women interfere in and generally disrupt the otherwise clear-cut, manly work of any number of stars in Ford films, although most often it's John Wayne. For example, Wayne's ardor for killing Japanese while making a name for himself in the Navy is sidetracked, time and again, by his affection for attractive (but not Hawksian) nurse Donna Reed in *They Were Expendable* (1945). In *She Wore a Yellow Ribbon* (1949), cavalry officers portrayed by Wayne, John Agar, and Harry Carey Jr. are constantly sidetracked in their work of assisting in the genocide of Native Americans because of various little dramas centering around a young, coquettish female (Joanne

Dru) back at the fort. In *Rio Grande* (1950), Cavalry Colonel Kirby Yorke's (Wayne) recently returned ex-wife (Maureen O'Hara), definitely a Hawksian type despite the phony airs she puts on, is the cause for considerably more troubles than the insurgent Apaches he's fighting. Another Hawksian woman played with gusto by O'Hara complicates Wayne's life yet again as he plays a prizefighter attempting to retire to a simple, peaceful life in rural Ireland in *The Quiet Man* (1952). Posing as a Madonna, Southern belle style, would-be spy Constance Towers does everything she can to undermine Wayne as a Union cavalry commander in Ford's Civil War film, *The Horse Soldiers* (1959). Giving Wayne a break, Ford casts Carroll Baker as a Quaker missionary and the humanistic thorn in the saddle of Richard Widmark, a cavalry officer just trying to do his job (see above regarding genocide), in *Cheyenne Autumn* (1964).

As many of Hawks's and Ford's films illustrate, the woman's intrusive presence disturbs and often upends the elite, macho world that men at war have designed for themselves, distracting them from what Richard Crenna's Navy gunboat captain described in *The Sand Pebbles* (1966) as "the give and take of death."

Because Hawksian women are sometimes allowed into the inner sanctum of the male fraternity, they must be transformed somewhat from the feminine. As mentioned earlier, this is accomplished in part by changing their names to nicknames or, if they're already shortened, like *Red River's* Tess, assigning them terse names at the screenwriting phase. Such women have nicknames like Feathers, Dallas, Nikki, or Slim, to better fit in or contrast with men such as Biff, Bo, Bubba, Skipper, Sparky, or Buzz. As David Boxwell explains,

> Certainly women are nicknamed in Hawks' films to indicate that they, too, have gained acceptance by men in groups on masculinist terms—they shed their conventional gender identities as passive, domestic, and feminine to become "Hawksian women" who are involved in male formations and institutions in something more than just peripheral [and passive] roles. The Hawksian woman's nickname signifies her status as a person permitted to join the men, if not on equal terms, then at least on terms that grant her something other than traditionally subordinate status. (Boxwell, 2002)

Molly Haskell agrees, writing that "the best woman was often an honorary male, and the highest accolade was that in performing some task, she was 'good.' [Rosalind] Russell's character, Hildy [in Hawks's *His Girl Friday* (1940)], quick-witted, resourceful and articulate, is repeatedly referred to as a 'great newspaper*man*'" (1997, 113).

Additionally, although many of these women were also love interests for male protagonists, the conventions of the Hawksian narrative forbade certain words. Brackett describes one of them:

> There are some other Hawksian conventions about men and women. The word
> "love" is not heard, and there is no scene where hero and heroine declare their
> tender feelings for each other. It's done obliquely . . . and marriage is not
> mentioned. . . . Hawks people are not domestic types; nobody ever talks about
> getting that little spread and settling down to raise a family. (1977, 196)

Of course, in *His Girl Friday,* due to male ego and to cement his male
hegemony in the journalistic arena, Cary Grant's managing editor character
keeps reminding the audience that Hildy was his protégée whom he taught
everything she knows about the newspaper business. He even mentions that
he hired her right out of journalism school to reinforce how "green" she was
before the Pygmalion-like changeover he engineered. Although Haskell is
quick to point out how adopting manlike behaviors is the ticket to acceptance
in a man's world, she also praises Hawksian women for establishing new
possibilities for women, which screenwriters of the twenty-first century cinema have built upon:

> Whatever defects the Hawksian worldview may be held to have in its compen-
> satory overvaluation of male heroics, its adolescent hierarchical rating of man-
> liness, stoicism and professionalism, Hawks has given us some of the most
> exhilarating, rambunctious and assertive heroines in cinema. They have out-
> lasted more pliant female characters, becoming prophetic representatives of a
> species of women who yearn for something beyond settling down and nesting,
> with or without marriage and family. (1997, 114)

This is an important point regarding the women's role. Hawksian women are
certainly closer to equality with men than, say, Madonnas usually are, but
they signify an important change. As Wise writes, "While she is still far from
the ideal, 'liberated' woman, she represents an important step toward that
ideal" (1996, 114).

AIR FORCE

As mentioned in chapter 2, although Faye Emerson's character, Susan, has
relatively little screen time in Hawks's *Air Force,* and at that speaks all her
lines while lying, wounded, in a hospital bed, dialogue about her reveals that
she was an impressive Hawksian woman. As mentioned earlier, she is the
cause of a misunderstanding among the flyers that for a time puts the war on
the back burner. In the aftermath of the Japanese attack on Pearl Harbor and
Hickam Field, the aforementioned crew of the B-17 bomber, the *Mary Ann,*
learn that Lt. Tommy McMartin's sister, Susan, was badly wounded. The
crew accompanies Tommy to the hospital to visit her. Obviously on pain
medication and not able to explain fully what happened, Susan is only able to
tell her brother not to get mad at fellow pilot "Tex" Rader, that "It's all my

fault. . . . He tried to make me get out of the car, but . . . I guess he'd better tell you." After that, she falls back into a drug-induced sleep, leaving the crew to think the worst of whatever Susan and Tex were doing in that car when the Japanese attacked. Once again, a Hawksian woman complicates the lives of a group of men who are just trying to do their jobs.

The men find Rader, asleep (another black mark against him), in an operations shack and at first give him what he calls "the third degree" over what went on between him and Tommy's sister. Not knowing exactly what the men think, and not quite awake yet, Tex says the worst possible thing to exacerbate the misunderstanding: "Don't believe her," he says. "It's my fault. I should have made her get out of that car right then." He explains that when the Japanese attack began, the two raced to Hickam Field, only to encounter Japanese fifth columnists with guns. Next, with Tex standing on the running board and hanging onto the side of the car, Susan had driven the car through the base toward some hangers. "The last time I saw her," Tex explains, "she was standing on the car, yelling and rooting like she was at a football game." That's when she was hit with Japanese machinegun fire.

Before Tex can also explain why he wasn't wounded, too, the crewmen depart, still angry and disgruntled, leaving him before they decide to knock his block off. Later, the chagrined flyers find out why Rader wasn't at Susan's side, protecting her from the Japanese: He was one of only three American pilots to get their fighters airborne during the attack and engage the enemy. Rader shot down four zeroes before he himself was shot down. Learning this, Tommy and the other crewmen were no longer angry. Later, flying onward toward the South Pacific, the crew gets the word that Susan will make a full recovery. At the end of the film, we learn that Rader, trained as a fighter pilot and thoroughly obnoxious through three-quarters of the picture about the pursuit plane's superiority over a bomber, now has changed his tune: He is the commander of one of these same big bombers, and is assigned to lead one of two bomber wings in an upcoming mission to bomb Tokyo.

A HAWKSIAN PROTOTYPE

If there was ever a prototype of the Hawksian woman, many writers and historians point toward Lauren Bacall's performance as Marie "Slim" Browning in Hawks's World War II espionage caper, *To Have and Have Not*, freely adapted by Jules Furthman and fellow novelist William Faulkner from Ernest Hemingway's novel. Geoffrey MacNab compares Slim to Lady Brett Ashley in Hemingway's *The Sun Also Rises* as "self-reliant, insolent, capable of running with the boys" (MacNab, 1997). When casting the part, Hawks was taken with the then-eighteen-year-old Bacall, and gave her the nickname "Slim," after Hawks's second wife. Some point to Nancy "Slim" Keith, adept at many manly sports including skeet shooting, as one of Hawks's prototypes for his ideal woman.

In *To Have and Have Not*, to understand how Slim insinuates herself into the narrative and then influences it, one has to go back to the beginning of the picture. This film, which has many plot points similar to *Casablanca*, is a film about a reluctant Bogart character "getting back into the war" by confounding Martinique's rather incompetent, gangster-like Vichy French authorities. However, *To Have and Have Not* begins like an adventure yarn about game fishing in the Caribbean. This is to establish the typical Hemingway/Hawks masculine milieu occupied by Bogart's character, Capt. Harry Morgan, and his sport fishing boat assistants, the drunkard Eddie (Walter Brennan) and crewman Horatio (Sir Lancelot). We open on the ocean near Fort de France, Martinique, with the sad results of the fifteenth day in a row in which Harry has taken client Mr. Johnson (Walter Sande) out on his boat, the *Queen Conch*, fishing for marlin, only to fail to haul in his catch. Despite what must have been two weeks of patiently coaching Johnson, the inept client still can't master the rather simple (but manly) skill of properly setting the drag on his casting reel and attaching it by hooks to his chair so a big fish won't jerk it out of his hands. When Johnson actually manages to hook onto a big marlin, he clumsily loses it—along with his rod and reel. In a Hawks picture, this establishes Johnson as an unmanly incompetent, out of place in a man's world. MacNab (1997) quotes documentary filmmaker Kevin Macdonald: "The only people he respected were those who could do their jobs properly." This theme runs through all Hawks's, Ford's, and William Wellman's films, to name a few, and explains why women, who complicate the successful completion of men's jobs, are clearly classed as "the other," whose presence makes a man's work more difficult and complicated.

Additionally, Hawks, a fighter pilot during World War I who was accustomed to being surrounded by manly men, always valued the company and camaraderie of other macho males while they did manly deeds. For example, the macho Hemingway and other manly Hollywood types, including William Faulkner, Victor Fleming, and John Wayne, were Hawks's hunting, fishing, and sailing companions. Yet in *To Have and Have Not*, Hawks shows that Johnson has fished this two-week charter alone, with only the crew to accompany and serve him. Apparently, Johnson, an abrasive fellow, has no buddies to invite on a fishing trip, perhaps because of his lack of personality and integrity.

To make matters worse, Hawks draws a picture of Johnson as a man of low character, perhaps a spoiled rich guy, who routinely blames his failures on others. In this instance, he blames his lack of success in catching marlin on everyone around him: the crew and its captain. But the audience clearly sees that it's Johnson's unmanly incompetence to blame. Another negative character trait is that since he blames the crew for his incompetence, Johnson plans to stiff Harry and the crew for their two-week charter bill. When Harry attempts to get Johnson to settle up, he claims he doesn't have enough cash in his wallet. He says he'll go to the bank at ten in the morning the next day when it opens and draw out Harry's money. But as we learn later, Johnson plans to catch an early morning plane off the island, skipping out without paying.

When Harry returns to the hotel where he lives in the city of Fort de France, he encounters a new hotel guest in the room across the hall: Marie Browning, newly arrived and almost broke, after unexplained but inferred sordid adventures in Rio de Janeiro and Trinidad. Brackett (1977) explains what comes next for Harry in the Hawks formula:

> The hero is woman-shy, living in a male world where he is comfortable with his relationships. When the new girl arrives, he tries at first to get rid of her. She insists on staying, and now she has to win her place in this closed group *as a man* (or asexual human being, if you prefer), proving that she is as honest and courageous and loyal as any of them. Somewhere along the line, she is likely to say to the hero, "Any time you want me to go, just tell me, and I'll go." In other words, no strings. When the hero can accept her as he would another man, with the masculine virtues he values, then he can start thinking about her as a woman. (195–96)

Harry and hotel/bar/restaurant owner Gerard (Marcel Dalio), whom Harry has given the nickname "Frenchy," are in Harry's room. Frenchy asks Harry to help him smuggle two Free French comrades of his onto the island, but Harry, as Bogart's Rick Blaine initially did in *Casablanca*, refuses to get involved with any of Frenchy's intrigues. Marie crosses the hall from the door of her room, drapes herself seductively in Harry's doorway and asks for a match. (If there is a way to seductively light and smoke a cigarette, modern-day vamps should take pointers from Slim.) To indicate that at least at first Harry is a bit wary and plans to steer clear of Marie, rather than cross over to her to light her cigarette, he tosses her a box of matches. She lights her smoke and tosses back the matches, and doesn't throw like a girl. This alone speaks volumes about her: Not offended, she lights her own cigarette like a man and tosses it back (good arm).

Almost immediately, Harry dubs Marie with her "Slim" nickname, perhaps in praise of her long legs, and so she remains from then on. Equal to the task, and for no good reason, Slim decides to call Harry "Steve." (As an homage to this, in Peter Bogdanovich's farce, *What's Up, Doc?* Barbra Streisand's Judy character also decides to nickname Ryan O'Neal's character, Dr. Howard Bannister, "Steve.") The initial meeting between Harry and Slim is short, as Harry has business to conduct, but he catches up with Slim later downstairs at the bar. Experienced in fending for herself, Slim has spotted

Johnson as a potential mark and is having a drink with him, while listening to Cricket (Hoagy Carmichael) play the piano and sing. But when Johnson (also awkward with women) tries to get affectionate too soon and reaches for her, Slim pulls away, covering her exit by slyly rising and crossing over to Cricket's piano. She joins Cricket in an impromptu duet of "Am I Blue," which becomes a de facto audition for joining Cricket and his band as a sultry singer, thus securing herself an income. Reaction shots show that Harry is amused by the way Slim handles herself with Johnson, and when she also relieves Johnson of his wallet and goes upstairs, he follows. OK with Slim's actions but concerned that he won't get paid for the charter, Harry threatens to frisk her by asking, "What's it gonna be?" In a typical Hawksian response, she tells Harry that she's intrigued by that possibility, but she nonetheless hands over Johnson's wallet. Slim explains that she was after boat fare to get out of Martinique and home to the United States, which she now regrets leaving in the first place. Another of the usual attributes of a Hawksian woman is that her experiences have made her sadder but wiser. As Harry examines Johnson's wallet, he discovers traveler's checks, cash, and a plane ticket for 6 a.m. the next morning, alerting him that Johnson planned on running out on his charter bill.

The two head downstairs, and an angry Harry has it in mind to confront Johnson. Upset with Johnson's trickery, and with an unlit cigarette dangling from his mouth, Harry is considering beginning his conversation with Johnson by socking him in the jaw. Instead, with perfect timing, Slim intervenes, lighting his cigarette, allowing Harry an extra moment to calm down. Harry becomes more impressed with Slim. So instead of assaulting him, Harry insists that Johnson sign over one of his travelers checks to him on the spot, and even provides the pen. Unfortunately, at this exact moment, a gun fight breaks out between pro- and anti-Vichy agents outside in the street, and while everyone including Harry and Slim are smart enough to duck and hit the floor, Johnson stupidly stands facing the street like a deer in the headlights, and catches two bullets in the chest. He is dead before signing the traveler's check; also deceased are Harry's chances of getting paid.

Next, security chief Capt. Renard (Dan Seymour) suspects Frenchy, Harry, and Slim of associating with anti-Vichy agents (which they did) and arrests them. When Renard asks why Slim is visiting Martinique, she gives him a smart aleck answer, "To buy a hat." This causes one of Renard's henchmen, Coyo (gangster character actor Sheldon Leonard) to slap her face. A tough Hawksian woman, she ignores Coyo and looks back at Renard as if nothing has happened. But Harry becomes incensed, only restraining himself from slugging Coyo because there are too many guns suddenly aimed in his direction. But a minute later he gets face-to-face with Coyo and with one of those highly malevolent Bogart grins, threateningly urges Coyo to try something like that on him. Later in the film, Harry gets the chance for some payback with the thug. But for the present, despite his anger, Harry has time to be impressed with how the Hawksian woman took the slap, assuming it's not the first time she has coolly endured abuse from men. While interrogating Harry, Renard confiscates all of Johnson's money along with all of Harry's. He is now both offended *and* broke.

In an earlier scene, drunken Eddie tells a story about stepping barefoot on a dead bee and getting stung nonetheless. It suddenly has new meaning to Harry. He has done nothing against the Vichy government but is still penalized. The combination of being furious with Renard and his gangster henchman, wishing to provide Slim with money for fare back to the United States, and being totally broke motivate Harry to change his mind about accepting Frenchy's job to smuggle his anti-Vichy friends onto the island.

But before he does so, on the way back to the hotel, Slim decides she's thirsty. Since Renard has closed Frenchy's bar for the evening (after all, it's supposed to be a crime scene), Harry takes her to another bar. But before they order, Harry realizes he has no money. So Slim takes off on her own, knowing that in a tavern full of men, she'll have no trouble getting someone to buy her a drink. Grinning, Harry walks home, knowing that in this environment, a woman like Slim can take care of herself. Sure enough, some time later, Slim shows up at Harry's door with a bottle!

What follows is a great deal of male-female sparring, including one of Slim's famous lines, "You know Steve, you're not very hard to figure, only at times. Sometimes I know exactly what you're going to say. Most of the time. The other times . . . the other times, you're just a stinker." Finally, the sparring over, she slinks onto his lap and kisses him. This comes so quickly that Harry doesn't participate much at first. When they come up for air, Harry asks, "What's the decision?" "I don't know yet," she replies, and kisses him again. This time, Harry kisses back. She gets off his lap, takes a well-timed Bacall pause and crosses toward the door. Then she stops, looks back seductively, and gives us another famous Bacall line. Referring to the kiss, she quips, "It's even better when you help." As she exits, she says the number one come-on line most quoted from this movie, complete with artful pauses for effect:

> **Slim:** You know you don't have to act with me, Steve. You don't have to say anything, and you don't have to do anything. Not a thing. . . . Oh, maybe just whistle. *(She turns to exit, stops, and turns back again.)* You know how to whistle, don't you, Steve? You just put your lips together and . . . blow. (*To Have and Have Not*, 1944)

After Slim exits, all Harry can manage is a bit of a dry-mouthed whistle and an amazed expression.

Later, with payment in advance from Frenchy, Harry purchases Slim a plane ticket back to the United States. This doesn't sit too well with Slim, because she thinks Harry's giving her the brush-off, which in a way he is. This ticket-buying would discourage a non-Hawksian woman, who would probably just give up, snivel a bit, and get on that plane in the morning. Instead, when Harry returns from his smuggling mission, he finds that Slim has not gone and is still hanging around. She tells him she's been hired as Cricket's new band singer. Not that easy to get rid of, she nonetheless tells Harry that she's still ready to travel, "Any time you are." This doesn't mean Slim is angling for an engagement ring and a house with a mortgage and a white picket fence. Brackett explains:

> His [Hawks's] heroes and heroines are what he calls "grown up." They don't expect the moon with a string around it [a veiled comparison to the more emotional and typical Hollywood love story in *It's a Wonderful Life* (1946)]. They do not expect or desire to own each other. They are content with what they have, for as long as they have it, and this is possible because the Hawksian woman is not husband-hunting or looking for "security." She is secure in herself, and she is giving her love as a free person, with open hands. (Brackett 1977, 198)

As it turns out, Harry's service to Frenchy and the Free French cause is not tidily complete. In smuggling two Free French, Paul and Helene DeBursac, to Martinique, Harry's boat comes under Vichy patrol boat fire and Paul is wounded in the shoulder. Harry, who somewhere in his ambiguous backstory has picked up a medical kit, along with instruments and significant experience treating gunshot wounds (perhaps, like Rick in *Casablanca*, Harry fought against the Fascists in Spain) is pressed into service, turning the hotel basement into a hospital. Not at all squeamish, Slim assists. When the fearful Helene asks who Slim is, she replies, "Nobody. Just a volunteer." Harry asks Helene to assist in the "operation" as well, to stand by with chloroform to drug her husband should he wake up while Harry probes the man's shoulder wound for the bullet. But when she sees the blood, Helene faints. Slim again looks disgusted with Helene. After Harry extracts the bullet, he tells Slim, "I gotta get nursie outta here (Helene has fallen on the floor next to the open bottle of chloroform) or she never will come to." As Slim looks on disapprovingly, Harry lifts the shapely Helene in his arms and seems to enjoy carrying her into the next room. Wondering where to put her down, Harry stands for a moment, holding Helene as Slim enters, capping the bottle of chloroform. "What are you trying to do, guess her weight?" she quips. "All right if I give her a little whiff of this?" (the chloroform) she adds. They both snicker as Harry finally puts Helene down.

The next morning, deciding that Helene does not seem like a trained agent, Harry asks why she's on this mission with her husband. The relatively helpless Madonna explains that the Free French thought that if Paul left her behind, the Germans might find out about her and take her hostage, or worse, compromising Paul's activities. Helene admits she's too afraid to be of any use to Paul on this mission, and, worse yet, fear for her safety is causing the usually intrepid Paul to be much more cautious, even acting afraid for the both of them. Madonnas are little use to heroes when they're along on the mission. Rather, their role is to be the symbolic inspiration back home, or at least away from the fighting. A Madonna's presence in the middle of a men's mission always makes a Hawksian woman unhappy, especially when an attractive Madonna makes small talk with her man.

But is Harry her man yet? Not quite, Harry thinks. Later, after staying up half the night tending to Paul, Harry decides to go back to his room for some sleep. Slim follows and tries to be somewhat domestic by helping him take off his shoes. She even asks if she can draw him a bath. Harry puts on the brakes. He orders her to stop trying to help him, and strides to the middle of the room. He tells her to walk in a circle around him. She does so, curiously, and when she is nearly finished her circle, she comprehends the purpose of the exercise. "You find anything?" he asks. She knowingly replies, courtesy of a response probably written by Brackett, "There are no strings tied to you." (She pauses.) "Not yet." In his last attempt to resist, he tries to usher her out of his room so he can nap in peace, but she mildly resists, and they end up kissing passionately. Then, with his usual bad timing, Frenchy interrupts them and Harry has to go. As he retreats, Slim says to his back as he exits down the hotel stairs, "Look out for those strings, Steve. You're liable to trip and break your neck."

Harry decides that he will shove off from Martinique and motor to Haiti with Eddie and Slim. When he asks, Slim replies with a line borrowed from Jean Arthur's character's response to Cary Grant in an earlier Hawks film, *Only Angels Have Wings:* "I'm hard to get: All you have to do is ask."

It looks like the beginning of a beautiful friendship.

To wrap things up, with Slim's help, Harry overcomes the Vichy agents (including clobbering Coyo) and turns these villains over to the Free French for disposal. He rescues Eddie, whom the Vichy were holding hostage, and arranges to transport Paul and Helene off the island so they can fulfill their mission. Harry, Slim, and Eddie will then take off in the *Queen Conch* for Haiti and more adventures.

HAWKSIAN BACALL VS. MADONNA DENEUVE

To make a point about a Hawksian woman vs. a typical Madonna of more modern times, critic Germaine Greer (2006) suggests that the classic era of Hawksian women has perhaps passed:

The Hawksian woman was an idea that flourished at a time of crisis, in the depression and during the war [WWII], when the full energies of women were needed if they were to survive. After the war she was supplanted by the female eunuch, weighed down with huge hair and false eyelashes, unequal to any challenge—all things to all men and nothing to herself.

Greer argues that Bacall was not a regular beauty, and that in contrast, the modern European beauty prototype, Catherine Deneuve, was a perfect, fair-skinned Barbie doll. Greer also points out that she could not remember any memorable line spoken by any character Deneuve ever played, and described her as "meek, passive, expressionless. With a brow never furrowed and not a single laugh line."

But perhaps Greer was a little hasty in pronouncing the era of the Hawksian woman over and done with. As this book continues its examination of female roles, we will point out both in this chapter and later ones roles played by modern Hawksian women, and a number of GI Janes who will prove to be equal to Hawks's highest standards of female companionship.

THE WIND AND THE LION

At first glance, in John Milius's *The Wind and the Lion* (1975), Candice Bergen's Eden Pedecaris appears to be a typical American Madonna, not a Hawksian woman, quietly presiding over her genteel home in what must be an upscale neighborhood for internationals in Tangier, Morocco. However, peace suddenly vanishes as wild, horse-riding Berber tribesmen attack, sacking the mansion, killing the servants and a visiting Englishman, and kidnapping not only Eden but also her two children, William (Simon Harrison) and Jennifer (Polly Gottesman).

Immediately, we see that our first impression of Eden was mistaken. Scrappy from the outset, she puts up a fight before finally being overcome and whisked away on horseback by the leader of the Berbers, Mulai Ahmed er Raisuli (Sean Connery). She is furious over the attack, especially with the attendant destruction and slaughter. Eventually, though, we will see her adapt to her captivity, even insinuating herself into the Raisuli's strategic deliberations, as his charm wins over Eden and her children. After all, they've been kidnapped by a tall, tan, bearded, dashing Sean Connery.

Eden appears to just be just chattel, a pawn in the war between Raisuli and the sultan (Marc Zuber) and his uncle, the bashaw of Tangier (Vladek Sheybal). Of course, Eden can't help being chattel, because her kidnapping has caused an international incident, which turns out to be Raisuli's intent from the outset. He wants to embarrass the sultan and the bashaw, and show them to be puppets of the European powers, thereby inciting all the Berbers in the Rif (mountainous northern Morocco) to rise up in a jihad and overthrow the sultan.

But Eden is no sniveling, cowering bundle of feminine chattel sitting in terror, waiting for men to come and rescue her. At the first opportunity, this Hawksian woman and her children attempt their own escape, bribing a venal Berber to help them sneak away and to guide them back to Tangier. But the Berber himself is a brigand, and instead leads them into a camp full of savage bandits, bent on mischief of a high order. Until they are rescued by the pursuing Raisuli, Eden still manages to kill one of the bandits and holds off the rest until Raisuli rides up, swinging a huge sword, dispatching the rest. All he says afterwards is, "Mrs. Pedecaris, you're a great deal of trouble."

Meanwhile, back in the United States, President Teddy Roosevelt is running for reelection. Raisuli's ransom demands, issued to the United States (since Eden and the children are Americans) are for gold, the head of the bashaw, and the overthrow of the sultan in favor of Raisuli. But instead, Roosevelt uses the kidnapping to brandish his "big stick" in campaign speeches, roaring, "Pedecaris alive or Raisuli dead!" The president orders a squadron of U.S. Marines to back up his ambassador and intervene in this crisis in Morocco, demonstrating American will and power to the world while improving his own standings in the polls.

When the United States offers Raisuli less than his demands, he decides to hold out. Eden interrupts him and argues that he should take the offer, because she's sure that the Europeans will use the crisis as an excuse to land more troops in Morocco. Raisuli defiantly refuses her advice, saying, "I do not need the counsel of women," and adds that he wouldn't even accept the counsel of his own wives. Nonetheless, he decides to agree to the U.S. offer because it pleases him to do it. Perhaps it's also to get rid of Eden, whose petulant presence is turning into more of a scene from the *Ransom of Red Chief* than the manly coup d'état that he had in mind.

Meanwhile, Roosevelt stirs the pot. Using his Marines and some sailors who land in Tangier, the Americans overcome the bashaw's palace guard and take the bashaw hostage. Now there is to be a hostage exchange: the bashaw for Eden and her children.

To go to make the exchange, Raisuli rides with his cousin, the sherif of Wazan (Nadim Sawaltha) and his men. Raisuli is still baffled by the female he has captured. She is not like any Arab or European woman he's ever encountered, refusing to be treated like anything but an equal. "I do not understand this woman," he complains to the sherif. "My entire education has been horses and the Koran. What have I learned? What have I become?" In many ways, Raisuli is simply not prepared to deal with the likes of a Hawksian woman, intellectually competitive with him. The sherif, a Berber of simple, traditional understanding, retreats to what he knows, declaring, "You are the lord of the Rif!" "Yes," Raisuli replies. "And you would think I would understand this woman." Raisuli finds himself in almost the same situation as John Wayne's Sheriff John T. Chance in *Rio Bravo* when he finds that in a few short days, Feathers (Angie Dickinson) has completely upset his male-only world and made him question many of his long-held beliefs.

When Raisuli, riding into the village where the hostage return is to take place, returns Eden and her children, there is no bashaw. Rather, he is betrayed by an alliance between German and Moroccan troops and is taken prisoner by the Germans. The American Marines do not interfere, because they have gotten what they came for, Eden and her children. But Eden won't stand for this treachery, and at the point of a shotgun, confronts Capt. Jerome (Steve Kanaly), the Marine squadron commander:

Eden: President Roosevelt made an agreement with that man [Raisuli] being held over there, and President Roosevelt keeps his agreements!

Jerome: What do you have in mind?

Eden: I intend to free the Raisuli.

Jerome: Alone, I suppose . . .

Eden: . . . With my children.

Jerome: *(smiling)* I'd like to throw in with you.

To a man, the rest of Jerome's Marine squadron grunt their enthusiastic approval. The Marines, no fans of the Germans, are eager to fight alongside this bellicose female. Eden, the children and the Marines, assisted by the sherif and Raisuli's Berbers, assault the location where the Germans are holding Raisuli.

During the battle, Eden personally shotguns a few Germans. Rescued, and his sword restored to him, Raisuli mounts a horse to lead the Berbers through the remainder of the battle. Since his men are outnumbered and are facing German Howitzers and other modern weapons, he thinks perhaps he may die. So when he takes his leave of Eden and the children, he says, "I'll see you again, Mrs. Pedecaris, when we're both like golden clouds on the wind." But he survives, soundly defeating the Germans, and rides off into the desert at the head of his band.

Milius's script and his movie may at first glance read like a Harlequin novel, but unlike many heroines of these paperbacks, Eden is no wimpy, simpering young woman frightened to her ripped bodice by the sheik of Araby. Milius's twist in this plot is that this time, Raisuli is vamped by a

Hawksian woman who stands her ground and puts up her dukes, ready to brawl with the fellas.

A GUY NAMED JOE

Hawksian women are reasonably comfortable in the world of men or quickly adapt, but a few additionally possess the male skill sets used in war. Until recently, women have seldom been trained or experienced in the art of war. But in the case of the fantasy World War II film, *A Guy Named Joe* (1943), a woman, a highly-skilled flyer, already has many of the abilities of the men in the film who fly bombing missions against the enemy. Dorinda Durston (Irene Dunne) is a WASP, a member of the Women's Airforce Service Pilots, whose mission in the war is to ferry warplanes from U.S. factories to war zones. Women pilots were not allowed in combat during World War II, and could only deliver the planes to the men who would do the fighting. Dorinda is nonetheless a skilled pilot and quite easily could have qualified for combat duty if she were a man. Although she does not have a nickname among the flyers, her lover, Pete Sandidge (Spencer Tracy), calls her "Kid." Dorinda is great friends with the men in Pete's bomber wing, especially Pete's best friend and flying comrade, Al Yackey (Ward Bond) and Col. "Nails" Kirkpatrick, Pete and Al's commander.

Admired because of both her personality and her flying ability, Dorinda fits right in among the men. She can take a ribbing as well as give a little back. But with Pete, Dorinda becomes much more pliable, not at all Hawksian. Pete's not a marrying man, but he'd consider tying the knot if Dorinda would agree to give up flying. She's an adventurous flyer, and cuts corners— much like Pete—and that's why he worries about her. But before Pete has a chance to fulfill his end of their bargain, he flies a bombing mission in which he tries to sink a German aircraft carrier (which would truly have been a fantasy, since during World War II the Germans never launched a carrier). But during the attack, Pete's plane is hit and crashes, and Pete is killed.

Now a ghost, Pete is ushered through the clouds before "The General" (Lionel Barrymore), who enlists him in becoming a spiritual companion for another pilot just undergoing flight training, Ted (Van Johnson). Now that he's a guardian angel of sorts, Pete's job is to help Ted learn to fly and to coach him. Pete can't be heard or seen, but Ted seems to sense Pete's instructions and reacts, as if by newly acquired instinct. Eventually, Ted is successful in flight training, gets his wings and grows in skill and experience as a P-38 pilot in the Pacific. Ted flies for Pete's flying buddy, now squadron commander, Al Yackey, and their commander is still Nails Kirkpatrick. With Pete as his ghostly copilot, Ted soon becomes an ace.

Dorinda has taken Pete's death very badly. Although she's still a WASP pilot, now ferrying planes to bases in the Pacific including Ted's, she is not interested in a new relationship. Al and Nails treat Dorinda like a daughter and hope she comes out of this "tail spin" of depression. But it takes Ted to bring her out of it. As the screenplay would have it, Dorinda resists Ted at first, but finally falls in love again. The ghostly Pete is upset that Dorinda has fallen in love with Ted, since Pete still thinks of her as "my girl." But finally Pete realizes that his time is over and that Dorinda deserves all the happiness she can have with Ted.

Dorinda overhears plans for Ted to fly a dangerous mission to bomb a Japanese munitions dump. Out of her love for Ted, and knowing that despite Ted's recent achievements in the air, she is still the better pilot, Dorinda steals Ted's plane and sacrificially flies the mission herself. This may be because of her love and concern that Ted might not come back, and she would have to mourn yet another lover. Of course, this is 1943, so Dorinda doesn't get to fly the mission alone. Instead, the ghostly Pete sits in the back seat of the P-38, acting as Dorinda's copilot, coaching her like a modern day football offensive coordinator radios plays into the quarterback's helmet. With Pete's help, Dorinda fires her machine guns and drops her bombs successfully on a huge enemy ammunition dump, and thanks to her superb flying ability, escapes safely and flies back to the air base and into Ted's arms. Pete's job with Ted is finished, and he'll be reassigned as a guardian angel to a new pilot.

Hardly a feminist icon, Dorinda can dish it out with the guys, but when she falls in love, her feminine side makes her vulnerable to men like Pete and Ted. Perhaps Dorinda could use some assertiveness training from Eden Pedecaris. But not all possess the complete Hawksian woman package, and not all such women have checkered pasts. A case in point is Cora Munro.

THE LAST OF THE MOHICANS

Taking into account what era Cora (Madeleine Stowe) was born into (1757), she could teach her own course in assertiveness training for chattel English-women of the era. Admittedly, as with the remainder of the women in this chapter, in Michael Mann's magnificent retelling of James Fenimore Cooper's *Last of the Mohicans* (1992), Cora is missing some of the usual lower-class, sadder but wiser Hawksian credentials. Instead, she comes from a privileged English/Scottish upper-class family. Her sister, Alice (Jodhi May), is a prototype effete English upper-class woman (read helpless Madonna), but Cora's temperament is quite different. Instead, as soon as the two arrive in colonial New York, something about the frontier greatly moves Cora's spirit, as if her soul has found its home. Later, it is clear that Cora has more in common with Alexandra Cameron (Tracey Ellis), a colonist farmer's wife, than with the stuffy Englishwomen who have raised her. We see this constantly in Madeline Stowe's acting, as director Mann cuts to Cora's reaction to events. There, instead of the wide-eyed panic and lack of understanding we see in Alice's eyes, in Cora's we see wonderment and appreciation.

This adventure begins as Cora and Alice are newly arrived from England and staying with friends in Albany, New York, during the third year of the French and Indian War. They expect to soon join their father, English Lt. Col. Edmund Munro (Maurice Roëves), commanding officer of Fort William Henry, located on the shore of Lake George. Maj. Duncan Howard (Steven Waddington), newly arrived from England, along with a company of British soldiers, is transporting the women through a forest to the fort. But their Native American guide, a scout called Magua who in actuality is working for their enemy, the French, leads the company into an ambush staged by a war party of the French's Native American allies, the Hurons. As the assault begins, the British soldiers, used to fighting on open ground, cannot adapt to an enemy hiding in the bushes and picking them off. Instead of taking cover, the British obligingly present themselves as easy targets by wearing red jackets and standing up in a row. The Hurons would have killed everyone, if not for the last-minute rescue of Cora, Alice, and Duncan by three men.

Mohican Indians Chingachgook (Russell Means); his son Uncas (Eric Schweig); and Chingachgook's adopted white son, Hawkeye (Daniel Day-Lewis), expert trackers, had been hunting nearby when they picked up the Hurons' trail. Concerned for their nearby settler friends in the proximity of a war party, the three follow the Hurons and happen upon the ambush at just the right moment. The three, aided by Duncan, the only surviving English soldier, skillfully attack and kill all the attacking Hurons except Magua, who escapes into the forest.

During the attack, as one would expect from a helpless Madonna, Alice shrinks to the ground and practically rolls herself up in a ball in fear. Having no weapon (for the only time in this film), Cora bravely puts her arms around her younger sister, as if she is a child, to shield her. A few times during the skirmish, Hurons get close to the women, but either one of the three or Duncan kills them. After the skirmish, Cora picks up a pistol and hides it in her skirt pocket, silently vowing to never be defenseless again. Later, on a few occasions, Cora ends up using her pistol to defend herself.

Hawkeye and the two Mohicans agree to guide the women and Duncan to the fort. They set out on foot, because horses would make too much noise. They assume correctly that when the dead Hurons are discovered, other hostiles will be after them. During the journey to the fort, they come upon the Cameron's farm. James Cameron (Justin Rice) has left his family at home and volunteered to fight in the colonial militia. Uncas and Chingachgook can tell that another Huron war party, accompanied by two Frenchmen, has been there ahead of them. Alexandra, Cameron's wife, and their children have been killed. Hawkeye and the two Mohicans instruct Duncan and the women to leave the bodies as they've fallen, and say that they must quickly get away from the farm. Cora insists that Hawkeye stop to bury the dead, but instead, he is adamant that they must leave immediately. Later that night, Hawkeye explains to Cora that if they would have buried the Camerons, other hostiles coming upon the scene would have known that they had been there, and would track them easier. Hawkeye chooses a place to spend the night very close to a Native American burial ground, which spooks one pursuing Huron war party into staying away.

Safe for the night, Cora and Hawkeye look up at the stars. Hawkeye relates an old Mohican legend:

Hawkeye: My father's people say that at the birth of the sun and of his brother the moon, their mother died. So the sun gave to the earth her body, from which was to spring all life. And he drew forth from her breast the stars, and the stars he threw into the night sky to remind him of her soul. So there's the Cameron's monument. My [deceased] folks' too, I guess.

Cora: You are right. We do not understand what is happening here. And it's not as I imagined it would be, thinking of it in Boston and in London. . . .

Hawkeye: Sorry to disappoint you.

Cora: No, on the contrary. It is more deeply stirring to my blood than any imagining could possibly have been. (*Last of the Mohicans*, 1992)

This is when Hawkeye begins to look at Cora differently. He is already attracted to her, and her words of wonder tell him that she is rapidly becoming the kind of woman who is suited for frontier life, a woman with the same vision of the world as himself. Before Chingachgook, Uncas, and Hawkeye encountered the Huron ambush, the three were about to head out to Kentucky, perhaps to stake out some land like the Camerons did, and perhaps (for Hawkeye and Uncas) to find the right kind of rugged, nature-loving frontier women (read Hawksian) to marry and to bear them children.

The next night, the men use a canoe for the women to infiltrate the French lines surrounding Fort William Henry and reunite Cora and Alice with their father. Munro had already sent a message to tell his daughters not to attempt to come to the fort, since they're under siege by the French. But none of Munro's messengers made it to Albany.

Hawkeye tells Munro that Huron war parties are likely attacking up and down the frontier, and tells him what they found at the Cameron farm.

Knowing that if this is true, his colonial militiamen will want to leave the fort to go protect their homes, Munro acts skeptical. Hawkeye asks Duncan to corroborate his story, but Duncan, beholden to Munro and not to the colonists, knows that Munro doesn't want to hear the truth. He lies about the Cameron massacre, chalking it up to thieves. Cora and Hawkeye are astounded by Duncan's duplicity.

Both back in England and as recently as a few days ago, Duncan has proposed to Cora, but she has continually put off giving him a final answer. Every time they have discussed it, Duncan has made it clear to Cora that the best standing she'd ever have in this relationship is as his chattel, which was customary in England at this time. Now, hearing Duncan lie about the massacre causes Cora to become angry, and she later tells Duncan her final answer is a firm "no." Earlier he had condescendingly urged her to accept her family's judgment regarding their union, as if her own judgment were just that of a mere woman's and could not be as sound as a man's. But Cora's decision is final, and as a recently minted Hawksian woman, she makes it clear that she won't be pushed around. Nonetheless, considering the era, she still is polite about it: "You've complimented me with your persistence and patience, but the decision I've come to is this. I would rather make the gravest of mistakes than surrender my own judgment." A few centuries later, other Hawksian women might very well have hauled off and socked him in the nose for his lack of character.

Besides, Cora now understands that the tall, dashing Duncan is really an empty red suit who pales by comparison to a man like Hawkeye, with whom she is rapidly falling in love. She knows that when the colonial militiamen escaped the fort, Hawkeye remained because of her. In one wonderfully underplayed scene, Cora is laboring as a volunteer nurse in the fort's surgery. Hawkeye finds Cora there and just stares at her. At first, her high-class English upbringing causes her to lower her eyes and coyly look away. But Hawkeye continues to stare at her, and we can see on her face that she's decided that she likes it. Soon, she's looking the frontiersman straight in the eyes and smiling. "What are you looking at, sir?" she asks. Hawkeye replies, also smiling broadly, "I'm looking at you, Miss." The hook is set.

Because Hawkeye urged the militiamen to escape the fort and even helped them do it, Munro has him arrested and charged with sedition. Cora becomes furious with both her father and Duncan and faces them down. She reminds the two that she, Alice, and Duncan would have been dead on the trail if it were not for Hawkeye and the Mohicans. Munro barks, "The man encouraged the colonials to desert in this very room and in my presence!"

Duncan argues that these colonials can't just do what they want in the face of English law:

Duncan: And who empowered these colonials to pass judgment on England's policies, and to come and go without so much as a "by your leave"?

Cora: *(angrier)* They do not live their lives "by your leave." They hack it out of the wilderness with their own two hands, bearing their children along the way! (*Last of the Mohicans*, 1992)

Duncan continues to argue, jealously stating that the only reason Cora is speaking in Hawkeye's defense is because she's infatuated with him. Cora politely but firmly cuts him off at the knees, saying, "Duncan, you are a man with a few admirable qualities, but taken as a whole, I was wrong to have thought so highly of you."

When her father remains intransigent about Hawkeye, arguing that Hawkeye is just receiving English justice, it's the colonel's turn to receive Cora's wrath:

Cora: Justice? If that's justice, than the sooner French guns blow the English out of America, the better it will be for the people here!

Munro: You do not know what you're saying, girl!

Cora: Yes I do, I know exactly what I'm saying, and if it is sedition, than I am guilty of sedition too! (*Last of the Mohicans*, 1992)

Cora stomps out of the room, and for once, the colonel wisely gives no reply.

But circumstances take over. The French siege has become so successful that many British will die unless they surrender. Munro has found out that the cowardly General Webb has betrayed him and will not send relief to the fort, even though Webb's entire army is only eighteen miles away. So Munro agrees to surrender the fort to Gen. Montcalm in return for not ending up prisoners of war. Instead, Munro agrees to take his men to New York, sail back to England, and fight the French no more.

After the British vacate the fort and turn it over to Montcalm, however, Magua and his Hurons, to settle Magua's old blood feud with Munro, stage a surprise attack on the British column as they march through the forest, killing Munro and massacring many British. Standing over Munro before he kills him, Magua has sworn that he will kill the colonel's children. This is because many years ago, Munro led an attack on Magua's village, resulting in the deaths of his children. After a chase, Magua also ends up capturing Duncan, Cora, and Alice. Magua and his followers march their prisoners to Huron country, to brag to the sachem, the Huron chief, about their "knives stained red" and to offer up Cora and Alice to be burned alive.

But before the captives are killed, Hawkeye boldly walks right into the Huron camp, offering his life for the captives. The Huron chief, disgusted with Magua and his "Yangee ways," acts like Solomon and splits the two sisters, banishing Magua but giving him Alice, and ordering Cora to die in the fire. Out of love, Hawkeye tries to persuade the sachem to take him in Cora's place and let Duncan and Cora go. Because Hawkeye doesn't speak French, Duncan must translate, and changes Hawkeye's words, substituting himself as the offering. The sachem seems to like the idea of burning a white man—especially a British officer—instead of a white woman, and agrees, sending Cora and Hawkeye, whom he admires, away.

As the two escape, they look back and see Duncan suffering in the fire, and Hawkeye fires a long distance musket shot to put Duncan out of his misery. Then the two, along with Uncas and Chingachgook, pursue Magua and his men to try to rescue Alice.

But Uncas runs far ahead of the others and heads off Magua's men. On a mountain ledge, he kills two of Magua's men, but is defeated by Magua, who kills Uncas by cutting his throat and throwing him over the cliff. Wrongly assuming she will never be rescued, Alice takes her own life by throwing herself over the cliff. Chingachgook arrives in time to see his son killed and roars his grief. With Hawkeye close behind, firing away, the two kill a number of Magua's men. Chingachgook kills Magua, too.

But it's too late. Chingachgook has lost his son, and he is now, truly, the last of the Mohicans. The story ends here, but the audience is sure that Hawkeye and Cora will be married and probably settle down together on a frontier farm in Kentucky. The adventure in America that has inspired Cora will continue.

HEARTBREAK RIDGE

The remaining women in this chapter have many Hawksian characteristics in common with Slim, Feathers, and Susan. The next two are the principal female roles in Clint Eastwood's *Heartbreak Ridge*, the 1986 story of a highly decorated Marine (Eastwood) almost at the end of his career, trying to finish well. Beginning a new assignment at a post where he served earlier in his career, Gunnery Sgt. Tom Highway is the sergeant of a reconnaissance platoon. After a first day meeting with his platoon, Highway realizes he has a huge and challenging job ahead of him trying to turn around an outfit with no motivation, no esprit de corps, little experience, and an attitude problem. Even the platoon leader, Lt. Ring (Boyd Gaines), is a rookie, right out of Marine Corps ROTC. Highway must find a way to retrain and motivate his platoon so he can "save their lives in combat."

Looking for a place to live off base, Highway heads for a little bar that caters to Marines called the Globe and Anchor, owned by his old and dear friend, Little Mary Jackson (Eileen Heckart), the first of two Hawksian women in this film. Mary is the widow of one of Highway's comrades-in-arms who was killed in Vietnam, fighting alongside Highway and his best friend Sergeant Major Choozoo (nicknamed "Chooz"; Arlen Dean Snyder). Later dialogue suggests that Mary, in her seventies, is herself a veteran of three wars, so she could have met her Marine husband while serving in the Woman's Marine Corps. The bar Mary owns is full of Marine Corps memorabilia. She also owns an apartment she occasionally rents out that is attached to the back of the bar, and after Highway was divorced, he rented it from Mary. Later in the film, we understand that Mary, nearly a generation older, is more of a mother figure to Highway. Every morning, Mary makes sure that Highway's clothes are laid out and his coffee is standing by. Naturally, looking for an off-base apartment, Highway enters the Globe and Anchor, looking for Mary. When he enters and spots Mary, Highway gives her his traditional humorous greeting: "Hey, baby: You fool around on the first date?" Complete with a big, toothy grin, Mary rushes around the bar and wraps Highway in a big hug. Next, she's back behind the bar, pouring him a beer.

Highway continues flirting, but Mary, continuing her mother role, and playing Cupid because she knows his ex-wife, Aggie (Marsha Mason), is living nearby, gives him some tough love advice:

Highway: You look great. They don't make 'em like you anymore, sweetheart.

Mary: Oh, sure they do . . . but if you want a lot from a woman, you have to give a lot.

Highway: Not this kid. It seems marriage and the Marine Corps weren't too compatible.

Mary: Panther piss. The best years of my life were with a Marine. If I was a little younger, I'd make you eat your words and curl your toes.

[Mary cares for Aggie, and it's obvious that she hopes the two will reconcile now that Highway is stationed in town.]

Mary: Aggie always kept a smile on your face.

Highway: That was pain.

Mary: Aggie's in town. She's "cocktailing" over at the Palace. (*Heartbreak Ridge*, 1986)

Highway assures Mary that he's definitely not going to go over to the Palace and look for Aggie. But Mary understands Highway, so she knows different-ly. And sure enough, as the next scene begins, Highway is in civilian clothes, entering the Palace, looking for Aggie.

Aggie had been Highway's girl since high school. Apparently, after grad-uation, Highway first joined the U.S. Army, as did Choozoo and Mary's late husband. But after the Korean War, they all transferred to the Marines. Either before or after Korea, Highway and Aggie were married. The backstory we glean from their conversations indicates that sometime after Highway's tour of duty in Vietnam, the two were divorced. Also, it seems apparent that Aggie, comfortable around Marines, likes hanging around a Marine post town, because she's still there. Her amorous adventures since she divorced Highway are open to speculation.

The Palace, where she works, is not what the name implies: This is a typical roadhouse, serving whiskey and beer and mostly featuring live enter-tainment of the redneck variety. But this environment doesn't seem to upset Aggie, and she seems to handle herself well around the two kinds of patrons at the Palace: rednecks and Marines. But one Marine in particular always arouses feelings in Aggie, both affectionate and homicidal. When Highway walks into the Palace after being absent from Aggie's life for some years, her first reaction is not one of affection. He orders a beer and is glad to see that the brand of long neck she serves him is his favorite. Trying to start a pleasant conversation, he thanks her for remembering his brand. "Bad whis-key, bad sex and bad men I never forget," she remarks. He smiles and replies, "You didn't talk dirty like that when we were married." She barks back, becoming increasingly prickly: "Always. Only you were never there to hear it." He tries to shake off this criticism, obviously the biggest complaint about him. He flirts some more, but Aggie is having none of it: "It's late, I'm tired and my feet hurt. Save the banter for the bimbos. What the hell are you doing here?" Highway explains that he's again stationed at the Marine base. Seeing that Aggie has been talking to Highway for a while and that she appears agitated, the tall, rugged, but obnoxious owner of the Palace, Roy (Bo Sven-son), approaches. Trying to lighten the introduction of Highway to her boy-friend, Aggie says to Roy, "I'd like you to meet one of my favorite exes." Unfortunately, Roy is not amused and is far from polite: "I heard all about you and your bullshit heroics." This is not the thing one says to a Marine like Highway, whose uniform sports a chestful of medals, topped by the highest service medal America bestows, the Medal of Honor. Thanks to Aggie, expe-rienced in keeping peace among roadhouse patrons, the two don't come to blows. But it's obvious that, as odd as it may seem in a Marine town, Roy is extremely anti-military. Roy seems an odd choice of beau for Aggie, who, as the movie continues, shows signs of deep affection for both Highway and the Marine Corps. Perhaps, in Highway's absence, and as an adaptable Hawk-

sian woman, Aggie has taken up with Roy for strictly pragmatic reasons: Roy
is well off, he's interested in her, and even if he has an abrasive personality,
he represents a secure future.

Highway has decided that at the end of his career, he wants things to be
the way they were at the start. To him that means two objectives, doing
something meaningful as a Marine and regaining the love of his life. Not
knowing that he will soon be involved in one more war (albeit a small, short
one), Highway decides that meaningfulness means turning his immature,
lazy platoon of unmotivated postadolescents into skilled, professional Marines. To find a way to reach out to Aggie, Highway starts reading women's
magazines. The first time Aggie sees Highway reading a pile of these magazines in the cab of his truck in the Palace's parking lot, she isn't buying any
of it: "You don't even know how to read," she says. He wants her to jump in
his truck and talk about such unusual things (to him) as feelings and communication, but Aggie still has her guard up, saying, "I'm not one of your troops
who can be bullied," and walks quickly away. This typical Hawksian woman
has now officially confused our hero as completely as Feathers confounded
Sheriff Chance.

What could be termed a flaw in the film's screenwriting is that Aggie's
character arc doesn't slowly rise from prickly to affectionate, it turns off and
on like a traffic light, except without the caution light in between. Aggie
spends half of the picture being approached by Highway in reconciliation
mode, while her anger for all those years of neglect keeps her from considering that perhaps you can teach an old dog new tricks. Suddenly, after their
biggest fight in the movie, she changes and becomes much more reasonable.
What both your authors wish had been inserted somewhere between Aggie
going from prickly to affectionate would be for Aggie to drop by Mary's bar
for a beer and a chat, during which Mary, one Hawksian woman to another,
urges her to give Highway one more chance.

Highway's company commander, Maj. Powers, is in his first combat
command, having asked and received a transfer to the recon battalion from
rear echelon duties as a supply officer. Unfortunately, rather than learn from
the sixty years of combined experience that Highway and Sgt. Maj. Choozoo
could teach him, Powers, an egotist with a personality worse than Roy's,
thinks he knows it all and goes his own way. Choozoo, also close to retirement, goes along quietly and patiently with his commander, but Highway is
more abrasive and bucks Powers at every turn. Many of Highway's conflicts
in the film are due to Maj. Powers.

The next time Choozoo enters Mary's bar, he spots Highway sitting and
drinking, so he quips, "You'll let anybody in here, won't ya?" Mary quips
back, "Have one [beer] on the house to ease your pain." The two Marines sit,
drink, and complain to each other about Powers, who has no use for older,
more experienced NCOs, and has just insulted Choozoo, reminding him that

he and Highway have yet to fight in a winning war. Having lost in Vietnam and "tied" in Korea, they as yet have nothing but a zero in the "win" column. Highway remarks that before he retires, he'd like one more chance to even the score at 1-1-1. Mary interrupts, telling the men that the base has called and that their unit is on alert. This often means that as Marines, their country needs them in some trouble spot in the world, and they will be quickly transported into a combat zone. The two quietly get up and leave the bar with no word of good-bye to Mary. Rather than become offended, Mary, who knows the men may soon be in combat, simply watches them exit and quietly says, "God bless."

But this alert turns out to be a combat readiness drill. Such drills sometimes are called when a real deployment is anticipated, as will occur shortly in this story. In the meantime, having read another pile of women's magazines, Highway decides to try to once again reach out to Aggie. He discovers that this is her day off, and, a six-pack of beer in hand, visits Aggie at her home. But Aggie is still prickly and doesn't trust Highway:

> **Aggie:** You come stompin' back into my life after all this time with no warning whatsoever, interfere with me in my place of work, damn near start a brawl, almost lost me the only crummy job I could find. And then you show up here, expecting me to just . . . smooth as silk, invite you in for a sit-down and a smile. . . . It's always the same, Highway: All balls, no brains. (*Heartbreak Ridge*, 1986)

But Highway's soothing, nonconfrontational style begins to at least temporarily soften Aggie's defenses. Sounding concerned, he asks about her aforementioned sore feet. "Well, I hop booths five nights a week, you know. There ain't no senior prom looming on my horizon." Highway continues his soothing approach, discussing his wish to conclude his Marine Corps career "as right as when I started." Continuing with pleasant conversation, Highway sits behind Aggie and begins to massage her shoulders and smell her hair. He asks her what she previously wanted from their marriage, and she, impressed that he's trying to communicate about something other than the Marines, blissfully recalls that they used to talk about starting an avocado ranch and buying a house with a barbecue in the back. Aggie qualifies this good memory by saying, "Then you volunteered for every goddamn war that came down the pike." She starts to moan softly with delight as his shoulder rubbing is having its effect. But then, suddenly, a look of realization comes over her, and she rises quickly to get away from him. Aggie's entire attitude snaps back to defiant and prickly. Volume rising, Aggie angrily says, "You changed tactics on me, didn't you? You gave up the old frontal assault and tried to outflank me. Well, I'm on to you and I want you out of here right now!" Highway counters from his limited readings from the women's magazines and says, "You're acting very undignified for a mature woman." *Wrong thing to say.* "Why you old Marine war horse! I'll show you dignified! You get out of here, you old bastard!" Shouting more obscenities, Aggie throws the confused Highway and his six-pack out the front door.

Here is where the screenplay becomes confused. Although we see no signs of remorse for her outburst against him, from now on in this film, Aggie seems to be a changed woman with regard to her ex-husband. After Aggie throws him out, Highway gets drunk and ends up in jail. Aggie, Choozoo, and one of the Marines in his squad, Cpl. Jones (Mario Van Peebles) bail Highway out of jail and take him over to Mary's to sober him up with coffee.

While they're at the Globe and Anchor, Choozoo tells Jones more of Highway's backstory: Choozoo says that there's no one better to be with in a hot landing zone than Highway. Mary, listening nearby, inserts two words into the conversation. "Heartbreak Ridge," Mary says with finality. Jones doesn't know about the story of the Korean War Battle of Heartbreak Ridge, partially because he wasn't born yet, and partially because it wasn't among traditional Marine Corps legends. It was an all-Army show. Highway, Choozoo, and Mary's late husband were in the Army, not the Marines, when they fought there. Choozoo explains that only these three men out of their entire company survived the battle. Highway received the Medal of Honor for heroism during this engagement, and afterward, all three transferred to the Marines. This transfer is probably a screenwriting ploy permitting the name Heartbreak Ridge, a bloody episode during the Korean War in which many entire companies were wiped out, to be adopted for a movie about Marines, who did not participate in that battle.

Meanwhile, since Highway is reasonably sober now, Aggie airs her principal grievance with Highway, the horrifying year (1968) she spent worrying about him while he was fighting in Vietnam. Finally understanding how traumatizing this was for Aggie, Highway guesses "There are worse things than getting shot at." Aggie's anger rages one last time, and she slaps his face twice. But then she throws her arms around Highway and cries some more. "That's all right, baby," he says, and they hold tight to each other.

In the next scene, wearing their black "dress blue" uniforms, Highway and Choozoo are attending an invitation dress ball for officers and senior enlisted men. Their battalion commander, Col. Meyers (Richard Venture), is impressed with the light blue ribbon on Highway's chest, signifying his Medal of Honor. But Highway is even more impressed with finding Aggie at the ball. She explains that she's "still on the mailing list." Their romance seems to grow, as they dance and reminisce about their senior prom. Their reverie includes the story that after the prom that they had their first sexual encounter. Smiling as they recall, Highway says, "You were a wild creature, I must say." She asks if he is still reading the women's magazines, and he responds, "Affirmative." "And what do they say about ex-wives," she asks. He responds, "Not too much: Just that sex is great, because you don't have to establish a relationship or be meaningful." They both laugh and continue a dialogue, until he wants to talk about that avocado farm, code for perhaps a future together after his retirement. But she tells him that Roy has proposed marriage. As movies do, the two never get a chance to finish this important conversation. Col. Meyers gets to a microphone and announces that the battalion is immediately going on alert. The all-important resolution of their relationship must wait. As it turns out, this Marine unit will be a part of the U.S. incursion into Grenada to rescue American citizens there.

Good things happen for Highway during this combat mission. Highway, his young lieutenant, and his men distinguish themselves in the eyes of Col. Meyers, and Meyers fires Maj. Powers, demoting him back to being a supply officer. In the final scene, the Marines are returning to their base, cheered on by grandstands full of civilians and families. Highway does not expect to find anyone waiting for him, but Aggie sits in the stands wearing a fetching white sundress. She's there for him, having chosen Highway over Roy. The two leave the festivities and walk away, side by side. At first, they don't touch, since Highway is carrying his M-16 in the hand closer to Aggie. But then, symbolically, he changes the rifle to his other hand and reaches his hand out to her. Then the two walk off together, holding hands.

THE WOMEN OF *TOP GUN*

It's odd to talk at all here about the women of Tony Scott's *Top Gun* (1986), because this film centers most of its attention on macho men and overflows with as much testosterone as *Navy SEALs*. But there are two important women playing two important roles that contain many character elements of the Hawksian woman. For most of the film, the first female, Top Gun instructor Dr. Charlotte Blackburn (Kelly McGillis), call sign (read Hawksian nickname) "Charlie," manages to hold her own nicely against a macho gaggle of young, oversexed Navy fighter pilots. But at the end of the film, Charlie gives up her job and a promotion to become the professional equivalent of a camp follower.

We first meet Charlie in the bar of a restaurant near Miramar Naval Air Station near San Diego, the 1980s home of the Navy's Fighter Weapons School (It has since changed its name to Naval Strike and Air Warfare Center and moved to NAS Fallon in Western Nevada, where some of the flight sequences for *Top Gun* were filmed). Two new students at the Fighter Weapons School, referred to as "Top Gun" by naval aviators, are about to play one of their usual betting games: a hunt for a quick score with some available chattel. Pilot Pete Mitchell (Tom Cruise), call sign "Maverick," is present, along with his constant companion and radar intercept officer (RIO) who sits in the cockpit right behind his pilot and assists with visual and radar identification of targets, among other more classified duties), Nick Bradshaw (Anthony Edwards), call sign "Goose." Maverick looks around, enjoying all the pretty young women, and exclaims, using aviator lingo,

Maverick: This is what I call a target-rich environment.

Goose: You live your life between your legs, Mav.

Maverick: Goose, even you could get laid in a place like this.

Goose: Hell, I'd be happy to just find a girl that would talk dirty to me. (*Top Gun*, 1986)

The two discuss the usual rules of this particular bet: To win, Maverick must have carnal knowledge of a woman this night within the confines of the restaurant. Ready to hunt, Maverick begins to search the crowded bar for his target of the evening. Once he spots the gorgeous Charlie, he decides to use a ruse he has used before to make a grand entrance:

Maverick: "She's lost that loving feeling."

Goose: *(kidding)* She's los . . . No, she hasn't.

Maverick: Yes, she has.

Goose: She not lost that lov . . .

Maverick: *(interrupting)* Goose, she's lost it, man.

Goose: Come on! *(to himself)* Aw, sh . . . I hate it when she does that. (*Top Gun*, 1986)

Maverick grabs a handy microphone, approaches Charlie, who's sitting at the bar, and begins singing this classic Righteous Brothers tune. Goose sings the Bobby Hatfield harmony to Maverick's Bill Medley lead, but both are terribly out of tune. As they sing, dozens of other Naval aviators gather around to watch and to sing both verbal and musical accompaniment to Maverick's lead. This goes on for a verse or so, until everyone, including Charlie, is laughing. She says to Maverick, taking the upper hand,

Charlie: Sit down! I love that song! How long have you two been doing this act?

Maverick: Oh, since uh . . .

Charlie: *(interrupting)* Puberty?

Maverick: *(grinning)* Right, puberty. (*Top Gun*, 1986)

She asks him how often he's done it, and he admits only twice, including this time. Maverick admits that the first time, he "crashed and burned," but this time, the second time he's used this ruse, "it's looking good so far." Pushing his position, Maverick introduces himself not by his real name, but as "Maverick." Charlie makes fun of his name, asking why his parents were so cruel. Maverick thinks for a moment he has encountered a babe in the woods and explains that it's his call sign. Charlie goes along, pretending to be impressed, asking if he's a pilot. Maverick corrects her terminology, responding proudly that he's a naval aviator. But then, before Maverick can make a real move, Charlie tells him that she's waiting for her date, who arrives and spoils the moment. But to cap off the encounter, Charlie leaves him with one last dig:

Charlie: Listen, can I ask you a personal question?

Maverick: That depends.

Charlie: Are you a good pilot?

Maverick: I can hold my own.

Charlie: Great, then I won't have to worry about you making your living as a singer.

Maverick: I'm going to need a beer to put these flames out. Yo! *(to himself)* Great, Mav, real slick. (*Top Gun*, 1986)

Later, Charlie leaves her date at the table and heads for the ladies room and Maverick follows her in. She understands that his reason in following her to the lavatory is to try to have some expeditious sex with her. Charlie, who because of her job has been sparring with come-ons from fighter pilots for some time, knows all their games, including the one in which they bet whether or not they can have sex with women in places like the ladies room. Also, in Hawksian fashion, Charlie enjoys these men, and unlike other women, is not insulted by their silly games. Typically direct and with little nonsense, Charlie gets right to the point:

Charlie: What do you wanna do? Just drop down on the tile *[floor]* and go for it?

Maverick: No, actually I had this counter in mind.

Charlie: *(sarcastically)* Great. That would be very, very comfortable, yeah.

Maverick: It could be. (*Top Gun*, 1986)

Sensing that a quick round of sex with Charlie is unlikely, Maverick wisely changes his tack, saying that he actually followed her to the ladies room so he could "save you from making a big mistake with that older guy [her date]." Again, beating Maverick to the punch, Charlie quips back, "Really? So I can go on to a bigger one with a young guy like yourself?"

Once again, Maverick is "in flames." On the way back to her table, Charlie passes Goose and decides to have some fun with him. She coos at Goose, saying, "Your friend was magnificent." Goose, flabbergasted, can only blubber, "Mah . . . " in amazement.

Charlie, who will be Maverick's love interest in the film, turns out to be one of the Top Gun instructors. She has a PhD in astrophysics and a top-secret security clearance. Charlie is also an expert in ACM (aerial combat maneuvering), the main subject taught at the school. In the first draft of Jim Cash and Jack Epps Jr.'s script for this film, Charlie was a Navy enlisted technician whom Maverick is attracted to and subsequently dates. But the Navy, which provided considerable amounts of men, locations, and equipment for this film, rejected this role, correctly noting that officers are forbidden to fraternize with enlisted personnel. That's when the writers discovered that the real Top Gun employs a number of civilian consultant-instructors. This creates additional conflict between Charlie and Maverick, even more attractive to the writers than their original characterization. As such, she clashes with Maverick the first day of training when he corrects her about one of the capabilities of the new Russian MiG-28. Then she learns that Maverick, who recently was the only American pilot to tangle with the fast, sharp-maneuvering MiG-28, knows about certain characteristics of the aircraft. Charlie is attracted to Maverick, impressed by his flying ability and also interested in picking his brain for everything he knows about the MiG-28. She's angling for a promotion in her government job, and thinks that exclusive information about the MiG-28 (portrayed in the movie by America's Northrup F-5 Freedom Fighter jets) will help her get a new, better job in Washington. Maverick tries to play her need to his advantage and asks her out, but Charlie's wise rule until now has been to not date students. He argues that yes, it could be complicated, but if the Navy trusts him with a $30 million fighter jet, she should trust him, too. Finally, both because of her attraction to Maverick and to press him for more data about the MiG, she invites him to her house for dinner. To avoid professional criticism, she asks that their date be kept "classified." This starts their romance. Later, after disagreeing publicly about Maverick's risky air combat tactic during one of his training sorties, Charlie explains her problem: "I see some real genius in your flying, Maverick, but I can't say that in there [the small auditorium where they review the video of each air encounter]. I'm afraid that everyone would see right through me. I just don't want anyone to know that I've fallen for you." They kiss, and next is their now-famous lovemaking scene, to the tune of "Take My Breath Away." Charlie has lowered her guard, a move that Hawks, Wellman, and Ford would probably judge as unprofessional conduct for a Top Gun instructor. But no Hawksian woman is perfect.

Scott does not devote a lot of screen time to the second woman's role of note in *Top Gun*, Goose's wife, Carole. Basically, she's in only three scenes. But from the little bit we see of her, we come to understand that if Carole could fly, she might well put her feet up on the table, guzzle another beer, and act much like the other fighter pilots. Carole is now mother to a small boy, and so we can only imagine what kind of crazy gal she was when she was single. From Goose's point of view, Carole's call sign is "Honey," and not even Charlie fits into this circle of masculinity as easily and effortlessly as Carole.

Like many of Hawks's female characters, Carole begins her role in the movie as someone not really welcome among the fraternity of men, but who decides she must be there. In this case, Carole and her young son arrive at Miramar at an awkward time, while her husband is totally preoccupied with the rigors of Top Gun training. Carole's first scene opens with Goose and Maverick waiting at a nearby municipal airport for Carole's plane to arrive. Goose is trying to explain to Maverick why Carole is coming in the first place: "I told her how tough it is here, you know, my ass dragging like an old, tired dog. I told her that *you* didn't even have a woman here. You know what she said? 'Oh, he probably doesn't have one, he has eight!'" In other words, Carole insists on coming, bringing their young son, despite the fact that Goose really doesn't want a woman interfering with his and Maverick's attempts at winning the Top Gun trophy, a closely contested race between themselves and another top team of pilot and RIO, "Iceman" (Val Kilmer) and "Slider" (Rick Rossovich).

Complicating matters for Goose, while he is the ego and superego of their team, Maverick is footloose and fancy free, the team's id. At one point, after the team was nearly expelled from Top Gun because pilot Maverick disobeyed one of the important rules of engagement followed by an unauthorized fly-by of the control tower, Goose gives Maverick a stern talking-to about how important to their careers the Top Gun opportunity is. Now, when

Goose is working so hard to keep their team out of trouble and to win the competition, his goofy wife arrives to distract him. A classic Hawksian dilemma, channeling *Only Angels Have Wings* or *Bringing Up Baby.* When Carole gets off the commuter airliner and spots Goose, she squeals with delight and throws her arms around him.

As they walk through the airport, Carole shows the audience a few telling behaviors: First of all, Goose isn't Nick and Maverick isn't Pete—they're their call signs, Goose and Maverick, and they remain that way nearly through the entire movie. Only once does she call either one of them by their first names, and this is when she talks about Maverick to Charlie, whom Carole is perhaps not yet convinced is a full-fledged member of the club. Carole is one of the boys, and around them she talks like one. It also doesn't take long for Carole, who doesn't always engage the brain before putting it in gear, complicates Goose's and Maverick's close relationship when she blurts out,

> **Carole:** So, Maverick: Goose tells me you're in love with one of your instructors.

> **Maverick:** *(amazed she knows about this)* Is that right?

> **Goose:** I didn't tell her that!

> **Carole:** *(matter of factly)* Yes, you did.

> **Goose:** *(aside to Carole, frustratingly)* I can't believe you said that! That was a secret! (*Top Gun*, 1986)

Goose kisses Carole on the mouth, perhaps to keep it from divulging any more secrets.

Next, Maverick and Charlie are in a restaurant, finishing lunch with Goose and family. Maverick and Charlie listen while Carole talks a lot and Goose is playing Jerry Lee Lewis's "Great Balls of Fire" on a nearby upright piano while their son, placed on top of the piano, is trying to sing along with Daddy. Carole asks if Goose ever embarrasses Maverick, and he replies in the negative. Then he thinks about it and begins a story, "Well, there was the time . . . " but Carole quickly interrupts and says, "Admiral's daughter. . . . He told me about the time you went ballistic [more pilot slang] with Penny Benjamin." Amazed not only that Carole would bring this up around Charlie, but also that Goose told her this deep, dark secret, Maverick replies, "Did he? That's great." She replies, "He tells me about all of 'em, Maverick. How my little angel, Goose goes home early for church, but you always go home with all the hot women." Now it's Charlie's turn to blush a little. Maverick tries to put an end to this all-too-revealing conversation by saying, "All right, thank you, Carole. I'm going to go embarrass myself with Goose for a while," and joins Goose in singing out of tune at the piano.

Now Carole has Charlie all to herself, and decides to make sure this newcomer knows all the ins and outs of who gets whom in the Navy: "I'd love to be able to warn you off about Maverick, but . . . *(she laughs and chomps a French fry)* I just love him to death! You know, I've known Pete for a lotta years now, and I'm telling you one thing for certain: *(stops to chew another fry)* There are hearts breaking all over the world tonight." Charlie asks "What?" "Because unless you are a fool, that boy is off the market. He is one hundred percent, prime-time in love with you." Then, without missing a beat, Carole yells to the men, "Hey, Goose, ya big stud!" Goose replies loudly over the noisy piano he continues to play, "That's me, honey!" She shouts, "Take me to bed or lose me forever!" Then the women rise and join their men at the piano for one last chorus in terrifying unison.

Later, Charlie and Maverick have been riding double—alone for the first time this night—on his motorcycle and are parked near the ocean. In a quiet but sexy voice, she repeats Carole's loud, brash love call: "Maverick, ya big stud, take me to bed or lose me forever." Charlie's catching on.

But then the tragedy occurs. Goose is killed in a training flight accident in a combat simulation. Disconsolate, Maverick boxes up Goose's belongings to give to Carole, who is sitting in the operations shack ready room. She has been crying for some time, but stops crying and wipes her eyes when Maverick enters. It wouldn't do for a member of the flying fraternity to weep. Heartbroken, Carole still takes the time to try to comfort Maverick: "God, he loved flying with you, Maverick." She puts her arms around him and gives him a hug. She continues, "He'd have flown anyway without you. He'd have hated it, but he would have done it." Carole knows that Maverick, speechless, is on the verge of doing the unmanly thing and showing tears. She just puts a hand to his cheek in acknowledgment, but then she is about to cry. It's her turn not to weep, and she rushes out of the room.

This is last the audience sees of Carole. Through much of the remainder of the film until the final air battle, Maverick cannot engage an opposing aircraft in combat. His grief is partly because of survivor guilt, partly because as pilot, he thinks he might have been able to do something to avoid the accident. Regardless, Goose's memory is what is keeping Maverick from continuing on.

Eventually Maverick gets over his inability to engage the enemy, and he saves his wingman, shooting down three enemy MiG-28s in the process. As a reward, Maverick is allowed to choose his next assignment. He picks the post of instructor back at Top Gun.

This is another instance in the film in which Hawks and company would find fault with Charlie. Hearing that Maverick was going back to teach at Top Gun, Charlie "unprofessionally" gives up her promotion and her new job

for Maverick, her love, and moves back to Miramar to be with him. Para-
phrasing the school's slogan about Top Gun teaching the very best pilots, she
says to Maverick,

Charlie: I heard the best of the best was going to be back here, so . . .

Maverick: *(grinning)* It could be complicated. . . . You know, on the first
one I crashed and burned.

Charlie: And the second?

Maverick: I don't know, but it's looking good so far. (*Top Gun*, 1986)

THE WOMEN OF *THE RIGHT STUFF*

The Right Stuff (1983) cannot be classified as a war film, since no real
combat takes place. Some combat is discussed, though, since many of the
planes the pilots test are fighter jets, and Chuck Yeager's war record as a
fighter pilot is also mentioned. However, the entire U.S.-Soviet space race of
the 1960s was initiated in response to the Cold War. Essentially, as Lyndon
Johnson put it, the race to put a man in space and then on the moon was—in
his reasoning—to avoid "going to bed every night by the light of a commu-
nist moon." As a senator, vice president, and later as president, LBJ was one
of the United States' most enthusiastic space program proponents. Johnson
was worried that if the Soviets gained superiority in outer space, they might
intimidate the free world with space platforms capable of dropping nuclear
bombs.

In this film, two women characters, both based on real individuals, spring
off the screen as prototypical Hawksian women: Glennis Yeager (Barbara
Hershey) and Pancho Barnes (Kim Stanley). At Pancho's Happy Bottom
Riding Club, a bar and grill located close to Edwards Air Force Base in the
California desert, test pilots gather to eat and drink and discuss everything
from who's at the "top of the pyramid" (the top test pilot) and whether or not
these young, less experienced pilots who have been chosen for the space
program are just "spam in a can."

Frequenting Pancho's, there appear to be three kinds of women: the
Hawksian kind who fit right in, young women looking to hook up with
handsome young pilots, and nervous wives whom their husbands have
dragged along and who look and feel out of place at Pancho's. The wives at
Pancho's either argue with their husbands about the dangers of test piloting
or are uncomfortable in an establishment brimming over with so much testosterone. One hopeful but ignorant young woman tries to flirt with the top
test pilot at Edwards, Chuck Yeager (Sam Shepard), but he ignores her. At

this moment, Yeager is in the process of following his Hawksian wife, Glennis, out of the bar to begin the "chase" portion of a little sexual game they play. Pancho herself advises the young lady that Yeager is married and that Glennis is his wife. On the other hand, Glennis is quite comfortable—even happy—in the company of these macho men, and later in the film says so. The excitement that these men emanate is part of the reason she was attracted to Yeager in the first place. We see no interaction of any kind between Glennis and other women, aside from some knowing looks between herself and Pancho. The flirty game between the couple starts when Yeager asks Glennis,

> **Yeager:** Honey, have you ever been caught on the desert alone?

> **Glennis:** *(boasting)* Never have. Never will. Never did meet the man who could catch me out there.

> **Yeager:** I'm a jackrabbit.

> **Glennis:** Forget it, flyboy. You'd never catch me.

> **Yeager:** *(smiling)* I believe I will.

> **Glennis:** Can't be done. (*The Right Stuff*, 1983)

And with that, Glennis is out the door of Pancho's, headed for her horse (both arrived at Pancho's, which is out in the middle of the desert, on horseback). Laughing, she rides off swiftly, her hair flying in the wind, with Yeager galloping off through the desert after her, full tilt. But on this occasion, Yeager doesn't succeed in catching Glennis, because he accidentally runs into a large cactus branch and is knocked off his horse, breaking two ribs. This is the first time we see Glennis complicate Yeager's life, because the following day he must try to break the sound barrier despite this injury.

Upon entering Pancho's, Yeager's usual greeting to its proprietor/bartender is friendly, although wordless. Pancho knows the ace flyer well: "Well, Yeager, you old bastard. Don't just stand there in the doorway like some old mouse shit sheep herder, come over here [to the bar] and have a drink." Yeager gives her a smooch as she hands him his drink. Pancho Barnes was real, not fictional, and her character in Tom Wolfe's book and in the movie were based on the real Florence Lowe "Pancho" Barnes. One of the first female pilots in the early days of aviation, Pancho founded the first test pilots union. Among other achievements, Pancho broke Amelia Earhart's air speed record in 1930. She was a member of the Ninety-Nines, an international union of female pilots, and raced planes in the Women's Air Derby. Always a colorful character, Pancho and one of her four husbands owned a ranch on which her bar and grill was built. There was once even a scandal when Pancho, who was in the middle of a heated negotiation over the ranch's sale to Edwards AFB for a planned runway expansion, was accused of running a house of ill repute on the ranch. This she always vigorously denied, and in colorful language.

In this film, when a civilian test pilot, "Slick" Goodlin (William Russ) turns down an offer to break the sound barrier (768 mph, designated "1" on the Mach meter), flying the X-1 experimental rocket jet unless the Air Force offers him $150,000, the Air Force offers Yeager the opportunity instead. Since the offer was made at the bar, Pancho grins and immediately shouts out this public offer: "The first fella who breaks the sound barrier's gonna get a free steak with all the trimmings!" Yeager responds, "I'll have mine medium rare, please." Glennis just looks at him and smiles, both proud and slightly worried. As the film's narrator says, a popular legend claimed that "there was a demon that lived in the air. They said whoever challenged him would die. Their controls would freeze up, their planes would buffet wildly, and they would disintegrate. The demon lived at Mach 1 on the meter, 750 miles an hour, where the air could no longer move out of the way. He lived behind a barrier through which they said no man could ever pass." But Yeager doesn't believe in such a barrier. So, along with Yeager's friends, Glennis, and other observers, Pancho appears on the flight line the next day to witness history. Glennis kisses him and tells him to "Punch a hole in the sky." As Yeager taxies away, Glennis waits calmly, arms folded, leaning on a piece of machinery. Yeager makes history, breaking Mach-1.

Later at Pancho's, the party begins, complete with a free steak and all the trimmings and a considerable amount of drinking. Outside the bar, an inebriated Yeager gazes up and howls at the moon like a coyote, one arm hoisting a drink and the other around Glennis for support.

PANCHO AND THE PUD KNOCKERS

Soon fearless fighter pilots from throughout the Air Force get transfers to Edwards to join this new "fellowship of speed." Among these pilots are future astronauts Gordon Cooper (Dennis Quaid) and Gus Grissom (Fred Ward). On their first visit to Pancho's, the two friends find out that this Hawksian woman is not to be trifled with, and that despite their achievements to date, these pilots have yet to become members of the club. When "Gordo," as Cooper is called, and Grissom reunite and sit down at the bar, Pancho approaches the two young pilots:

Pancho: What are you two rookies gonna have?

Gordo: Rookies? Now hold on, sis. You're lookin' at a whole new ball game here, now. In fact, in a couple of years, you're gonna immortalize us by puttin' our pictures up there on your wall. *(Bar patrons look askance at Gordo, and he senses he has broken some local taboo.)* What? I say something wrong here?

Behind the bar, Pancho has decorated a wall with photos of Edwards test pilots who have died in the line of duty.

Pancho: *(chomping on a cigar)* See, we got two categories of pilots around here. You got your prime pilots who get all the hot planes, and then you got your pud knockers, who dream about gettin' all the hot planes. So, what are you two pud knockers gonna have, eh? *(The Right Stuff,* 1983)

A few years later, Yeager's Mach 1 record is broken when Scott Crossfield breaks the Mach 2 barrier. Again, there is a celebration and Pancho grills up a free steak for Scott. Although Yeager is on hand on the flight line and at Pancho's afterward to happily congratulate Crossfield, Glennis is concerned for her husband's state of mind. During the celebration at Pancho's, the music is playing, so she asks him to dance. Yeager is encouraged to get back to the top of the pyramid. Later, when Yeager does break Crossfield's Mach 2 record with Mach 2.3, Pancho somehow has tapped into Yeager's radio transmissions to listen in (including Yeager's boastful "Sorry, Scott") and pipes it through the loudspeakers.

After the Soviets' Sputnik was launched and a panicky U.S. government swiftly launched a space program, President Eisenhower insists that astronauts be test pilots. Two Washington bureaucrats (Jeff Goldblum and Harry Shearer), looking to recruit astronaut candidates, travel to Edwards to meet with Edwards's test program liaison (David Clennon). The meeting, interestingly, is set at Pancho's. The clueless bureaucrats think they know exactly what kind of men they're looking for, whom they now refer to as pilots with "the right stuff." Amazingly, they reject Edwards's best test pilot, Yeager, both because he didn't go to college before enlisting in the Army Air Corps during World War II, and because of his less-than-positive attitude about NASA's first space capsules. These were not functioning "spacecraft" (as they later became), but as the United States' chief space scientist (played by Scott Beach and modeled after America's top rocket scientist Wernher von Braun) describes them, they are just pods to launch "specimens." Most importantly, such a design did not permit a pilot to fly it, and the older, more experienced pilots at Edwards have rejected this idea. Hence they coined the term, "spam in a can" for whoever would be locked inside of one of these capsules and hurled at the top of a fiery missile into outer space. Instead, the bureaucrats choose ambitious "rookie" test pilots from Edwards. But before these bureaucrats leave Pancho's, they will hear a few chosen words from its Hawksian proprietor. Pancho contemptuously quips, "You know, there are some things you can't change: Some peckerwood's gotta take the beast up, and some peckerwood's gotta land the sonofabitch. And that peckerwood's called a [pause for emphasis] *pilot*." The flyers drinking at the bar toast her.

Later in the film, Yeager feels forgotten, as Soviet and American astronauts orbiting as fast as 17,000 miles per hour dwarf what he and Crossfield have accomplished. Glennis sees her husband's growing depression, and over a drink at Pancho's decides to give him a tough love pep talk: She explains that although they don't have much in the way of life insurance, she has always admired his fearless work as a test pilot. But she says that if she ever saw him turn into a defeated man mired in the past, she'd be out the door, and he'd never catch her. Smiling, Yeager says, "You know, I'm a fearless man, but I'm scared to death of you." "No, you're not, but you ought to be," she replies.

With the no-nonsense words of his Hawksian woman to inspire him, with no speed records he can set and his admission to the astronaut club forbidden, Yeager decides to try to break the Soviet aircraft altitude record in the new F-104 he's testing. He throttles the jet upward for near ballistic flight, right out of the Earth's atmosphere, as did the Soviet pilot, but that's as far as he can go. The airplane, which still requires air for its engine, eventually flames out when the air gets too thin. Unfortunately, before he can restart the engine, the aircraft falls into a flat spin from which not even Yeager can recover, and he's forced to eject from a great height and parachute to the ground. But in a way, thanks to Glennis's urging, Yeager has matched the Soviet pilot and joined the astronauts, flying to the very edge of space.

This chapter has investigated the characteristics of Hawksian women and examined the different roles such women can play in war and action genres. The next chapter changes emphasis from such women and instead discusses females who have become warriors by profession or have been forced by circumstances to set aside the apron and pick up a rifle to battle an invading enemy.

Chapter Six

GI Jane and Female Resistance Fighters

Due primarily to socialization, violence has always been socially determined to be antithetical to females, trained by their mothers to nurture and give care and shelter to their families. Lucy Komisar (1976) concurs, stating,

> Testosterone notwithstanding, male aggressiveness and female passivity are learned traits. . . . The values of masculinity and femininity [and their behaviors] are drummed into them by parents, teachers, the media and other agents of socialization (212). . . . Little boys learn the connection between violence and manhood very early in life. Fathers indulge in mock prizefights and wrestling matches with eight-year-olds. Boys play cowboys and Indians with guns and bows and arrows proffered by their elders. . . . They are encouraged to "fight back," and bloodied noses and black eyes become trophies of their pint-sized virility. (202)

This is the social soil from which prohibitions against female warriors stem.

But change is inevitable. Herbert Sussman (2012) asserts that the essential dilemma for the modern male is to maintain his masculine identity in the face of a culture that makes equality the norm (15). In ancient times, membership in the warrior caste gave men the identity of superiority that human males require. Today it's called male ego. Ego is a personality construct inherent in both men and women. The modern-day pop culture definition describes ego in the male as an attitude of false pride and arrogance. Interestingly, as equality in women evolved in the twentieth century, the egos of both the female and the male have caused interpersonal conflict both psychologically and socially between the sexes in our culture. Now both men and women are attempting to define themselves and defend their positions.

Warrior castes still exist today, even within the U.S. Armed Forces, such as the Marine Corps Force Recon, the Navy SEALs, and the Army Special

Forces (Green Berets). If women attempted to join an elite caste, they'd be seen by many men serving in these units as sex-role usurpers. But in recent years, as women have been accepted into elite fighting units, Sussman credits the fact that "warfare no longer depends on physical strength" (15). But there are other reasons. For example, a number of American women have distinguished themselves in recent wars, have been wounded, and even have died in wars despite prohibitions put in place designed to shield them from direct combat.

Add to this the political and social movements in the United States that have contributed to the rapid evolution of the roles played by women in combat. For some years, American servicewomen have been allowed to fly all types of aircraft, including fighter jets and helicopter gunships, and at this writing, the Department of Defense (DOD) has announced that it will permit women to fight alongside men on the ground. And just prior to the DOD's 2013 lifting of the combat ban for females, in December of 2012, in a case of life imitating art (such as in the film *G.I. Jane*), two female officers at Fort Leonard Wood in Missouri graduated from combat training formerly closed to women, the Army's grueling Sapper Leader Course for combat engineers. Despite a number of men dropping out of this rigorous training, these two women managed it, and proudly stood at graduation beside their brothers. The point has now been made. As Komisar puts it,

> Today women are demanding new definitions of masculine and feminine that do not require the dominance of one sex over the other. We have rejected all the myths about masculine aggression and feminine passivity and we seek to replace them with values that encourage human relations based on equality, compassion and respect. (1976, 214)

Although twenty-first-century women are allowed to fly aircraft in combat, in World War II, no matter how skillful, no matter how many flight hours women logged with a stick and rudder, the most females were allowed to do was to ferry aircraft to combat bases. In *A Guy Named Joe*, discussed in chapter 5, we learned that Hawksian woman Dorinda Durston (Irene Dunne) is a highly experienced pilot. When her fiancé, Ted Randall (Van Johnson), volunteers for an important but risky mission to bomb an enemy installation, Dorinda, who knows that she's a better pilot, steals his P-38 Lightning and flies the bombing mission herself.

In *Top Gun* (1986), although Charlie (Kelly McGillis) is never shown actually flying an aircraft, this Hawksian woman serves her country as a senior civilian air-to-air combat instructor at this Navy school for highly skilled, testosterone-fueled male fighter pilots. Charlie is an expert in modern fighter combat tactics, and as such, is in the odd and virtually unique position—for a female in war films, anyway—of teaching men how to fight more efficiently. But Charlie sacrifices her own career interests for love, giving up a big promotion and a chance to serve in Washington so she can remain at Miramar Naval Air Station in California with the man she loves.

Such choices by career women in the movies present viewers with the essential conflict of the career woman: a fulfilling career vs. a loving relationship with a husband and the chance to have children. In *I Hate You— Don't Leave Me*, Jerold Kreisman and Hal Straus discuss the changing roles and expectations for both men and women. Women have to choose between a myriad of roles and expectations spanning the continuum from the traditional nurturing role of mother and wife to the career woman or "supermom" who attempts to successfully combine both. Men are also experiencing a changing of roles and expectations in which they are expected to be more open and sensitive, taking a larger part in the child rearing process than their fathers and grandfathers were required to do. Unfortunately, this "larger part" men are being asked to do often still has a long way to go before it becomes an equal partnership between husband and wife (Kreisman and Straus 1989, 71–74).

In 2013, in an interview on Katie Couric's morning talk show, Supreme Court Justice Sonia Sotomayor—who is unmarried—called "nonsense" the notion that a woman can "have it all," that is, being totally satisfied as both a career woman and a mother. Justice Sotomayor said that such a woman is either successful on the job but wondering what events in her children's life she's missing while she's at the office or is a stay-at-home mom who sometimes sadly reflects on what self-actualizing events and achievements in a career outside the home she has passed up.

Having it all is one issue often found in the themes of films in the war genre and in many others, but through the years, there are other themes regarding women warriors. Although the next film we will discuss was produced in this century, it hails back to prejudices faced by women of previous generations who wanted to fight.

WARBIRDS

Although here we're discussing one particularly poorly made and ridiculously fictional film about Women's Air Force Service Pilots (WASPs) during World War II, *Warbirds* (2008), the more realistic themes introduced are important. A detachment of WASP pilots is given a top secret mission: to deliver the B-29 carrying the first atomic bomb to Tinian Island. First a factcheck: History tells us that the first and second A-bombs dropped on Japan and parts for the assembly of a third A-bomb—not used due to the Japanese surrender—were delivered to Tinian unassembled on board a number of transport aircraft and the Navy cruiser USS *Indianapolis*. However, historical accuracy is tossed aside in *Warbirds*, since the film's two antagonists include a small detachment of Japanese and a few thousand flying, fire-breathing, prehistoric dragons.

In this film, a crew of the 2008 descendants of Dorinda Durston is assigned to this top-secret transport duty, although if the U.S government would have actually transported a fully assembled A-bomb anywhere, they assuredly would assign some of their best bomber flight crews, not women who transport aircraft. In 1945, no other decision could have been made. But in this dream world created by writer-director Kevin Gendreau, Maxine West (Jamie Elle Mann) and her fellow female pilots serve as the crew flying this top-secret mission under the command of OSS Col. Jack Taller (Brian Krause), a complete male chauvinist pig who refers to Maxine, who holds military rank in the WASPS, only as "Miss."

Throughout the film, Maxine and her fellow pilots receive nothing but disrespect from Taller. The worst of these incidents occurs when he won't listen to reason when they encounter a terrible storm along the way to Tinian. Taller won't allow Maxine to deviate from their course to avoid the storm and land on some other base close to Tinian. This and an attack on the bomber by an unidentified flying object, which we later learn was one of the dragons, causes them to land on an island somewhere in the Pacific. The island has a tiny airfield, and skilled pilot Maxine is trying to land a huge bomber on the equivalent of a postage stamp. Determined, she says as she maneuvers the plane in for a wheels-down landing, "I promised myself I'd die happy in Clark Gable's bed and I ain't breaking that promise." She manages a skillful landing on the small strip with minimum damage to the huge B-29, itself probably an impossibility. But, after all, this is a fantasy.

Under an order of total radio silence, Col. Taller won't radio for help. He wants to swiftly repair the plane and take off again for Tinian. Set aside the facts that an airfield only large enough for Japanese Zero fighter planes is not long enough for a B-29 to land, much less take off, loaded down with the extra weight of America's first A-bomb.

Next the group encounters, subdues, and captures a small detachment of Japanese airmen and discovers that the enemy is also stranded on the island. Although the Japanese have four functioning Mitsubishi Zero fighters, they can't take off and affect an escape because anything flying around the island is attacked by these highly aggressive flying dragons. The colonel is still unwilling to share the secret of the B-29's cargo with anyone, including Maxine, and says that anyone who gets nosy about their cargo will be shot. The prickly Maxine quips to one of her flyers, "It'd be a damn shame if that man walked into a spinning propeller." Eventually, though, the secret of the A-bomb is revealed to everyone. With Maxine's help, they develop a plan to use one of the Zeroes to fly to the nearest Allied-held territory to get help. They plan to use the other three Zeroes as fighter escorts for the messenger

Zero, to be flown by "Hoodzie" Smith (Lucy Faust) because weight and fuel are factors and Hoodzie weighs the least. The Zero has been stripped of all its heavy armaments to obtain the longest possible range. The last orders Max smilingly gives Hoodzie are, "You better make it, or Momma's gonna kick your ass." During this attempt, the women shoot down a number of dragons pursuing Hoodzie's plane. As Max shoots down one dragon, she happily quips, "You just got your ass kicked by a girl." Up until then, the women have been doing battle with only a dozen dragons. But then, just when they think their sortie will work, another one hundred dragons join the air battle and Hoodzie's plane goes down.

When they return to the island, the Japanese officer in command, Capt. Ozu (Tohoru Masamune) reveals that they, too, tried the same kind of sortie, but were also overcome by dragons. Furious because Ozu didn't share this with the Americans before their attempt, Maxine wants to shoot him, but Taller won't let her: "But I promise when the time comes, you can pull the trigger," he says. "Agreed," the steely-eyed Maxine replies.

Next they decide to do the impossible and use the B-29 to take off from the island with the two remaining Zeroes flying escort cover for them. With Maxine at the controls, they achieve the impossible lift-off of the huge bomber. Another of Maxine's pilots dies in her Zero protecting the B-29 from the dragons. To add more wild ideas to an already ridiculous story, Col. Taller decides to drop their A-bomb on the island to wipe out the dragons. To heck with the Japanese, apparently. At the conclusion, Taller finally admits that Max and her pilots are "good soldiers." It apparently takes some men quite a while to see something that's obvious.

What's probably most interesting about this film is the co-opting of a genre film usually populated by men with perhaps a woman along as a love interest, and then turning things upside down, casting women in roles usually reserved for men. Reminding us that Hollywood has often done this, Jeanine Basinger explains that not much has changed when they do it:

> At the lowest level, taking a genre and populating it with women instead of men was nothing but a variation that freshened up the action or gave the studio a chance to work all of its female stars. But no such variation would ever have been employed unless it fit the basic generic mold or unless it had broad audience appeal. . . . If women weren't supposed to do men's jobs, act like men or be like men, why were these movies acceptable? What happens when a woman takes over a male genre? The feminizing of an established genre was a standard Hollywood device. Although genres such as the western, the gangster film, the prison movie, the combat film, the pirate/swashbuckler story, were all thought of as stories about men in an action-oriented universe, female versions of all do exist. (Basinger 1993, 463)

FIGHTING ALONGSIDE THE MEN

In films such as *Top Gun*, women serve the country officially as "noncombatants," but in recent years, there is a growing list of women in war and related action-genre films who are officially permitted to fight alongside the men. On the Helium website, the writer with the nom de plume of Charlotte Starlet credits the evolution of the female at war to twenty-first-century men's wishes that their women become more empowered:

> Now men are looking for intelligent, confident, empowered "ass-kicking babes" who manage to look perfect even after 15-minute fights with chainsaw-wielding robots/flesh-eating zombies/indestructible cyborgs. As one member of filmthreat.com stated, "Chicks can indeed be tough. It is indeed inspiring to women in that it makes us think we can do more than we are taught to do." (Starlet 2007)

As demonstrated by the name of this chapter, certain films like *G.I. Jane* place a woman firmly in the role of hero, the actor, rather than the heroine, someone who is acted upon. In *The World War II Combat Film: Anatomy of a Genre*, Basinger creates four ground rules for a woman becoming a hero in the war film rather than a heroine. She becomes a hero when her role complies with one of four conditions:

1. A woman who defies conventional roles and redefines her life on her own terms, even if she ultimately chooses to be a wife and mother. She undergoes a process of questioning, as a hero would.
2. A woman who defies society itself, not just the conventions of society. She settles for nothing less than the possession of her own life, even if she is destroyed in the fight. A man who fights this way is a hero.
3. A woman who by choice or accident finds herself in a situation or a profession that commonly would be restricted to male participation, and she functions ably within it.
4. A woman who forms and maintains a positive sisterly relationship, a healthy mother/daughter relationship, or who joins a group of women in an important professional endeavor. (227)

G.I. Jane

A relatively recent film (1997) looms huge in America's social history. As we will continue to discuss, the roles and situations audiences are shown as reality often become reality, as evidenced by what has occurred at the Defense Department sixteen years later. In *G.I. Jane*, a feminist U.S. senator (Anne Bancroft) pushes her political campaign for total gender integration in the U.S. military by bullying the Secretary of the Navy into admitting the first female in history into Navy SEAL training. Although there is a 60 percent dropout rate among the men, a young, ambitious intelligence officer, Lieutenant Jordan O'Neil (Demi Moore), applies to be the first woman to undergo the rigorous SEAL program. But, unlike the senator, O'Neil is not really a feminist crusader: She's simply ambitious, and knows that any naval officer without "operational experience" is destined to a mediocre career with little possibility of promotion to the senior ranks. To obtain operational experience, O'Neil has already requested duty on board a submarine, but was refused because subs don't have special toilets for women . . . at least that's the nonsense O'Neil was told.

Before she takes on all the men in her SEAL training, we learn that O'Neil is up to the task of dishing it. In a scene in which she and her Navy boyfriend, Royce (Jason Beghe) are sharing a bathtub discussing O'Neil's application for SEAL training, he asks, "You're doing shit hot in intel: Why do you want to go play soldier girl?" These are odd words for a beau who would not be tolerated if he were a true male chauvinist, but they probably reveal his conflict in the matter. Knowing that success in SEAL training means a three-year tour and a great deal of separation, she asks if Royce will be around for the long run. He gets out of the tub and tells her he can't make that decision so fast. She retorts, "Get your dick back in here," as the scene ends.

Especially in 1997, the year this film was released and in which *G.I. Jane's* story is set, O'Neil knows that she must overcome a considerable amount of entrenched male prejudice against her if she is to succeed. Throughout O'Neil's training, Master Chief John James Urgayle (Viggo Mortensen) persecutes her, constantly encouraging her to drop out. At least he has the honesty to tell her why he objects to the idea of a female SEAL. Channeling Howard Hawks, Urgayle believes that men working with women in combat won't do their job as efficiently, and SEAL missions and lives could be endangered. The main reason he believes this is that in his view, male SEALs would be handicapped because they would always be concerned about protecting female SEALs on their team.

It's not surprising Urgayle thinks this way. His attitude is ingrained in our culture. Men are socialized by parents and media to act as women's protectors. So many plots in all genres of motion pictures end up with a man rescuing a woman from something. Examples of this mind-set include the case of the high school male wrestler in the Midwest who feared hurting a female to such an extent that he forfeited his match rather than wrestle the girl he drew in the tournament. In the Aurora, Colorado, movie theater shootings, several male victims lost their lives protecting their female companions.

As soldiers are socialized through their rigorous training to rely on their comrades in life-and-death situations and help each other, one would hope this would apply, whether the other combat team members were male or female. In a combat situation the impulsive reaction for self-preservation could inherently blind a person to gender differences. In a foxhole, a soldier wants and even expects his comrade to watch his back, and at that life-or-death moment doesn't care whether that comrade is a man or a woman. Survival instinct takes over.

At the outset of O'Neil's training, it is apparent that there are two standards: one for the men and another for "the girl." Urgayle calls it "gender norming." When she learns that she will be held to less-than-male standards during her training, O'Neil realizes that even if she finishes the course, she won't be taken seriously and her entire ordeal will be meaningless. O'Neil understands that most of this second-class citizenship is the work of a resentful SEAL training base commander (Scott Wilson). But the commander's attitude doesn't stop O'Neil. Going right up the chain of command, a furious O'Neil confronts the sarcastic, resentful SEAL commander in his office:

O'Neil: I mean really, sir, why don't you just issue me a pink petticoat to wear around the base?

C.O. Salem: Did you just have a brain fart, Lieutenant?

O'Neil: Begging your pardon, sir?

Salem: Did you just waltz in here and bark at your commanding officer? Because if you did, I would call that a bona fide brain fart, and I resent it when people *fart* inside my office!

O'Neil: I think you've resented me from the start, sir.

Salem: What I resent, Lieutenant, is some politician using my base as a test tube for her grand social experiment. What I resent, is the sensitivity training that is now mandatory for all of my men. The ob-gyn I now have to keep on staff just to keep track of your personal pap smears. But most of all what I resent, is your perfume, however subtle, interfering with the scent of my fine three-dollar-and-seventy-nine-cent cigar, which I will put out this instant if the phallic nature of it happens to offend your goddamn fragile sensibilities! Does it?

O'Neil: No, sir.

Salem: *(loudly)* "No, sir" *what?*

O'Neil: The shape doesn't bother me. Just the goddamn sweet stench. (*G.I. Jane*, 1997)

As typical when women attempt to do what society has defined as men's work, to gain respect and assure equal treatment O'Neil has to give up most of what defines a woman, from her hair (which she shaves down to a buzz cut), to no makeup or women's clothes, and even to her conduct. She resolves to act and react as much as possible as a man, even when conversing with a female Navy doctor:

Lt. Blondell: Lieutenant, why are you doing this [training for the SEALs]?

O'Neil: Do you ask the men the same question?

Blondell: As a matter of fact: yes, I do ask them.

O'Neil: And what do they say?

Blondell: 'Cause I get to blow shit up.

O'Neil: Well, there you go. (*G.I. Jane*, 1997)

As testosterone-filled and appealing to both sexes as *G.I. Jane* is, it can still be defined as a woman's film, because, as Basinger asserts, the scenario "forces women to make a choice. If she makes the wrong one, she is punished for it. Thus the women's film demonstrates society's way of repressing the woman" (1986, 228).

O'Neil survives her training, even a grueling capstone exercise called "SERE" (Survival, Evasion, Resistance, and Escape) training. In SERE, her trainee team is "captured" and tortured for information. This is where Urgayle thinks O'Neil will crack, and he and other SEAL trainers beat her unmercifully. Instead of giving up, she staggers to her feet, turns to her abusers and yells, "Suck my dick!" The other trainee prisoners begin chanting her macho mantra, and a frustrated Urgayle realizes that nothing will stop O'Neil. Although many trainees initially had shown resentment toward O'Neil, this incident crystallizes all the trainees and assures that she is accepted as one of them.

After the grueling exercise is over, O'Neil, sporting bruises from her ordeal, is invited to drink beer with the trainees. Trainee Cortez (David Vadim) has been intolerant of O'Neil prior to the SERE exercise. In a much more friendly manner than before, Cortez kids her, "I like you better when you drink." She retorts, "You know, Cortez, I like you better when I drink." Later, in the ladies' room of the tavern, a civilian woman is appalled by O'Neil's bruised appearance and says, "Ain't really none of my business, but I say, leave the bastard." O'Neil just laughs.

In the film's climax, O'Neil finds herself on a real combat mission in North Africa, along with a team of SEALs and the master chief. In this mission, it is Urgayle—perhaps subconsciously making his own point—who fouls up on the mission, breaking protocol trying to needlessly protect O'Neil when he should have trusted her to do the job he trained her to do. O'Neil is about to quietly kill an enemy soldier with her knife. The soldier is a large, muscular man, and Urgayle doesn't have sufficient faith in O'Neil's strength and skill to do the job. So he shoots the enemy soldier, revealing their position to a larger enemy force. Eventually, in escaping from the enemy, Urgayle is wounded and O'Neil drags and carries him to safety. Throughout SEAL training, Urgayle has also maintained that females are usually too small and weak to handle the weight of rescuing a big man if she had to carry one. But in the end, O'Neil does just that: She hauls the hefty Urgayle out of harm's way. Later, sheepishly, he complains, "I'll never live this down."

But as we delight in O'Neil's success "infiltrating" the male world of the SEALs, Basinger poses an interesting caveat. She notes that when women take over male jobs and roles in genres such as the combat film, they still must sacrifice their female identities:

> The point is that if a woman is allowed to enter what is presumably a male genre and participate in it by playing what would ordinarily be the hero's role, then it has been somehow suggested that women can be men. We cannot call this progress, and feminists have posited the concept that one of the few options to women in film viewing is the transference of their identity into maleness, the loss of themselves as women. (1993, 485)

However, Basinger also asserts that films like *G.I. Jane* do the cause of feminism a service, in this case putting in the minds of the public the notion that perhaps a woman *could* qualify to become a Navy SEAL: "By making it possible and putting it on the screen as if it were a reality, it begins to make it probable. The impossible then becomes possible and finally inevitable" (1986, 228).

Courage under Fire

Another important drama about women in combat was introduced in chapter 1. In *Courage under Fire*, Capt. Karen Walden (Meg Ryan) flies a rescue helicopter during the first Iraq war. While on a rescue mission, she ingeniously destroys an Iraqi tank that's shelling some Americans huddled around their own downed chopper. When other Iraqis shoot down her chopper, Capt. Walden fights bravely on the ground beside her men. Although not all the men under her command take her seriously, she does. At the end of the film, when the true story of her actions is revealed, Capt. Walden receives a posthumous Medal of Honor, fictionally characterized as the first time America's highest decoration for combat heroics was bestowed on a woman.

But this summary of events doesn't quite tell the entire story. The film is both about Lt. Col. Nat Serling and his PTSD, described in chapter 2, and the *Rashomon*-like compilation of accounts of the events in Iraq by the surviving members of Walden's crew. Serling's first interview, with Warrant Officer Rady (Tim Guinee), paralyzed from the waist down in the crash of Walden's helicopter, shows that he and his wife have had many arguments about the incident. It is inferred that Rady's wife, Annie (Amy Hathaway), spitefully blames Walden's initiative in destroying the Iraqi tank for her husband's wounds and lifetime incapacitation. As Annie sees it, Walden is to blame for the fact that her husband must spend the rest of his life in a wheelchair. A woman of unliberated views on sex roles, the spiteful wife says, "You always defend her. She was so butch . . . one of those women who want to be officers." Rady firmly tells his wife to shut up: "She gave her life for those men. She was a soldier."

Serling's next interview with helicopter crewman Ilario (Matt Damon), tells essentially the same story, adding illustrations of Walden's professionalism, such as her barking orders at the men to inventory their ammunition and create a defensive perimeter while they hold off Iraqi ground attacks and wait for rescue. But Ilario lies on one key point: Once on the ground, he and another crewman, Monfriez (Lou Diamond Phillips) were afraid, did not want to wait to be rescued and wanted to leave the wounded Rady and run, but Walden, who refuses to leave anyone behind, was having none of it. Monfriez, not a regular crewman on Walden's chopper but a last-minute tag along, doesn't know Walden. He is openly scornful of women in combat. But under the duress of battle, it's Walden who appears better suited for a firefight and Monfriez, his macho airs a cover-up for his own insecurities, who appears cowardly. At one point, Monfriez, insisting on deserting the wounded Rady and running, aims his rifle at Walden just as the Iraqis attack their position. Right over Monfriez's head, as he sits with his back to the Iraqi position, Walden shoots an enemy soldier who tries to infiltrate their position. When she shoots her weapon, Monfriez thinks for one split second that she's shooting at him, so he instinctively pulls the trigger and seriously wounds Walden.

The next day, when their rescuers land their helicopter a hundred yards away, Walden is too badly hurt to make a run for it and orders Monfriez and Ilario to carry Rady to the chopper and come back for her with a stretcher. She bravely continues firing at the Iraqi position to cover her men's retreat. Because Monfriez knows that he and Ilario will be court-martialed for their mutinous behavior the night before, instead of coming back for her, Monfriez tells the rescue chopper pilot that Walden is dead. Ilario is shocked at this, but out of a sense of self-preservation, he remains silent and goes along with

Monfriez. Since there are still plenty of Iraqis nearby, the rescue chopper pilot takes Monfriez at his word and orders in an air strike. Walden dies when an A-10 napalms the entire area.

Later, when Serling interviews Monfriez, and his false story of an incompetent, scared Walden, who had to be propped up by his own courageous actions, seems so different than the other crewmen's versions of events, the officer is sure that someone is lying. So Serling re-interviews Ilario, who since his initial interview with Serling has gone absent without leave. Although addicted to drugs to self-medicate away his survivor guilt, this time Ilario tells Serling the truth of what happened, which later causes Monfriez to commit suicide rather than admit his cowardice and mutiny to a court-martial.

Walden's heroic story ends as her young daughter receives her mother's Medal of Honor in a White House ceremony.

Among the many complimentary reports Serling sorts through in Walden's personnel records is the statement, "Capt. Walden is an officer of exceptional moral courage." This certainly comes across in Meg Ryan's convincing performance. As such, roles such as those dramatized in *Courage under Fire* and *G.I. Jane* lend substance to the belief that women cannot only fight alongside the men but distinguish themselves as well and that, as Basinger says, exposing audiences to such stories will hasten the time when they will come true. So in *Courage under Fire*, one more woman's story—fictional though it may be—helps lay the groundwork for the 2013 Defense Department's removal of the ban against women in combat roles.

The Lucky Ones

Not all GI Janes are as intelligent as Lt. O'Neil or as tough and resourceful as Capt. Walden. In *The Lucky Ones* (2008), we find another GI Jane in Colee Dunn (Rachel McAdams), stationed in Iraq and wounded in the leg when an IED exploded under her truck. When we meet her, Colee has just arrived stateside at a New York airport to begin a thirty-day convalescent leave. Due to flight cancellations, Colee; T. K. Poole (Michael Peña), also on convalescent leave; and Fred Cheaver (Tim Robbins), who has been granted a medical discharge after a porta-john fell on him, have decided to share the rent on a car and drive from New York to St. Louis, Fred's home. From there, Colee and T. K. should be able to catch flights to their intended destinations in Las Vegas.

T. K.'s war wound has resulted in impotence, and he has convinced himself that if anybody can snap him out it, it's the kind of hookers for whom Las Vegas is famous. Colee carries a guitar, which she plans to return to the family in Las Vegas of her friend and secret lover, Randy, who was killed rescuing her from the truck when she was wounded. Colee is estranged from her only relative, her mother, who kicked her out of the house a few years earlier. Not a candidate for Mensa, Colee believes that when she, Randy's wartime lover, shows up in Vegas, Randy's family will automatically embrace her and offer her a home with them when she leaves the Army. Colee is devoted to Randy's memory, although later in the film we learn that he was a terrible liar. He told Colee that he was a felon who enlisted in the Army before the cops caught up with him. Hearing Colee tell this story, T. K. makes the mistake of commenting that Randy sounds like "lowlife trash," causing Colee to go ballistic, throwing a soft drink all over him, yelling, "Randy saved my fucking life! He pulled me out of that truck when I got shot (she's pounding on T. K. during this tirade) and took a fucking bullet for me! All I got left is his fucking guitar! I oughta kick your ass!" Later T. K. half-apologizes.

Stopped at an Indiana roadhouse for a lavatory and beer break, the three encounter a rowdy group of university students. Insulted by a snotty coed, Colee, ignoring the fact that she is heavily outnumbered, starts a fight, and has to be rescued by T. K. and Cheaver. Later, Colee characterizes the fight as, "[We] Kicked *their* college asses! Just glad I didn't have my weapon." Simply put, the impulsive Colee is quite capable of acting and sounding like an idiot. Simple-minded and naive, she says that if someone drinks booze through a straw, they get drunker. Asked how, she doesn't know, but Colee questions nothing. In many ways, she reminds us of the young woman in the humorous State Farm commercial who believes that everything posted on the Internet has to be true, and that her new date, whom she met on the Internet, is a French model, despite his inability to really speak French.

After a disaster in St. Louis, in which Cheaver learns that he no longer has either a wife or a job to return to, the three drive on west together. T. K. and Colee are still headed for Las Vegas and Cheaver goes along, hoping to eventually end up in Salt Lake City to ask his brother, who lives there, for a job. On the road, his injured back bothering him, Cheaver takes too many pills while driving and has an accident. In the accident, Colee's leg wound opens up a little and it must be repaired. In a discussion afterward, we learn more of Colee's crazy ideas. She thinks perhaps Cheaver was trying to commit suicide (he wasn't), and that would be bad because if a person kills himself, he's condemned to the "lake of fire." Her idea is so preposterous that the opinionated T. K. is stunned and says nothing, and Cheaver quips, "I feel like I'm in it now."

Later, while their car is being repaired, Colee disappears. The men find her across the street at a church meeting. During the meeting, demonstrating that she has no sense at all and rarely engages her brain before speaking, Colee stands up to testify that T. K. needs healing because he was wounded in his "private parts" in Iraq. Invited to a dinner party by patriotic church-goers, Colee asks T. K. if he'd dance with her. T. K. has to remind her that dancing would not be too bright a thing to do with her injured leg. As they drive on toward the Rocky Mountains, Colee again forgets she's wounded and tells the men that she'd like to go hiking and picnicking in the Rockies. T. K. just says "no," but they end up stopping for the picnic portion of her whim anyway.

Going for picnic supplies, the weather swiftly changes, and T. K and Colee encounter a tornado. Pulled over and hiding in a deep ditch and huddled together for protection, T. K. discovers that he is impotent no longer. Of course, later, Colee cannot keep the good news to herself, regardless of how sensitive, and blurts out the news to Cheaver:

Colee: Hey, Cheave! Guess what?

Cheaver: What?

Colee: His penis works! *(She points at T. K.)*

Cheaver: *(at T. K.)* What do you mean? You got wood?

Colee: Yeah, definitely wood!

Cheaver: You don't need these [Las Vegas] ladies anymore?

Colee: No. He's all fixed up. He could pound a nail with that thing.

Cheaver: Pound a nail? How do you know that? Have you touched it?

Colee: No, I didn't have to. It was just poking right into me [when they were huddling together in the ditch]. It's a miracle! (*The Lucky Ones*, 2008)

When the friends finally arrive in Las Vegas, Colee is still convinced that when she lands on Randy's family's doorstep, that they will magically take her in like she's Cinderella. When Colee meets Randy's family, she discovers that every last thing Randy told her was a lie, beginning with his nonexistent criminal past and ending with the fact that he was married and had a baby. Meeting Randy's widow and child, Colee makes the pretense that she was just a war buddy, not a girlfriend that he lied to and slept with. Of course, this fools nearly no one, especially Randy's mother. The family is very kind to her, but—in a rare moment of clarity—Colee realizes she doesn't belong. Leaving, she takes the guitar with her.

Later, Cheaver decides to reenlist, and a month later all three are back together on a troop plane for Iraq. T. K.'s "private parts" have completely recovered and Cheaver will use his reenlistment bonus to help put his son through college. Colee, perhaps a teeny bit wiser for her experiences, will try once again to learn something from her mistakes. Although a GI Jane, Colee takes no ground for the women's movement in her role in the armed forces. She's essentially cannon fodder who fills a place in the Army's supply chain.

Battleship

In the 2012 adaptation of the tabletop board game and the video game, *Battleship*, a GI Jane doesn't figure in a leading role. However, two women assist the traditional male hero in achieving the final victory. Upon the deaths of all his senior officers, a young Navy lieutenant becomes the hero when he takes command of a destroyer and is principally responsible for the defeat of a detachment of alien invaders who have landed on and near the Hawaiian island of Oahu. Two petty officers, one male and one female, are key in assisting Lt. Alex Hopper (Taylor Kitsch) in overcoming the invading aliens. Hopper gains much of his courage and conviction from Chief Petty Officer Walter "The Beast" Lynch (John Tui), whom Hopper leans on and counts on to inspire him to step up and take charge of the situation. Hopper's other reliable ally is the first of the two women who will combine with Hopper to defeat the enemy. Petty Officer Cora "WEPS" (weapons officer) Raikes (played by the recording artist Rihanna), is a highly skilled, courageous, and capable weapons officer. Sitting at a computer screen in the destroyer's fire control center, Raikes efficiently targets and fires on the alien ships. When Hopper is detailed to command a launch armed with a minigun to make contact with the enemy, it's Raikes who shows she's more than a computer button-pusher as she "mans" the gun. Throughout the film, whenever Hopper needs assistance firing any number of different kinds of guns, rockets, and other weapons on board his destroyer, it's Raikes who gets the job done. And after taking out three of the invaders' vessels but losing his destroyer in the process, Hopper and some of his crew commandeer the mothballed battleship *Missouri* to continue the fight against the invaders. The calm, competent Raikes is once again the person Hopper calls upon to take charge of figuring out how to operate and fire the World War II–era battleship's big guns. Throughout, Raikes's behavior is as brave and bold as the men, showing a female WEPS is boldly equal to the task described by *G.I. Jane*'s O'Neil as "blowing shit up."

The second female begins the film as what appears to be just a shapely blond love interest: Hopper's attractive girlfriend, an admiral's daughter. But later we learn that Sam (Brooklyn Decker) is also a skilled physical therapist working at a hospital helping wounded veterans recover from catastrophic injuries. In that capacity, trying to motivate Lt. Col. Mick Canales (Gregory Gadson), who has lost both legs in Iraq, Sam has taken Canales on his new prosthetic legs on a hike up one of Oahu's mountains. Coincidentally, on this mountain is a high-powered radio transmitter array that recently was created to transmit signals to an Earth-like planet that astronomers had just discovered in hopes of contacting friendly extraterrestrial life. This project has, of course, backfired, as the Earth gets an invasion in return for reaching out and touching someone across the heavens.

When the aliens attack, Sam figures out that since the invaders' communications array crash-landed, the enemy will need to commandeer the humans' radio transmitter array to maintain command and control communications with their home planet. Sam contacts Hopper on board the *Missouri* and warns him that the radio transmitter site must be destroyed. To delay invaders who are about to use the transmitter, Sam bravely rams a car into a control room in the facility. This prevents the alien transmission long enough for Hopper and Raikes on board the *Missouri* to fire its big guns and blow up part of the array. Navy carrier-based jets destroy the rest of the facility and the Earth is saved from the aliens.

GI JANES FROM MANY COUNTRIES

Beyond American women, just as tough as O'Neil and Walden are the female Soviet soldiers in Sam Peckinpah's *Cross of Iron*, as discussed in chapter 3. As we will see, other countries produce their own versions of GI Janes.

Enemy at the Gates

Beyond American women, just as tough as O'Neil and Walden are the female Soviet soldiers in Sam Peckinpah's *Cross of Iron*, discussed in chapter 3. More female Soviet soldiers fight Germans in *Enemy at the Gates* (2001). In this film, a handful of female troops assigned as snipers are among many Russian men and women under the command of Nikita Khrushchev, holding the line against invading Germans in this relatively factual World War II story about the siege of Stalingrad. The first Soviet GI Jane of note is named Ludmilla (Sophie Rois). We know little about her, except that she's a soldier who happens to be an excellent shot and who has also been trained to use stealth techniques to sneak up on kills. A good sniper can also lie motionless for hours, patiently waiting for the right time to shoot his or her victim. However, in this case, Ludmilla is not very professional, not at all the disciplined sniper she's supposed to be, and not at all in the same league with an expert German sniper like German Maj. Konig (Ed Harris). The reason Konig has been brought to Stalingrad is because the Germans want him to kill Vassili Zaitsev (Jude Law), the Russians' newest, youngest, and most deadly sniper, who has been knocking off Germans all over the city with great regularity. Over his career, the real Vasily Zaytsev was responsible for the deaths of 225 enemy soldiers and was hailed as a "Hero of the Soviet Union." In reality and in the film, the propaganda the Russians have put out about Zaitsev explains that the young man is a great hero of the proletariat who learned shooting and stealth techniques from his grandfather while hunting for game and killing off wolves in Russia's Ural Mountains.

Ludmilla is teamed with Zaitsev for this day's sniper mission in the bombed-out city center of Stalingrad. They spot a target in one of the windows of a department store and shoot. Then they go inside the store to look for a body and to retrieve his identity tags. This is when Ludmilla and Zaitsev realize that they are not the predator, but the prey. The two become pinned down by Konig, who is ensconced safely one floor above, and who is very much alive. The target Ludmilla and Zaitsev saw in the window was a trap to lure them in. To make matters worse, the Germans are bombing the city. Instead of staying still and keeping cover, Ludmilla, showing fear, panics and runs and Konig shoots her. Zaitsev had tried to warn Ludmilla to remain calm and patient, and not to move, but she was too frightened to listen. The more experienced Zaitsev doesn't move and eventually escapes Konig's trap.

College-educated Tania Chernova (Rachel Weisz) begins her stint in the Russian Army as a regular soldier until a commissar named Danilov (Joseph Fiennes) discovers that she can speak German and transfers her to their intelligence service, where she works as a radio intercept operator and translator. But Tania wants more than to translate: She has a personal score to settle with the Nazis. Her Jewish mother and father were captured and killed by the Nazis. Since Tania is also a good shot, she wants a transfer from intelligence to sniper duty for the chance to experience some personal payback for her parents. Danilov, in love with Tania, tries to get her friend Zaitsev to persuade her to remain in the relative safety of her intelligence work. Danilov doesn't understand two things: Tania and Zaitsev are in love with each other, and Tania is insistent about a transfer to sniper duty for more reasons than revenge. Finally Tania gets her wish. One of Zaitsev's sniper friends and mentors, Koulikov (Ron Perlman), has just been shot by Konig, and so Zaitsev welcomes Tania to their deadly fraternity by making her a gift of Koulikov's sniper rifle.

The Soviet Army treats snipers better than their regular infantrymen, herded toward the front lines like cattle to die, some without even being issued a rifle. Despite their loftier status, Soviet snipers still aren't quartered at the Ritz. They roll up in blankets and sleep on the floor next to each other. At one point, Zaitsev, and Tania make love rolled up in blankets just feet away from the others. It's interesting to note that amid all this, another female sniper nearby, just to keep a vestige of her femininity, takes a minute to put on eye shadow and primps in a mirror. It isn't much, but it's all she can do to remind herself that she's still a woman.

Later, Tania and Zaitsev team up in an attempt to shoot Konig, but only manage to wound him in the hand. Attempting to help evacuate a woman neighbor across the Volga-don Canal, Tania is wounded. She is evacuated to a hospital, but Danilov and Zaitsev believe that she's been killed. Konig sets a trap for Zaitsev and almost succeeds, killing Danilov, but Konig makes a mistake and Zaitsev kills him. Later, Zaitsev learns that Tania is alive, and after the siege of Stalingrad is lifted, he finds her in the hospital and the two soldier-snipers are reunited.

Female Viet Cong Soldiers

As with the Soviet female soldiers, no quarter is asked or given to women soldiers fighting in two Vietnam War films. In *Full Metal Jacket*, in the Tet Offensive battle for the city of Hue, a crafty female Viet Cong sniper (Ngoc Le) positioned a few floors up in a half-destroyed building, has shot a number of U.S. Marines. Spread out through the building to ferret out the sniper, Pvt. Joker (Matthew Modine) finally locates and tries to shoot her, but at the critical moment, his rifle jams. Spinning around, pigtails flying, the sniper tries to shoot Joker, but he finds cover behind a beam as he desperately tries to clear his M-16's jam. Pvt. Rafterman (Kevin M. Howard) hears the shooting and arrives in time to shoot the sniper. Standing over the fatally wounded woman, Pvt. Joker is initially conflicted about finishing her off, even though she's obviously dying. Desiring payback for the comrades she's killed, the other Marines want her dead, but a few are opposed to killing her quickly. Animal Mother (Adam Baldwin), newly in charge by rank due to the fact that the sniper has just shot their squad leader, weighs in on the question, "And I say that we leave the gook for the mother-lovin' rats." Others say, "Fuck her. Let her rot," hoping to prolong her suffering. But finally, after the female VC repeatedly begs him to finish her off, Joker pulls the trigger and ends her life.

In *The Iron Triangle* (1989), serving among the men in a company of Viet Cong, women fight as near equals. But none is shown serving in leadership positions or has the temerity to speak out with authority in the company's political meetings. That is left for the men. At the end of the picture, however, in a climactic firefight against an overwhelming force of Americans, female VC soldiers fight fiercely and die as bravely as do the men in their unit.

A third female Viet Cong fighter ends up receiving better treatment from an American than the *Full Metal Jacket* sniper. VC soldier Vo Mai (Jane Le) appears toward the end of *Tunnel Rats* (2008). Whether or not she has other duties above ground is not shown in this film, because she spends most of her screen time defending a VC tunnel against invading Americans. Tunnel rats are U.S. Army soldiers whose dangerous job it is to enter the maze of tunnels used by the VC to hide from the Americans. The highly dangerous (some called it suicidal) job of a tunnel rat is to ferret out the enemy in dark, booby-trapped underground labyrinths and kill them, destroying these effective VC hiding places. In one scene, just as an American finds an exit to one of these tunnels, Vo Mai, who's been lying in wait, spears him through the neck. Like the Russian women who stabbed the young German soldier, Vo Mai is a tough, experienced VC, but this gruesome killing sickens even her. Later, in an ambush, she kills yet another American in another tunnel. But at the climax of the film, the last remaining American tunnel rat blunders out of a tunnel into a hollowed-out cave area, apparently the underground "home" of Vo Mai and her two children. This encounter becomes a standoff, because the American won't shoot the woman, but can't communicate with her, either. He speaks no Vietnamese and she knows no English, and she holds him off with a knife. All the American wants to do is cross over to where Vo Mai and the children are crouching and exit the cave through the tunnel behind them. But he can't make his peaceful intent understood. Then a U.S. air strike above causes a massive cave-in. The children scamper out of the cave and down the tunnel to safety, just as another cave-in closes both entrance and exit tunnels, trapping the soldier and his enemy. Together, no longer menacing each other with weapons, the American and the woman VC work together to try to dig out and clear the passageway, but sadly they run out of air and die of asphyxiation.

Operation Crossbow

In *Operation Crossbow* (1965), British WAAF Flight Officer Constance Smith (Sylvia Syms) also serves, although she never is in combat. The first half of the film is about British efforts to discover if and where the Germans might be developing and testing rockets. These weapons would go on to become the world's first operational ballistic missiles. Based on a true story, the Germans were, indeed, using a remote seaside location in Germany called Peenemünde to test their V-1 and V-2 rockets, subsequently launched on London.

Based on the achievements of the real Constance Babington Smith, the film character's role is as an officer working in photo intelligence. She spots something that could be used as a rocket launching platform and shows it to her male superiors, who, somewhat chauvinistically, think that this woman's imagination might be getting the better of her. But after additional photoreconnaissance, she identifies the vertical launch tower for the V-2. As a result of Smith's intelligence efforts, the Allies first launch a preemptive air strike on Peenemünde, killing many Germans working on the project, destroying their facilities, and delaying Nazi rocket attacks on London. Later, thanks to Smith's initial intelligence work, the film portrays the efforts of a group of courageous and self-sacrificing spies who target another ballistic missile construction and launch site inside Germany and destroy it in an Allied bombing raid.

FEMALE COMMANDERS

In American films about wars taking place in the twentieth and twenty-first centuries, nearly all women serve in subordinate positions to male officers. However, perhaps because science fiction films like *Wing Commander* (1999) and *Starship Troopers* are set in the distant future, women are allowed nearly complete equality with males, and are even allowed to command huge starships. In *Wing Commander*, Lt. Cmdr. "Angel" Devereaux (Saffron Burrows) is the title character. However, one thing hasn't changed since Lt. O'Neil in *G.I. Jane* or Capt. Walden in *Courage under Fire.* The price women who wish to command must pay includes shedding most of their female behaviors. To command male respect, they must dress, act, and speak more like men. On this starship version of a contemporary aircraft carrier, Angel must maintain a manly exterior, fitting into the macho culture of her mostly male fighter pilots. So, when she catches the men squabbling, just on the verge of a fistfight, she insults their manhood, saying, "If you *ladies* don't stand down, you'll have a problem with me," implying that in a fight, she could subdue both men. This further implies that there are two kinds of women in this society of the future, women like Angel and lesser creatures referred to as ladies, who have no place on a starship. Later, when another pilot objects to the unpopular Lt. Blair (Freddie Prinze Jr.) being assigned to fly on his wing, Angel channels John Wayne's same leadership decision in 1951's *Flying Leathernecks* and assigns Blair to be her wingman. Blair questions this assignment, asking her if she's sure, implying that her decision may have been emotional (read female) rather than militarily sound (read male). Quickly she stiffens and responds, asserting the commander-subordinate relationship: "Did I just give you a suggestion or an order?"

In this film, everything that occurs in the pilots' ready room exists in a male mode of metaphorical discourse. Courage and daring is referred to throughout the film as "balls," as evidenced by this conversation between hotshot pilot Lt. Todd "Maniac" Marshall (Matthew Lillard) and Lt. Rosie Forbes (Gilly Holder). When Marshall, a newcomer, boldly brags that although he's a rookie, he's still the best pilot on the carrier, the more experienced Rosie is amused by his bravado and also physically attracted to him. Nonetheless she responds using male ready room banter:

Rosie: You've got balls.

Marshall: *(slyly)* You should see 'em.

Rosie: *(brashly)* Mine are bigger.

Marshall: I've been told size doesn't matter.

Rosie: She lied.

Angel is quite capable of making hard decisions and disciplining her men. When her best friend Rosie's fighter crashes on the flight deck, Angel must give the order to push the fighter's wreckage off the flight deck so that the rest of her pilots can bring in their ships, which are low on fuel. Rosie may or may not still be alive in the tangle of wreckage, but regardless, the order must be given. Rosie's ship was damaged in the first place when she and Marshall disobeyed standard safety procedures. Always trying to better each other in the most outrageous flying maneuvers, Rosie and Marshall were still competing when Rosie suffered her fatal accident. Later, confronting Marshall on the flight deck, Angel draws her weapon and almost executes Marshall on the spot. She relents, but coldly warns the young officer, "If you ever endanger another pilot, you're dead."

Later, Angel sacrifices herself to protect the carrier and to help Lt. Blair complete their mission: to inform the fleet of an imminent enemy attack. Since her fighter is badly damaged, she must eject in an escape pod, but the pod will probably run out of oxygen before she can be rescued. She gives what she thinks is her last command, ordering Lt. Blair not to waste valuable time trying to rescue her, but to continue on his mission to warn the fleet. Later a ship from the carrier finds the escape pod, and Angel, out of air and unconscious, is rescued and revived.

Starship Troopers

Again, in *A Woman's View*, Basinger would posit that even in a future that promises female equality, Angel's choices mean that she must stay relatively unattached and somewhat aloof to merit a command assignment (1993, 485). In *Starship Troopers*, another woman seeking promotion within planet Earth's Federation Fleet Service must sacrifice any traditional relationship with her infantryman boyfriend to pursue her career goal of becoming a starship captain. As her female captain provides her with an example of living an apparently unmarried and aloof life as a starship commander, Carmen Ibanez (Denise Richards) realizes that she will have to pay what a man would not have to pay for the privilege of rank. Basinger reminds us of this distinction:

> When women hold these occupations [those reserved for men], they encounter grief for being in them. They are told [as in *Courage under Fire*] by characters in the movie that these jobs are not appropriate women's work. Even though

these movies show the woman doing the man's job, and thus provide covert
liberation through depiction, their plots are strongly geared toward taking the
woman out of such jobs for antifeminist reasons. (1993, 452)

In the three *Starship Troopers* sci-fi war films, women appear to have
complete parity with men enlisted in Federation service. In training, men and
women work together, room together in a common dorm and even take
showers together! In the initial film, by virtue of her superior ability in math
at school, Carmen gets the chance to train at fleet academy and become a
starship officer. Johnny Rico (Casper Van Dien), her boyfriend at school,
also enlists. But he is subpar in academics and is assigned, essentially, to be a
riflemen in the federal infantry, a futuristic form of the Marines. As a pilot,
Carmen serves under another female and role model, Captain Deladier
(Brenda Strong), commander of the starship *Rodger Young*. At the end of the
first *Troopers* picture, after Deladier's death, Carmen, outstanding at her job
and also due to heroism in battle, is promoted and, despite her youth, gets to
command her own starship.

However, sexism in this futuristic military organization is not entirely
absent. Rico has just been given a field promotion, and in his first command
decision, he favors an unqualified male over a more qualified woman. Earlier
in the film, Rico witnesses squad leader Pvt. Ace Levy (Jake Busey), flus-
tered in the ferocity of battle, unable to make important decisions. But when
Rico, just promoted from sergeant to lieutenant, must appoint his own suc-
cessor, instead of choosing the more qualified woman, "Dizzy" Flores (Dina
Meyer), he first asks Levy if he wants the job. Levy, wisely knowing his own
limitations, passes on the promotion, citing his inability to command under
stress. Only then does Rico offer the job to Dizzy. Like Master Chief Urgayle, Rico cannot set aside Dizzy's femaleness and assess her abilities fairly. To make matters worse, Rico *knew* that Dizzy would be an excellent
choice to command troops. Earlier in the film, we see the tough, quick-
thinking Dizzy playing quarterback of Rico's arena football team at school.
A leader, Dizzy shouts out orders, selects plays, and leads her team—com-
posed otherwise entirely of men—to victory. After graduation, she is offered
the chance to become a professional football player, but instead, since she is
in love with Rico, follows him into the infantry. During basic training, Dizzy
shows her leadership abilities during training exercises. She conjures up
"plays" (tactics based on football) and feeds them to Rico, who executes
them with the team and then earns all the credit, including promotion to
squad leader. Although Dizzy and Rico finally become lovers, in an enemy
ambush, she heroically sacrifices her life to provide covering fire so the rest
of her troops—including her beloved Rico—can escape overwhelming enemy odds.

In *Starship Troopers 2: Hero of the Federation*, a platoon of Federation soldiers survives a massacre and holds up with a Federation general (Ed Lauter) in an installation that resembles a horror film castle more than a Federation outpost. In this derivative iteration on the old *Ten Little Indians* plot, we begin with a platoon of troopers and end up with only one survivor. But in this film, the roles of two women soldiers stand out: Pvt. Lei Sahara (Colleen Porch) and Sgt. Dede Rake, again portrayed by Brenda Strong. In the initial battle scenes, Sgt. Rake, a by-the-book noncom, is stuck with obeying orders from the incompetent Lt. Dill (Lawrence Monoson), who seems to have been absent during officers' training when the subject of organizing defense perimeters was taught. Rake, a consummate professional, is unable to get Dill to listen to her sound advice. As a result, a number of troopers are killed.

Later in the film, we learn that the enemy bugs have developed a new way to combat their human enemies. Since there are no new ideas in this screenplay, screenwriter Edward Neumeier uses a variation on the tired, old sci-fi/horror "pod people" story, in which a person is inhabited by a bug that takes him or her over and makes the victim do its bidding. The enemy's plan, which they carry out well, is to inhabit the general and as many troopers as they can, and when the troopers and the general are rescued and returned to Earth, they can infiltrate the highest levels of the Federation, inhabiting more senior officers and as many other human leaders as possible.

Since the first *Starship Troopers* film, we have learned that the Federation has discovered the value of psychics to the intelligence service, and many units, including this stranded outfit, have one. The psychic, Pvt. Sahara, touches one of the bug-possessed troopers and her vision tells her that this trooper is controlled by the enemy. Sahara reports the possessions to Rake, but the doubting noncom, prejudiced against psychics, doesn't believe her. Thus the usual horror plot convention continues, guaranteeing that since no one believes Sahara, more troopers will be possessed and the situation will worsen before the real threat is uncovered. When Sahara reports the infestation to Lt. Dill, he believes her, but when he tries to do something about it, he is killed.

Finally, after killing off a number of bug-infested troopers, only three remain alive to be rescued, Sahara, the possessed general, and Capt. Dax (Richard Burgi). Dax was already under arrest for killing his colonel, who, like the lieutenant, was responsible for the unnecessary deaths of a number of Dax's men. In the climax, Dax and Saraha end up bravely fighting off swarms of bugs on the roof of the castle, waiting for an airborne rescue. To avoid infesting Earth with bug-possessed humans, Dax kills the general, and since he thinks that he will go to jail for shooting two senior officers, he decides to stay. He fights a delaying effort against the enemy, allowing Sahara to escape with the news of this most recent bug threat. What Dax didn't realize was that the ever-present propaganda arm of the Federation, always looking for good P.R., turns him posthumously—and Sahara—into Federation heroes.

In the third iteration of this film series, *Starship Troopers 3: Marauder*, Johnny Rico is back, now a famous hero with the rank of colonel, again leading his "roughneck" infantrymen in battle. In this film, the *Troopers* story is getting old, as Neumeier, now both writer and director, rehashes old themes and borrows from other combat scenes in earlier movies. But through all the bad writing, there are two very different and interesting female roles to explore. The first is another starship captain, Lola Beck (Jolene Blalock), whose spacecraft is assigned to transport the Federation's Sky Marshal Anoke (Stephen Hogan) to a planet named Roko San. After a bug attack on this planet, Beck assists Anoke in escaping the planet, but her vessel is shot down by the bugs. Now Beck must lead a ragtag group of people, most of whom are inexperienced in survival tactics or combat, plus Anoke, through a peril-filled wasteland inhabited by bugs. Beck proves to be not only a talented starship pilot but also a soldier capable of clever infantry tactics and courage under fire.

The other interesting female role is Admiral Enolo Phid (Amanda Donohoe), second in command of Federation forces. Throughout the film, the scheming admiral appears to be one of the villains of the film, as she plots to overthrow and succeed Sky Marshal Anoke, thus becoming the most powerful military leader in the Federation. But in this warped, fascist universe, Phid ends up a hero, because as Neumeier's plot would have it, Anoke is possessed by a super-powerful "brain bug," which forces the sky marshal to commit sabotage against the Federation. With Phid's and Beck's assistance, Johnny Rico and his roughnecks attack and destroy the brain bug and his cohort with new weapons, called "Marauders," giant bipedal robotic walkers borrowed artlessly (and shamelessly) from various combat walker models in the six *Star Wars* films and scores of video games.

Star Trek Women Commanders

Mixed genre science fiction/war films have consistently created roles in which females command men. Basinger would remind us that such films reinforce the proposition that women are quite capable of doing an excellent job in the captain's chair. Frequently discussed in this regard is Captain Kathryn Janeway of the starship *Voyager*, the most famous of literally dozens of female starship commanders in the *Star Trek* universe of television series and feature films. On her own in the Delta Quadrant, thousands of light years away from second-guessing male superiors in Star Fleet, Capt. Janeway handles things—including situations of mortal combat—as well as any male. And like many other women in command, she often finds herself in situations in which she must stifle her female side and act more like John Wayne. Shortly after she cleverly uses a Borg transwarp conduit (whatever that is) to return the *Voyager* safely to Earth, she is promoted to the rank of admiral. In her "Bio-psychological profile," StarTrek.com describes her this way:

> Janeway is a tough captain who is not afraid to take chances, while her intelligence, thoughtfulness, dedication and diplomacy have earned her respect and recognition as one of the best in Starfleet. Her talents in engineering and science allow her hands-on expertise, if necessary; as such she has shown a tendency to defy the Starfleet protocol against beam-down of commanding officers into unsecured away team missions. She prefers to be addressed as "Captain" rather than either the gender-based "sir" or "ma'am."

Zoë and River

In the science fiction/war film *Serenity* and in the short-lived Fox TV series *Firefly*, four women on board a spaceship provide audiences with three very different roles. Inara Serra (Morena Baccarin) is a prostitute, but in this futuristic era, much of the stigma of the "whore" seems to have been removed in the way Inara practices her profession. In this futuristic universe, prostitution has become a sisterhood full of ritual and ceremony, more similar in training, qualification, and practice to the Japanese geisha than to the typical American call girl. There is great sexual tension and attraction between Inara and *Serenity*'s captain, Mal Reynolds (Nathan Fillion), but Mal can never mentally put Inara's profession aside and deal with her simply as a man and a woman.

Kaylee Frye, a "country girl" from a frontier planet, has a genius for engineering, and signed on to *Serenity* to keep the old and rickety spaceship aloft as its chief engineer. Unsophisticated and sometimes embarrassingly honest, the delightfully youthful almost-Madonna Kaylee often provides audiences with their own take on circumstances. A hopeless romantic, Kaylee is always rooting for the sparks to fly between Mal and Inara. Kaylee herself is head over heels in lust for Simon, a passenger/doctor/crewmember on board *Serenity*. At one point, Kaylee's frankness and honesty in discussing sex spills into a conversation, to traditionalist Mal's embarrassment. Explaining that she, too, needs some loving, Kaylee blurts out, "Goin' on a year now I ain't had nothin' 'twixt my nethers weren't run on batteries!"

A woman known only by "Zoë" is the second-in-command and extremely capable right fist of Mal. Zoë (Gina Torres), a skilled professional soldier, served alongside Mal in an ultimately futile war for independence waged by colonists from many planets against a huge combination of commercial concerns and governments known as the Alliance. Later, when Mal acquired the cargo ship *Serenity*, Zoë followed him into the postwar soldier-of-fortune/

smuggler business. Having come out on the losing side of the war, Mal, Zoë, and the rest of the crew try to make a living while staying one step ahead, and out of the gun sights, of the malevolent Alliance. Superior to Mal in a fight, Zoë is portrayed as both Mal's WEPS (weapons officer) and as a universal soldier. Fiercely loyal to Mal, Zoë always has his back. Typically, she does so in a subtle way until needed. In the middle of one kerfuffle, when Mal begins to look like he may need assistance, producer-director Joss Whedon cuts to Zoë, fingering the handle of the pistol on her hip, preparing to intervene. In another scene, Mal realizes that Inara is in the hands of an agent of the Alliance and he must rescue her. He also realizes, as he tells Kaylee, that he just had a reasonably long conversation with Inara without it turning into an argument, so he knows that if he goes there, he'll be heading into a trap. Typical for Mal, he tells Zoë that if he doesn't come back to the ship within an hour, she should come and rescue him. Always the military tactician, Zoë responds, "And risk the ship?" But Mal, concerned more for his safety than the ship's, offhandedly quips, "It's mighty cold out there."

As a woman, after any battle is over, Zoë finds time to dial back the soldier side of her personality and act female. She has married *Serenity*'s highly skilled pilot, Hoban "Wash" Washburn (Alan Tudyk). Wash and Zoë make an interesting pair, but Wash, always the comedian, makes life around him lively. For example, at one point, he tells Mal, "This landing is gonna get pretty interesting." Mal asks, "Define 'interesting.'" Wash responds, in a deadpan manner, "Oh, God, Oh, God, we're all going to die." Or, on another occasion, Mal orders him to "Just get us on the ground." "That part'll happen pretty definitely," Wash snarks back. But Wash leaves most of the sarcasm for the captain, and concentrates his unwavering affection on Zoë. And when Zoë lets down her soldierly pose for a moment, her love for *Serenity*'s pilot is evident.

Sgt. Jayne Cobb (Adam Baldwin), a soldier of fortune of doubtful morality who signed on to *Serenity* to add his gun to Zoë's when fighting situations arise, is more concerned about money than people, although his occasional benevolent actions surprise and shock everyone on board the ship. But at one point of contention, removing River Tam (Summer Glau), a fugitive being pursued by the Alliance, from the ship, Jayne is insistently arguing with Mal. Mal knows that River is a victim of the Alliance, and just can't see himself abandoning her to sure death if the Alliance ever lays hands on her. In a shouting match, Jayne is insistent, and the altercation is probably heading toward a gunfight. But Zoë intervenes in the most threatening manner she does in the entire film as she fingers her sidearm and eyeballs Jayne, saying, "You want to *leave* this room?" The firmness and finality with which Zoë confronts this fierce soldier makes it clear that she'll be drawing down on him any second and that he will die. Showing his respect and outright fear of

Zoë's combat abilities, Jayne emphatically says, "Damn right I do," and quickly exits.

Although Jayne and Zoë can handle themselves in a fight, the abilities of another female character dwarf them both. Because the Alliance discovered the superior psychic abilities of River Tam, she was kidnapped from her family as a child and put through traumatic medical treatments and psychological conditioning that turned her into a super-warrior. When motivated, River becomes a one-woman combat unit capable of killing dozens of bigger, stronger, better-armed male opponents. In this way, River takes on the attributes of a number of male "GI Joes" and becomes almost a superhero in abilities. In a bar, she shows her prowess by dispatching dozens of larger, stronger, and presumably well-trained male combatants. When Jayne, a much larger, muscled soldier, takes it upon himself to single-handedly remove River from *Serenity*, the diminutive "ninety-pound girl" displays greatly superior hand-to-hand skills and knocks him silly. Later, in the film's climax, Zoë leads the crew in fighting a rearguard action against the particularly savage and psychotic beings known as Reavers while Mal fights his way to a transmitter to broadcast to the galaxy a terrible secret that the Alliance has been trying to cover up. During the battle, River, using swords, hand-to-hand prowess, and psychic skills, single-handedly slaughters dozens of Reavers. In the epilogue, Wash having died in the battle, River also takes on the role of *Serenity*'s pilot and surprises Mal with her skill at the controls.

Although the above women of sci-fi, Angel, Carmen, Kathryn, Zoë, and River became GI Jane–type soldiers or leaders of men in combat in their respective universes, it's important to remember the earlier prototypes on whom many of these more recently created characters draw their strength and ability to compete in a world of men. These proto–GI Janes are Ellen Ripley in the Alien series of films as well as a crewmember named Vasquez in the one combat film among the four, *Aliens*, the second in the series (which we'll focus on here), and Sarah Connor in the Terminator films and spinoff television series. Interestingly, neither Ripley nor Connor, either by training, temperament, or ambition, begins as a soldier.

Ripley

In the original film of the series, *Alien* (1979), Ellen Ripley (Sigourney Weaver) is a commercial flight officer on a futuristic ore-carrying space vessel called the *Nostromo*. She is essentially the *Nostromo*'s third officer, in line behind two men. Ripley and all her fellow crewmembers will encounter the alien monster whose menace will subsequently dominate her life.

In *Alien*, essentially a gothic horror film set within the confines of a spaceship, the crew is picked off, one by one, by the monster. Finally Ripley is the only surviving human. Her plan is to set the auto-destruct device on the

Nostromo and escape in the vessel's shuttlecraft, thus killing the alien. Unfortunately, unknown to Ripley, the monster has concealed itself on board her shuttlecraft. After the *Nostromo* is destroyed, Ripley discovers her stowaway and must do battle with the monster. She succeeds by ejecting the creature out of the shuttlecraft's airlock and finishing it off by burning it with a blast from the ship's engines. Then Ripley puts herself into hypersleep for the journey back to Earth, but the vessel misses its home target and drifts for fifty-seven years with Ripley in suspended animation on board. After her shuttlecraft is recovered by a salvage vessel, Ripley finds herself back on Earth, relating a story about the doomed *Nostromo* that no one believes. Thus the story of the sequel, *Aliens* (1986), written and directed by *The Terminator*'s James Cameron, begins. Advertised with the logline, "This time it's war," *Aliens* is actually an allegory of the United States' hubris in its conduct of the Vietnam War. *Aliens* relates how Ripley is persuaded to sign on as a "consultant" to a colonial Marine expedition that will return to the planet where the *Nostromo* picked up the first alien monster. Why? During the fifty-seven years since Ripley's crew set down on the planet, Earth people had begun terra-forming (creating a breathable atmosphere) and colonizing this planet. But the colonists have abruptly quit responding to radio communication, and Earth authorities finally begin to wonder whether Ripley's incredible story of monsters might be true.

The Marine platoon is led by a relatively inexperienced officer, Lt. Gorman (William Hope) and the older Platoon Sergeant Apone (Al Matthews), whose advice the officer, of course, never heeds. Neither does Gorman listen to Ripley's admonitions. The Marine platoon is made up of the usual compliment of griping jarheads, who have had some experience on other planets protecting Earth colonists against aggressive alien species. But what they call "bug hunts" does not prepare the Marines for the fight of their lives against this particularly bellicose species of extraterrestrial. No amount of caution Ripley advises is heeded, as hubris rules the day.

Part of the problem is that, at first, Ripley is considered an outsider, an amateur, and a non-GI female, so in the minds of both the male and even the female Marines she's just another "colonist's daughter" or other helpless Madonna they usually are assigned to save but not take seriously. One Marine describes her as "Snow White," and another quips that Ripley is along on this mission "because she saw an alien once." Ripley doesn't help herself when Lt. Gorman asks her to address the Marines about the kind of enemy they will face. She starts and stops and repeats herself in a disorganized discourse, interrupted by one arrogant female Marine who just wants to know where they are so she can shoot them. Ripley hasn't learned yet that these Marines respond to football coach–style oversimplified messages laced with fight metaphors such as those provided by Sgt. Apone. Later, after Ripley assumes leadership of the surviving Marines, she will adopt Apone's macho/coach's style.

As in Vietnam, the Marines assume that because they are armed with their advanced weaponry, they can "kick ass" against any enemy they encounter. But like the Viet Cong, the aliens don't come out and fight the Marines in the open. Instead, lying in wait in the dark subterranean recesses of the terraforming facility, the enemy will use concealment and surprise to swoop down from the ceilings and overcome the Marines before they see them. As one Marine, Hudson (Bill Paxton), reports, "They're coming outta the walls! They coming outta the goddam walls! Let's book!" Soon it is obvious that despite all their technology, firepower, and training, the Marines are no match for the swarms of aliens arrayed against them. After their first incursion into the alien hive, most of the Marines are either dead or swept up by the monsters and impregnated with alien embryos, helpless live cocoons to breed more aliens.

Ripley, empowered, yells at Lt. Gorman to get the surviving marines out of the hive, but the panicked young officer just becomes more helpless. Finally, Ripley, never one to suffer fools lightly, is out of patience and takes charge. She drives the attack vehicle through an alien-constructed wall of organic material to provide the now cut-off Marine survivors a way out. During this escape, the vehicle encounters more aliens, but Ripley just runs them over. In the process, Gorman hits his head and suffers a concussion. By the time Gorman awakens, Ripley, with the help and co-leadership of Cpl. Hicks (Michael Biehn) has effectively taken charge of the operation and gives most of the orders.

Finally, the surviving and now grateful Marines listen carefully to Ripley's advice. They cannot expect help from Earth in time. When Hudson, the platoon's electronics specialist, panics over the situation, Ripley begins to bark orders like Sgt. Apone with her new, tough approach: "You better just start dealing with it, Hudson! Listen to me! Hudson, just deal with it because we need you and I'm sick of your bullshit!" Used to listening to harsh language from his superiors, Hudson, just a follower, focuses, gets to work, and quits complaining as much.

Cut off from the Marine combat vessel orbiting around the planet because the aliens have also attacked and destroyed the Marines' shuttlecraft, Ripley and the Marines' plan is to contact the vessel by computer uplink and remotely launch another shuttle drop vehicle from the ship to rescue them and to "nuke" the entire facility from orbit. Complications arise, including the discovery of the only surviving colonist, a little girl named Newt (Carrie Henn).

However, getting the shuttle down to the surface will take time, and the aliens are not content to wait patiently for the humans to depart. The survivors must use all available resources to defend themselves while they wait for the shuttle to arrive. Using a blueprint of the facility and taking inventory of their remaining firepower, Ripley advises Hicks how they should set up their fortifications and defense weapons. Impressed, Hicks says "Outstanding. . . . We've got a purpose . . . now all we need is a deck of cards." Finally, the aliens attack the facility. In the ensuing firefight, all but one Marine are killed, and Ripley and little Newt become separated. Ripley, in full combat mode by this time, still displays affection and protectiveness for the little girl. In later director's cuts of *Aliens*, audiences discover that in the storyline of the original *Alien*, Ripley had an eleven-year-old daughter whom she left behind on Earth for a journey that was to be only a few months. When she was rescued in suspended animation fifty-seven years later, her daughter had already lived her life and had died. This helps to explain Ripley's sad, motherly affection for Newt.

Ripley and Hicks cannot find Newt, who has been captured by the aliens and taken to their hive where she will be impregnated with an alien embryo and will serve as a human cocoon like the others, until the gestated monster bursts from her chest, killing her. Ripley; Hicks (who has by this time become injured); and Bishop, the android (Lance Henriksen), can escape on the attack shuttlecraft and execute their plan for the facility and the hive to be "nuked," but Ripley will have none of it. Armed to the teeth and determined to invade the hive and rescue Newt, Ripley bravely goes back alone. Along the way she fights off many aliens, including a fourteen-foot-tall, highly enraged alien queen.

Earlier they discovered that the atomic reactor that powers the facility has been damaged and is melting down, which will effectively "nuke" the entire area without the aid of the Marine's attack shuttlecraft. As Bishop explains, "In nineteen minutes, this area's gonna be a cloud of vapor the size of Nebraska." But Ripley and Newt make it back to the ship and take off with just seconds to spare. Unfortunately, as occurred in the first movie of the Alien series, an alien, this time the highly resourceful giant queen manages to hitch a ride on the shuttlecraft back up to the mother ship. This precipitates the famous scene in which Ripley, now equal in strength to the alien queen inside a large, motorized exosuit called a power loader, does "hand-to-hand" battle with the monster. Ripley's oft-quoted line, which precipitates this encounter, challenges the queen to a fight, distracting her from pursuing Newt: "Get away from her, you bitch!"

Ripley uses the same tactic she had employed in *Alien*, battling the queen into an airlock and then expelling the monster out into space. Once again, the film ends as the survivors go into suspended animation for the long voyage home.

Sigourney Weaver, decked out as Ripley the warrior before she assaults the hive to rescue Newt, was featured on the covers of national magazines that year, dubbed a "Rambette," or female counterpart to Sylvester Stallone's iconic warrior, John Rambo. Critic and producer Richard Schickel agrees with Basinger's statement quoted earlier as he writes about Ripley in an essay in *Time* magazine,

> Yet all this splendid craftsmanship, popular moviemaking at its best, is in the service of building rooting interest in the story of a woman who keeps finding ways to transcend the limits that unexamined custom often imposes on her sex. In action pictures, women are supposed to swoon or retreat to a safe corner (or, at best, praise the lord and pass the ammunition) while the male lead protects them and defends Western civilization as we know it. In *Aliens*, it's the guys who are all out of action at the climax and Ripley who is in a death duel with evil. (1986, 3)

Vasquez

As a civilian advisor in *Aliens*, Ripley has a much more difficult time fitting in with the Marines than if she were a member of the "club" like one of the three female colonial Marines in the story. One woman is the pilot of the assault shuttlecraft and contributes little besides maintaining a derisive attitude toward civilian Ripley. Another woman serves alongside the men, rifle in hand, but is killed early in the film without uttering anything significant besides her death scream. But the other female character is singled out in the screenplay for her toughness and unwillingness to accept anything besides parity with male Marines. Having much in common with the persona O'Neil displayed around the other SEALS in *G.I. Jane*, she is known simply as Vasquez, one of the two Marines in the platoon chosen to heft a much heavier and larger-caliber weapon than the standard pulse rifles the rest of the men carry. Actress Jenette Goldstein was cast for the role for a number of good reasons, including her acting ability, but also because she could show off some rippling biceps, since she was a body builder.

As soon as the Marines arrive in orbit around the alien planet and are awakened from hypersleep, while other Marines are moaning and complaining about the hangover-like aftereffects of spending months sleeping in a suspended animation tube, we see Vasquez doing chin-ups on a handy horizontal bar alongside her combat soul mate and fellow heavy rifle carrier, Drake (Mark Rolston). It is obvious from the start that the two have more than a professional relationship. Demonstrating Vasquez's toughness, when Pvt. Hudson spies Vasquez's bulging biceps flexing as she exercises, he quips, "Hey, Vasquez: Have you ever been mistaken for a man?" She quickly retorts, "No. Have you?" Drake laughs, bumps fists with Vasquez and says, admiringly, "You're bad!"

When someone with a sure trigger finger and a courageous attitude is needed to go on point (the person who bravely precedes the rest of the squad into an unsecured area), Sgt. Apone calls on Vasquez. Vasquez is a no-

nonsense pro, every bit as *macho* as the men. She is intolerant of the platoon's inexperienced and (in her mind) cowardly Lt. Gorman, who uses video technology to order his people into danger while he stays behind in relative safety in the assault vehicle watching a bank of video monitors and giving orders through a radio headset. At one point, after the Marines sweep an unknown but deserted area inside the facility, Gorman announces over the radio that the area is secure and he's coming in. Disgusted that Gorman doesn't lead the platoon from the front, Vasquez turns to Drake and calls Gorman the Spanish word, *pendejo* (stupid or irresponsible). But toward the end of the film, as Ripley, Newt, and the surviving Marines attempt an escape from the facility, Vasquez becomes wounded and falls behind the rest. Gorman tells the others to go on while he goes back for Vasquez, and together (although to the very end she still calls him an asshole) the two unlikely heroes fight a murderous delaying action against overwhelming swarms of aliens. Finally out of ammunition and about to be killed by the monsters, the two overlap hands as they grab a high powered grenade and detonate it, killing themselves along with scores of aliens.

The Terminator

The Terminator film series chronicles an apocalyptic war between machines and men, precipitated when Skynet, the United States' master computer, becomes self-aware, takes control of all machines on Earth, and turns on its human creators, using the U.S. arsenal of atomic weapons to destroy most of humankind. In the initial film of the series, in 1984, Sarah Connor (Linda Hamilton) was the total opposite of a GI Jane. She was a young waitress, more concerned with her hair, clothes, makeup, young men, and where she was going out dancing and drinking on Friday night than with almost single-handedly saving the human race from annihilation. But Sarah is the unknowing future mother of John Connor, who, with Sarah's help and training, would lead humankind back from the brink of extinction to organize a resistance force against the robot rulers of Earth. In this initial Terminator movie, the machines have realized that they are losing the war of resistance to their human opponents, and that this human military force has been organized and led by John Connor. Creatively for a bunch of computers, the machines send one of their own, a nearly indestructible "Terminator" model human cyborg (Arnold Schwarzenegger), back in time to kill Sarah, preventing John from ever being born, thus depriving humans of their great leader. Like Ripley, Sarah at first is not prepared or even willing to become a combatant, but, like Ripley, Sarah learns quickly. By the sequel, *Terminator 2* (1991), Sarah's character arc has changed significantly. Although somewhat mentally unbalanced by this time, Sarah has become a skillful soldier and survivalist, much more highly skilled in war—especially guerilla war—than Ripley. In *T-2*, we learn what Sarah has done in the fourteen years between son John's birth and the present. Sarah spent time in Mexico and in the desert of the American Southwest, associating with survivalists and paramilitary types, sometimes sleeping with such men so she could learn all she could from them—many of whom being disillusioned veterans—about guns, explosives, combat tactics, and "living off the grid." Then, Sarah would teach what she learned to her son. We learn in *T-2* that Sarah has many friends off the grid, and has even cached weapons, ammunition, and other munitions in these wastelands, all in preparation for the time when humans mistakenly give machines control of atomic weapons and the machines turn on them and use these weapons in a war to eradicate mankind. In *T-2*, trying to use the machines' tactics and hopeful she can perhaps reverse the course of history by keeping human computer experts from ever creating Skynet in the first place, she stages a one-woman commando raid on the home of the scientist responsible for developing this master computer.

Although Sarah dies of cancer before the third Terminator movie, *Terminator 3: The Rise of the Machines* (2003), Sarah's martial preparedness and presence are still felt: In one scene, her son, John; his wife-to-be; plus a "good terminator" cyborg, again played by Schwarzenegger, raid a cemetery mausoleum to disinter what apparently was Sarah's coffin. But the coffin, instead of containing Sarah's remains, has been stocked full of weapons, cached in this safe place for John's use.

In 2008–2009, the Terminator films were morphed into a Fox Network television series and inserted into the time line between films *Terminator 2* and *Terminator 3*. In this series, called *Terminator: The Sarah Connor Chronicles*, Sarah (Lena Headey); her high school–age son, John (Thomas Dekker); and another good-guy terminator called Cameron—ironically played by *Serenity*'s Summer Glau—continue to try to prevent the creation of Skynet.

Battle: Los Angeles

Although not necessarily trained to be a rough, tough Marine like Vasquez, another Rambette-type GI Jane stands out in a much more "realistic" sci-fi/war genre film. In *Battle: Los Angeles* (2011), Elena Santos (Michelle Rodriguez) is actually a U.S. Air Force Technical Sergeant, an expert in electronics and communications. In this film, she will contribute her technical expertise to the mission, but also demonstrate her kick-ass sisterhood with the scrappy Vasquez of *Aliens*.

In this film, set in downtown Los Angeles to create a highly believable setting for an alien invasion film, a U.S. Marine recon platoon led by SSgt. Michael Nantz (Aaron Eckhart) joins thousands of other Army, Marine, and Air Force fighters defending the city from an invasion of alien troops. The platoon's initial mission is to rescue civilians hiding in a police station in an area behind enemy lines. Fighting their way, city block by city block, to their objective against a much stronger alien army, some of Nantz's men are killed or wounded. At one point, Nantz and his surviving men come across four non-Marine soldiers, including TSgt. Santos. At first Nantz and his men don't know what to make of her, and treat her like the colonial Marines treated Ripley. They doubt if this "zoomie" (slang for Air Force) chick is going to be more than just one more burdensome "civilian," like the people they were assigned to rescue. Marines would say that the Air Force doesn't really train their personnel to be fighters as much as technicians and button-pushers, and thus, as the macho men of the U.S. armed forces, Marines look down their noses at zoomies. Nantz points to her weapon and asks Santos whether she knows how to use it. But she is having none of this nonsense. Offended, she barks back, "I didn't get to where I am on my good looks. I'm ready for some payback (for her dead USAF buddies), sergeant." Nantz likes her attitude, at least.

When they reach the civilians at the police station, one of them volunteers to examine the body of an alien that the Marines have killed. Santos shows she doesn't mind a little gore and guts by helping out with this ad hoc autopsy. Together they find an area on the alien's chest that is a good "kill spot." From now on, everyone will aim for this spot, because the rest of the alien's bodies seem impervious, covered with thick armor. Santos continues to impress the Marines when later, in a firefight with the aliens, she muscles her way in beside two Marines, saying, "You need another gun." Skillfully firing, she kills the leading alien soldier. "Hell, you can take all the room you need," one Marine responds happily.

Later, rescue mission accomplished, the few survivors of the Marine platoon and Santos catch a ride on a chopper behind the battle lines, to a place of relative safety. Along the way, Nantz and Santos spy what they think may be part of an alien command and control (C and C) center, vital to operating the hundreds of alien drone attack airships providing the aliens an edge against American forces throughout the city. Rather than remain in the rear, Nantz decides to go look for the C and C center alone. But the rest of Nantz's squad, including Santos, are having none of that and join him. This is where Santos's Air Force training adds something to Nantz's recon squad besides her skill with a rifle. Using her electronic training, Santos helps Nantz locate the C and C center. And during this portion of their recon mission, Santos ends up in a hand-to-hand fight with a much larger, armored alien soldier. Undeterred, channeling Vasquez in *Aliens*, Santos bayonets him, then shoots off a couple of rounds into him. When the alien finally falls, she kicks him in the head, yelling, "Sonofabitch! (then sarcastically) 'That hurt?" Then, while Nantz is using a laser to "paint" (pinpoint) the C and C center for an Air

Force rocket attack, Santos takes out an alien drone attacking Nantz's position.

Finally extracted and back at the base in the rear, Nantz and the squad are congratulated and offered some downtime for sleep and food. But again, the Marines and Santos are not willing to sit out the fight. The Marines and one rough, tough GI Jane jump on board the nearest chopper heading back to the action in the fight to retake L.A.

Lara Croft as "Butt-Kicking Babe"

Although the Lara Croft pictures are not of the war film genre, they remain the action-adventure equivalent, and represent an entire class of films that feature women adventurers as sole protagonists. This class of films exploits sex as well as violence to attract their audiences. It is rare when reviewers and critics discuss the modern female action hero in any genre and do not bring up Angelina Jolie's roles in *Tomb Raider* (2001) and *Lara Croft Tomb Raider: The Cradle of Life* (2003). For example, when *Tomb Raider* was released, Mary Spicuzza (2001) wrote on *Alternet*, "Jolie's sex-kitten Croft in *Tomb Raider* . . . leaps into action as the latest addition to an undeniable trend in the evolution of today's action hero, the butt-kicking babe." In these films, Jolie indeed is cast as an action protagonist, but as Benshoff and Griffin (2009) remind us, to keep male audience members' eyes on the screen, Jolie does it "in skimpy and fetishistic clothing. . . . This does not liberate women: They are still sex objects vying for objectives in a game in which men make the rules and women play by them" (300). Spicuzza (2001) adds, "Critics say the trouble is [that] plenty of butt-kicking women on the screen are ultimately most concerned with being sexy, finding a man who can make their lives complete, and settling down. They say that women heroines are less concerned with female liberation than satisfying male fantasy."

FEMALE RESISTANCE FIGHTERS

In war films, there have always been women, both in and out of uniform, who find a way to do their bit in the fight for truth, right, and justice. Although like Dorinda in *A Guy Named Joe*, they are often not always allowed to enlist in the army to fight, they still find ways to serve. Many of these women are portrayed in the subgenre of the war film called the "occupied countries" films. In a film that has many reverse parallels with the U.S. occupation of Iraq, *The Moon Is Down* (1943) chronicles a fictional story of the Nazi occupation of a town in Norway. At first, the Nazis and the townspeople try to make the best of a bad situation, but when it is obvious that peaceful coexistence with the Germans is impossible, a resistance movement

forms, and little-by-little nearly the entire town sets itself against the inter-
lopers. As sabotage and the killing of German soldiers rises (including some
by women who pretend to be romantically interested in Germans, only to kill
them when they are alone in an intimate setting), so do the inevitable Nazi
reprisals. Similarly, a generation later in the 1979 film, *Hanover Street*, a
French farm girl (Suzanne Bertish) pretends to be attracted to a German
officer. She lures him into her barn, kisses him and pretends she wants to
make love. Instead, she shoots him. We later learn that the Germans killed
her brother, and that the systematic extermination of overly amorous German
officers is her way to aid the resistance movement.

As mentioned earlier, in *Edge of Darkness*, when the German commandant allows his soldiers to act "normally," that is, to resume acting like the
thugs they are and mistreat the people of the Norwegian fishing village with
no restraints, one woman is raped and her father ferrets out and shoots the
offending Nazi. In reprisal, the Germans plan to hang suspected resistance
leaders in the town square. But, as often happens—especially in the propa-
ganda-saturated American war films made during World War II—the heroic
Norwegian citizenry rise up. Both men *and* women (including one white-
haired grandmother), with weapons provided in secret by the British, attack
the Nazis, and wipe out their entire garrison.

Character Arc in Occupied Countries War Films

At first, in some occupied countries films, some women are not sympathetic
enough to pitch in to aid the Allied cause. Although other women in films
made during World War II are initially committed to resistance or at least
lined up opposed to their occupiers, many Hollywood screenwriters chose to
develop a character arc in which Madonnas who are either noncommittal or
even opposed to the resistance jump off the fence and join the fight. Usually
this broad character arc is in response to the despicable deeds of the occupiers, but sometimes, as in *Joan of Paris* (1942), change occurs after meeting
an Allied soldier or flyer. In this film, Joan (Michelle Morgan) is a waitress
in occupied Paris who has a chance encounter with a group of downed RAF
pilots, and meets the dashing Free French flyer, Paul Lavallier (Paul Henreid). The flyers, one of whom is badly wounded, are in need of help, shelter,
and contact with the French Resistance, who then can make arrangements to
transport them back to England.

The Gestapo is on the flyers' trail, and desperately wants to capture them.
Since they are wearing civilian clothes as a disguise, the Gestapo plans to
shoot them all as spies. While Joan helps with arrangements to evacuate
these flyers, she is found out and arrested by the Gestapo, and brought before
crafty Herr Funk (Laird Cregar). But Funk wants more than just to nab a
waitress, and makes a deal with Joan to spare Paul's life if she will lead them

to the other flyers. Instead, Joan leads the Germans on a wild goose chase, allowing all the flyers to escape. For this, Joan faces a Gestapo firing squad.

Similarly, in *Tonight We Raid Calais* (1943), Odette (Annabella) actually hates the Allies because her brother, forced to fight for the Vichy French, died fighting the British. But eventually, she becomes yet another woman living in occupied French territory who learns about German treachery. Odette had agreed to help the Germans in return for their sparing her parents, whom the Germans arrested for their involvement in the French Resistance. But the Germans execute them anyway. Infuriated, Odette kills a few Germans of her own and assists a group of salty French farm women in the burning of their own wheat fields that surround a secret German munitions factory, lighting the way for an Allied bombing raid. Basinger writes, "Their faces light up in delight as they rampage across the countryside, and in the end, Odette calmly hands [her dead brother's] baby to the hero, who is returning to England. She'll be too busy fighting the war to take care of a child." (1993, 446)

In a twist on this conversion formula, the story of the film *Resistance* (2003) centers less on a woman joining the Resistance than having the Resistance thrust upon her. It's also an illicit love story about a downed American reconnaissance pilot named Maj. Ted Brice (Bill Paxton) and Claire Dussois (Julia Ormond), the wife of an occasional member of the French Resistance during World War II. Although other women in her rural village perform various services for the cause, such as hiding and operating short-wave radios used to communicate with London and, in one case, slitting the throats of a few German soldiers, Claire has not yet done anything to aid Resistance efforts against their German occupiers. She's just married to someone who occasionally lends the Resistance a hand. But all this changes when Brice, injured when his plane crashes, is delivered to her home. Claire and her husband, Henri (Phillipe Volter) hide him from the Germans in a secret room/closet in their farm house. As Brice recovers, he falls in love with Claire, and vice-versa, and a torrid affair begins. Eventually, Henri, a brutish and not too bright fellow, finds out about the affair. Furious and not considering outcomes, Henri betrays Brice to the Germans. In return, the Germans shoot Henri (he was, after all, both a traitorous Resistance member as well as an enemy of the Reich) and torture Brice and Claire for information. Claire refuses to betray the Resistance and eventually, Brice gives the Germans false information in return for Claire's release to the Red Cross.

Dragon Seed

In a culture in which Chinese women were expected to quietly obey their husbands, Katharine Hepburn's portrayal of Jade Tan in *Dragon Seed* (1944) breaks the rules. In an adaptation of the Pearl Buck novel, the intellectually curious Jade first teaches herself to read, a skill not required or even expected of Chinese women. Even though she knows that Jade is different, her old-fashioned mother is surprised when Jade wants to learn to read, since she says that women have no need of an education. Actually, only one person in their village, an old man, is literate. But Jade's father and husband both recognize that she is different, and her husband purchases Jade her great desire, her own book.

When the Japanese invade their valley, Jade joins her brothers to suggest that they must resist. But her father, Ling Tan (Walter Huston), cannot understand the idea of coveting another's land or crops or possessions, and thinks that his family and his neighbors should be able to coexist with invaders. Soon, however, even Ling realizes that when it comes to the murderous, rapacious Japanese, this is impossible. While some members of the family stay on their farm, Jade; her husband, Lao (Turhan Bey); and two brothers travel west to enlist in the Chinese Resistance movement. They return to the valley to help organize local resistance and to make sure that like the Chinese in other Eastern provinces, when harvest time comes, they will destroy their crops, homes and towns to leave nothing behind on which the Japanese can subsist. But this terrible act will take much persuasion.

Meanwhile, their membership in the Resistance has been noticed by their brother-in-law, the venal merchant Wu Lien (Akim Tamiroff). They learn that soon Wu will feather his own collaborationist nest and betray them to the Japanese. The older men argue about what to do, since Wu, after all, is married to Ling's eldest daughter. The young men are away in the west, and will not be back in time to help. But Jade's mother, in a discussion with her daughter, despises Wu and says, simply, "Women must act while men waste time and talk." Jade decides to act, so she walks into town and buys poison from an apothecary. Then she goes to visit Wu, who as a collaborator, for his own safety, now lives with his family in a big house in a Japanese-protected compound. Jade tries, but cannot find the opportunity to poison Wu, who is called away to supervise a Japanese banquet. Jade follows him, but again cannot find any way to kill him. Finally, she pretends she's starving and says she will offer her body to the chief Japanese chef (J. Carroll Naish) in return for food. The chef is looking forward to taking advantage of Jade, but first he must finish the cooking, so he tells Jade to wait. When no one is looking, she dumps the poison into a vat of duck sauce, knowing that all the Japanese officers are looking forward to this, Wu's main dish. Then she escapes. The duck, complete with sauce, is served to the Japanese, who all are sickened and are dying. Before he dies, one officer blames collaborator Wu for the poisoning and shoots him.

After this, as Jade's character arc continues to rise, she finally has the temerity to challenge her father, insisting that they, too, burn their houses and fields. She tells him that half measures in war just prolong the suffering and aid the enemy, and that they must sacrifice if this terrible conflict is ever going to end. This finally has the desired effect, and as an example to the rest, Ling burns his fields and ancestral home. Following Ling, the rest of the farmers in the area do the same. Then they all leave their homes, moving west to what they call "Free China" to grow rice for themselves and to feed the Chinese Resistance, out of reach of the Japanese. Ling and his wife, on their way to these new lands, part company with Jade and Lao, who leave their young son with his grandparents for safety, since Jade and Lao, rifles on their shoulders, will stay on to fight a guerilla war against the invaders.

The Guns of Navarone

No quarter is given to either Allied or German combatants and spies in *The Guns of Navarone*. Two female Greek resistance agents are assigned to work with an Allied commando team sent to the town of Navarone. Their mission is to destroy two giant German artillery guns, strategically mounted within a mountainside cave that cannot be destroyed using traditional bombing attacks. The threat of these guns prevents Allied warships from passing by on their way to assist Allied soldiers on Crete. One Greek resistance fighter, Maria Pappadimos (Irene Papas), is introduced after she sneaks up in the dark and gets the drop on the whole assault team (of men). They were expecting her father, but she explains that the Germans have captured him, and, she quickly adds, "He won't talk." Maria explains that she will replace her father on the mission. At first, the men doubt whether a woman can do the job, but quickly they discover that Maria is a skilled, tough fighter and guide, an asset to their mission.

Coincidentally, one of the Allied team is her own brother, Spiro (James Darren), who has been living in the United States since he was a boy. Maria is at first glad to see him, but then slaps his face. "What did you do that for?" he yelps. "To remind you to write letters occasionally," she replies. He defends his lack of correspondence by arguing, "There happens to be a war on." "I mean, before the war," she interrupts. "I promised myself I would do this when I see you again. I'm sorry, brother." Then they hug. She also introduces Anna (Gia Scala), another resistance agent who has not spoken since she was captured and supposedly tortured by the Germans. Actually, she will turn out to be a double agent working for the enemy. Anna is the reason the Germans always seem to be one step ahead of them, showing up where the team goes next.

Later, during a German air attack, another team member, a native Greek named Andrea (Anthony Quinn) yells out something obscene at the enemy. Then he notices Maria and apologizes for his language. She replies, saying something in Greek that tells Andrea that his language is not a bother. This sparks a relationship between these two freedom fighters that begins as mutual admiration between warriors and grows throughout the movie into affection.

Maria is unflappable. Acting as the team's guide, nothing seems to bother her. This calm continues when the Germans capture the team and they are threatened with execution. But Andrea creates a diversion and the team overcomes their German captors and escapes. Maria drives the team at high speeds over dangerous mountain roads to make good their escape. Demonstrating that women can multitask better than men, as she drives along at a breakneck pace, Maria calmly asks Andrea if he's married. Andrea explains that his wife and children were killed in the war. Next, she asks if he's killed many men. Andrea admits he's killed many, but all were Germans or Italians. This pleases her. She responds simply and firmly, "I like you." Andrea, also pleased, says, "I like you, too." Later, at a hideout, she watches Andrea shave, admires the way he looks cleaned up, and smiles. So does he.

When it is discovered that Anna is actually a traitor working for the Germans, the men argue among themselves whether they should—or could—shoot a woman, regardless of her crime, a scene similar to the one twenty-six years later in *Full Metal Jacket.* The team members wouldn't hesitate to shoot a man in the same situation, but most are squeamish about killing Anna. There is no alternative, because they don't dare tie up Anna and leave her. If she were to escape, she'd betray their entire mission. When the men seem at an impasse over what to do, Maria, the no-nonsense resistance fighter, furious with Anna's betrayal, shoots her, and unlike the Russian woman in *Cross of Iron*, doesn't shed a tear.

Later, after the guns are destroyed and the mission over, Maria steals a motor launch and transports the three surviving team members to a British destroyer, but she tells the team that she won't be coming with them to Crete. "I must go back. . . . Navarone will pay heavily for your success tonight," and it is implied that she will make sure that the Germans pay heavily for any reprisals. Andrea decides to go back with Maria to fight alongside her. The last we see of Andrea and Maria, they're on the launch together, heading back to Navarone, grinning happily at each other.

The Longest Day

Although *The Longest Day* (1962) is a story about thousands of men at war, there is one woman, a French Resistance fighter, who stands out for her brave actions. Interestingly, unlike Maria above, who appears more menacing than sexy, this dedicated Resistance fighter uses her female wiles to fool oversexed/underloved German soldiers. If she wasn't working with the Resistance, you could categorize her role in war films as a spy. But clearly in this film, Janine Boitard (Irina Demick), is talented at her job. Plus, she's a character based on a real person, a sexy civilian-clad soldier for France: The real Janine Boitard is revered to this day as a Resistance heroine of her country.

One of the few women shown in *The Longest Day*, Janine appears to work full time for the Resistance in Caen. In her first scene, the beautiful Janine rides up to a German roadblock on a bicycle, wearing a dress with an alluring split skirt and low-cut across the breasts. She is completely charming and distracting for the two German soldiers who are supposed to be searching a hay wagon that has also just pulled up to the roadblock. But this is a con job set up by the Resistance to get the hay wagon through the roadblock unsearched: Janine arrives at the roadblock right after the hay wagon. When he sees her draw the attention of the Germans away from him, the driver of the hay wagon pesters the Germans to finish with him. The Germans prefer to spend a few moments ogling and talking to the charming, smiling Janine, so they tell the driver that he may go. Janine continues passing the time of day with the Germans, allowing the hay wagon, which actually contains a few downed Allied flyers hiding deep in the hay, to get away.

Later, in a cellar used by the Resistance to stash weapons and radio, and at this time also serving as a temporary hiding place for the flyers, Janine and her fellow Resistance fighters listen to shortwave radio from London for their nightly coded messages. The message, coded for their Resistance unit, will tell them when to strike their assigned targets to sabotage German D-Day defenses. They hear their message and immediately spring into action, grabbing weapons from their hiding places in the cellar and scurrying out. Janine tells the flyers that all the Resistance fighters must go, and that they should remain hidden in the cellar until they return.

Janine's assignment on the night before D-Day is first to go to a drop zone to meet French paratroopers whose assignment is to blow up a German train as it crosses an important bridge. Once again, Janine poses as a distraction for German sentries, walking along the train track near the bridge with her bicycle. One German soldier takes her in one direction while the other spots something he wants to check out on the railroad track. A French paratrooper kills this German with a knife, which alerts the other, who tries to signal the oncoming train to stop. The brave Janine attacks him and they struggle, eventually causing both to fall off the bridge into the water below. The German tries to drown Janine, but one of the paratroopers shoots him. The train full of German reinforcements is demolished.

The Heroes of Telemark

Although many of the GI Jane resistance fighters in World War II are French, women of many countries fought and died to drive the Nazis off their land. They included women in the Norwegian Resistance, as portrayed in the film, *The Heroes of Telemark* (1965). The Anthony Mann film was based on the story of a group of real-life British-trained Norwegians who helped delay Germany's production of heavy water and Nazi development of an atomic bomb.

Initially, Dr. Rolf Pedersen (Kirk Douglas), a physics professor, is alerted to the research the Germans are working on in Norway and as a result, is recruited to the Resistance by Knut Straud (Richard Harris). Initially reluctant to become involved, when Rolf finds out what the Nazis are doing in a top-secret facility in the small town of Rjukan in Telemark, Norway, he commits to the fight. He realizes that the Nazis are going to use the heavy water to create a nuclear bomb, and that this could easily tip the outcome of the war in Germany's favor. Soon Rolf is reunited with his ex-wife, Anna (Ulla Jacobsson), who with her uncle (Michael Redgrave) are also Resistance fighters.

Because the facility is situated so close to Rjukan, a town of six thousand, they first decide not to try to destroy it in a bombing raid. Rolf, Knut, Anna, Uncle, and another five Resistance fighters prepare to welcome a commando assault team, which is supposed to land in a nearby valley, but the plane is shot down and the entire assault force is killed. Undeterred, the nine organize their own assault on the facility. Although this assault is successful, the Germans quickly rebuild the parts of the factory that were damaged in the raid.

After more close calls with the Germans, who are trying to ferret out resistance fighters, a bombing raid on the heavy water factory occurs. Unfortunately, the raid manages very little damage. Frustrated, the group next learns that the Germans have produced a great amount of heavy water, which they soon plan to transport to Germany. But they will have to use a ferry boat to transport the water across a deep fjord to a railroad line that leads to Germany. Sinking the ferry in the deepest part of the fjord is how Rolf decides they can destroy the heavy water. But Anna stands firmly against this, because many civilians use the ferry every day. Realizing the importance of scuttling the ferry, Rolf rudely tells Anna, "Try to get into your head: What counts is not who's going to die on the ferry, but how many millions will be saved if the ferry's sunk." Demonstrating the lack of civil communication that (along with his infidelities) probably precipitated their divorce in the first place, Rolf makes it clear to Anna that her concern for civilian casualties is sentimental and short-sighted, a peacetime luxury that in their present circumstances they cannot afford. To placate her, Rolf and Knut radio to London for their approval "to share the responsibility."

After placing the bomb below decks in the ferry, Rolf stays on board, and when the blast goes off and the ferry sinks as planned, he helps women and children into lifeboats. Anna and Knut rescue others in a rowboat.

The theme of the latter part of this film is illustrated by Anna's qualms about the killing of civilians. She has no trouble killing Germans, but the idea of killing Norwegians to achieve tactical and strategic objectives in war is another thing. Anna's humanitarian (female) concerns compete with Rolf's emotionless (male) orientation to complete the mission at any cost, and the Norwegians who lost their lives in the operation become real casualties of war. This is a debate not reserved for the Telemark operation or for this or more recent wars, but is as current as tomorrow's news reports about casualties in American drone attacks in Afghanistan and Pakistan.

The Steel Claw

Finally, in a B picture produced, directed by and starring George Montgomery called *The Steel Claw* (1961), we find one last interesting variation of the role of female resistance fighter. Her name is Rosa (Carmen Austin), and the role she plays appears to be about half stereotypical Mexican bandito and half World War II Filipino Resistance leader. In this film, a recently handicapped Capt. John Larsen (Montgomery), with a handmade hook replacing his missing hand, uses his doubtful persuasive abilities along with a great deal of money to cajole/bribe the leaders of two guerilla bands, Santana (Mario Barri) and Rosa, to help him rescue an American general who's been captured by the Japanese.

Santana and Rosa are old colleagues in the brigand trade and have been lovers in the past. But Santana was not faithful, and now they seem to be spiteful competitors in the business of killing Japanese and looting whatever enemy resources they can for fun and profit. At the start, Rosa, tough as nails, would just as soon shoot Santana, but Larsen persuades her with money to bury the hatchet for now, so Santana's and Rosa's bands can work together to assault a Japanese railhead where intelligence says the general is being held. Rosa is smart, brave, and a good tactician as well, better than Santana, whom she still refuses to let closer than bolo (machete) length to her. However, at one point, Rosa is wounded and when Santana picks her up, saying, "You are my woman," she shakes off her wound and says, "I am a woman, but I can still fight." Santana laughs in admiration, and as they fight side by side, Rosa begins to soften a little toward her former lover.

Their mission changes when Larsen discovers that the general is dead and a sergeant has been impersonating him, hoping for better treatment from his captors. By the end of the film, all is sorted out, and Rosa and Santana go off into the sunset together, presumably for some more combined banditry, sex, and battles with the Japanese.

These have been examples of various GI Jane roles appearing in war films over the last century and the beginning of this one. In the next chapter, we will discuss a somewhat different role for women in war, as spies in war films. These clandestine GI Janes will risk their lives to get information and complete secret missions behind enemy lines, all the while pretending to be someone else.

Chapter Seven

The Female Spy, or "Mata Hari"

An important cousin of the GI Jane and resistance fighter roles is the female spy. Male and female spies appear often in war films, but of course Hollywood has seen to it that spies in general have their own genre. In this we find suave, multitalented secret agents risking their lives for queen, country, or personal profit in elaborately plotted scenarios of international intrigue. To a certain degree, roles acted out by superspy characters like James Bond and Jason Bourne inform the way these spies are expected to behave in other genres, such as war films. But in the war genre, we also see a class of spy not bred to the trench coat, Walther PPK, or vodka martini. Rather, when we look at women in war films, besides a class of intelligence professionals, females from many normal walks of life, from wife and mother to high-heeled, sophisticated businesswoman, are recruited into spy work by intelligence professionals (mostly males) who are looking for individuals who can pass for "civilians" and are also intelligent and/or skilled enough to be trained for various kinds of spy missions.

Since female roles in war and spy genres interact with each other in terms of audience expectations, it's important to lay the groundwork before examining the history of female spies in war films. To do this, we will use the screenwriter's tactic of reversing event chronologies and see what roles and behaviors we can currently expect for females in spy-genre films.

As discussed earlier, one can't discuss female action heroes today without paying homage to roles played by Angelina Jolie. Additionally, in the current decade, Jolie has appeared in more than one spy role, including a film that may be a prototype for Bond-like women superspies of the next decade. In *Salt* (2010), Jolie is cast in a role that was originally written for *Mission: Impossible*'s nimble superspy, Tom Cruise. As Cruise has done in earlier pictures, playing a discredited CIA agent who's on the run, looking for evidence to disprove the accusation that she's a double agent, Jolie's character deftly avoids her own pursuing colleagues while searching for the real truth.

The actress establishes herself as a legitimate female superspy, according to Ann Hornaday (2010) of the *Washington Post*: "Jolie may even be on the cusp of a spy franchise that will make Evelyn Salt the first female name on a list that has included James Bond, Jack Ryan, and Jason Bourne." In laying claim to a new role among mythic characters like 007, Jolie's superspy makes such female behaviors and roles more believable for audiences, including the antics of spies in future war-genre pictures. There are certainly other superspy actress roles to note besides Jolie's, such as Russian agent XXX, Maj. Anya Amasova (Barbara Bach) in the Bond film *The Spy Who Loved Me* (1977). Also consider a woman even more liberated and spectacular than Bach's, martial arts star Michelle Yeoh, the Malaysian native who went on to fame in *Crouching Tiger, Hidden Dragon* (2000). In 1997, she played Chinese superspy Wai Lin, an agent equal to Jolie in accomplishments, dexterously matching feats of daring with James Bond in *Tomorrow Never Dies* (1997). Compared to Bach, Wai Lin loses only a few feminist points for poor underwater escape skills, because in the climax of the film, Bond (Pierce Brosnan) must rescue her. But for the rest of the picture, Yeoh's character matches Bond's in stunt after amazing spy stunt. Regardless of which woman we discuss, Jolie, Bach, Yeoh or others, Homaday makes the case for a reconsideration of the roles of women in spy and war/spy genres: "By starring in the kind of movie that made Sean Connery, Harrison Ford, and Matt Damon household names, Jolie [as well as others] has undertaken no less an audacious feat than redefining female stardom itself" (2010).

ZERO DARK THIRTY

It's important to note that like spies in war films, not all contemporary spy-genre heroines take on superhuman personae like Jolie or Yeoh. Most recently, we have been introduced to the character of the intellectual CIA agent, Maya, the role portrayed by Jessica Chastain, for which she secured one of the multiple Oscar nominations garnered by the picture *Zero Dark Thirty* (2012). One can define this film as either a spy or war picture, because at this writing, the United States still maintains a state of war against terrorism, represented chiefly by the late Osama bin Laden and al-Qaeda. The film's Maya character is based on an unnamed but honest-to-goodness CIA spy, so she doesn't do backflips to effortlessly put away gangs of thuggish antagonist minions with her bare hands. She is in many ways the cerebral opposite of Jolie's or Yeoh's athletic characters.

Zero Dark Thirty is about a CIA agent whose intelligence and tenacity over a twelve-year period resulted in the raid that killed Osama bin Laden.

In the post-9/11 war against terror, the foot soldiers in this fight are and were not in uniform and don't march in a straight line. Instead they are agents like Maya, whose real name has apparently been withheld to protect her and her family from subsequent al-Qaeda revenge attacks. As we learn later in the film, she was recruited out of high school for a CIA-sponsored college scholarship. There she studied important subjects required of a CIA agent, including Middle East culture and the Arabic and Farsi languages. Then she became an intelligence analyst with the CIA. Maya is first shown reporting for duty in Pakistan as a full-fledged agent some years after this. She takes up work on the CIA's biggest challenge, the hunt for the elusive leader of al-Qaeda, Osama bin Laden. The Pakistan-based CIA's mission was soon after made clear to everyone, as shouted to them at one point by their chief, George (Mark Strong), "I want targets. Do your fucking jobs. Bring me people to kill."

At first, she finds the torture of captured al-Qaeda members to extract little shards of information sickening, and her reactions show that, she finds these CIA black operation tactics extremely repugnant. But Maya also knows that she is a woman doing "a man's job," as inferred constantly by her male superiors. So as best she can, she keeps her feelings to herself, learning to act more "butch," refusing to show her mentor and the chief interrogator, Dan (Jason Clarke), her dislike for these savage interrogation tactics. At the outset, Dan is enthusiastic and somewhat sadistic in his use of waterboarding and other torture tactics. His standard line to his victims is, "When you lie to me, I hurt you." He even uses Maya's presence in the torture chamber as a way to embarrass his victims by stripping them from the waist down, a psychological torture technique quite hurtful to a macho Middle Eastern male.

However, two interesting phenomena develop as these torture sessions continue. Maya becomes desensitized to the torture while Dan becomes more disgusted with his role. Dan can no longer stand his position as chief torturer, and eventually he requests reassignment from Pakistan back to CIA head-quarters at Langley, Virginia. But even in explaining to Maya, a coworker, why he wants to give up torturing people, Dan must keep up a he-man front. His lame excuse is that since he's always stripping prisoners from the waist down, he's tired of looking at their "junk" (genitals) all day long. Later, after the U.S. Congress objects to CIA black ops and torture, Dan gets back into the action as more of a 007 kind of spy, bribing a Kuwaiti businessman with a Lamborghini for information (a phone number and address) of the relative of an important al-Qaeda suspect.

Due to the torture experiences and by learning important spy behavior from a somewhat older female mentor, Jessica (Jennifer Ehle), Maya be-

comes increasingly hardened and cynical. Sometime after an experience in
which she and Jessica were almost killed when al-Qaeda bombed a hotel
frequented by foreigners, a young CIA female rookie who looks up to Maya
asks if they might share dinner. Maya tersely responds that eating at a restaurant is too dangerous. Indeed, later, leaving her own fortified house, al-Qaeda
gunmen try to assassinate her. Fortunately, she travels in a car with bullet-
proof glass, so she survives. Among other experiences, Maya is shocked
when Jessica is killed after she sets up a meeting with an informant she has
come to trust. The informant gets out of his car, mumbles "Allahu Akbar"
(God is great) and blows up himself and a group of CIA agents. From this,
Maya resolves never to trust anyone. Her calm cold comment about the
incident is, "I'm going to smoke [kill] everyone involved in this op, and then
I'm going to kill Osama bin Laden." Maya has completed a transformation
from a woman with feelings to one hell-bent on a mission of revenge.

Maya has a single goal in life, to the exclusion of everything else: assassinate bin Laden. One might say that it has become an obsession, but on the
other hand, it is also her job. She is a spy. Doing as little other intelligence
work as possible, she focuses her efforts on turning tiny shards of information into a road map leading to bin Laden. First of all, she openly opposes the
so-called prevailing wisdom of the agency, which is that bin Laden is still
hiding in a "fortress" somewhere in the mountains of southeast Afghanistan.
She argues logically, "You can't run a global network of interconnected cells
from a cave." When her Pakistan station chief wants to reassign her to other
duties, Maya threatens to blackmail him, asking what Langley—or Congress—would do to the career of a CIA official who let Osama bin Laden slip
through his fingers. The craven CIA official backs down. Perhaps coincidentally in the film's time line, he is soon replaced as station chief.

Eventually, other CIA spies take Maya much more seriously, and later, at
least one operative decides to comply with her wishes for intensifying a
search for an important al-Qaeda operative because the word is that it's best
not to buck Maya.

She reasons that bin Laden is headquartered close to a city. Then, via
couriers, he can safely and quickly communicate throughout the outside
world. Through torture, one al-Qaeda prisoner has given up the name of a top
bin Laden courier. At least a half hour of the movie documents Maya's
efforts to identify the courier, whose nom de guerre is Abu Ahmed. But
Maya must buck resistance from some quarters because Ahmed has been
declared dead by another tortured prisoner. On the one hand, no one totally
believes information obtained by torture; on the other, some of the information turns out to be legitimate. Eventually, Maya's research uncovers why
some prisoners think Ahmed is dead: Ahmed and his many brothers look
nearly identical, and with bushy beards one could easily be mistaken for the
other. Acting on the theory that the tortured al-Qaeda prisoner witnessed the

death and burial of one of Ahmed's brothers, and using electronic spying techniques, Maya tracks Ahmed to northern Pakistan. Eventually this tracking effort leads Maya's people right to the door of bin Laden's compound in Abbottabad, Pakistan.

Next comes the most difficult of all of Maya's spying accomplishments. Back at Langley, she must nearly singlehandedly convince skeptical male superiors that a raid on the Abbottabad compound will at least capture or kill some high-level al-Qaeda operatives, and this compound might just be the home of bin Laden. For over one hundred days, politicians in Washington and equally wary officials in the CIA debate the issue, sometimes in Maya's presence and sometimes behind her back, simply referring to her as "the girl." Admittedly she is young looking, but after college, CIA training, and twelve years with the agency, one would think that a nonsexist leadership would at least refer to her with more respect. In a big senior staff meeting, the director of the CIA asks for the odds of bin Laden being present in the Abbottabad compound. Stating that, after all, their conclusions are only deductive reasoning, most top staffers give their chances as 60 percent. Perhaps not doing her case much good, Maya chimes in "100 percent," but defers to administrators' phobia for absolutes by rating the chances at 95 percent.

Still days go by, and with it Maya's patience. Every day, she scribbles on the glass door of her supervisor's office how many days have elapsed since they discovered the Abbottabad compound. Occasionally she seasons this frustrated act with a comment, such as that the odds that bin Laden is still in the compound decrease day by day. Although as frustrated as Maya with the top bosses' reluctance to raid the compound, the supervisor, George, can only sit and wait while the president of the United States and all of his politicians decide if they can trust "the girl." Finally, the president must have asked the director of the CIA (James Gandolfini) to give him his final judgment on the matter, because the director comes down to the employees' cafeteria to chat with her. After some small talk, the director makes up his mind that Maya has the goods, and the president orders a strike on Abbottabad.

On station on a U.S. base in nearby Afghanistan, Maya tells the SEAL team leader the truth about her recommendation on how to assault this stronghold:

Maya: Quite frankly, I didn't even want to use you guys, with your dip and velcro and all your gear bullshit. I wanted to drop a bomb. But people didn't believe in this lead enough to drop a bomb. So they're using you guys as canaries. And, in theory, if bin Laden isn't there, you can sneak away and no one will be the wiser. But bin Laden is there. And you're going to kill him for me. (*Zero Dark Thirty*, 2012)

For political reasons, no one with the CIA wants to stick out his neck in Maya's support, so if she's wrong, they can blame it all on her. However, the SEAL team can smell administrator BS, and they find none on her. They also seem impressed with her intelligence, leadership skills, and even her manly attitude. As Maya stands nearby, within earshot, watching the SEALs drink beer and pitch horseshoes before the raid, she overhears a conversation between SEAL Justin and team leader Patrick:

> **Justin:** So Patrick, be honest with me. You really believe this story? I mean (*turns to Maya*) no offense, no offense. . . . I don't. (*turns back to Patrick*) But . . . Osama bin Laden?
>
> **Patrick:** Yeah.
>
> **Justin:** What part convinced you?
>
> **Patrick:** Her confidence.
>
> **Justin:** (*half sarcastically and half with bravado*) That's the kind of concrete data point I'm looking for. I'll tell you buddy, if her confidence is the one thing that's keeping me from getting ass-raped in a Pakistani prison, I'm gonna be honest with you, bro. I'm cool with it. (*Zero Dark Thirty*, 2012)

The team carries out a successful raid, killing bin Laden and two other assistants, one of whom was Maya's long-pursued courier. The SEALs put bin Laden's body in a body bag and take it away with them. The raid was marred only by the engine failure followed by the intentional destruction of one of their top-secret stealth helicopters. They also retrieve a roomful of intelligence information (papers, tapes, hard drives) that they will turn over to the CIA, which are probably still being evaluated and used against al-Qaeda.

Back at the raid's staging area in Afghanistan, Maya unzips the body bag to stare into the dead eyes of Osama bin Laden. She positively identifies the al-Qaeda patriarch. Reminding us that regardless of this great victory, Maya's status remains the same, we hear on the radio the SEAL team leader, Patrick, telling Langley and the president, ensconced in his War Room in Washington, that the on-site CIA representative had positively identified Osama bin Laden. "The girl?" someone from Langley replies. "Yes," says Patrick.

Despite being labeled "the girl," Maya has the distinction that usually no female spy (except perhaps the Bond movies' fictional superspy code named "M") has in motion pictures like this about spies and war. The other female agents discussed in this chapter are directed by older male operatives and simply follow their controls' orders to achieve specific missions. Maya, on the other hand, although beginning her spy career as an underling, grows in knowledge and experience, and is admired not only (and usually somewhat grudgingly) by her male superiors, but also by younger female agents, who wish to imitate her style and behavior.

On the entertainment website *Moviephone*, Annette Bourdeau differentiates between this more cerebral kind of modern intelligence operative and female superspies in action and war/action films:

> Maya isn't like the other female spies we see portrayed most often in film and TV. She doesn't run around in stilettos seducing sources like we've seen done by the leading ladies of *Covert Affairs*, *Alias* and *Nikita*. She doesn't rely on her female wiles to get what she needs. Instead, she leverages her considerable smarts and a lot of good old-fashioned hard work. . . . [Because she is a spy in a male-dominated organization], Maya has to work extra hard to prove herself, and that may be one of the driving forces behind her successful quest to find Osama bin Laden. That, and her well-above-average IQ and impeccably refined BS detector and a total lack of personal life. (Bourdeau, 2013)

HEARTS OF THE WORLD

This, then, is the present role status in spy or spy/war films, from the sexy superspy of the Bond films to a tough CIA intellectual proving her worth among men who undervalue and disrespect her. But female espionage agents in war films did not begin with much flair or even serve on the side of the good guys when D. W. Griffith added one to his World War I epic, *Hearts of the World*, in 1918. As in many films set in occupied countries to follow, filmmakers have sometimes identified a venal person dedicated to money and business and portrayed him or her as a collaborator. As the innkeeper in a French village, Fay Holderness's character helps the Germans by radioing them reports of French troop movements. The film is not clear on how the innkeeper is turned, but audiences can assume that she was probably recruited by Von Strom (George Siegmann), a German spy who did reconnaissance in the area before the war. Regardless, the innkeeper character spies for the Germans, and Griffith shows his dislike for collaborators by including a scene in which Von Strom pays her off in cash—her thirty pieces of silver—for betraying France.

Military men on both sides are shown spying in *Hearts of the World*, but no women are shown doing intelligence work, either in or out of uniform, except for the innkeeper.

TRUTH AND FICTION ABOUT MATA HARI

One notorious woman is remembered for her espionage efforts during World War I, and was famously executed in 1917, charged with spying against France and its Allies for the Germans. Her name has since become synonymous with espionage, hence our chapter title. Her real name was Margaretha Zelle MacLeod, born in the Netherlands. An internationally famous exotic dancer and courtesan, her made-up press story was that she learned Oriental dancing growing up as a Java princess of Hindu birth. A contemporary of Isadora Duncan, the flirty, promiscuous Mata Hari traveled frequently around Europe before and during World War I, doing her sensual dances for well-heeled audiences, and easily crossing borders using her Dutch passport. Traveling around Europe as a citizen of a neutral country made more believable the accusation at her trial that she carried war secrets back and forth to German agents. At one point, Britain's Scotland Yard arrested and questioned her, but she denied working for Germany and claimed to be providing intelligence to France, Britain's ally. Later, however, with somewhat flimsy evidence at the time, the French arrested Mata Hari in Paris, convicted her, and executed her by firing squad. German documents uncovered in 1970 certified that Mata Hari did, indeed, spy for the Germans.

There have been two films of note about the espionage activities of Mata Hari, *Mata Hari*, starring Greta Garbo in 1931, and another film made in 1985 that was as much a soft porn vehicle for sex kitten Sylvia Kristel as it was a spy drama. These films utilize Mata's reputation to their dramatic advantage, but don't approach the real story of Margaretha Zelle MacLeod, made as they were with the creative license of filmmakers interested in making another Garbo romantic tragedy (in 1931) and an R-rated sexploitationer (in 1985).

Garbo's version is essentially another of the famous Swedish actress's tragic romances. In it, she plays a German spy whose exotic dancing captivates General Shubin (Lionel Barrymore), an older man enamored with the young woman. Although the general deeply regrets the secrets he has revealed to her, he is helpless to resist. Meanwhile, Mata is also busy vamping young Lt. Alexis Rosanoff (Ramon Novarro), a dashing flyer. At one point, in a somewhat daring scene for the era, she sleeps with Rosanoff to delay his departure on a secret mission to deliver important war dispatches. The dispatches are secretly copied while Rosanoff is otherwise occupied. The next day he has no idea that he has been betrayed.

But here is where the great spy meets her Waterloo. Unprofessionally for a spy, Mata falls in love with Rosanoff, and even feels guilty for involving him in her intrigues. She tries to quit the spy game, but her handler won't let her leave Germany's service alive. She knows too much. Ironically, before the Germans can manage to kill Mata, she is arrested by the French and convicted of spying. The French execute her by firing squad, which is probably the closest this version of the story gets to the facts.

The 1985 version, Sylvia Kristel's *Mata Hari*, is designed more to show off Kristel's naked body than anything else. Mata is persuaded to spy for Germany at the outset of the war. The audience is never told why or how she is persuaded. From here on, any resemblance to the truth about her life is sacrificed on the altar of R-rated expediency. First, she seduces a French officer named Ladoux (Oliver Tobias). Next, she's in bed with a German spy in Paris, Karl von Byerling. Mata begins to fall in love with Karl, so much so that she rents a country house so that their trysts can remain secret. Unfortunately for Mata, French intelligence discovers who she's entertaining at the villa, and they arrest her. To placate the French, she agrees to spy for them, and goes to Madrid to spy on Karl. But Karl is not available, so she ends up romancing another German, a naval officer, and learning what she can from him. She also agrees to spy on a French nobleman who appears to be playing both sides. This encounter is probably the most confusing, but also, considering it's an orgy, the most sex-charged scene in the film. Then the Germans convey her in disguise back into France to assist Karl, who has been wounded and captured. The rest of the film is a rather silly plot about a bomb in a cathedral that Mata diffuses. Then the French arrest and execute her.

Basically, neither of these films is very helpful in either establishing the truth of Mata's life or in setting any kind of example for other female wartime spies to follow.

SPYING IN WORLD WAR II

During World War II, the U.S. War Activities Committee of the Motion Picture Industry asked Hollywood to make some films praising our then ally the Soviet Union in its fight against Germany. One of the lesser films in this category is an independent B movie called *Miss V from Moscow* (1942). Vera Marova (Lola Lane), who works in counterespionage for the Soviet Union, is perhaps the earliest version of a "Natasha," a female Russian spy, that would eventually evolve a generation later into Barbara Bach's Agent Triple X. In *Miss V from Moscow*, the cool and highly skilled spy Vera is ordered by her handler to pose as a deceased German spy. Vera bears an uncanny resemblance to this German, and the enemy does not yet have any idea that their agent is dead.

Once about her spy activities, however, Vera is arrested by the Gestapo, but Col. Heinrich (John Vosper), a victim of hubris, having knowledge of the German agent but not of her death, is convinced that Vera is indeed their spy, and believes her suavely told story that she's working on a counterespionage mission. So she's a Russian spy, pretending to be a German spy who's supposed to be ferreting out Allied spies. What Vera is really doing is uncovering information that will save American convoys on their way to Russia from German submarine wolf packs.

Also, Col. Heinrich is quite taken by the attractive Vera, and she alternately flirts with him and then plays hard to get. Finally she agrees to dine with him and then intentionally stands him up. To keep Heinrich off balance, Vera actually shows up for their next dinner date. Basically, to use an expression from the 1940s, she has the colonel wrapped around her little finger. So even when he notices a few slipups, he interprets them in her favor, angering a German SS officer who's equally convinced that Vera is really working for the Allies. Vera continues to extract valuable information from the colonel until she disappears, leaving the hapless German officer holding the bag. The colonel ends up being executed for revealing secrets to the enemy.

As a World War II propaganda film, it shows German officers to be egotistical and relatively stupid, and demonstrates how easy it is for an attractive woman to pull the wool over their eyes.

Where Eagles Dare

In the World War II film, *Where Eagles Dare* (1968), two highly professional spies, Mary Elison (Mary Ure) and Heidi (Ingrid Pitt) are Allied secret agents, working undercover deep behind enemy lines. Heidi poses as a barmaid in a tavern frequented by German soldiers, and Mary, who has been spying in Italy but is pulled out of that assignment to help with this one, pretends to be Heidi's cousin who has come to visit her. Both have been assigned by Allied intelligence to back up a commando unit tasked with penetrating a highly defended castle, the Schloss Adler, which is serving as a German provincial headquarters. The two attractive women risk their lives as they infiltrate this headquarters, posing as domestic workers who must endure the nosy questions and sexual harassment of an obnoxious SS officer. But while this officer (Derren Nesbitt) is busy sniffing around the women, his absence works to the commando team's advantage because he does not pay attention to all the intrigue going on at the castle until it's too late. Although working under the orders of team leader Maj. Smith (Richard Burton), the two women spies ably assist the commandos in completing their mission, and they escape with the men when the job is done. At various times during the film, Mary and/or Heidi demonstrate their characters' skills by making a risky night parachute drop, rappelling down the outside of the castle, deftly firing machine guns to help the commandos hold off pursuing Germans and using their charms to skillfully manipulate the SS officer.

For a while, Mary is Maj. Smith's secret from the rest of the team. Smith knows that a few members of his team are actually German double agents, and the main goal of their mission is to discover who the British double agents are. So after the team parachutes from the plane, Mary, who has been hidden from the team in the cockpit, is escorted to the open door and parachutes on her own into the night. When she lands, the intrepid Mary hides from the other team members and makes her way alone to a secret rendezvous point with Smith.

There is a more than a hint of a relationship between Mary and Smith. First of all, the two were bought in on this operation because they were spying together in Italy, and their boss, Adm. Rolland (Michael Hordern), was assured that they were loyal. At one point, Mary tells Smith that she loves him, but expects nothing in return, because until instructions are given and they're ready for the next phase of the operation, Smith is all business. But before they part company, he gives her a kiss.

Mary is a pro, speaks fluent German, and is ready on a mission to do anything necessary to achieve their objectives. This includes using her charms to distract and manipulate the aforementioned SS officer. The foolish officer is so smitten with Heidi and Mary that he personally escorts the two of them from the village up to the castle by cable car. Little does the officer know that hidden in Mary's suitcase, which he helps her carry at one point, are ropes and explosives and other equipment that the team will need for their stealthy assault on the castle.

On the unofficial website of *Where Eagles Dare* (WED), describing the impact of Mary Ure's and her exemplary performances in the film, Ingrid Pitt expressed satisfaction that they were allowed to show off their toughness and ability to fight alongside the men:

> When WED came out, the cinema was beginning to realize that there was a place in films for strong women. Women in war films usually played a supporting role. Either suffering or betraying. Even [biopics of real WWII female British spies] were based on how the men stoically allowed the little woman to drop into enemy territory and how they muddled through in spite of the fact that it was against their nature. I think WED showed that the fairer sex could operate in a hostile environment without being patronized by men. (whereeaglesdare.com)

The Big Red One . . . Once Again

As previously mentioned in chapter 2, a number of women play Madonna and prostitute roles in *The Big Red One: The Reconstruction.* But those aren't the only two roles for women in this picture. One of the most bizarre and ironic sequences in a film full of bizarre and ironic sequences takes place in the collaboration between a female Allied spy and the film's GI protagonists. The spy is a Walloon (a French-speaking person who comes from Wallonia in Belgium, portrayed by French film star Stephanie Audran) currently posing as an inmate in an insane asylum. She was ordered to infiltrate the asylum because the Germans are using the asylum's tower—the highest point in the area—for observation. She has been ordered to wait until Sarge's (Lee Marvin) infantry squad arrives, and then, trying not to kill any of the patients, dispose of all the Germans who occupy it. Sarge's men are always complaining about something, and this time, as he describes their orders, someone points out that they could get killed on this assignment and the question is asked why the Army doesn't just bomb it. Sarge replies, "Killing insane people isn't good for public relations." Griff sarcastically retorts, "[But] killing sane people's OK." The Sarge stoically replies, "Right."

The stealthy assault begins when the Walloon spots Sarge silently killing a sleeping German guard. Taking this as her cue for action, the spy begins to prance around, dancing with a doll like the crazy woman she's supposed to be. Two more German guards, used to the odd behavior of the patients, watch the shapely woman dance for a few seconds, but ultimately ignore her. Out of her doll's dress, she pulls a razor and expertly and quickly cuts the throats of the two Germans. Continuing her act, singing in English, which none of the Germans understand, she smiles as she chants, "The Americans are coming" as she kills yet a third German. The crafty spy signals Sarge, who has been admiringly watching her work, to follow her. Many of the inmates watch as the American soldiers quietly infiltrate the hospital and kill Germans, but they pay them little mind. The Walloon spy leads Sarge upstairs to the tower, distracts the German observer and they silently kill him as well.

The squad still undiscovered, most of the remaining Germans are next shown eating lunch along with the patients in the refectory. To distract the Germans, the Walloon does her crazy dance with the doll again, this time showing off some leg as she prances on one of the picnic-type tables. This distracts some of the Germans, but some entering the refectory finally spot the Americans. A firefight ensues. With all the bullets flying around, infantryman Griff (Mark Hamill), chivalrously concerned about the Walloon's safety, throws her to the ground and lies on top of her, shielding her with his body. Watching the firefight curiously as they eat, many of the patients enjoy the commotion and even laugh at the bloody floor show. But one patient, seeing these soldiers slaughter one another, has an epiphany. He grabs a Schmeisser (automatic rifle) from a dead German and starts shooting at everyone, yelling, "I am one of you! I am sane!" Griff later narrates how absurd it was to have to shoot this patient.

Finally, all the Germans are dead, the patients are settled in for the night and Sarge's squad is bivouacking at the hospital, sleeping on the floor. Griff approaches the Walloon spy, who, smilingly, appreciates Griff's earlier concern for her welfare. Affectionately, she says, "I'll be tender," and the two make love on the floor—quietly—surrounded by a roomful of sleeping GIs and crazy people.

Amateur and "Professional" Spies in *Inglourious Basterds*

In Quentin Tarantino's *Inglourious Basterds* (2009), Shosanna Dreyfus (Mélanie Laurent) plays an unlikely spy heroine. Like many resistance heroines we discussed in the last chapter, the situation is often thrust upon a character, and normal, untrained civilians simply rise to the occasion and do the job. The reason Shosanna is doubly unlikely in this film is because when we first meet her, she is not an undercover agent. She is instead a victim, a teenage Jewish girl hiding from the Nazis under the floorboards of a French farmhouse. Then the evil Nazi Col. Hans Landa (Christoph Waltz), nicknamed the "Jew Hunter," comes to call at the farmhouse. He smilingly toys with the farmer for a while, knowing all along that Jews are hiding below the floorboards on which they stand. Landa then brings his SS men into the farmhouse to machinegun the floor, killing everyone except Shosanna. She barely escapes and runs across an open field. Landa, watching her run away, could have shot at her or ordered his minions to chase her down, but instead, he laughingly lets her go. It's unclear why, but the audience is sure of one thing: charity really has nothing to do with it.

Four years later, Shosanna reappears, living under the name of Emmanuelle Mimieux, a young, beautiful proprietor of a medium-sized movie theater in Paris. Although hateful toward French collaborators, Shosanna appears content to run her theater, be sympathetic toward the French Resistance and wait for the Allies, soon to land on Normandy, to liberate her country. But a new situation presents itself, in the person of Pvt. Fredrick Zoller, a recent German hero. In three days, Zoller (Daniel Brühl), a sniper, while perched in a bell tower, was responsible for shooting over three hundred enemy soldiers. For this, Nazi Chief of Propaganda Joseph Goebbels (Sylvester Groth) has turned Zoller into a hero of the Fatherland. Goebbels has even produced a new film that dramatizes Zoller's exploits.

One evening, as Shosanna works at her theater, Zoller walks up to her and strikes up a conversation about the movies. Zoller is attracted to Shosanna, but she does everything she can to politely brush him off. She knows that the French can't be too rude to their occupiers, or they'll likely be whisked away to a concentration camp. This may be what Shosanna thinks is happening the next day, when a car arrives and two disdainful Nazis pick up Shosanna. But she's not really under arrest: The next thing she knows, Shosanna is sitting across a restaurant table from Zoller and Nazi chief propagandist Joseph Goebbels. In hopes of impressing Shosanna in return for later sexual favors, Zoller has convinced Goebbels to move the premiere of *Nation's Pride*, the movie Goebbels' propaganda filmmakers made about his sniper exploits, from a larger movie house to Shosanna's theater. Since many Nazi dignitaries would attend, Shosanna must then endure a scary interview over schnitzel with Landa, in charge of security for the premiere. For all she knows, this conversation over schnitzel could have been the Jew Hunter toying with another hapless victim he is about to execute. But actually, Landa, who never got a good look at Shosanna the last time, has no idea that he's eating dessert with the young Jewish girl he spared four years earlier. After Landa leaves her, Shosanna has a panic attack, so sure she was that she was about to be arrested and killed like her family.

Next Shosanna decides that she can finally take revenge for her family's murder and in the same stroke, exterminate a theater full of top Nazis. With the help of her lover, who is connected with the French Resistance and who also works with her in the theater, she concocts a plan. While the Nazis are watching the film's premiere, she will set the theater ablaze. It will likely cost them both their lives, but she doesn't care. Shosanna has a collection of highly flammable nitrate films in her storeroom, which means that she won't even have to find hard-to-get gasoline to set her theater on fire. Then it's a matter of locking the exit doors at the right time and flicking a cigarette into a pile of film. Shosanna even films a short, taunting clip that she will project to announce to the Nazis that they are about to have the tables turned: to be burned to death by a Jew.

While Shosanna is busy with her preparations, in Tarantino's strange, pseudo Coen Brothers–type scenario, another character, a female intelligence agent (which in this case may be oxymoronic, as she is not very smart) in league with British intelligence, is making similar murderous plans. Only in the British plan, they will kill the Nazis with explosives and machine guns. Bridget von Hammersmark (Diane Kruger), a German movie star, is the Allied secret agent. Aware of this chance to kill many top Nazi officials in one bold strike, British intelligence has ordered Bridget to attend this premiere and to use her prominence to gain admittance to the theater for some of her "friends." These friends are actually to be a British commando and German-speaking members of the Basterds team. Once inside the theater, the plan is for them to plant dynamite charges, block the doors, and machine gun all the top Nazis they can. Unfortunately, this plan is derailed due to the inexperience of the dim-witted female agent and the hubris of the commando, who speaks German with a noticeable accent.

After the British commando Lt. Archie Hicox (Michael Fassbender) parachutes into France and meets up with the Basterds, all that remains is connecting with Bridget. For his rendezvous, Bridget has chosen as a meeting place the worst possible location: a tavern frequented by German soldiers. Worse yet, as Basterds leader Lt. Aldo Raine (Brad Pitt) comments, there's only one entrance to the tavern, which is in the basement of an inn. Additionally, this entrance is via an awkward spiral staircase. Aldo complains about the arrangements to Archie:

Aldo: You didn't say the goddam rendezvous was in a fuckin' basement.

Archie: I didn't know.

Aldo: You said it was in a tavern.

Archie: It is a tavern.

Aldo: Yeah, in a basement. You know, fightin' in a basement offers a lot of difficulties. Number one bein', you're fighting in a basement!

Later, another Basterd, Sgt. Donny Donowitz (Eli Roth), chimes in:

Donny: Speaking of Frau von Hammersmark, whose idea was it for the death trap rendezvous?

Archie: She chose the spot.

Donny: *(sarcastically)* Well, isn't that just dandy.

Archie: Look, she's not a military strategist. She's just an actress.

Donny: Well, you don't got to be Stonewall Jackson to know you don't want to fight in a basement. (*Inglourious Basterds*, 2009)

Arrogantly, Archie thinks his German-language skills will pass inspection, but as previously mentioned, his spoken German has an odd accent that immediately draws the attention of an SS agent who also happens to be enjoying a beer in the tavern. Archie's less-than-perfect German betrays him as an Englishman, and a firefight ensues between Germans and agents in the bar. Only Bridget survives, although she suffers a bullet in her leg. The remaining Basterds, who were not in the basement bar, rescue her, but in the confusion, they forget one of her shoes, which Landa later will trace back to her, trying it on her foot like Cinderella. Aldo and the others see to her wound. To cover up the fact that she's been shot, the Basterds arrange to put Bridget in a cast. They concoct a silly cover story that she broke her leg mountain climbing. How she did this in Paris was equally ill thought out. It's decided that a team of Basterds will still accompany Bridget to the premiere, but all the German-speaking Basterds were killed in the tavern firefight. They thus plan to pose as members of an Italian film crew who are friends of hers from the movie business.

The Basterds' ability to speak any Italian is limited, and worse yet, Aldo speaks the few Italian words he knows with a terrible Southern drawl. Of course, the erudite Col. Landa, fluent in Italian, is not fooled for a minute. Aldo and one of the Basterds are arrested and Landa takes Bridget into an office in the theater where he uses the shoe to quickly discover that she is a spy. He strangles her.

This leaves only Shosanna and two Basterds who escaped Landa's round-up to kill all the Nazis, made more important by the surprise attendance of Adolf Hitler himself! Shosanna and her lover bravely manage to set the theater on fire and lock the doors, and the two Basterds spray the dignitaries—including *der Fuehrer*—with bullets from their machine guns and set off dynamite charges, likely killing everyone in the theater. Unfortunately for Shosanna, right before the fire was set, Zoller accosts her in the projection booth, expecting his sexual reward for putting her theater in the Nazi lime-light. Shosanna has finally had enough of Zoller and shoots him. Although fatally wounded, Zoller still manages to shoot back and kills Shosanna. Thus in this film, the amateur spy manages the fictional assassination of the entire leadership of the Third Reich, while the inept male and female professional spies both are killed before they nearly foul up the entire operation.

In this fiasco, it's hard to decide whose hubris was worse, Bridget's or Archie's. Although an official Allied agent, Bridget was clearly an intelligence dilettante, a rich movie star playing at spying as if she were portraying a role in the movies. Archie, a writer and film critic before the war, was a terrible egotist with a much-inflated opinion of himself—especially his ability to pass himself off as a German. It is clear that neither of these agents ended up being worth one well-meaning, motivated amateur.

Blood on the Sun

A much more professional female spy is a pre–Pearl Harbor double agent in the combination newspaper caper/spy film, *Blood on the Sun* (1945). The MacGuffin of this film pursued by everyone is a copy of the apocryphal document that is supposed to be evidence that in 1927, then Japanese prime minister Giichi Tanaka (John Emery) presented to Emperor Hirohito a plan for Japanese world domination. Sylvia Sidney plays Iris Hilliard, a secretive, mysterious Asian/American who initially appears to newspaper editor Nick Condon (James Cagney) to be either Tanaka's assistant or his mistress, or both. Actually, Iris is much more than she appears. Not only is she spying on Tanaka, but she is also an advocate for women's rights in Asia.

Iris gets her hands on a copy of the Tanaka Plan and, while dodging the Japanese secret police, helps Condon verify it. She does this by taking Condon to see Prince Tatsugi (Frank Puglia), a pacifist member of the royal family who sadly admits that the plan is real. Shortly after he makes this admission to Condon and Iris, the secret police murder him. Then the chase is on to apprehend the two. Finally, Condon devises a way to make sure that Iris and the document escape Japan and make it to America. While Iris boards a ship on her way to the United States, Condon leads the Japanese agents on a chase to apprehend him as if he had the document. This cat-and-mouse game ends a few dozen yards from the American embassy, with a wounded Condon lying in the street, encircled by secret police. But a U.S. diplomat comes out of the embassy and claims Condon, helping him inside the embassy. Later, his wound healed, Condon is able to get to America himself, retrieve the document from Iris and get it published as proof of Japan's plans for aggression throughout the world.

Throughout the film, Iris plays a cool customer, keeping Condon wondering if she really is on the U.S. side. In the twisted, mysterious style of the *film noir* genre that will soon evolve in American cinema, only toward the end of the film does Iris's true identity and purpose as an agent for the United States become clear. Her role through most of the picture is to be as inscrutable as possible and keep the audience wondering which side she's on. Only when Tanaka, who has bugged her apartment, overhears her tell Condon whose side she's really on do we also know for sure.

During the 1940s, there were many women who played spy roles for the Allies in the war against the Axis. In *Back to Bataan*, as discussed in chapter 3, Dalisay Delgado (Fely Franquelli) appears to be just the quisling Filipino radio network mouthpiece of the occupying Japanese Army, but in actuality, she is a spy for the Allies, assisting guerilla forces by informing them where and when Japanese soldiers will turn up. Similarly, in *Bombs over Burma* (1942), Lin Ying (Anna May Wong) appears to be a Chungking schoolteacher, but she's actually a Chinese spy gathering intelligence for the Chinese Resistance. In this story, Lin appears to be on a school inspection trip, but it's really because she and another Chinese agent have been assigned to ferret out an agent for the Japanese who's posing as a British nobleman. They turn the collaborator over to Chinese peasants who make short work of him. Then Lin goes back to Chungking and calmly takes up teaching again, until the next opportunity to fight the Japanese arises.

Lady from Chungking

Anna May Wong's character in *Lady from Chungking* (1942) hails from the same city as Lin Yang the schoolteacher. Her role is also as a spy, but the resemblance stops there in this propagandistic, sloppily made B movie. Rather than just show a Chinese spy working against the Japanese, *Lady from Chungking*'s melodramatic ending beats the audience over the head with a long anti-Japanese, pro–Chinese Resistance speech designed to whip up support among American audiences for America's allies, the Chinese.

Kwan Mei (Anna) leads a group of Chinese peasants who appear to the Japanese to be knuckling under to their Japanese occupiers, content to be slaves to their oppressors. But when the time is right, Kwan's men kill their overseer and attempt to rescue two downed Flying Tiger pilots. One of these

Americans is injured and is hidden by Kwan's men, but the Japanese capture the other.

Kwan, posing as a Chinese aristocrat, tries to infiltrate the headquarters of Gen. Kaimura (Harold Huber). Kaimura, dismissive of all conquered Chinese, is nonetheless impressed by this noblewoman. Kwan plans to rescue the captured flyer while she also gathers intelligence about the general's next offensive. At first, however, she must endure the leering, salacious Lt. Shimoto (Ted Hecht), who has his own predatory plans for Kwan. But as soon as Gen. Kaimura spots her, he does the senior officer's version of calling "dibs" on the Chinese beauty, rank having its usual privileges in the Japanese Army as well. At the time, Kaimura's favorite female is an itinerant entertainer named Lavara (Mae Clarke), but when he meets Kwan, the general is charmed both by the Chinese aristocrat's beauty and her noble lineage. Kwan flatters and romances the general and finds out his plans, which she reports to her men. When a Japanese soldier follows her to her meeting with her men, Kwan knifes him, greatly impressing the men, who until then were a little unsure about following a mere woman. Kwan also turns Lavara into a spy as well, and recruits her to help rescue the captured pilot, to whom she also repeats the general's plans. All the pilot can say about Kwan is "What a woman!"

But eventually Kwan is found out and captured. As the embarrassed general questions her, they hear bombs in the distance. Kwan tells the general that what he hears is "your troop train being bombed." Her intelligence information had gotten through and Kaimura's men are being slaughtered. The general is disgraced. But before he thinks about his own doubtful future, Kaimura makes sure that his firing squad makes Kwan pay the price. Kwan nevertheless still manages to give the usual propaganda message that condemned Allied soldiers give in these movies:

Kwan: You cannot kill me. You cannot kill China. Not even a million deaths can crush the soul of China, for the soul of China is eternal. When I die, a million will take my place, and nothing can stop them, neither hunger nor torture nor firing squads. We will live on, until the enemy is driven back over scorched lands and hurled into the sea. That time will come soon, for the armies of decency and liberty are on the march. China's destiny is victory. It will live because human freedom will not perish. Out of the ashes of ruin and old hatreds, the force of peace will prevail until the world is again safe and pure. (*Lady from Chungking*, 1942)

In war films made in the United States during World War II, many protagonists about to be executed utter such a speech, but very few of these overblown orations, delivered by Americans or anyone else, were allowed to be spoken by a woman. Her rhetoric is stereotypical of this kind of propaganda film, but it is refreshing to hear Anna May Wong say it.

FEMALE AGENTS IN VIETNAM

In the Vietnam War film *The Green Berets* (1968), a sympathetic South Vietnamese woman (Irene Tsu) becomes a spy and sacrifices her virtue by sleeping with a Viet Cong (V.C.) commander at his villa, distracting him so that the American Green Berets can break in and kidnap him. In another, better-made, Vietnam War film, *Go Tell the Spartans* (1978), a young Viet Cong agent named Butterfly (Denise Kumagai) joins a peasant farmer and his family loyal to the V.C. to pose as refugees to gain access to an American-held firebase. Later, Butterfly assists the V.C. family in acts of sabotage against the Americans. Finally, she guides the Viet Cong through the base's labyrinthine defenses, helping them to overrun and kill the Americans and the South Vietnamese irregulars they commanded.

"SEMI-PRO" SPIES

This variety of female spy role describes women who don't initially set out to be spies, but for one reason or another, volunteer for or are recruited to clandestine service. The first example is probably not the best or the worst wartime spy film, but it's certainly among the most critically despised. *Shining Through* (1992) has the dubious distinction of nearly sweeping the infamous Razzie Awards for that year, "winning" Worst Picture, Worst Actress, and Worst Director, plus nominations for Worst Actor and Screenplay and chalking up a very low score on the movie criticism website, *Rotten Tomatoes*. Ouch. Major criticisms of the picture included the inappropriate casting of Melanie Griffith in the starring role of secretary-turned spy Linda Voss. Criticisms also noted the unbelievable situations Linda survives and some bad choices made in writing the screenplay adaptation, which reportedly left out some of the best parts of the Susan Isaacs book.

But for our purposes, *Shining Through* demonstrates that even when it comes to clandestine operations, women as well as men could choose to step up and volunteer to put their lives in danger to help win World War II. The daughter of German Jews living in the United States, Griffith's character, Linda, is hired as a legal secretary to international attorney Ed Leland (Michael Douglas), largely because of her ability to speak fluent German. But Leland is much more than he appears: Besides being an attorney, he is an OSS (Office of Special Services) spy. The OSS is America's predecessor to the CIA. Since he travels a lot in Europe for his legal work, Leland is in a perfect position to spy for the government. Working closely together, Linda and Leland eventually become lovers.

The intelligent and resourceful Linda soon figures out that the secretive Leland is a spy, and sometime after the United States declares war with the Axis powers, she leaves the law firm and goes to work for him in Washington at the OSS. But Linda thinks she can do more for her country than take dictation and run errands around Washington. She volunteers to go into Germany on intelligence missions. At first, Leland refuses to approve her request, but she eventually persuades him. "You know what you're getting yourself into, Linda?" he asks. "Yeah," she firmly replies. "The war."

Because Linda is not only an expert speaker of German but also, thanks to her upbringing, an excellent German cook, Leland's contacts in Germany get her a job cooking in the home of an important Nazi. It is hoped that she can break into the Nazi's home office and perhaps photograph secret papers. But, unfortunately, due to circumstances beyond her control, the dishes she cooks for her first big dinner party for a number of high-ranking Nazis are a disaster, and she is fired on the first day. But one of the party's guests, a German general and single father (Liam Neeson), who is attracted to Linda, offers her a job as nanny for his two children. She accepts the job because the general is an important official in the Third Reich, and perhaps she can uncover some secrets in his home office. But oddly she finds nothing. Although he appears to bring work home, there seems to be nothing of value in his office. There is so little in this office that Linda suspects that he hides his government papers somewhere else. Later the children let it slip that in his home, the general has a secret room in their basement. Linda breaks into the room and finds and photographs plans for the V-1 and V-2 rockets the Germans are testing in northern France. When an acquaintance accidentally reveals Linda to be a spy, she escapes with the film of the plans and takes refuge in the apartment of Margrete (Joely Richardson), a woman all the Allies think is their agent, but who turns out to be a double agent who has recently betrayed Linda's own Jewish cousins to the Gestapo. While Linda is in another room, Margrete reports her to the Gestapo. While the Gestapo is on the way to arrest Linda, she figures out that she has been betrayed. Again using her wits, she manages to kill Margrete, but Linda is badly wounded. Amazingly, she escapes the Gestapo by letting herself down a laundry chute. And even more amazingly, the Gestapo doesn't completely search the house and fails to discover the unconscious Linda sprawled in a large laundry basket in the basement. Later Leland arrives and finds her quickly, and in a suspenseful climactic scene, he transports the wounded Linda and her secret film across the Swiss border. At the end, once again, the man must save the woman.

Later, despite the actual historical facts, the film states that the information from Linda's spy camera was used to alert the Allies to the threat from the German rockets, and the German rocket facility in Peenemünde is bombed. The film concludes many years later, as Linda tells the story of their wartime exploits in a television interview. Behind the cameras watching the interview is Leland and the couple's grown-up children.

Compared to other female spies, the free-thinking Linda seems to consider most orders from her handlers to be more like suggestions. When she finds out that she has Jewish relatives being hidden from the Gestapo by some good-hearted Germans, Linda immediately puts saving her relatives before completing the mission, or even before being extracted from Germany herself. She only reverts to putting the mission first when she finds out that her relatives have already been arrested.

Carve Her Name with Pride

The respectful 1958 biopic about Violette Szabo (Virginia McKenna), a real-life British spy in World War II, received much better reviews than *Shining Through*. *Carve Her Name with Pride* is the story of an English girl who had a French mother. She falls in love with a French officer, Etienne Szabo (Alain Sury), while he is stationed in England. They marry and have a little girl, but Etienne is later killed fighting in North Africa. To assist the war effort, Violette receives a commission as an officer in a British auxiliary corps. She drives ambulances and manages canteens for the troops. Later, Violette is recruited to British intelligence because she speaks French like a native, is an outstanding track and field athlete, and also happens to be a crack shot. Violette would use her auxiliary corps job as a cover. Only later did her family and friends find out that she actually worked in British intelligence.

After recruitment, Violette endures a rigorous training course that includes, besides the usual physical training, hand-to-hand combat, demolition, and airborne parachute instruction. After graduation, Violette and fellow spy, Tony Frazer (Paul Scofield), go together on a mission to occupied France. She is ordered to try to make contact with members of a spy cell that has recently been compromised. Next, she organizes them to engage in the demolition of a viaduct used by the Germans to transport supplies. Later, she is arrested and questioned by the Gestapo, but is released. Violette escapes to Paris, meets up with Tony again and the two are transported back to England. Working again on her cover job, Violette is contacted by intelligence and prepared for another mission. It's now D-Day plus one, and Violette and Tony parachute into France. However, on a mission, Violette is captured and interrogated by the Germans in Paris. She obstinately refuses to divulge the information they want, which is a poem, a secret code key between her and her control in London. Violette is sleep-deprived and beaten. Two other women who went through spy training with Violette (Denise Bloch and Lilian Rolfe), who worked in France as radio operators for the Resistance, are put in her cell. Later, the three are transported by train to a concentration camp. Unfortunately, shortly before the Allies retake France and they would be liberated, the Gestapo executes Violette and her two comrades by firing squad. The film ends as Violette's daughter receives the George Cross medal from the king, the second-highest medal bestowed on British citizens, for her mother's bravery and service to British.

Throughout the film, Virginia McKenna portrays Violette as an average person, not a superspy, who gets nervous and fearful and sometimes doubts her own ability. But, like the British in World War II, Violette, with a stiff upper lip, finds a way to do the job and, if possible, complete the mission. McKenna's performance in this film helps demonstrate that *real* secret agents are quite different from the James Bond or Agent XXX kind of spy.

Charlotte Gray

The fictional film *Charlotte Gray* (2001) is a picture with many similarities to *Carve Her Name with Pride*. The composite character Charlotte is actually based on four real British agents during World War II: Pearl Witherington Cornioley, Nancy Wake, Odette Sansom Hallowes, and Violette Szabo. Cornioley served as a secret courier between Britain and France, and after D-Day helped organize Resistance groups into combat teams. At one point the Nazis put a price of one million francs on her head. An even higher valued Gestapo target was Nancy Wake. An Australian, the Gestapo code named Nancy "The White Mouse" because she always escaped them. She helped deliver arms to *Maqui* (Resistance) units and fought beside them to weaken the German Army before D-Day. Odette Sansom Hallowes was a nurse and a courier and worked with the Resistance in France's Burgundy region. Betrayed by a double agent, Odette and fellow spy Peter Churchill were arrested, brutally tortured, and interrogated. Sentenced to death and sent to the Ravensbrueck concentration camp to be executed, they concocted the story that they were married and that Peter was a nephew of British prime minister Winston Churchill. As a result, they were not killed, because the camp commander, Fritz Suhren, feared he would be subject to a war crimes trial after the war. Instead, the two were escorted to the American lines in an attempt by Suhren to get leniency. But Odette and Peter had witnessed many deaths at the camp on Suhren's orders and denounced him. After the war, following his trial at Nuremberg, Suhren was hanged. Odette was named a Member of the Order of the British Empire (MBE) and also received the George Cross. For her bravery in captivity, Odette also received the French Legion of Honor. Two films in the 1950s were made about Odette, but the makers of *Charlotte Gray* in 2001 just used pieces of her story for this composite heroine.

In the movie, Charlotte Gray (Cate Blanchett) is a Scotswoman fluent in French who enlists to train for courier duty between England and France. A main motivation for Charlotte to get over to France is that her lover, Peter (Rupert Penry-Jones), an RAF pilot, was shot down and declared missing in action somewhere in northern France. She also seemed to harbor a romantic notion about being a hero in the war.

Charlotte dyes her hair brunette and parachutes into France with a simple mission: deliver a small parcel containing two vacuum tubes (presumably impossible-to-find parts for a Resistance shortwave radio) to another female agent. She makes her delivery, but almost immediately the agent is arrested, and we do not learn her fate. Rather than return to England, Charlotte poses as a housekeeper for a farmer and Resistance member, Lavade (Michael Gambon). Lavade is hiding two Jewish boys whose parents have been arrested and taken away to a concentration camp. While hiding out with the crusty Lavade, Charlotte works with his son, Julien (Billy Crudup), to organize a sabotage mission in which she, Julien, and the local Resistance mine railroad tracks and blow up a German train. The Germans crack down on the local Resistance after this, and some are killed in an ambush. Charlotte just misses the ambush because she's meeting with her control, who tells her the devastating news that Peter has reportedly died.

A collaborator informs the Germans about the two Jewish boys, and Charlotte and Julien relocate them. But eventually, the Germans catch the boys and put them on a train to what is likely to be the same terrible fate as their parents. Furious, Julien kills the traitor and his girlfriend, also a collaborator. Julien becomes a wanted man and the Germans shoot Lavade.

Charlotte returns to England and works to find aid and shelter for victims of the Blitz. Later, she receives a letter saying that her flyer/boyfriend Peter is alive, but by this time, she feels more connection with Julien than Peter. Later, in 1945, after France's liberation, she returns to France and heads for Julien's family farm. Julien is glad to see her, surprised to see that her hair color is now its natural blonde. For the first time she introduces herself to Julien as Charlotte Gray and they kiss.

Tom Grealis, a critic from RTE, the Irish television network, called *Charlotte Gray* "An adaptation that is often confused as to whether it's a love story set in wartime or a war story with a love angle" (2002). Most reviews of *Charlotte Gray* were also uncomplimentary. It's a shame that the many heroic exploits of the four real female spies were not placed in the forefront of this film, rather than loop a few of their combined accomplishments around a disjointed and uninspiring love story. The story of women as intelligence agents in wartime would have been better and more accurately served—and the memories of these four brave agents better remembered—if it were shown that these women's minds were on the mission, not their boyfriends.

There is one more major role to consider in the treatment of women in war films. It's an auxiliary but vitally important role: women as nurses and doctors. We will discuss them next.

Chapter Eight

Female Nurses and Doctors

In D. O. Selznick's *Since You Went Away*, discussed in chapter 2, Anne's hypocritical, snobby socialite friend Emily rebukes her, saying that it's inappropriate for her daughter Jane, a young, unmarried woman, to volunteer as a nurse's aide tending to young men severely wounded in the war. Quickly Jane interrupts, saying that the boys at the hospital who lost their arms and legs weren't too young to serve, so why shouldn't she? Emily's elitist response is that there must be "other women"—implying nursing is for the lower classes—who are better suited to such work. Although the nursing profession seems to be too proletarian for the likes of a phony like Emily, we know it is an honorable profession practiced by many women of all ages and classes. As adjuncts to the military, female nurses and doctors are a vital part of any nation's war effort. "By definition a noncombatant," writes Yvonne Tasker (2011), "the nurse is associated [in war films] with healing and nurturing and also with sacrifice. Her selfless devotion to her patients provides a mirror for men's selfless sacrifice in combat. The nobility of war and care are thus twined while being divided into separate, gendered spheres of action" (72–73).

In war films, nurses are portrayed as various varieties of Madonna, chattel, and even women capable of the loosest morality. Probably the prototype Madonna caregiver was nurse Sandy in *They Were Expendable*, appropriately played by Donna Reed, Jimmy Stewart's sweet, loving helpmate in *It's a Wonderful Life* and the ideal 1950s–1960s housewife on *The Donna Reed Show*. Sandy was the sweet, virtuous, and professional nurse who reminded American men fighting in the Philippines of what they were fighting for. Fifty-six years later, in the film *Pearl Harbor* (2001), we are shown a group of nurses eager to serve, but who are also more actively on the hunt to have a good time and to snag boyfriends and eventually husbands. These young women have some commonalities in style and personality with Sandy, but, as befits a twenty-first-century portrayal of an earlier generation, the new nurses appear much more open about love and sexuality. This notable exception is the main difference between these nurses and nurse Madonna Sandy: their willingness to let their boyfriends get well beyond first base. In Robert Altman's film *M*A*S*H*, a comedy war film about the Korean War made during the sexually liberated early 1970s, we also encounter a much looser (virtue-wise), collection of sexually liberated, fun-loving nurses working at the 4077th Mobile Army Surgical Hospital. Likewise, the nurses we meet in the Vietnam War combat romance *Purple Hearts* (1984) are open to romance, and unlike the virtuous Sandy, are open to the possibility of sleeping with their men. In *They Were Expendable*, one simply can't imagine a love scene between John Wayne and Donna Reed that would go any further than an affectionate kiss. As director John Ford stages it, a corny salute in which the PT boat squadron's crewmen serenade Sandy with a love song called "Dear Old Girl" (a curious choice) in her honor places her securely up on that pedestal.

A FAREWELL TO ARMS

The history of nursing is one of evolving legitimacy for the profession and respect for the (mostly) women who chose this vocation. In the United States, nursing as a profession became more formalized after the Civil War. Doris Weatherford (n.d.) of the National Women's History Museum writes, "Often called 'sisters' (as British nurses still are), [nurses'] lives were indeed similar to those of nuns. Forbidden to marry, they were cloistered in 'nurses' homes' on hospital grounds, where every aspect of life was strictly disciplined." This is reflected in one of the earliest films about nurses in war, *A Farewell to Arms* (1932), based on the Ernest Hemingway novel. In the film, an American ambulance attendant, Frederic Henry (Gary Cooper), falls in love with a nurse, Catherine Barkley (Helen Hayes) amid the carnage of World War I. Prior to the entrance of the United States into the war, the two both joined the Italian Army, which is fighting on the side of the Allies against the Germans. Most of the film is a relatively standard love story of a soldier and a nurse, but these lovers are star-crossed. The two are secretly married by a sympathetic chaplain, and as the film goes on, Catherine becomes pregnant. The war separates the two for some time, then Frederic finally finds her. But the story ends on a sad note: The baby is stillborn and Catherine dies of childbirth complications.

For the most part, Catherine's character reads as a Madonna who falls from her pedestal. Her values are as wholesome as any Madonna, but she suffers from a psychological wound. Like any average young woman of the time, she yearns for love and romance, but for Catherine, the yearning is affected by a deep, inner urgency. Before she enlisted in the Army, Catherine was engaged to a soldier and waited faithfully for him in England while he went off to fight the Germans. Then she learned of his tragic death. That's why Catherine decides to join the fight and to devote herself to nursing wounded soldiers back to health. When she meets and falls for the charming Frederic, Catherine decides not to again wait for the "right time" like she did with her deceased soldier. Thus, like the Emily character many years later in *The Americanization of Emily*, Catherine throws caution to the wind and allows Frederic too many liberties with her. Later, when the two are married, she feels much better about herself. The marriage must remain a secret, though, because of regulations. If she's found out, Catherine will be dismissed from the service and sent home, separating her from Frederic. Although male doctors may be married, nurses, like nuns, must be virtually celibate, watched over like teenage schoolgirls by older head nurses. The way Hemingway's story goes, it seems that when the two lovers break these rules, fate steps in to punish them. Nurse-soldier relationships in later films often permit such lovers to break rules and not pay the price.

In films about World War I, the only exception that we have discovered to the rule that requires that nurses be celibate takes place in *The Blue Max*, and on the German side. In this film, Elfi Heidemann (Loni von Friedl) is the wife of Col. Otto Heidemann, commander of a squadron of fighters doing combat in the air and in support of ground forces. Perhaps because Heidemann is from a noble Prussian family like most of the pilots in his squadron, Elfi, although married, is permitted to serve as a volunteer nurse in a military hospital in Berlin. Perhaps being a volunteer exempts her from the celibacy requirement. Also, the German High Command uses Elfi for their propaganda purposes. On one occasion, Lt. Bruno Stachel (George Peppard), one of the new young aces in Col. Heidemann's squadron, suffers a minor wound on his forearm. Stachel is a special case, as he comes from the common people, while most of the pilots in his squadron are rich and come from Germany's aristocracy. The German propaganda machine has turned this young pilot, who has distinguished himself by the number of Allied planes he has shot down, into a folk hero. Although he could recuperate just as well in his own billet at the aerodrome, Stachel is instead transported to Berlin and given a nice, clean hospital room all to himself, with Elfi as his nurse. There they take publicity pictures of this hero of the Fatherland being tended to by his commander's wife. At least for Elfi's sake, this publicity stunt gives Stachel the chance to give her the latest word from the aerodrome, and he tells her that her husband is well. For Elfi, who quietly resents being taken away from her many patients in the otherwise overcrowded hospital to "play act" in this private room with Stachel, it is a break from the constant horrors of an understaffed hospital serving too many wounded soldiers.

We see Elfi one more time in this film. In a sequence discussed in chapter 3, dressed elegantly in a wool suit and hat, not in a nurse's uniform, Elfi is on the arm of her husband, Otto, at an airfield in Berlin as Lt. Stachel takes the test flight in the experimental monoplane that results in his death.

SO PROUDLY WE HAIL AND CRY "HAVOC"

Most war films relegate nurses to the background, concentrating on the men doing the fighting. Only occasionally, as with Sandy in *They Were Expendable*, are nurses trotted out to the foreground, and mostly then to serve as the love interest. After they have served their purpose, nurses dissolve into the background as we follow the men heading back out to do the fighting. But in discussing two different kinds of films about nurses, the World War II dramas *So Proudly We Hail* and *Cry "Havoc,"* both released in 1943, Basinger writes about the advantages and disadvantages of a different type of nurse's story in war films, in which the women, not the men, are the protagonists, and the men, rarely shown fighting, are the ones shoved into the background:

> Although the generic setting of such movies is combat, the primary issues are those concerned with the women's world, not the war. The women are worrying about love, romance, sex and clothing. In *So Proudly We Hail*, there's a dance, a scene of childbirth, a wedding ceremony and a honeymoon night. [In *So Proudly*] rape becomes the primary combat threat. . . . What happens is that the basic objective of women in combat is clearly seen to be *taking care of men*, not fighting the war itself. . . . One can see that if the male genre is feminized, it allows women a chance for freedom and heroism, but also maintains a status quo in which the women cannot, for example, win the war, only wait for the men to win it for them. (1993, 477)

In another book, Basinger reminds us that even if women manage to be the protagonists in combat films, that at least for them, "the issues of the war are love, motherhood, sex and choice, four things the women's film is always about, whether it is set in the West, in the home, in a prison or in combat" (1986, 227).

For example, in *So Proudly We Hail*, Lt. Janet "Davy" Davidson (Claudette Colbert) is faced with the inevitable choice women must make: put off her happiness until after the war or reach out for it and marry the man she loves, Lt. John Summers (George Reeves), knowing that this is really the wrong time to get married, since neither of them may survive the siege of Corregidor. She decides that love is her choice, so the two are married. But, as with Frederick and Catherine a generation earlier, when she chooses love in a war zone, as Basinger writes, "she brings down the inevitable punishment of death for her husband and catatonia for herself." In this film, after all the action is behind them, others tell Davy's story in flashback, as she sits, staring blankly, on a deck chair of a medical ship headed back to the United States. As Basinger says, "She makes a wrong choice. She can be a soldier or a lover, but she can't be both. Only men can be both" (1986, 230).

In *Cry "Havoc,"* the same decision faces "Smitty," as nurse Lt. Mary Smith (Margaret Sullavan) is nicknamed. The audience doesn't find out until later in the picture, but the reason Smitty doesn't permit herself to be evacuated from the Philippines to be treated in Australia for malignant malaria is that she's secretly married to communications officer Lt. Holt (Addison Randall). There's another reason she won't go: Smitty is sorely needed in this hospital near the fighting because the new recruits who have just arrived are far from a group of trained nurses. Instead, they are volunteers, including a number of female character stereotypes plucked out of various Hollywood women's pictures in the 1930s, such as a spoiled Southern belle, a waitress, and a stripper. Included is Pat (Ann Sothern), who has held many kinds of jobs, none for very long (probably) because of her prickly personality and affinity to create drama everywhere she goes. Rankled by Smitty's exercising authority over her, Pat, who might today be called a borderline personality, has never worked well with others. Making waves, Pat complains that she isn't used to "taking orders from a dame." In fact, for most of the film, the only time Pat shows an attractive side is when she makes a play for Smitty's husband. Since Pat is a troublemaker with a loose tongue, no one who knows about the marriage wants to tell her the truth until later in the picture, when Pat shapes up a little and turns into a good—but still highly abrasive—team member.

Little by little, most of the new women adapt, learn how to work as nurses' aides, and contribute to the objective of serving the men who desperately are holding on against the onrushing Japanese. But eventually, the Japanese overrun their hospital, and in the last scene, those who survive are taken prisoner and are marched off to a fearful, uncertain future.

Both the beginning and the conclusion of *So Proudly We Hail* exemplify the difference between men's war films and women's. At the start, we see eight bedraggled, combat-tested women of the Army Nurse Corps being evacuated from Corregidor by airplane. What does the narration over this scene call them? "Girls." Not once, but twice. At the end, Davy is cured from her catatonic state when a friend reads her a newly discovered letter from her late husband, advising her to leave the military and go home to America to his farm and "make things grow," the perfect job for a nurturer like Davy. Of course, a man's ending, especially in a 1943 war film just following Corregidor's fall, would be to vow like Gen. Douglas MacArthur to return to the Philippines, retake Bataan and Corregidor and the other islands, and wreak fearful revenge on the Japanese.

The difference is clear in the contrasting objectives of the men versus the women in this film. Men's objectives are apparent from the outset and are much simpler than the women's: Men have a job to do, to delay the advance of the Japanese until reinforcements can arrive from the United States, and then together they can start to take back the rest of the Philippines. That's the work that has to be done, and men are mostly about their work. From the start, women's objectives have little to do with combat tactics and strategies to defeat the Japanese. Certainly they're there to nurse fighting men back to health, but from their conversations, most of their day-in, day-out concerns are about attracting men, relationships with men, their unfortunate appearances in the sack-like military overalls that the nurses must wear at the front, their relationships with other women, and even one nurse's hope of finding a decent beauty parlor!

Among the women, there is only one nurse whose primary concern reads like a man's. Olivia (Veronica Lake) has a hard, unfriendly attitude that the other women find difficult. Davy finally finds out the reason: Olivia's fiancé was killed at Pearl Harbor. Because of this, Olivia oozes hate for the Japanese and wants nothing more than to personally kill as many of the enemy as she can. Later, Olivia asks a supervisor who doesn't know her backstory if she can be assigned to the hospital ward for wounded Japanese prisoners. Her intent is to wait until she's alone and then to kill them all, but at the critical moment, she looks at these helpless men and can't do it. Later, Olivia does get to have her moment of revenge, but she pays a great price. As the Japanese advance on their hospital on Bataan, the women are all attempting to evacuate, but the enemy cuts off the retreat of the last truck full of nurses. Olivia, after all, is beautiful and knows how to distract men, so she loosens a few buttons on her overalls and lets down her long blonde hair. Hiding a hand grenade in her bosom, she walks toward the Japanese. Half-drooling enemy soldiers gather around her anticipating gang rape, then Olivia reaches into her shirt and pulls the pin on the grenade, causing it to explode, killing everyone. This combination of sacrifice and revenge allows the other women to tearfully make their escape.

Even though the nurses are all Army officers, there is a significant difference in the mind of their commander, Col. White (James Bell), between the men and the women under his command. Although he's looking at uniformed female officers, all that he really sees are Madonnas from back home. At present he can't evacuate the nurses to Corregidor, but he promises Davy that he'll get them all out, "Or I couldn't look at my wife or any other woman in the face again."

THE NURSES OF *PEARL HARBOR*

Although in *Pearl Harbor* we are shown many scenes featuring just the nurses, the film's content falls short of qualifying as one of Basinger's women's films set in combat, like *So Proudly We Hail* or *Cry "Havoc."* Although some of the scenes Basinger describes in these two earlier films exist in *Pearl Harbor*, combined they amount to a series of delightful B- and C-plots. For example, on one occasion, a nurse explains why she joined the Army Nurse Corps: "I'm here to do my patriotic duty," she says, "and to meet guys." On another occasion, coming back from church where she's gone to confession, Betty (Jaime King) says, "I can't help thinking when I'm up there getting my slate wiped clean how I'm going to dirty it up again." Betty and an Army pilot nicknamed Red (Ewen Bremner) end up being the first in this group of pilots and nurses to become engaged. "Betty beat us all to the post," one nurse comments. Marriage, apparently, is these nurses' endgame.

But the dominant plot, called by screenwriters the A-plot, of *Pearl Harbor* is not directly concerned with the women: It's the "bromance" between two pilots, Rafe McCawley (Ben Affleck) and Danny Walker (Josh Hartnett), who play lifelong friends and flying enthusiasts. But the men's friendship is strained because of a love triangle between them and nurse Evelyn Johnson (Kate Beckinsale). But all that is set aside when Rafe and Danny hop in behind a stick and rudder and start doing the job they do so well. By taking huge liberties with history, the screenplay places them in two of the very few undamaged P-40 Warhawk fighters that got off the ground during the Pearl Harbor attack. Using their outstanding flying skills, they shoot down a few of the attacking Japanese planes. Also ignoring history, the script crams more adventure into the film by putting these fighter pilots into the captains' seats of two of the B-25 bombers that participated in the famous Jimmy Doolittle Raid on Tokyo. As often happens in war film love triangles, Danny is killed, and Rafe inherits nurse Evelyn.

IN HARM'S WAY

In Harm's Way (1965) features a Hawksian woman who is a nurse. Navy nurse Lt. Maggie Haynes is at ease with men, and as an experienced nurse, she's quite capable of dishing it out. How else could this middle-aged nurse (Patricia Neal) corral the older, cautious bachelor Capt. (soon to be Admiral) Rockwell Torrey (John Wayne)? In the same film, another nurse, young Ens. Annalee Dorne (Jill Haworth), initially appears to be a Madonna or chattel type. But, young and sexually inexperienced, Annalee is a tease, and her attraction to the wild side in older, sadder Cmdr. Paul Eddington (Kirk Douglas) results in her downfall. Although engaged to a young Navy ensign who treats her like a Madonna on a pedestal, nurse Annalee agrees to go on a beach trip with Eddington, who, unbeknownst to Annalee, has severe psychological problems related to his late, unfaithful wife. Inexperienced, Annalee thinks she's safe with him. She flirts and teases, but, as we discussed earlier, this behavior sets off his inner demons. He attacks and rapes her. Later, feeling disgraced and having discovered she's pregnant, a despondent Annalee takes her own life.

THE GI NURSE FANTASY

Often, GIs in foxholes have fantasies about sexual encounters with nurses. Perhaps this is because nurses, being close at hand, are the closest representatives of the women they left behind. A typical fantasy is voiced in *Platoon* when Chris Taylor (Charlie Sheen) is wounded and in shock. He asks an older, experienced soldier, Big Harold (Forest Whitaker) about his situation and receives a nurse fantasy to distract him from his wound:

> **Chris:** Big Harold, do you know if . . . if you're gonna die? Do you feel like everything's just gonna be fine?

> **Big Harold:** Don't gimme that morbid bullshit! You're about to get outta here. [be shipped out of the jungle to a hospital in Saigon] They're gonna give you three hot meals a day . . . white sheets. . . . Them pretty white nurses'll give you blow jobs if you pay 'em enough! (*Platoon*, 1986)

NURSE MADONNA ROLE MODELS

In a few films, nurse Madonnas do more than serve selflessly and professionally and provide ideal women for soldiers' love interests. On a few occasions, these nurses serve as change agents to provide the examples necessary to affect character transformations in male protagonists. Such a nurse is Brooke Elliot (Anna Lee) in *Flying Tigers* (1942). Although she is the girlfriend of Capt. Jim Gordon (John Wayne), of late Gordon has been taking Brooke for granted. Perhaps because he is too busy running the squadron to pay proper attention to her, Brooke becomes mildly attracted to Woody Jason (John Carroll), the flashy new pilot in Gordon's squadron. Perhaps she thinks that a little competition will light a fire under Gordon. Jason, selfish and self-centered, sees Brooke as just a "dame" to romance, but he soon is impressed for other reasons. He sees that she is principled, not a pushover, and a truly good person. It is often said that a good woman can help an immature man grow up, and this is certainly the case with Brooke and Jason. Brooke introduces Jason to a hospital full of Chinese orphans to whom she has dedicated her life. Brooke has even gone to the trouble to learn Chinese. For perhaps the first time, Jason sees what true, unselfish love and service are all about. Showing a little of his newfound unselfishness, in a conversation with deceased flyer Blackie Bales's (Edmund MacDonald) widow (Mae Clarke),

Jason lies and tells her how many Japanese planes her husband shot down. He actually shot down the planes. He also tells the widow about how the quiet, reserved Blackie was really the funniest, most admired pilot in the squadron. Jason pulls out a wad of cash, bounty from the planes he has shot down, and gives Blackie's widow all of it, claiming that this was his commission money. Later in the film, Jason shows he has learned his lesson when he performs the greatest unselfish act, sacrificing his life on a bombing mission with Gordon.

In a B movie called *The Shores of Tripoli* (1942), irresponsible playboy Chris Winters (John Payne) is a new Marine recruit who has developed an instant crush on a Navy nurse, Mary Carter (Maureen O'Hara). Despite the fact that Winters is an enlisted man and she's an officer, which forbids her from consorting with him, Mary is attracted to the brash, young Marine. During the course of his Marine training, Winters tries a number of hare-brained tactics in hopes of winning Mary over, but although she likes him, Mary is all Navy and all professional dedication and will not give in. During this time, Mary's behavior and good example continue to impress Winters, but not enough for him to reform. Meanwhile, Winters has made some mistakes and may choose to get out of the Marines (it's not explained how—perhaps due to influence in high places) and take a civilian job in Washington. Mary, full of esprit de corps, tries to convince him to stay in the Marines, and at the last, Mary's urging and good example coupled with the news that the Japanese have attacked Pearl Harbor convince Winters to remain in the Marines. Finally, they all ship out together to "go shoot Japs." As Tasker writes, this dedicated nurse "offers playboy Chris Winters a glimpse at a better life" (2011, 75).

Purple Hearts

In the Vietnam War film *Purple Hearts* (1984), another nurse provides an initially distasteful character, a doctor this time, with a glimpse at a better life. A playboy doctor, Don Jardian (Ken Wahl), is in the Navy only to obtain trauma surgery experience unique to wartime. He plans to use this experience, plus the financial resources of a rich fiancée, to set up a million-dollar plastic surgery practice after his service in the war is completed. Enter a nurse, Deborah Solomon (Cheryl Ladd), who is the polar opposite. She's all service, compassion, and generosity, especially when it comes to wounded soldiers. We find out later that, like Catherine in *A Farewell to Arms*, before she met Jardian, Deborah was in love with a soldier who was killed. But unlike Catherine, this experience has left Deborah less willing to commit herself to another love relationship. She fears that in Vietnam, if she falls in love again, her new man will also die. So in this film, Jardian helps Deborah take the chance to love again and Deborah shows Jardian how to live a better, less selfish life, to learn the true meaning of their shared profession: caregiving. But initially, Deborah sees what Jardian is up to, both in pursuing her for casual, meaningless sex and in his plan to get trauma surgery experience for his own professional benefit. In their first meeting, Jardian has just arrived at the hospital in Da Nang. He has come straight from the battlefield aid station on a chopper and is reeking of body odor. He is instantly attracted to Deborah and asks her out for a drink. Because he smells so bad, Deborah refuses to go out with Jardian until he cleans up. As he finishes showering, we meet another nurse, Deborah's roommate, the cheery, cheeky Lt. Hallaway (Annie McEnroe). A Hawksian woman, Hallaway is quite different, being flirty, apparently open for anything, especially sex with the likes of handsome hunk Jardian. While he showers and Deborah checks on the condition of the wounded Marine whom Jardian has brought in from the bush, Hallaway steals Jardian a fresh uniform. She delivers the uniform to Jardian just as he steps out of the shower. As she gets an eyeful, Hallaway grins and says, "Good to meet ya!" Hallaway appears periodically in the film, providing sexy comedy relief and a friend for Deborah to confide in. At one point, after the couple's love affair deepens, the immodest roommate does her own nearly nude scene when Jardian thinks it's Deborah in the bathroom, but Hallaway emerges with her hair in a towel, wearing nothing but a pair of panties, her dog tags, and a big grin, causing Jardian to throw back his head and laugh. But Jardian has eyes only for Deborah, who begins to have another kind of effect on him. She tells him about *her* quite different postwar plans. She speaks disdainfully about her father, who is, simply put, "a medical corporation," and her brother, also an MD, a lawyer specializing in medical malpractice suits. Deborah is in medicine for an entirely different reason. Mostly because she feels great compassion for wounded soldiers, Deborah plans to put her Vietnam experience to work in a relatively low-paying nursing job at a veteran's hospital in Washington State, in a place called American Lake. She tells Jardian that she tried six months of medical school at Johns Hopkins, and "had already learned to strut around like a little god." Part of this, to be sure, seems to be a reaction and rebellion against her unfeeling, greedy father, but Deborah is in medicine because she's a true caregiver: "[I] couldn't stand that cool, professional distance: Treat the patient, but don't get involved with the people." Because Deborah refused to become a corporation, she left med school and went into nursing, where the real care happens. This impresses Jardian, who becomes even more attracted. He also wants to sleep with her, just for comfort and to make the war go away for a while. But (as we will discover later in this chapter) Deborah is not one of those loose-virtue nurses from *M*A*S*H*. This does not dissuade Jardian, who continues to find ways—sometimes risky ways—to get to Da Nang to be close to her. He knows that Deborah is well known as an expert "scrounger," able to reach out all over Vietnam, even to the black market, to find scarce medical equipment and drugs for her patients. So Jardian decides he needs a rare kind of surgical retractor, and cons his commander into going to Da Nang to acquire it. As time goes on, Jardian's growing love for Deborah and his admiration for her begin to change his attitude toward everything he believed and planned on when he arrived in the country. Meanwhile, Deborah falls in love with Jardian, and after seeing the change in Jardian, they finally make love.

In the climax of this war/romance film, a series of strange coincidences occurs. For a time, Jardian, who volunteered for a dangerous secret mission, is declared missing in action and presumed dead. Deborah finishes her tour in Vietnam and sadly flies home, believing that she's lost yet another man she loved. But Jardian and two SEAL operatives actually have survived a helicopter crash in enemy territory and slowly are making their way back to American-held South Vietnam. Later, he arrives at Deborah's hospital in Da Nang just after a VC rocket attack has killed a number of hospital people, including some nurses. Lt. Hallaway was killed and her face badly disfigured in this rocket attack. But Hallaway was wearing a nurse's uniform with Deborah's name tag sewn on it because Deborah gave Hallaway her uniforms when she separated from the service and returned to the U.S. Because Hallaway hadn't changed the name tag yet, initially it was thought that Deborah was the one who was killed. So both Jardian and Deborah leave Vietnam convinced that the other had been killed.

Jardian's character arc continues to show great change. He returns to the U.S. completely transformed. He breaks his engagement with his rich fiancée and gives up his plans for the million dollar plastic surgery practice. Instead, for two reasons, Jardian decides to follow Deborah's lead and work at the veterans hospital at American Lake: The first reason is to honor her, and the second is because his own experiences in Vietnam have left him with a dedication to improving the lives of wounded and handicapped servicemen. The veterans hospital chief of surgery is amazed but delighted that Jardian has chosen to join them. He knows that with Jardian's experience in wartime trauma surgery, the young doctor could do much better financially at other hospitals, and compliments him for his unselfish choice. But then the chief's chance mention of a certain second floor nurse whom he describes as a highly resourceful scrounger causes Jardian to wonder, so he goes upstairs to investigate. There he finds Deborah. The film ends as the lovers are happily (and tearfully) reunited.

THE NURSES OF *M*A*S*H*

In 1969, timid studio heads were still too afraid to make a full-blown anti-Vietnam war movie. Later in the 1970s, this attitude would change significantly, in part due to the popular and commercial success of Fox's 1970 Vietnam allegory, *M*A*S*H*. This was a time like few others in American history, when literally brother stood against brother at odds over this increasingly unpopular war. When director Robert Altman showed studio executives his first cut, they laughed at all the right moments, but they also insisted that he change the beginning of the film to add a clear statement saying in no uncertain terms that the era was 1951 and the place was Korea, so no one in the audience would possibly confuse it with Vietnam. Anyone who has seen the film knows how Altman took this disclaimer, along with other bits in the movie, to ludicrous excess, making even this craven studio statement funny. Fox executives didn't seem to care if, on the face of it, Altman's film appeared to criticize the culture and the military-industrial complex of the previous generation. In their dim-wittedness, they thought that this premise would protect them in public opinion from the faction in the country that continued to insist that the United States waste more young lives in the quagmire of Vietnam. Of course, when *M*A*S*H* was released in 1970, every critic and most of the public clearly saw that what critic Emanuel Levy (2007) summarized in this review applied as much to Vietnam as to the Korean War:

> Impudent and bold, M.A.S.H. satirizes the glorification of war, military bureaucracy, social hypocrisy, repressed sexuality, and other old-fashioned norms that have lost their validity. Like other counter-cultural films of the era, it shows distrust and disrespect for any kind of authority—military or civilian—and any type of morality—religious or secular.

For our purposes, the female authority figure who sums up for Altman and screenwriter Ring Lardner Jr. what was wrongheaded about the military in 1951 and still applied two decades later is the 4077th Mobile Army Surgical Hospital's new chief nurse, Maj. Margaret Houlihan (Sally Kellerman). Her first scene is a silly, Chaplinesque bit when she arrives by helicopter, showing off her stocking and garter belt-clad legs as she disembarks, crouching and trying to salute MASH commanding officer Lt. Col. Henry Blake (Roger Bowen) right underneath the chopper's low-slung rotor blades. One realizes that as Hawkeye Pierce (Donald Sutherland) would later state, Margaret was just one of those "regular Army clowns."

Roderick Heath (2012), in writing about the subversive nature of the film, explains how Margaret ends up as an object of derision until later, when her character and role in the film completely change:

> Another key radical idea driving M*A*S*H [was] the notion that the willfully undisciplined, individualist heroes are actually better at their jobs than conformist, uptight people who hide within institutions. [Maj. Frank] Burns [an inept surgeon and a symbol of religious fanaticism, hypocrisy and mean-spirit-

edness] is soon given more support by the arrival of uptight, un-right head nurse Maj. Margaret O'Houlihan, who quickly announces her admiration for Burns to Hawkeye because he's a good "military surgeon," upbraids Hawkeye for letting the nurses call him by his nickname, and smudges the grin on his face when she answers his question about where she comes from with, "I like to think of the Army as my home!"

In the script, Hawkeye dismisses Margaret and places her clearly as the opposition:

Hawkeye Pierce: Oh come off it, Major. You put me right off my fresh fried lobster, do you realize that? I'm now going to go back to my bed, I'm going to put away the best part of a bottle of scotch. . . . And under normal circumstances, you being normally what I would call a very attractive woman, I would have invited you back to share my little bed with me. You might possibly have come. But you really put me off. I mean you . . . you're what we call a regular army clown. (*M*A*S*H*, 1970)

In a fascinating website devoted to defending the image of professional nurses against what they characterize as unfair media characterizations of their profession, Harry Jacobs Summers (2003) summarizes both the negative image of women and specifically the image of Margaret Houlihan at the beginning of the picture:

But as with too many other great movies of its era, M*A*S*H is infused with hostility to women—and all the significant female characters are nurses. Among nurse characters in American film, only Nurse Ratched [villain of *One Flew over the Cuckoo's Nest* (1975)] is more influential than the martinet "Hot Lips" [Margaret's nickname imposed on her later in the movie] Houlihan, who was also a key figure in the long-running television series that followed. Houlihan is far better than Ratched, but the film's depiction of nurses is nothing to celebrate.

Interestingly, one of the most significant differences between the roles played by Loretta Swit as Margaret in the TV series and Sally Kellerman as Margaret in the movie relates to Margaret's sexuality. In the film, Sally's Margaret begins full of pent-up, denied sexuality, hidden neatly behind the stiff collar of military-style hypocrisy. In the TV series, Loretta's Margaret comes to the 4077th MASH as a woman with a relatively well-known, promiscuous past, notorious for her torrid affairs with senior officers as she slept her way up through the junior ranks of army nurses. But in the movie, Sally's Margaret, in seeking out the only other officer as uptight and tradition-bound as she, finds a kindred spirit in Frank Burns. At first they hide their growing sexual attraction to each other behind a façade of religious righteousness. Together they write a secret letter of complaint to deliver up the chain of command to Henry Blake's boss, criticizing the fact that Henry does not clamp down on the hijinks of Hawkeye, Trapper John (Elliott Gould), Duke (Tom Skerritt) and the other hard-drinking, free-loving, "nonmilitary" doctors and nurses of the 4077th. During her last conspiratorial meeting with Burns in her tent, Margaret and Burns finally give in to sex, and try clumsily to make love in what Summers calls "a cringe-inducing affair." Two inches from each other, they are about to kiss, when Frank says,

Burns: God meant us to find each other.

Margaret: *(enthusiastically opening her blouse, revealing her breasts and throwing her head back)* His will be done!

Unfortunately for Margaret and Burns, the whole camp knows about their assignation, and to make matters much worse, Radar (Gary Burghoff) slips a microphone into her tent, under Margaret's bunk. As Margaret cries out and moans for Burns to "kiss my hot lips" (hence her subsequent nickname), their pornographic performance is being broadcast by loudspeaker throughout the entire camp. While a number of doctors and nurses are gathered in Radar's office, listening to the "broadcast" and laughing, Fr. John "Dago Red" Mulcahey (Rene Auberjonois), the 4077th's totally clueless chaplain, walks in. Thinking they're listening to Armed Forces Radio's shortwave of a stateside radio comedy show, he asks, "Is this *The Bickersons*? I love them."

The next day in the mess hall, when Burns is kidded unmercifully by Hawkeye about their lovemaking, the revelation that he is not the religious "sky pilot" that he pretends to be, coupled with his embarrassment and anger, he explodes in anger, diving across the mess hall table and assaulting Hawkeye, much to the amusement of the other doctors and nurses. Afterward, now catatonic and trussed in a straight jacket, Burns is carted away to some unnamed mental hospital. This leaves Margaret with no ally and a new, embarrassing nickname.

Making matters even worse, Margaret's next indignity involves the doctors—egged on by Duke, who is not-so-secretly attracted to Margaret—wagering whether or not Hot Lips is a real blonde. Betting a serious amount of money on it, they know there's only one way to find out for sure whether she gets the blonde tresses on the top of her head from a bottle. In collusion with the other nurses, most of the camp collectively witnesses an event in which the flap of the bathing tent is pulled open, revealing Margaret while showering. Once everyone is satisfied and bets are paid, the other nurse conspirators rush in with towels and a robe to help cover up Margaret. But when she storms out of the shower area and bursts into Henry Blake's tent to complain, Margaret finds the commander naked in bed with pretty nurse Leslie (Indus Arthur). Frothing like Donald Duck, Margaret ignores the assignation she has just disturbed and babbles on about the lack of discipline and how it's all Blake's fault. Finally, in a manner in which a child might threaten to hold her breath until she gets her way, Margaret threatens the ultimate act if he doesn't immediately arrest Hawkeye and the rest:

Margaret: If you don't turn them over to the MPs this minute, I . . . I'm going to resign my commission!

Blake: Goddamnit, Hot Lips, *resign* your goddamn commission!

Margaret: *(stares, then turns to leave, wailing and staggering)* My commission . . . my commission . . . my commission . . .

Colonel Blake: *(calmly to nurse Leslie)* Little more wine, my dear? (*M*A*S*H*, 1970)

After this incident, Margaret's entire role in the film changes. As if the shower tent scene turns off one Margaret character and flips on the switch of another, for the rest of the film she seems to have become resigned to the new role as "Hot Lips." Instead of the uptight military authority figure, Margaret turns into yet one more sexually submissive nurse "babe" around the camp. Soon after, we see her sneaking away from the "Swamp," the tent Hawkeye, Trapper, Duke, and others share, after an assignation with Duke. Their affair now in the open, a subsequent scene shows Duke playing poker with the other doctors, Margaret draped coolly and seductively next to him. With the exception of acting like an idiot while cheerleading for the camp's football team in a game with an evacuation hospital's staff, Margaret turns into Duke's cool-behaving mistress.

Few if any nurses keep their virtue for long after arriving at the 4077th. Heath describes a few of the stock company of loose nurses: "No character seems too small to have meaning for Altman, from Capt. 'Knocko' (Tamara Horrocks) who sits trembling with randy excitement as she listens to Burns and Hot Lips shagging, to Capt. Storch (Dawne Damon) who lays claim to (simpleton Pvt.) Boone [Bud Cort]."

Summers describes the toga party–like atmosphere that pervades the camp:

M*A*S*H is a male movie. . . . While the film shows little nursing, it certainly shows nurses. They fall into several overlapping categories. There are the strict bureaucrats, embodied by Houlihan and a couple of starched specimens Hawkeye and Trapper encounter when they barge into a military ward in Tokyo looking for a VIP patient. There are the naughty nurses . . . who do sexual favors for the surgeons, notably Lt. Dish (Jo Ann Pflug)—yes, a nurse [nick-]named "Dish." Hawkeye pimps Dish for the sexual salvation of "Painless" (John Schuck), the camp dentist who plans to commit suicide because an

episode of erectile dysfunction has convinced him he's gay. . . . Hawkeye
persuades Dish to have sex with Painless in part by suggesting it's a nursing
responsibility.

Poor Lt. Dish, so nicknamed by Hawkeye the first time he meets her in
the mess hall, who tries to act "married" in the midst of all the bacchanalia.
Struggling to remain faithful to her husband throughout her tour in Korea,
Dish, otherwise a "good sport," fights a losing battle. Much earlier in the
film, she almost succumbs to Hawkeye's seduction as they hide away in a
tent and begin to strip off each other's clothes. But suddenly Hawkeye is
called away. Apparently for nearly the rest of the movie, Dish refuses to give
in to temptation and remains faithful. But on Painless's fateful night, which
is also Dish's last evening at the 4077th before being rotated home, Hawkeye
persuades her to meet him for what she assumes is the passionate conclusion
of that earlier interrupted tryst. Something about the finality of leaving Korea
seems to have convinced Dish that all the blood and guts and suffering she's
labored through since arriving at the MASH allows her to rationalize one
selfish moment. Perhaps, thinking about sex for the rest of her life with just
her husband, Dish wants to have this memory, which she will lock away deep
in her heart and share with no one. But Dish is in for an even *bigger* memory:
This is when Hawkeye shows her what he has in mind and manages to
persuade Dish to, so to speak, "take one for the team." Since the sleeping
Painless is by all reports the most well-endowed dentist in the Army, when
Hawkeye raises his bed sheet and Dish takes a long gaze at his private parts,
the music soars to something akin to angel's song, her eyes open wide and
she gives in. The camera then tastefully backs off and leaves the scene. The
next day, as Dish sits in the helicopter a few moments before liftoff, her
expression is somewhere between catatonic and noncommittal. Then, right
before the chopper rises to the heavens, her expression changes to a huge grin
as a heavenly chorus crescendos. In M*A*S*H, nothing is sacred except the
laugh.

"ANGELS OF MERCY"

There are more film nurses whose roles as "angels of mercy" extend to more
than sponge baths. For example, after Shears (William Holden) escapes from
the Japanese prison camp in *The Bridge on the River Kwai* (1957), he suffers
from malaria and malnutrition and is recovering in a military hospital. We
never see Shears with his nurse (Ann Sears) at his side in a hospital bed,
though. When we see the two, they're frolicking on the beach in bathing
suits, enjoying a picnic basket and each other. It's obvious by their familiar-
ity that they are having a torrid affair.

Similarly, in *Windtalkers* (2002), while Marine Sgt. Joe Enders (Nicolas Cage) is recovering in the hospital from injuries suffered when he was nearly killed in a mortar explosion on Guadalcanal, he is having an affair with Nurse Rita (Frances O'Connor). Enders has survivor guilt over decisions he made that cost the lives of all the men in his squad on Guadalcanal. He did the right thing—obeyed orders—but he believes that if he had found some other way, his men might be alive. So despite the fact that due to the explosion he lost hearing in one ear, he wants to obtain a clean bill of health—rather than the medical discharge he deserves—so he can return to the fighting. Nurse Rita aids Enders in faking the results of his hearing test, allowing him the chance to redeem himself on the battlefield.

Such soldier-nurse relationships are not reserved for Americans. In *Cross of Iron*, German Sgt. Rolf Steiner (James Coburn) also is wounded, a result of a mortar explosion. With a concussion and a few other wounds, Steiner is transported to a field hospital. After some time in the hospital, although ambulatory, Steiner's consciousness drifts in and out of reality, seeing dead comrades and other wounded soldiers both whole and healthy and then wounded, bandaged, some missing limbs. We always see Sister Eva (Senta Berger) at his side, including during an incident in which Steiner jumps in a nearby pond and poor Eva has to jump in to get him out.

Scenes that follow show that Sister Eva is more than Steiner's nurse. He sits in a wheelchair at one reception for patients with the faithful Eva pushing him. Steiner grabs a bottle of wine from a table, and Eva follows him to make sure in his addled state of mind that he doesn't hurt himself or anyone else. During the reception, the two dance together. Once, in private in his room, she wears his uniform tunic. Later, after Steiner and Eva have made love, he spies one of his men, recovered from his wound, who's headed back to the front. Loyal to his men and dedicated to their survival, Steiner decides to go back to the war with the soldier. Upset, Eva asks Steiner why he doesn't go home, since his injuries rate a home leave. He answers, "What home?" She replies, "My home, our home." Apparently Steiner has made some promises. Eva cries and plays psychologist for a moment, asking if he loves the war, or is afraid of what he would be without the war. Steiner doesn't answer, but gathers his things, finishes dressing and prepares to leave. Eva decides his leaving is inspired by patriotism, not knowing how cynical Steiner is about the war and especially the Nazis. As he silently exits, she says, "Long live Germany!"

One real life Dutch woman who became a nurse out of necessity is remembered as the "angel of Arnhem," and is immortalized in Richard Attenborough's epic recounting of the World War II Operation Market Garden, *A Bridge Too Far* (1977). Based on the real Mrs. Kate ter Horst and played subtly but sympathetically in the film by Liv Ullmann, Kate was an attorney's wife who gave her permission for the British First Airborne Division to set up a hospital in her spacious home. Allied soldiers there were surrounded and outnumbered by the Germans, and the battle was a disaster. With little help, Kate compassionately cared for 250 wounded British paratroopers during the eight-day battle.

FEMALE DOCTORS

In war films, there are very few instances in which women doctors, rather than nurses, are featured. One of them was in *Corregidor*, a 1943 romance/combat picture. Dr. Royce Stockman (Elissa Landi) has the bad timing to arrive in the Philippines December 6, 1941, the day before the Japanese attacked Pearl Harbor and the Philippines. At first, in all the confusion of enemy air and ground attacks, she and her new husband, Jan (Otto Kruger), also a doctor, are on their own in the jungle. They encounter a squad of U.S. Army soldiers and take up with them. Both of these physicians offer their medical services to the embattled Americans as the soldiers valiantly defend Corregidor against the invading Japanese. Royce gamely serves as a combat surgeon, and, after Jan is killed and Japanese victory is imminent, she and other female medical personnel are evacuated by seaplane off "the rock" to safety in Australia. As the film ends, we see Royce in Australia, looking out sadly over the water. Preposterously and incomprehensively, once evacuated to Australia, Dr. Royce seems to have been demoted from the status of doctor, because this board-certified surgeon is wearing the starched white uniform and head cap of a nurse!

Two wars later, in the Vietnam War film, *The Siege of Firebase Gloria*, Capt. Kathy Flanagan (Margi Gerard), an army doctor, doesn't get much more respect from the Marines in charge of a rural firebase to which she is assigned. Newly arrived, Kathy appears unsuited to her current assignment at this firebase, presently under assault by the Viet Cong. At one point, she has just finished patching up a wounded Viet Cong prisoner. Cpl. Joseph DiNardo (Wings Hauser) begins questioning this prisoner in Vietnamese about the nature of the VC battalion laying siege to their firebase. He pokes the prisoner's newly bandaged wound, causing the man to cry out in great pain. Flanaigan objects.

DiNardo: Lady [not calling her "doctor" or "captain"], this is called "extracting information." 'You understand that?

Flanaigan: So we torture prisoners now, do we?"

DiNardo: You're goddam right. This ain't Nebraska, lady.

Flanaigan: Don't do it in my hospital.

(Ignoring Flanaigan's order, DiNardo continues to poke and prod the prisoner's wound, and he continues to cry out.)

Flanaigan: *(furious)* What kind of animal are you?

DiNardo: *(angrier at her now than at the stubborn VC)* Lady, do you have any idea if Charlie got in here what he would do? He would rape you and your nurses until you were dead. But you know what? They'd have to kill me first. Animal? I'm not an animal. (*The Siege of Firebase Gloria*, 1989)

DiNardo is incensed that this woman doctor dares to question his doing his job, and so in much more graphic terms than he has to, he explains what the fortunes of this kind of war would have in store for her and her nurses. Besides her name-calling, Susan Jeffords has an opinion about why DiNardo comes down so hard on Flanaigan: "The very word 'woman' signifies all those qualities which the masculine mind splits off from itself . . . and in the female live all the qualities the male has decided are inferior and suspect. This repression of the feminine is at the heart of . . . much Vietnam literature" (2003, 432). And it is at the heart of the war genre itself, which finds little utility in the feminine perspective, since it runs counter to executing the manly "job" of war.

Later, Flanaigan's aid station is indeed overrun by VC soldiers. Suitably frightened about what DiNardo told her, Dr. Flanigan realizes that she's in a kill-or-be-killed situation: She lays aside the Hippocratic Oath, picks up an M-16 and starts shooting.

A difference of opinion with DiNardo isn't the only disrespect that Flanaigan must deal with while serving on Firebase Gloria. At one point, concerned about some of her patients, Flanaigan objects to Sgt. Hafner's (R. Lee Ermey) order that the walking wounded be patched up and sent back to the trenches to shore up their defense. Almost ignoring her concerns entirely, the crusty NCO replies, "I'm not too crazy about you ladies (Flanaigan and a few female nurses) being on my firebase in the first place, but I guess I'm gonna have to learn to live with it. Good morning, *Miss* Flanaigan. She quickly replies, "Captain. The rank's captain." Hafner sarcastically wisecracks, "I'm real impressed. Maybe you ought to be the CO (commanding officer)." Later, Flanigan complains to Hafner that she's run out of medical supplies. Hafner barks that there will be no resupply because the communication bunker's "history." She looks at him as if to say, "What do I do now?" Too busy to hold her hand, Hafner says, "You're a captain. Be a goddam captain." During the VC assault on her hospital bunker, she does indeed become a goddam captain.

Chapter Nine

A Few Concluding Thoughts

Molly Haskell's judgment about that opposite gender with whom women share this planet seems to conclude that like Sam Peckinpah's, most men's image of women remains unchangeable:

> As Peckinpah said in a *Playboy* interview, "There are women and there's pussy," a statement that not only overlooks the fact that there's a little of both, like the virgin and the whore, in all women, but that misinterprets Peckinpah's feelings, so viscerally apparent in film after film, that all women, way down deep, are pussy. (Haskell 1973, 363)

There will always be a certain percentage of men for whom such Neanderthal beliefs will never change. But as we have discussed, the great majority of citizens, affected so relatively easily by what they see on TV and in the movies, can change their opinions. Producers of commercial media products devoted to the management of consumer demand know how to persuade the public to "buy" anything they want them to purchase, because they understand how much and how the mass media affect their audiences. If consumers can be persuaded to buy things, we can also be moved to think differently about any number of issues.

Internet searches reveal literally thousands of pages in which entire websites, articles, blogs, and public responses to discussion questions wrestle with issues dealing with the real or perceived effects of film and television. Most of this emphasis is on negative effects. Most scholars who research and write on this subject agree with George Gerbner's cultivation theory, which asserts that people's perceptions of reality are informed and altered by the mediated versions of "reality" that they see on film and television (Cohen and Weimann 2000). Some older, more simplistic notions about media effects imagine direct cause-and-effect relationships between, for example,

241

viewed media violence and subsequent audience behaviors. Others hold with mainstream media effects research that suggests that behaviors such as violence may be influenced by specific media images and models, but cannot motivate nonviolent people to become violent. However, few, if any, mainstream social scientists would assert that the media models we see in the movies or TV have no effect at all. What we see in media, especially TV and the movies, becomes a part of our life experience, and any such experience could alter any number of changes in perceptions and even beliefs.

For example, when television sets became fixtures in American households in the 1950s and 1960s, characterizations of gay people or homosexual behavior were not allowed. Today, in part because gay characters have appeared and even starred in network TV shows during the last two decades, polls show that the majority of Americans accept gay marriage and full rights and benefits for gay people. This support was reinforced in 2013 by two U.S. Supreme Court decisions—declaring that restrictions on gays in the Defense of Marriage Act were unconstitutional, and overthrowing California's Proposition 8, a prohibition against gay marriage. Once people who perhaps have not knowingly even been acquainted with a gay person "get to know them" through gay roles sympathetically portrayed on television, they seem less apprehensive about allowing those with alternate lifestyles the right to enter the mainstream of American society and share in society's rights and privileges.

Another sea change in societal attitudes and norms over the last forty years pertains to women. Females have been appearing with greater frequency in TV series and motion pictures as soldiers who fight right alongside or against men. And unlike Basinger's earlier models for women in war and adventure films, some of these motion pictures or TV programs do not necessarily require women to give up all their femininity or follow the men's rules. Both in soldierly portrayals of America's wars and in fictional or science fiction wars, women both fight and even command male soldiers. This, plus viewing TV news and documentary images of women serving in harm's way in Iraq and Afghanistan have subtly informed and altered public opinion on women in war. This year (2013), as discussed in chapter 6, undoubtedly predisposed due to polls that advocate a change, the U.S. Defense Department has removed the last restrictions barring women in combat.

MANY FEMALE ROLES

In this book, we have introduced a dozen major roles that women play in films about war: the Madonnas; women as chattel; prostitutes, loose women, camp followers, and the unfaithful; the Hawksian woman; GI Janes and female resistance fighters; Mata Haris; and nurses and doctors. But within these roomy categories, we have discovered a considerable amount of variation in characters that provide alternative visions for future female characters in war and adventure films. Some of the roles we have discussed reflect the restrictions on women dictated by the eras in which the films were made. Other women boldly stepped far forward for their eras, suggesting the kind of women who were yet to be born, much less liberated from the constraints of films like *Hearts of the World*. Women's roles of the last twenty years especially have added a considerable amount of food for thought for our cultures, as we recall, courtesy of Jeanine Basinger, their cumulative effect: "By making it possible and putting it on the screen as if it were a reality, it begins to make it probable. The impossible then becomes possible and finally inevitable" (1986, 228).

STILL "THE OTHER"

Women in war films come in several varieties, but through the years, they still all share one common identity: They are the "other" to whom men compare themselves and whom they draw distinctions with, fight for, or pursue for both legitimate and illegitimate intentions. Hollywood's women in war have evolved considerably since their limited roles early in the last century, currently permitting them opportunities to fight alongside men and even to command men in combat. In men's perceptions, however, women still remain that other entity, who, as Hawks would say, distract men from the job of war. But in the twenty-first century, the women in our war films will continue to assert that they, too, can stand fast on the battle line and kill the enemy. They will also continue to remind us all that they are just as human as men.

Annotated Filmography of War Films

Note: Some of these plot synopses contain spoilers.

ACT OF VALOR (2012)

Directors: Mike McCoy, Scott Waugh
Screenplay: Kurt Johnstad
Cast: Roarke Denver, Duncan Smith, Roselyn Sanchez, Alex Veadov, Sonny Manson, Nestor Serrano
Oscars: None
DVD: Relativity Media

Story of a Navy SEAL team rescuing a CIA agent and then thwarting a jihadist terrorism cell before they can invade the U.S. and explode a number of suicide vest bombs in public places in the United States. Includes real Navy SEALs portraying themselves.

Film's treatment of femininity: There is both a long-suffering Madonna who must hide the tears as she bids her husband good-bye as he leaves on a dangerous mission and a CIA Mata Hari who is kidnapped by terrorists and beaten and tortured for information.

AIR FORCE (1943)

Director: Howard Hawks
Screenplay: Dudley Nichols
Cast: John Ridgely, Gig Young, Harry Carey, Arthur Kennedy, John Garfield

Oscars: Nominations for Original Screenplay, Black-and-White Cinematography and Special Effects; Oscar for Film Editing
DVD: Warner Home Video

Classic U.S. World War II propaganda film about the adventures of a B-17
crew that arrives at Hickam Air Base right after the attack on Pearl Harbor.
The aircrew hops from Hawaii to Wake Island and the Philippines, seemingly pursued constantly by the Japanese, and ends up dropping bombs on
enemy ships in the Battle of the Coral Sea.

Won the Oscar for Best Editing and received three other Oscar nominations: Best Original Screenplay, Best Cinematography (Black-and-White),
Best Effects, Special Effects.

Film's treatment of femininity: Displays both the Madonna character in
one flyer's mother and the Madonna who probably used to be a Hawksian
woman in the bomber commander's wife. Also, the Hawksian woman as
seen in Sue, McMartin's sister.

ALIEN (1979)

Director: Ridley Scott
Screenplay: Dan O'Bannon and Ronald Shusett
Cast: Sigourney Weaver, Tom Skerritt, John Hurt, Ian Holm, Veronica
    Cartwright, Yaphet Kotto, Harry Dean Stanton
Oscars: Nominated for Art Direction; Oscar for Visual Effects
DVD: Twentieth Century Fox

Ordered to set their spaceship down on an apparently lifeless planet, the crew
of the ore transport vessel *Nostromo* encounter a deadly alien, which they
take on board their vessel. On the trip back to earth, the alien kills the crew,
one-by-one, as in a *Ten Little Indians* horror story, until only one human is
left to battle for her life with the monster.

Film's treatment of femininity: Ripley's character is given the opportunity for a tremendous character arc throughout the picture, and in the end, she
is empowered to do battle with the monster. Ripley's clever method of expelling the creature from her shuttlecraft is used in the climaxes of three of the
Alien films as the standard method of killing the beast.

ALIENS (1986)

Director: James Cameron
Screenplay: James Cameron; story by David Giler, and Walter Hill

Cast: Sigourney Weaver, Michael Biehn, Paul Reiser, Bill Paxton, Lance Henrickson

Oscars: Nominations for Best Actress, Original Score, Film Editing, Art Direction, and Sound; Oscars for Visual Effects and Sound Effects Editing

DVD: Twentieth Century Fox

An Oscar-winning (Best Visual Effects, Best Sound Effects Editing) science fiction film, *Aliens* is a thinly veiled Vietnam War allegory that also is deeply critical of America's military-industrial complex. Futuristic colonial marines, arrogant and overconfident in their firepower, lose every encounter with powerful, intelligent, well-organized "bug" creatures. Nearly all the humans are killed, and only the heroine of the original film, *Alien*, Ellen Ripley, and a few others survive the encounter. The film received five other Oscar nominations (Best Editing, Original Score, Art Direction/Set Decoration, Sound) including one for Weaver as Best Actress, a rarity for a science fiction/action film.

Film's treatment of femininity: When traditional males (Marines) fail, a GI Jane character evolves with the skill, intelligence, and courage to defeat the aliens.

THE AMERICANIZATION OF EMILY (1964)

Director: Arthur Hiller

Screenplay: Paddy Chayefsky, based on the novel by William Bradford Huie

Cast: James Garner, Julie Andrews, Melvyn Douglas, James Coburn, Keenan Wynn

Oscars: Nominations for Black-and-White Cinematography and Art Direction

DVD: Warner Home Video

A comedy about a U.S. Navy officer, an aide to an important admiral, with a unique approach to his job in World War II: to avoid fighting at all costs while living the good life in London in the weeks prior to D-Day. He falls in love with a British woman who has a much more traditional view of war. During the D-Day invasion, the officer becomes an accidental hero, and must find a way to come to grips with his beliefs.

Film's treatment of femininity: Features a fallen Madonna, plus her conversion from worshipping fallen heroes to the love of a self-professed coward, or as she happily puts it, a man who's "craven through and through."

APOCALYPSE NOW (1979)

Director: Francis Ford Coppola
Screenplay: John Milius, Francis Ford Coppola, Michael Herr, based on the novella *Heart of Darkness* by Joseph Conrad
Cast: Martin Sheen, Marlon Brando, Robert Duvall, Frederic Forrest, Dennis Hopper
Oscars: Nominations for Best Picture, Supporting Actor, Director, Adapted Screenplay, Film Editing, and Art Direction; Oscars for Cinematography and Sound
DVD: Lions Gate

Coppola's adaptation of Joseph Conrad's *Heart of Darkness*, set during the Vietnam War, received eight Academy Award nominations, including Best Picture, Director, and Adapted Screenplay and won two Oscars (Best Cinematography, Best Sound). An Army Special Forces assassin is ordered to venture upriver to Cambodia to "terminate with extreme prejudice" (kill) an insane American officer running amok throughout the countryside with local tribesmen, engaging in savage, unrestrained attacks. However, typical events in the war that the assassin experiences during his adventure create doubt that what his target is doing merits assassination.

Film's treatment of femininity: Madonnas at home briefly discussed.

BACK TO BATAAN (1945)

Director: Edward Dmytryk
Screenplay: Ben Barzman, Richard H. Landau (Story: Aeneas MacKenzie, William Gordon)
Cast: John Wayne, Anthony Quinn, Beulah Bondi, Philip Ahn, Lawrence Tierney, Fely Franquelli
Oscars: None
DVD: Warner Home Video

An American Army colonel leads a guerilla force of Filipino soldiers and civilians against the Japanese occupation. They rescue a Filipino officer—son of a famous Filipino military leader—from the Bataan Death March to assist them in their efforts and rally civilians to the cause. At first reluctant, the rescued officer witnesses the commitment of his people to the struggle and also becomes committed to the cause.

Film's treatment of femininity: Brave Mata Hari spies right under the nose of the Japanese command.

BAND OF BROTHERS (HBO MINISERIES, 2001)

Directors: Phil Alden Robinson, Richard Loncraine, Mikael Salomon, David Nutter, Tom Hanks, David Leland, David Frankel, Tony To
Screenplay: Tom Hanks, Erik Jendreson, E. Max Frye, Graham Yost, Bruce C. McKenna, Erik Bork, John Orloff
Cast: Damian Lewis, Ron Livingston, Scott Grimes, Shane Taylor, Donnie Wahlberg, Peter Youngblood Hills, Nicholas Aaron, Philip Barantini, Michael Cudlitz, Neal McDonough
Emmys and Golden Globe: Won thirteen Emmys; six additional nominations; Golden Globe for Best Miniseries; also nominated for Best Actor and Best Supporting Actor
DVD: HBO Home Video

Based on Stephen Ambrose's history of Easy Company, 101st Airborne Division, this ten-episode miniseries chronicles the gritty, realistic story of these average American soldiers from paratrooper training in the United States, through their amazing experiences during D-Day, Operation Market Garden, the Battle of the Bulge, the capture of Hitler's Eagle's Nest, and the end of the war. Winner of multiple Emmys, including Outstanding Miniseries.

Film's treatment of femininity: Chronicles the fates of female collaborators in occupied countries after the countries are liberated. Also, the men experience minor encounters with German women during the last phase of the war in Europe.

BATTLE: LOS ANGELES (2011)

Director: Jonathan Liebesman
Screenplay: Christopher Bertolini
Cast: Aaron Eckhart, Michelle Rodriguez, Bridget Moynahan, Ramon Rodriguez, Wil Rothhaar, Cory Hardrict
Oscars: None
DVD: Columbia

A Marine staff sergeant leads a platoon against formidable aliens who invade Los Angeles. Thanks to a woman, an Air Force Technical Sergeant at that, the platoon is able to find the alien command and control center and destroy it.

Film's treatment of femininity: Among the civilians whom the Marines saved are both men and women, but the real female star is a tough, no-

nonsense Air Force GI Jane who proves to some doubting Marines that she knows her tech and is also very good in a firefight.

BATTLE OF BRITAIN (1969)

Director: Guy Hamilton
Screenplay: James Kennaway, Wilfred Greatorex
Cast: Michael Caine, Trevor Howard, Ian McShane, Laurence Olivier, Christopher Plummer, Michael Redgrave, Ralph Richardson, Robert Shaw, Susannah York
Oscars: None
DVD: MGM Video

A historically consistent chronicle of the early days of the air war between Britain and Germany, resulting in Germany's inability to invade Great Britain.

Film's treatment of femininity: The most interesting story is about the conflict between an RAF officer and his wife. The officer wants her home, tending the petunias, while she enjoys the independence of her job in RAF Air Operations and won't quit.

BATTLESHIP (2012)

Director: Peter Berg
Screenplay: Jon and Eric Hoeber
Cast: Taylor Kitsch, Alexander Skarsgård, Rihanna, Brooklyn Decker, Liam Neeson, John Tui
Oscars: None
DVD: Universal

Based on the board game and the video game, *Battleship* tells the story of an alien invasion thwarted by U.S. Navy personnel, using destroyers and in the climax, pressing the Battleship *Missouri* back into service.

Film's treatment of femininity: There are two women in supporting roles. The first is the girlfriend of the hero whose actions identify the target that must be destroyed to thwart the plans of the invaders. The second is a female petty officer who supports the hero as his weapons officer.

THE BEST YEARS OF OUR LIVES (1946)

Director: William Wyler

Screenplay: Robert E. Sherwood from a novel by MacKinlay Kantor
Cast: Fredric March, Dana Andrews, Myrna Loy, Teresa Wright, Harold
    Russell, and Cathy O'Donnell
Oscars: Nominated for Sound Recording; Oscars for Best Picture, Actor,
    Supporting Actor, Director, Adapted Screenplay, Music, Film Editing,
    and a special Oscar for wounded veteran Harold Russell
DVD: MGM Video

The unforgettable and intertwined stories of three veterans coming home
after World War II to restart their lives. Al, a banker, goes back to his post,
but the war has afflicted him with an alcohol problem. Fred has no job, and
his wife deserted him. Homer, having lost both arms in battle, has the hardest
readjustment.

Film's treatment of femininity: A sampling of female types, it includes
the all-wise and loving middle-aged Madonna, two young Madonnas-in-
training to act as love interests for Fred and Homer, and Fred's unfaithful ex-
wife, who perhaps never stood upon the pedestal.

THE BIG RED ONE: THE RECONSTRUCTION (ORIGINAL RELEASE IN 1980, RECONSTRUCTION IN 2005)

Director: Samuel Fuller
Screenplay: Samuel Fuller
Cast: Lee Marvin, Mark Hamill, Robert Carradine, Bobby Di Cicco, Kel-
    ly Ward, Stephane Audran, Siegfried Rauch
Oscars: None
DVD: Warner Home Video

The story of a sergeant, a veteran of World War I, and four soldiers of his
squad and their adventures in World War II. Beginning with the disastrous
Battle of the Kasserine Pass in North Africa, these soldiers experience the
war in Sicily, the devastation of D-Day, an ironic firefight with the Germans
in an insane asylum in Belgium, and the liberation of a Nazi death camp at
the end of the war.

Film's treatment of femininity: A Sicilian boy risking everything trying to
bury his dead mother; the men enjoying being treated like sons by a group of
older Italian women they rescued from the Germans; delivering a baby in the
shot-out ruins of a tank; partying with prostitutes in Belgium.

BLOOD ON THE SUN (1945)

Director: Frank Lloyd
Screenplay: Lester Cole and Nathaniel Curtis
Cast: James Cagney, Sylvia Sidney, Porter Hall, Robert Armstrong, Wallace Ford, John Halloran
Oscars: Best Black-and-White Art Direction
DVD: Image Entertainment

A newspaperman and a double agent team up to transport a copy of the Tanaka Memorial Plan out of Japan so it can be published in the United States and throughout the world. The fictional document was purported to detail Prime Minister Giichi Tanaka's secret campaign for Japanese world domination.

Film's treatment of femininity: Iris is a clever, mysterious, and sultry spy, ostensibly working for Tanaka, but actually an American agent. A Chinese-American, she also advocates for humane and equal treatment for Asian women.

THE BLUE MAX (1966)

Director: John Guillermin
Screenplay: Ben Barzman, based on the novel by Jack Hunter
Cast: George Peppard, James Mason, Ursula Andress, Jeremy Kemp, Karl Michael Vogler
Oscars: None
DVD: Twentieth Century Fox

World War I story of a common soldier who applies to be a combat aviator. He turns out to be an exceptional pilot, skillful in air combat. But the ranks of German combat aviation are reserved for the aristocrat class, and this commoner, despite his flying skill, is shunned by most of his comrades. Nonetheless, his success in the air leads to fame and glory, and earns him the coveted Blue Max medal. But his torrid affair with the unstable wife of an aristocratic general eventually leads to his undoing and death.

Film's treatment of femininity: A general's trophy wife learns the extent of her freedom and the true meaning of being chattel, and a squadron commander's wife is allowed the dubious privilege of working long hours volunteering in a Berlin military hospital in spite of being married.

BOMBS OVER BURMA (1942)

Director: Joseph H. Lewis
Screenplay: Joseph H. Lewis, George W. Pardy, Milton Raison
Cast: Anna May Wong, Noel Madison, Leslie Denison, Nedrick Young,
   Dan Seymour
Oscars: None
DVD: Alpha Video

In early World War II, a schoolteacher ostensibly on a school inspection trip and a man posing as a monk attempt to find out who among a group of stranded bus passengers is really an agent working for the Japanese. They eventually discover the culprit and turn him over to Chinese peasants for summary justice.

Film's treatment of femininity: The film shows that a schoolteacher, and a woman teacher at that, can be effective in the fight against the enemy. Wong in this film shows that a secret agent can also be a skilled detective.

THE BRIDGE ON THE RIVER KWAI (1957)

Director: David Lean
Screenplay: Carl Foreman and Michael Wilson, based on the novel by
   Pierre Boulle
Cast: William Holden, Alec Guinness, Jack Hawkins, Sessue Hayakawa,
   James Donald
Oscars: Nominated for Best Supporting Actor; Oscars for Best Picture,
   Actor, Director, Adapted Screenplay, Music Score, Film Editing, and
   Cinematography.
DVD: Columbia Tri/Star

Bridge is the story of two battles of wills and personalities: the first, a British colonel stubbornly standing on principle against a Japanese colonel fanatically adhering to his *bushido* warrior's code; the other battle being between an American slacker whose humanism and instinct to survive the war clashes with the duty he finds himself obliged to perform.

Film's treatment of femininity: Burmese women serve as bearers during the expedition to blow the bridge treat the men like masters, even washing them when the group stops by a river. Also, Spears and a nurse have an affair.

A BRIDGE TOO FAR (1977)

Director: Richard Attenborough
Screenplay: William Goldman, based on the book by Cornelius Ryan
Cast: Dirk Bogarde, James Caan, Michael Caine, Sean Connery, Edward
  Fox, Elliott Gould, Gene Hackman, Anthony Hopkins, Laurence
  Olivier, Ryan O'Neal, Robert Redford, Maximilian Schell
Oscars: None
DVD: MGM

Attenborough's epic account of World War II Field Marshall Montgomery's disastrous plan to "end the war by Christmas." An all-star cast dramatizes a factual account of Operation Market Garden, an attempt to drop thousands of Allied paratroopers into Holland and gain access to bridges across the Rhine into Germany. A half-dozen key Allied blunders and the chance presence of two German Panzer divisions in Holland foil the attempt.

Film's treatment of femininity: A Madonna opens her home to nurse wounded soldiers. Like *Band of Brothers,* the film details the fates of female collaborators in occupied countries after the countries are liberated.

CARVE HER NAME WITH PRIDE (1958)

Director: Lewis Gilbert
Screenplay: Vernon Harris and Lewis Gilbert from the R. J. Minney book
Cast: Virginia McKenna, Paul Scofield, Maurice Ronet, Jack Warner,
  Denis Grey, Anne Leon
Oscars: None
DVD: VCI Entertainment

To revenge her husband who was killed in North Africa and to assist the war effort, Violette, an Englishwoman, is recruited to British Intelligence because she speaks French like a native, is an outstanding track and field athlete, and also happens to be a crack shot. After spy training, Violette is ordered to make contact with members of a French Resistance cell that has recently been compromised. She organizes the cell to sabotage a German train. She returns to England, but is parachuted back into France after D-Day. Violette begins another mission, but is captured and interrogated by the Germans in Paris. Despite torture, Violette obstinately refuses to divulge the information they want. Later she and two other captured female British spies are transported by train to a concentration camp where the three are executed by firing squad.

CASABLANCA (1943)

Director: Michael Curtiz

Screenplay: Julius J. Epstein, Philip G. Epstein, Howard Koch, from the play *Everybody Comes to Rick's* by Joan Alison and Murray Burnett

Cast: Humphrey Bogart, Ingrid Bergman, Paul Henreid, Claude Rains, Conrad Veidt, Peter Lorre, Sydney Greenstreet, Dooley Wilson

Oscars: Nominations for Best Actor, Supporting Actor, Music, Film Editing, and Black-and-White Cinematography; Oscars for Best Picture, Director, and Adapted Screenplay

DVD: Warner Home Video

One of the greatest classic films and perhaps the best screenplay yet written, the story is set in unoccupied North Africa during World War II. Rick's café is the setting for intrigue, black marketeering, and refugees trying to get exit visas to Lisbon and, perhaps, America. Rick meets up with two such refugees, one of whom, Ilsa, is his former lover. Against his usual neutral principles ("I stick my neck out for nobody"), Rick makes an exception and helps Ilsa and her freedom-fighting husband escape to Lisbon. As her husband Victor says to Rick, "Welcome back to the fight."

Film's treatment of femininity: During wartime, women are not in control of their fates, and love becomes much more complicated.

CASUALTIES OF WAR (1989)

Director: Brian DePalma

Screenplay: David Rabe, based on the book by Daniel Lang

Cast: Michael J. Fox, Sean Penn, John C. Reilly, Don Harvey, John Leguizamo, Erik King

Oscars: None

DVD: Sony Pictures

In one movie-long posttraumatic flashback, a tragic Vietnam War story unfolds, in which a long-range reconnaissance patrol kidnaps, rapes, and murders a young Vietnamese girl. One member of the patrol refuses to participate and tries to protect the girl, but must do so at the risk of being murdered by the other men. Eventually he turns them in, and the men are court-martialed and convicted.

Film's treatment of femininity: Soldiers consider a Vietnamese woman as chattel to dispose of as they please.

CATCH-22 (1970)

Director: Mike Nichols
Screenplay: Buck Henry, based on the novel by Joseph Heller
Cast: Alan Arkin, Martin Balsam, Richard Benjamin, Art Garfunkel, Jack
    Gilford, Buck Henry, Bob Newhart, Anthony Perkins, Martin Sheen,
    Jon Voight, Orson Welles
Oscars: None
DVD: Paramount

Buck Henry's screenplay from Joseph Heller's novel satirizes the military
mentality and the military-industrial complex. It's the tale of a World War II
bombardier who, desperate to be grounded, appeals to the flight surgeon to
ground him for medical reasons. As the screenplay puts it, "In order to be
grounded, I've got to be crazy. And I must be crazy to keep flying. But if I
ask to be grounded, that means I'm not crazy anymore, and I have to keep
flying. . . . That's some catch, that Catch-22."

Film's treatment of femininity: To survive, women in the middle of war
must turn to prostitution and do the best they can under the circumstances.

CHARLOTTE GRAY (2001)

Director: Gillian Armstrong
Screenplay: Jeremy Brock from the Sebastian Faulks novel
Cast: Cate Blanchett, Billy Crudup, Charlie Condou, David Birkin, John
    Pierce Jones, Louise Vincent
Oscars: None
DVD: Warner Home Video

In a film based very loosely on several Allied female spies who carried on
espionage missions in occupied France, Charlotte is a Scotswoman fluent in
French who enlists to become an agent operating in France. Charlotte parachutes into France and poses as a housekeeper for a farmer and Resistance
member, who is also hiding two Jewish boys whose parents have been arrested and taken away to a concentration camp. Charlotte collaborates with
the farmer's son, Julien, also a Resistance member, to organize a sabotage
mission to mine railroad tracks and blow up a German train. Charlotte returns
to England and works to find aid and shelter for victims of the Blitz. After
France is liberated, she returns and is reunited with Julien, with whom she
has fallen in love.

CHINA (1943)

Director: John Farrow
Screenplay: Frank Butler, based on the play by Archibald Forbes
Cast: Loretta Young, Alan Ladd, William Bendix, Philip Ahn, Richard Loo
Oscars: None
VHS: Universal Studios

In pre-World War II China, an American oil profiteer changes from heel to freedom fighter when he meets a beautiful schoolteacher and witnesses Japanese atrocities against the Chinese people. He joins Chinese guerilla fighters and, with their help, ambushes and destroys a large Japanese Army convoy.

Film's treatment of femininity: Similar to *Casualties of War*, Chinese women are victimized by marauding Japanese soldiers.

COMING HOME (1978)

Director: Hal Ashby
Screenplay: Robert C. Jones, Waldo Salt (Story: Nancy C. Dowd)
Cast: Jane Fonda, John Voight, Bruce Dern, Penelope Milford, Robert Carradine
Oscars: Nominations for Best Picture, Supporting Actor, Supporting Actress, Director, and Film Editing; Oscars for Best Actor, Actress, and Original Screenplay
DVD: MGM

While her Marine husband is fighting in Vietnam, a woman busies herself by volunteering in a veterans' hospital. She falls in love with a paraplegic veteran and her whole life changes. Her husband comes home from his tour of duty, suffering from acute posttraumatic stress disorder. Realizing he has lost his wife, and riddled with guilt for supposed atrocities he has committed in Vietnam, he commits suicide. Winner of three Oscars: Best Actor (Voight), Actress (Fonda), and Best Original Screenplay. Nominated for five more: Best Picture, Director, Supporting Actor (Dern), Supporting Actress (Milford), Editing.

Film's treatment of femininity: A Madonna kept as chattel by her husband finds and exercises new freedom when he's off to war and she's on her own.

CORREGIDOR (1943)

Director: William Nigh
Screenplay: Doris Malloy and Edgar G. Ulmer
Cast: Otto Kruger, Elissa Landi, Donald Woods, Frank Jenks, Rick Vallin, Wanda McKay
Oscars: None
DVD: Alpha Video

Clumsily written B movie about a civilian doctor, Jan Kruger, and his new wife, Royce, also a doctor, who are caught in the middle of the Japanese invasion of the Philippines. After adventures in the jungle, the two make their way to the U.S. Army and volunteer to serve in the military hospital, where coincidentally Royce runs into an old flame, also a surgeon. Despite a few romantic sidesteps, they labor on until Jan is killed and Royce, along with the nurses on Corregidor, is evacuated to Australia.

Film's treatment of femininity: From the start, the Army hospital authorities nearly ignore Royce, as if they don't respect her as a doctor despite her qualifications and the surgeries she performs alongside the male doctors. Then, in an inexplicable final scene, a sad and lonely Royce looks out over the ocean from her new hospital in Australia, dressed in a nurse's uniform and cap!

COURAGE UNDER FIRE (1996)

Director: Edward Zwick
Screenplay: Patrick Sheane Duncan
Cast: Denzel Washington, Meg Ryan, Lou Diamond Phillips, Michael Moriarty, Matt Damon
Oscars: None
DVD: Twentieth Century Fox

Following the Iraq war, an Army officer from the Pentagon investigates whether a female helicopter pilot should receive the Medal of Honor posthumously. But as he interviews various soldiers who witnessed the event, he finds himself in a *Rashomon*-like situation: Every soldier tells a different story. Adding to this is another story, this officer's own battles with posttraumatic stress following a "friendly fire" incident.

Film's treatment of femininity: When a GI Jane commands men, some men display antifemale attitudes while others are compliant.

CROSS OF IRON (1976)

Director: Sam Peckinpah
Screenplay: Julius J. Epstein, James Hamilton, Walter Kelley, based on the novel by Willi Heinrich
Cast: James Coburn, Maximilian Schell, James Mason, David Warner, Senta Berger
Oscars: None
DVD: EMI Films

In 1943 on the Russian front, an arrogant, aristocratic replacement officer reports for duty with a single goal: to earn Germany's Iron Cross, a medal awarded for valor. Unfortunately, he is not well suited for combat, and spends most of his time hiding away in his bunker. But when he claims to have heroically led a counterattack against the Russians, an action that would lead to earning his Iron Cross, the officer comes into conflict with a sergeant who knows the truth and refuses to go along with him.

Film's treatment of femininity: A nurse falls in love with her patient and imagines them living together back home in Germany, but her patient is drawn back to war and his men and abandons her.

CRY "HAVOC" (1943)

Director: Richard Thorpe
Screenplay: Paul Osborn from the Allan Kenward play
Cast: Margaret Sullavan, Ann Sothern, Joan Blondell, Fay Bainter, Marsha Hunt, Ella Raines, Frances Gifford
Oscars: None
DVD: Warner Brothers

Story of a group of volunteer nurses' aides in the Philippines after Pearl Harbor. These women, of various backgrounds, learn how to care for the wounded and coexist with each other as they do their best to tend to wounded soldiers. At the end, all that survive are captured by the Japanese.

Film's treatment of femininity: Except for a "kick butt" GI Jane, nearly all the various roles portrayed by women in war films appear in this single picture.

THE DEER HUNTER (1978)

Director: Michael Cimino

Screenplay: Deric Washburn, based on a short story by Quinn Redeker

Cast: Robert De Niro, John Cazale, John Savage, Meryl Streep, Christopher Walken, George Dzundza

Oscars: Nominations for Best Actor, Supporting Actress, Original Screenplay, and Cinematography; Oscars for Best Picture, Supporting Actor, Director, Film Editing, and Sound

DVD: MCA/Universal Home Video

Nominated for nine Oscars and winner of five, including Best Picture, Best Director, and Best Supporting Actor (Walken), this film takes three young men from their hometown to the horrors of Vietnam and back again. The two survivors, one disabled, try as best they can to adjust to life after the war, to the loss of their deceased friend, and to the meaning of it all.

Film's treatment of femininity: A Madonna on a shaky pedestal waits for two men to return from the war.

DESTINATION TOKYO (1943)

Director: Delmer Daves

Screenplay: Delmer Daves, Albert Maltz, based on a story by Steve Fisher

Cast: Cary Grant, John Garfield, Alan Hale, John Ridgely, Dane Clark, Robert Hutton

Oscars: Nominated for Best Original Story

DVD: Warner Home Video

Oscar-nominated story of a World War II American submarine on a mission to sneak into Tokyo harbor to obtain weather and other intelligence information to support the Doolittle bombing raid on Tokyo. Screenplay by Delmer Daves and Albert Maltz provides not-too-subtle propaganda against the enemy, the Japanese.

Film's treatment of femininity: Single men at war dream—and tell wild stories—of women as chattel, while married men daydream about their Madonnas.

THE D.I. (1957)

Director: Jack Webb

Screenplay: James Lee Barrett

Cast: Jack Webb, Don Dubbins, Jackie Loughery, Lin McCarthy, Virginia Gregg

Oscars: None
DVD: Warners

GSgt. Moore has a problem: One of his recruits is a foul-up, a young man who doesn't seem to be Marine material. But Moore has faith in him, and spends most of the film trying to get him to grow up and become a Marine.

Film's treatment of femininity: Women in this film are either chattel as off-post love interests or a Madonna, the recruit's mother.

THE DIRTY DOZEN (1967)

Director: Robert Aldrich
Screenplay: Nunnally Johnson, Lukas Heller, based on the novel by E. M. Nathanson
Cast: Lee Marvin, John Cassavetes, Charles Bronson, Jim Brown, George Kennedy, Telly Savalas, Donald Sutherland, Ernest Borgnine, Robert Ryan
Oscars: Nominations for Best Supporting Actor, Film Editing, and Sound; Oscar for Best Sound Effects
DVD: MGM

An insubordinate U.S. Army major is assigned the task of training and leading a group of bedraggled, rebellious convicts on a dangerous mission behind German lines right before D-Day. The film was nominated for four Oscars, including a Best Supporting Actor nod to Cassavetes, and won for Best Sound Effects.

Film's treatment of femininity: *All* women shown in this picture, British and German, are prostitutes.

DRAGON SEED (1944)

Directors: Harold S. Bucquet and Jack Conway
Screenplay: Marguerite Roberts and Jane Murfin, from the Pearl S. Buck novel
Cast: Katharine Hepburn, Walter Huston, Aline Mac Mahon, Turhan Bey, Akim Tamiroff
Oscars: Nominations for Best Supporting Actress and Black-and-White Cinematography

During the 1930s invasion of China by the Japanese, a Chinese farming family, content in their isolation and their ancient ways, has their entire world shaken and torn apart by the invading Japanese. Many—especially women and children—die, as the peaceful peasants learn that they cannot coexist with their evil occupiers. Their response is to form a resistance, denying their crops and homes to the enemy by burning them to the ground, leaving the Japanese only scorched earth and no way to subsist. Many peasants migrate a thousand miles West, to what they call "free China," to grow crops to feed the resistance fighters, while the resistance, both men and many women, stay on to fight a guerilla war.

EAGLE SQUADRON (1942)

Director: Arthur Lubin
Screenplay: Norman Reilly Raine (Story: C. S. Forester)
Cast: Robert Stack, Diana Barrymore, Jon Hall, Eddie Albert, Nigel Bruce, John Loder
Oscars: None
DVD: Universal Pictures

In a propaganda film designed to convince the American people that the United States should support their ally in the Battle of Britain, a headstrong, young American pilot joins the Eagle Squadron, the contingent of American flyers who enlisted in the RAF before their country declared war on Germany. Through his experiences, American audiences were shown Britain's desperate circumstances and their brave fight against the German onslaught.

Film's treatment of femininity: Especially during the Battle of Britain, English women pitch in to help.

THE EDGE OF DARKNESS (1943)

Director: Lewis Milestone
Screenplay: Robert Rossen, based on the novel by William Woods
Cast: Errol Flynn, Ann Sheridan, Walter Huston, Helmut Dantine, Judith Anderson, Ruth Gordon
Oscars: None
DVD: Warner Home Video

A U.S. anti-Nazi propaganda film about the decision the people of a Norwegian fishing village had to make in the face of German occupation. They either could meekly and selfishly comply with their conquerors, as the German commander believes they will, or rise up as one to crush the invaders. The Nazis make the townspeople's decision easy by acting "normally," that is, mistreating and assaulting the villagers, goading them into collective action.

Film's treatment of femininity: As in *Casualties of War*, when an occupying force considers women as chattel to rape or mistreat as they please, there are consequences.

ENEMY AT THE GATES (2001)

Director: Jean-Jacques Annaud
Screenplay: Jean-Jacques Annaud and Alain Godard
Cast: Jude Law, Ed Harris, Rachel Weisz, Joseph Fiennes, Bob Hoskins, Ron Perlman
Oscars: None

Based on historical characters, *Enemy* is the story of famous Soviet sniper Vassili Zaitsev, the hero of the battle of Stalingrad during World War II. Beginning as a conscript soldier who wasn't even issued a rifle, Zaitsev, as his last name is spelled in the movie, grabs a weapon from a dead soldier and begins killing Germans. He is transferred for duty as a sniper, and becomes famous for killing dozens of Germans. Eventually, Zaitsev meets his match in the top enemy sniper, Maj. Konig, and only barely escapes his own death before he shoots the German.

Film's treatment of femininity: The film features two Soviet GI Janes, one of whom is well-suited to the job of sniper and soldier and one whose lack of professionalism and courage causes her own death.

A FAREWELL TO ARMS (1932)

Director: Frank Borzage
Screenplay: Benjamin Glazer and Oliver H. P. Garrett from the Ernest Hemingway novel
Cast: Gary Cooper, Helen Hayes, Adolphe Menjou, Mary Phillips, Jack LaRue
Oscars: Nominations for Best Picture, Supporting Actor, and Art Direction; Oscars for Best Cinematography and Sound Recording

This film begins as a standard romance between an ambulance attendant and a nurse during World War I, but becomes a tragedy. The two fall in love and are married, and—to circumvent regulations—must try to keep it a secret. The story ends badly when the nurse becomes pregnant, the two are separated for a time by the war, and finally, as she gives birth, both she and the child die.

Film's treatment of femininity: The nurse and almost all the other nurses in the film fulfill fairly standard Madonna roles. There is really only one other female character of note, a prostitute with whom the hero flirts before he meets the nurse. But all we ever see of the prostitute is her bare leg.

THE FIGHTING SEABEES (1944)

Director: Edward Ludwig
Screenplay: Borden Chase, Aeneas MacKenzie
Cast: John Wayne, Dennis O'Keefe, Susan Hayward, William Frawley, Paul Fix
Oscars: Nomination for best music
DVD: Republic Pictures.

A World War II propaganda film, the story involves a construction company building installations in the Pacific for the U.S. Navy, faced with the difficulty of doing heavy construction while Japanese forces try to prevent them. In response, the Navy creates Construction Battalions and recruits and trains these skilled workers to build and then fight to protect the installations they create. Through the experiences and mistakes made by one obnoxious contractor turned Seabee officer, the film preaches the virtue of cooperation between nominal civilians and the military.

Film's treatment of femininity: A female war correspondent yearns to experience war firsthand.

FIVE GRAVES TO CAIRO (1943)

Director: Billy Wilder
Screenplay: Charles Bracket, Billy Wilder
Cast: Anne Baxter, Franchot Tone, Akim Tamiroff, Erich von Stroheim, Peter van Eyck, Fortunio Bonanova
Oscars: Nominations for Best Black-and-White Art Direction, Cinematography, and Film Editing
DVD: Universal

During its march across North Africa, Field Marshal Erwin Rommel's Afrika Corps stops at a small hotel and makes it their temporary headquarters. Unknown to Rommel, a British soldier is pretending to be a waiter, and with the help of a French maid, obtains important intelligence information that he passes on to British Field Marshal Montgomery's headquarters. This information turns the tide in North Africa and Rommel is defeated.

Film's treatment of femininity: The French maid, Mouche, who is trying to save her wounded brother, a prisoner of war of the Germans, is manipulated by a German officer who promises to help. Actually, he just wants to have sex with her, and her brother has already died.

FLIGHT OF THE INTRUDER (1991)

Director: John Milius
Screenplay: Robert Dillon from the Stephen Coonts novel
Cast: Brad Johnson, Danny Glover, Willem Dafoe, Rosanna Arquette, Tom Sizemore
Oscars: None
DVD: Paramount

Upset over unrealistic, political restrictions on their bombing targets during the Vietnam War, Navy flyers dream about bombing the restricted "SAM City" target in Hanoi, the storage place for North Vietnam's stockpile of surface-to-air missiles. These SAMs have caused more deaths among these flyers' comrades than any other enemy weapon. Two pilots decide to disobey orders and make a trip to "Sam City."

Film's treatment of femininity: Rosanna Arquette's portrayal of a Madonna slipped from the pedestal is a good example of this role.

FLYBOYS (2006)

Director: Tony Bill
Screenplay: Phil Sears, Blake T. Evans, David S. Ward
Cast: James Franco, Martin Henderson, Jean Reno, David Ellison, Jennifer Decker, Abdul Salis
Oscars: None
DVD: MGM

Fact-based story of a group of young Americans who join the French Air Force during World War I. Members of the Lafayette Escadrille, as the American contingent of the French Air Force was called, learn to fly and fight against the Germans prior to the United States' entrance into the war.

Film's treatment of femininity: Traditional Madonna to be rescued from marauding Germans by our hero.

FLYING LEATHERNECKS (1951)

Director: Nicholas Ray
Screenplay: James Edward Grant (Story: Kenneth Gamet)
Cast: John Wayne, Robert Ryan, Don Taylor, J. C. Flippen, Janis Carter
Oscars: None
DVD: Warner Home Video

A Marine squadron commander proves his theory of close air support of ground forces while he tries to "toughen up" his executive officer who is too close to his men to make sound, hard-nosed decisions. Typical for this kind of John Wayne 1950s war film (think *Sands of Iwo Jima*), finally, the subordinate adopts the mind-set and values of his superior, and merits a promotion to squadron commander.

Film's treatment of femininity: Madonna wives of Marine pilots must courageously hold down the fort while their men are off fighting, act as the cheerful and affectionate helpmate when their men return, and don't cry too much when their leaves are over and they're off to war again.

FLYING TIGERS (1942)

Director: David Miller
Screenplay: Kenneth Gamet, Barry Trivers
Cast: John Wayne, John Carroll, Anna Lee, Paul Kelly, Gordon Jones, Mae Clarke, Edmund MacDonald
Oscars: Nominations for Best Score, Special Effects, and Sound Recording
DVD: Republic Pictures

Nominated for three Oscars (Best Scoring of a Dramatic or Comedy Picture, Best Visual Effects, Best Sound), this film tells the story of a band of American mercenaries who, like the Lafayette Escadrille against the Germans in World War I, joined the Chinese Air Force to fight the Japanese prior to Pearl Harbor and America's entrance into the war. This story centers on a selfish, playboy pilot whose actions threaten good squadron discipline and even result in the death of one member of the squadron. Finally, under the influence of John Wayne's character, the pilot realizes his mistakes and atones for his sins, flying a suicide mission.

Film's treatment of femininity: Two varieties of women in this film, the Madonna who waits for her man to come home and the loving Madonna nurse who pitches in to help right there in the war zone.

FORCE OF ARMS (AKA *A GIRL FOR JOE*) (1951)

Director: Michael Curtiz
Screenplay: Orin Jannings and Richard Tregaskis
Cast: William Holden, Nancy Olson, Frank Lovejoy, Dick Wesson, Paul Picerni, Katherine Warren, Gene Evans
Oscars: None
DVD: Warner Brothers Video

This is a mixed-genre love story/combat film about a soldier who meets and falls in love with a WAC in Italy during World War II. The soldier, promoted from sergeant to lieutenant for his bravery and leadership, loses both when he becomes over cautious and afraid once he falls in love. Although wounded and eligible to rotate back to the United States, his PTSD causes him to return to combat to regain his manhood.

Film's treatment of femininity: The lead female character is a Madonna who has slipped slightly from her pedestal in the past and is trying to right herself. But she throws caution to the wind when she meets and falls in love with a soldier.

FROM HERE TO ETERNITY (1953)

Director: Fred Zinnemann
Screenplay: Daniel Taradash, based on the novel by James Jones
Cast: Burt Lancaster, Montgomery Clift, Deborah Kerr, Donna Reed, Frank Sinatra, Ernest Borgnine
Oscars: Nominations for Best Actress, two for Best Actor, Music, and Black-and-White Costume Design; Oscars for Best Picture, Supporting Actor, Supporting Actress, Director, Adapted Screenplay, Film Editing, Black-and-White Cinematography, and Sound Recording
DVD: Sony Pictures

Winner of eight Oscars (out of twelve nominations) including Best Picture, Director, Screenplay, Supporting Actor (Sinatra), and Supporting Actress (Reed), this adaptation of the National Book Award–winning James Jones novel tells the story of a group of people in and around Schofield Barracks in Hawaii in the months just prior to the attack on Pearl Harbor. One hard-headed soldier, an expert boxer, refuses easy duty and promotion because he refuses to fight anymore. Meanwhile, his first sergeant is having an affair with the neglected wife of his company commander, and a young GI ends up in the stockade, tortured by a sadistic jailer. No one wins.

Film's treatment of femininity: Two women's roles: One is a prostitute who has a star-crossed love affair with a soldier. The other is an unfaithful wife, suffering in a loveless marriage. Having fallen far from the pedestal, she has had numerous assignations with other men and is currently having an affair with an enlisted man who is the first sergeant of the company her husband commands.

FULL METAL JACKET (1987)

Director: Stanley Kubrick
Screenplay: Stanley Kubrick, Michael Herr, Gustav Hasford, based on the novel *The Short Timers* by Hasford
Cast: Matthew Modine, Adam Baldwin, Vincent D'Onofrio, R. Lee Ermey, Arliss Howard
Oscars: Nominated for Best Adapted Screenplay
DVD: Warner Home Video.

Nominated for an Oscar for Best Adapted Screenplay, *Full Metal Jacket* represents Kubrick's unique version of the adventures of the Vietnam Generation in "their war." As with *Dr. Strangelove*, Kubrick provides his typical sarcastic and critical views of the military and its leadership as he relates the adventures of a character nicknamed "Joker" and his friend, "Cowboy," from basic training to combat during the Tet Offensive of 1968.

Film's treatment of femininity: Two kinds of women appear or are mentioned in this film: The first is the "wet dream fantasy" girlfriend waiting for the troops back home and the other is an expert Viet Cong sniper out to kill them.

G.I. JANE (1997)

Director: Ridley Scott
Screenplay: David Twohy and Danielle Alexandra
Cast: Demi Moore, Viggo Mortensen, Anne Bancroft, Jason Beghe, James Caviezel
Oscars: None
DVD: Walt Disney Video

A U.S. senator with a feminist political agenda manages to place a female officer in Navy SEAL training, which has heretofore been reserved only for males. The officer, Jordan O'Neil, must overcome male prejudice as well as herself to succeed in this rigorous form of training. Later, on an actual mission, O'Neil distinguishes herself, rescuing the SEAL who has been her chief critic throughout training.

Film's treatment of femininity: A woman tries to achieve a goal that few men are capable of: becoming a Navy SEAL.

GO TELL THE SPARTANS (1978)

Director: Ted Post
Screenplay: Wendell Mayes and Daniel Ford from Ford's novel
Cast: Burt Lancaster, Craig Wasson, Jonathan Goldsmith, Marc Singer, Joe Unger, Denise Kumagai
Oscars: None
DVD: HBO Home Video

A detachment from a company of U.S. Army advisors, early in the American involvement in Vietnam, tries in vain to occupy a firebase that once was the site of a massacre of French soldiers. Although the company commander knows that America's presence and helping the corrupt South Vietnamese Army is a mistake, the audience sees how the hubris of senior American commanders will soon lead the U.S. into an escalated war that they still cannot win.

Film's treatment of femininity: There are a few mistresses of the local Army of Vietnam commander. However, the interesting female role is Butterfly, a Viet Cong spy. Butterfly attaches herself to a family of peasants so she can infiltrate the U.S. firebase. From there, she organizes acts of sabotage and escapes the camp so she can lead VC troops safely back through the maze of barbed wire and booby traps the Americans have set.

THE GREEN BERETS (1968)

Directors Ray Kellogg, John Wayne (uncredited: Mervyn LeRoy)
Screenplay: James Lee Barrett, based on the novel by Robin Moore
Cast: John Wayne, David Janssen, Jim Hutton, Aldo Ray, Bruce Cabot, Jack Soo, George Takei
Oscars: None
DVD: Warner Home Video.

Perhaps the worst of the very few pro-Vietnam War propaganda films, this obvious defense of an indefensible Vietnam policy centers on the men of the Army's Special Forces on missions to defend a firebase and kidnap a North

Vietnamese general. Ends spectacularly as one sarcastic review puts it, as "the sun slowly sets into the East."

Film's treatment of femininity: A Mata Hari infiltrates an Army firebase, commits acts of sabotage and later leads the Viet Cong attack to overrun the base.

GUADALCANAL DIARY (1943)

Director: Lewis Seiler

Screenplay: Lamar Trotti, Jerome Cady, based on the book by Richard Tregaskis

Cast: Preston Foster, Lloyd Nolan, William Bendix, Richard Conte, Anthony Quinn, Richard Jaeckel, Lionel Stander

Oscars: None

DVD: Twentieth Century Fox.

Based on American war correspondent Richard Tregaskis's fact-based account, the film follows a Marine company on the campaign to take the island of Guadalcanal, the first major Allied land offensive against the Japanese in World War II. Concentrating on the men's personal experiences and interactions, the Marines mature into combat veterans as they do combat with a fierce and treacherous enemy.

Film's treatment of femininity: A Marine assumes a young soldier is writing to his girlfriend. Actually, he's writing home to his mother, but implies to his buddy that this nonexistent girlfriend is submissive chattel.

THE GUNS OF NAVARONE (1961)

Director: J. Lee Thompson

Screenplay: Carl Foreman, based on the novel by Alistair MacLean

Cast: Gregory Peck, David Niven, Anthony Quinn, Stanley Baker, Anthony Quayle, James Darren, Irene Papas

Oscars: Nominations for Best Picture, Director, Adapted Screenplay, Music, Film Editing, and Sound; Oscar for Best Special Effects

DVD: Sony Pictures

Based on Alistair MacLean's novel, this high adventure involves a British commando team and Greek partisans tasked with taking out a pair of massive cannons threatening the evacuation of 2,000 British troops from Kiros, an Aegean island. Built into the side of a mountain and highly fortified, the target becomes even more difficult to destroy when a traitor tips off the

Germans to their every move. Finally the traitor is discovered and dispatched, and the objective destroyed. Nominated for seven Oscars including Best Picture, Best Director, and Best Screenplay, the film's lone win was for Best Special Effects.

Film's treatment of femininity: Two women are featured: a tough Greek resistance fighter and another, posing as another member of the resistance who's actually a double agent.

A GUY NAMED JOE (1943)

Director: Victor Fleming
Screenplay: Dalton Trumbo, Frederick Hazlett Brennan (Story: Chandler Sprague, David Boehm)
Cast: Spencer Tracy, Irene Dunne, Van Johnson, Ward Bond, James Gleason, Lionel Barrymore
Oscars: Nominated for Best Original Story
VHS: MGM

Fantasy film about a World War II bomber pilot, killed near the beginning of the film, who returns as a spirit mentor (read: guardian angel) of a newly-commissioned P-38 pilot. Under the "angel's" guidance, the new pilot advances in flying and combat skills and becomes an ace. Complicating matters is when the young aviator begins romancing his own angel's girlfriend.

Film's treatment of femininity: A member of the Women's Air Force Service Pilots (WASPs) usually ferries planes to war zones, and then the men fly the missions. However, this woman actually flies a combat mission, reversing roles, to protect her lover. Why? Because she's convinced she's a better pilot and has a better chance to survive this dangerous mission.

HAMBURGER HILL (1987)

Director: John Irvin
Screenplay: James Carabatsos
Cast: Steven Weber, Dylan McDermott, Courtney B. Vance, Don Cheadle, Michael Boatman, Anthony Barrile
Oscars: None
DVD: Lions Gate

Bloody but truthful recreation of the 1969 battle for a nameless hill in the A Shau Valley of Vietnam between soldiers of the U.S. 101st Airborne and North Vietnamese soldiers, told mostly through the characters of one 101st squad. Between assaults on the hill, the Americans reveal the thoughts of the young soldiers of the Vietnam era. Film conveys their feeling of camaraderie awkwardly mixed together with the conflicts between their various personal backgrounds and force-blended American cultures, especially between the "brothers" of the company (the black soldiers) and the rest. Eventually, these differences blend into a brotherhood-in-arms.

Film's treatment of femininity: Women in this film are prostitutes, loyal to whichever side's soldiers have money to spend on them.

HANOVER STREET (1979)

Director: Peter Hyams
Screenplay: Peter Hyams
Cast: Harrison Ford, Lesley-Anne Down, Christopher Plummer, Richard
    Masur, Patsy Kensit
Oscars: None
DVD: Sony Pictures

Romance and action blend awkwardly with an interesting discussion of how circumstance creates heroes in this film about a World War II-era illicit romance between an American bomber pilot and a married British woman. Plot becomes complicated when the pilot realizes that as his plane is shot down over occupied France, the British spy with whom he has parachuted to safety is his lover's husband.

Film's treatment of femininity: In a study of guilt and romance, a Madonna tumbles off her pedestal when she falls in love with a flyer and has an affair with him.

TO HAVE AND HAVE NOT (1944)

Director: Howard Hawks
Screenplay: Jules Furthman and William Faulkner
Cast: Humphrey Bogart, Lauren Bacall, Walter Brennan, Hoagy Carmi-
    chael, Marcel Dalio, Sheldon Leonard
Oscars: None
DVD: Warner Brothers Video

Against his better judgment, Morgan, an American fishing boat captain, assists the Free French Underground on Martinique by smuggling a Resistance fighter and his wife onto the island. When he returns, his life becomes more complicated when he meets a young, beautiful American expatriate whom he nicknames Slim. Then, as they avoid Vichy French authorities, Morgan, the Underground, and Slim try to make arrangements to transport the couple to Devil's Island, where they hope to help another French patriot escape.

Film's treatment of femininity: For a young woman, Slim already has led an eventful life. She is mostly a mystery to Morgan, full of wisecracks and backtalk. In one way, she is a woman with a past, but in another, she's just what Morgan needs: more of a sense of purpose.

HEARTBREAK RIDGE (1986)

Director: Clint Eastwood
Screenplay: James Carabatsos
Cast: Clint Eastwood, Marsha Mason, Everett McGill, Eileen Heckart, Mario Van Peebles, Arlen Dean Snyder
Oscars: None
DVD: Warner Bros.

Veteran Marine Gunnery Sergeant Highway is about to retire, but he wants to go out with a win (speaking of wars). He is 0-1-1 in sports terms: No wins, one tie (Korean War), and one loss (Vietnam). Before he retires, Highway would like to get his ex-wife back and even the score at 1-1-1. This film allows him to attempt to do both.

Film's treatment of femininity: *Heartbreak Ridge* has two significant women, one the widow of a Marine and a veteran herself, and the other the long-suffering ex-wife of Gunner Highway. Both are in many ways Hawksian women.

HEARTS OF THE WORLD (1918)

Director: D. W. Griffith
Screenplay: D. W. Griffith
Cast: Lillian Gish, Dorothy Gish, Mary Gish, Ben Alexander, Robert Harron, Erich von Stroheim, Noël Coward
Oscars: None
VHS: Lions Gate

Story of the people of a French village suddenly and brutally occupied by the Germans during World War I. To create his propaganda film, commissioned by the British, Griffith uses his usual melodrama, such as a hero preventing a "beast of Berlin" from raping Lillian Gish, and a climactic race against time to the rescue, as he portrays the Germans as monsters finally driven off as the French Army retakes the town.

Film's treatment of femininity: Two women, a Madonna and a traveling gypsy of slightly dubious repute, cope with life in occupied France during World War I.

THE HEROES OF TELEMARK (1965)

Director: Anthony Mann
Screenplay: Ivan Moffat and Ben Barzman from novels by John Drummond and Knut Haukelid
Cast: Kirk Douglas, Richard Harris, Ulla Jacobsson, Michael Redgrave, David Weston
Oscars: None
DVD: Sony Pictures

Based on actual events, a small group of Norwegian Resistance fighters carries on Allied-coordinated raids on a top-secret German heavy water plant, trying to destroy or delay Germany's creation of an atomic bomb. Finally, the Norwegians sink a ferry containing the plant's entire production of heavy water to the bottom of a fjord.

Film's treatment of femininity: One woman, a bloodied, veteran member of the Norwegian Resistance, is willing to kill Germans, but has qualms about civilian casualties.

THE HORSE SOLDIERS (1959)

Director: John Ford
Screenplay: John Lee Mahin and Martin Rackin
Cast: John Wayne, William Holden, Constance Towers, Judson Pratt, Hoot Gibson
Oscars: None
DVD: MGM/UA Video

Based on a true story (minus the love interest), during the Civil War, a battalion of Union Cavalry behind enemy lines drives through the South, destroying Confederate railroad assets. Along the way there are conflicts between the humanistic chief medical officer of the unit and its tough, no-nonsense commander. Complicating matters, they must transport a Confederate woman with them, because she found out the battalion's plans and would reveal them to the Confederates if she could. The commander is job- and mission objective–oriented, and could shoot her as a spy, but his sense of chivalry forbids it. Besides, she is attractive to the commander, and vice versa.

Film's treatment of femininity: A Madonna, a daughter of the South, tries to play Mata Hari and is discovered. Rather than shoot her, the Union battalion she spied upon takes her along with them so she won't reveal their plans to the Confederates.

THE HUNTERS (1958)

Director: Dick Powell
Screenplay: Wendell Mayes, based on the novel by James Salter
Cast: Robert Mitchum, Robert Wagner, Richard Egan, Mai Britt, Lee
   Phillips
Oscars: None
DVD: Twentieth Century Fox

A study of the reality and true meaning of courage, this Korean War story follows a veteran fighter pilot after he joins a squadron flying F-86's against the enemy. On leave in Japan, the veteran meets and falls in love with the wife of another pilot, who is out of her favor because he is fighting off the fear he feels between missions with alcohol. After this pilot is shot down, the veteran's true sense of honor requires him to rescue his romantic rival, re-uniting him with his wife.

Film's treatment of femininity: A Madonna falls off her pedestal and almost has an extramarital affair with an Air Force flyer. Eventually, she must make a decision between the two men she loves.

THE HURT LOCKER (2008)

Director: Kathryn Bigelow
Screenplay: Mark Boal
Cast: Jeremy Renner, Anthony Mackie, Guy Pearce, David Morse, Brian
   Geraghty
Oscars: Nominations for Best Actor, Cinematography, and Original
   Score; Oscars for Best Picture, Director, Film Editing, Sound Editing,
   Sound Mixing, and Original Screenplay
DVD: Summit Entertainment

A new U.S. Army NCO is assigned to lead a bomb disposal team during the worst of the combat against insurgents in Iraq and surprises them with his apparent irresponsibility. Putting himself in harm's way more than the rest, Sgt. James still endangers the bomb team, other GIs, and civilians with his recklessness. The usual modern scenario is that soldiers try to achieve mission objectives while protecting themselves and their buddies as best they can, but James seems hell-bent on danger, regardless of the cost.

Film's treatment of femininity: One Madonna stands out as the long-suffering wife back home who cannot compete with the thrill James gets from his job.

HELL'S ANGELS (1930)

Director: Howard Hughes

Screenplay: Marshal Neilan, Joseph M. March, Howard Estabrook, Harry Behn

Cast: Jean Harlow, Monte Rutledge, Roy Rutledge, Karl Armstedt, Roy Wilson

Oscars: Nomination for Best Cinematography

DVD: Universal Home Video

Two brothers, Roy and Monte, attending university in England join the Royal Flying Corps to fight in World War I. They both are fond of a young woman who, for thrills, follows them to France as a canteen hostess. Only Roy is serious about serving. Monte is more self-serving. This gets him into a good deal of trouble. Finally, the two are shot down and captured by the Germans. Monte is willing to give the enemy valuable information in return for his life, but Roy shoots him before he has a chance to betray his country. Dying in his brother's arms, Monte comforts Roy, saying he did the right thing.

Film's treatment of femininity: A stereotypical example of a hedonistic camp follower with loose morals.

INGLOURIOUS BASTERDS (2009)

Director: Quentin Tarantino

Screenplay: Quentin Tarantino

Cast: Brad Pitt, Christoph Waltz, Melanie Laurent, Eli Roth, Diane Kruger, Michael Fassbender

Oscars: Nominated for Best Picture, Screenplay, Cinematography, Directing, Film Editing, Sound Editing, and Sound Mixing; Oscar for Best Supporting Actor

DVD: Universal

A squad of American Army soldiers of Jewish extraction, called the "Basterds," operates behind German lines as if they were terrorists, flamboyantly assassinating as many Nazis as they can. To make themselves more fearful, the Basterds act like Indians and scalp their victims. The squad becomes so successful that even Adolf Hitler is furious. The Basterds later are supposed to team up with British spies to blow up a theater in Paris they know will contain a number of high-ranking Nazis gathered for a movie premiere. Unknown to the Basterds and the spies, a French woman, Shosanna, who is Jewish, has her own plans for these Nazis. She plots to burn down her own theater and trap all the Nazis inside. But before they can act, the Basterds and a female spy are discovered, and all but two are killed or arrested. However, Shosanna's operation succeeds. Between Shosanna's and the two surviving Basterds' actions, everyone in the theater is killed.

Film's treatment of femininity: Two main female roles have speaking parts in this film. Shosanna is the sole survivor of a Nazi Jew hunter's slaughter of her entire family. As a victim of the Nazis, posing as a non-Jew operating a movie theater, she has joined the Resistance. When the Nazis take over her theater for the movie premiere, Shosanna seizes the chance to fight for France and also exact fiery revenge for her family. The second role is that of a German woman, Bridget, who is a famous movie star but also an Allied agent. Unfortunately, Bridget is not very bright, and her choice of a poor place to meet up with the Basterds causes a number of Americans and other spies to be killed. Bridget and the Basterds have barely arrived at the theater when a Nazi colonel discovers her true identity and kills her.

IN HARM' S WAY (1965)

Director: Otto Preminger
Screenplay: Wendell Mayes, based on the novel by James Bassett
Cast: John Wayne, Kirk Douglas, Patricia Neal, Tom Tryon, Brandon de Wilde, Paula Prentiss
Oscars: Nomination for Best Black-and-White Cinematography
DVD: Paramount

Right after the Japanese attack on Pearl Harbor, a cruiser commander takes the initiative, throws away the "book," and pursues the enemy, but his ship is torpedoed. He loses his command and is relegated to a staff job, but distinguishes himself and is forgiven. Promoted to rear admiral, he heads up a task force in a crucial part of the war in the Pacific. There, he must not only fight the Japanese, but avoid interference from another admiral, an inept dandy who tries to jump in and take all the credit. Nominated for an Oscar (Best Cinematography, Black-and-White).

Film's treatment of femininity: The film includes three women: a middle-aged nurse actively pursuing a hesitant, middle-aged Navy officer; a young nurse playing hard to get with two quite different men; and a Madonna wife in the mold of *Flying Leathernecks*.

THE IRON TRIANGLE (1989)

Director: Eric Weston
Screenplay: John A. Bushelman and Larry Hilbrand
Cast: Beau Bridges, Haing S. Ngor, Liem Whatley, Johnny Hallyday, Sophie Trang, Lilana B'tiste
Oscars: None
DVD: MGM Video

An American officer working as an advisor to Vietnamese forces is captured by a VC named Ho, who ethically considers his prisoner his responsibility and won't allow others to harm him, even at risk of his own life. Eventually, the American escapes and ends up opposite Ho in a firefight for control of a village. Ho dies in this fight. The story is essentially a true one, from the diary of a young VC soldier actually recovered from his body.

Film's treatment of femininity: The two interesting women in this film inhabit a small amount of screen time, but are nonetheless fascinating. Lai is a Viet Cong soldier, who in classic GI Jane fashion, fits right into the VC battalion and is treated in most ways like a man. Khan Li is a propaganda agitator working for the Saigon government. With a former French Foreign Legionnaire as her bodyguard, Khan Li is a powerful speaker as she tours the villages, but she has evil designs. If she spots any villagers who may object to Saigon, she has the Frenchman dispose of them. A regular Dragon Lady.

JARHEAD (2005)

Director: Sam Mendes
Screenplay: William Broyles Jr., based on the book by Anthony Swofford
Cast: Jake Gyllenhaal, Peter Sarsgaard, Jamie Foxx, Lucas Black, Chris Cooper, Dennis Haysbert
Oscars: None
DVD: Universal Studios

An adaptation of Marine Anthony Swofford's best seller, this classic war film plot begins—a la *Full Metal Jacket*—as Marines are insulted and brutalized by their drill instructor in basic training. Swofford becomes a sniper and is deployed to Iraq to fight in the first Gulf War. In the deserts of Kuwait, as they impatiently wait and train for combat against Saddam Hussein's forces, the men revert to typical frat house behavior with typical sophomoric results. Finally ordered into action, the men encounter death and destruction, but after the fact. Eager to finally get into the action, Swofford and his spotter are dispatched to do a sniper's job, but at the last second are ordered to stand down. Then, suddenly, the "war" is over, and after all he has experienced, Swofford never gets the chance to fire a shot in combat.

Film's treatment of femininity: The women in this film fall into two categories, Madonnas who patiently wait at home for their men to return from war and girlfriends/wives who are unfaithful to their Marines and send them various kinds of "Dear John" letters.

JOAN OF PARIS (1942)

Director: Robert Stevenson
Screenplay: Charles Bennett and Ellis St. Joseph
Cast: Michelle Morgan, Paul Henreid, Thomas Mitchell, Laird Cregar, Alan Ladd
Oscars: Nomination for Best Picture
DVD: Warner Home Video

During World War II, downed RAF pilots on the run from the Germans encounter a waitress named Joan, who like many other women in films set in occupied countries at this time was a Madonna, uninvolved in the French Resistance, just trying to survive the war. But Joan falls in love with one of the pilots, and with the assistance of a priest, helps the flyers make contact with the Resistance and arrange transport for them back to England. Arrested by the Gestapo, Joan lies to them, allowing the flyers time to escape, but is executed.

Film's treatment of femininity: Like many such films, especially those made during the war, Madonnas experience Nazi crimes against their people, causing them to join the resistance. In this case, due to both love for one of the flyers and her willingness to risk it all for France, a Madonna joins the Resistance and helps free the pilots to fight again.

KELLY'S HEROES (1970)

Director: Brian G. Hutton
Screenplay: Troy Kennedy Martin
Cast: Clint Eastwood, Telly Savalas, Don Rickles, Carroll O'Connor, Donald Sutherland, Gavin MacLeod, Stuart Margolin, Harry Dean Stanton
Oscars: None
DVD: Warner Home Video

As much of a "big caper" picture as it is a Vietnam era satire on the military, *Kelly's Heroes* tells the story of a pick-up squad of tired, disillusioned soldiers who desert their World War II duties and run off to capture millions in gold bullion behind German lines. War genre antihero performances by the cynical Eastwood as their leader, Rickles as the crooked supply sergeant financier of the expedition, Sutherland as a beatnik (too early in history to be a hippie) tank commander, and O'Connor spoofing a Patton-like general who thinks the illicit operation is for real and roots for their success like a football fan.

Film's treatment of femininity: There is only one small role for a female character in this film: the comely French sex object the U.S. tank commander.

LADY FROM CHUNGKING (1942)

Director: William Nigh
Story (No credit given for Screenplay): Milton Raison and Sam Robins
Cast: Anna May Wong, Harold Huber, Mae Clarke, Rick Vallin, Paul Bryar, Ted Hecht
Oscars: None
DVD: Alpha Video

The female leader of a Chinese Resistance group goes undercover in a Japanese general's headquarters with two missions in mind: To gather intelligence about the general's next offensive and to rescue a captured American pilot. She succeeds in both but is eventually executed when the general finds out he's been played for a fool.

Film's treatment of femininity: The film demonstrates that a woman, even in China, can take a leadership role. It also shows that Japanese "men are pigs" as well. Everything the Chinese woman is able to achieve is due to the enemy underestimating her and treating her like a sex object.

THE LAST OF THE MOHICANS (1992)

Director: Michael Mann

Screenplay: Michael Mann and Christopher Crowe from the James Fenimore Cooper novel

Cast: Daniel Day-Lewis, Madeleine Stowe, Russell Means, Eric Schweig, Jodhi May, Steven Waddington, Wes Studi, Maurice Roëves

Oscar: Best Sound

DVD: Fox

Cooper's story is about a once-orphaned colonist's son, now called Hawkeye, and his adoptive Native American Mohican family who rescue two Englishwomen and a British officer from attacking Indians and convey them to Fort William Henry, where the women's father commands the garrison. But the fort is under siege in this French and Indian War story, and the British reluctantly surrender to the overwhelming forces of the French. The French general, Montcalm, allows the British to leave the fort with their weapons, but renegade Indians later attack the British column and many are slaughtered. Hawkeye and his two Mohicans rescue one of the women, but their heroism is not without cost. The younger Mohican, Uncas, dies trying to save Alice, one of the two Englishwomen. This leaves his father, Chingachgook, as the last of his tribe.

Film's treatment of femininity: Three women have speaking roles in this classic film: the two Englishwomen, Cora and Alice, and a frontier wife named Alexandra. Two of the three are quite similar, although Cora doesn't know it yet. A Hawksian woman who is expected by effete English custom to act either as a Madonna or as chattel, the headstrong and capable Cora has much in common with Alexandra, the frontier wife. Alice, however, is a helpless Madonna who must be tended to, coddled, and constantly helped. Even their enemy, the Indian renegade Magua, notices this and criticizes how badly Alice is spoiled.

LAWRENCE OF ARABIA (1962)

Director: David Lean

Screenplay: Robert Bolt, Michael Wilson, based on the writings of T. E. Lawrence

Cast: Peter O'Toole, Omar Sharif, Alec Guinness, Anthony Quinn, Jack Hawkins, José Ferrer, Anthony Quayle, Claude Rains

Oscars: Nominations for Best Actor, Supporting Actor, and Adapted Screenplay; Oscars for Best Picture, Director, Music, Film Editing, Color Cinematography, Art Direction, and Sound

DVD: Columbia Tri/Star

Based on the exploits of T. E. Lawrence, this winner of seven Oscars, including Best Picture and Best Director, tells the story of a British intelligence officer who is ordered to "consult" with the Arab army in their fight against the Turks during World War I. Soon Lawrence is given command of this Arab army, and recruits other Arabs to fight a successful guerilla war for two years, eventually contributing to the fall of the Ottoman Empire. But at the end, when the establishment of an independent Arab state is within their grasp, and despite Lawrence's best efforts to broker an alliance, the Arabs' own inter-tribal hatreds and prejudices prevent them from organizing, and they succumb to European colonial powers.

Film's treatment of femininity: Arab women appear briefly in this film as veiled supportive wives, mothers, and sweethearts cheering their men off to war with the Turks, or as the bodies of raped and murdered women left by the Turks as they retreat.

THE LONGEST DAY (1962)

Directors: Ken Annakin, Andrew Marton, Bernhard Wicki
Screenplay: Cornelius Ryan, Romain Gary, James Jones, David Pursall, Jack Seddon, based on the book by Ryan
Cast: Eddie Albert, Paul Anka, Richard Burton, Red Buttons, Sean Connery, Henry Fonda, Jeffrey Hunter, Peter Lawford, Roddy McDowall, Robert Mitchum, Edmund O'Brien, Robert Ryan, George Segal, Rod Steiger, Richard Todd, Tom Tryon, Robert Wagner, John Wayne
Oscars: Nominations for Best Picture, Film Editing, and Black-and-White Art Direction; Oscars for Best Cinematography and Special Effects
DVD: Twentieth Century Fox

This film tells the story of D-Day, the Normandy Invasion that paved the way to Allied victory in Europe during World War II. It retells this story through the experiences of many participants, both German and Allied, from their commanders to common soldiers. Nominated for five Oscars, including Best Picture, the film won two (Best Cinematography, Best Special Effects).

Film's treatment of femininity: One brave woman, a true Resistance GI Jane, stands out in this picture, a member of the French resistance who uses her attractiveness to distract German guards so the men can sneak downed flyers through a roadblock. Another time, she distracts and then assaults a German sentry so French paratroopers can blow up a railway.

THE LUCKY ONES (2008)

Director: Neil Burger
Screenplay: Neil Burger, Dirk Whittenborn
Cast: Rachel McAdams, Tim Robbins, Michael Peña, Anne Corley, John Diehl, John Heard
Oscars: None
DVD: Lions Gate

This is the story of three soldiers who have recovered from wounds suffered during the Iraq War. They become friends on the trip back to the United States, but end up stranded in a New York airport. They decide to rent a car and travel across the country together. In this character study we experience their posttraumatic stress and some of the typical problems experienced by returning soldiers. Finally, although at the outset they were not planning on it, all three end up deciding to return to Iraq for another tour.

Film's treatment of femininity: A GI Jane, recovering from war wounds, must decide what to do with the rest of her life. Also, a wife tells her husband, just returned from duty in Iraq, that she's better off without him and that she wants a divorce.

*M*A*S*H* (THE FILM, 1970)

Director: Robert Altman
Screenplay: Ring Lardner Jr., based on the novel by Richard Hooker (H. Richard Hornberger)
Cast: Donald Sutherland, Elliott Gould, Tom Skerritt, Sally Kellerman, Robert Duvall, Roger Bowen, Gary Burghoff
Oscars: Best Screenplay Adaptation
DVD: Twentieth Century Fox

Black comedy is featured in this Vietnam War allegory about a group of medical personnel serving together in a mobile army surgical hospital in the Korean War. As per the TV series that followed, Hawkeye and Trapper keep things light as they persecute head nurse Houlihan and holier-than-thou surgeon Frank Burns. Nominated for five Academy Awards, including Best Picture and Best Director, it lost in both categories to *Patton*. However, the film did win the Oscar for Best Screenplay Adaptation.

Film's treatment of femininity: Nurses in this film eventually all become sex objects for the doctors, even uptight Army lifer Margaret Houlihan.

M*A*S*H (THE TELEVISION SERIES, 1972–1983)

Directors Gene Reynolds, Larry Gelbart, et al.
Teleplays: Gene Reynolds, Larry Gelbart, Alan Alda, etc.
Cast: Alan Alda, Wayne Rogers, Mike Farrell, Loretta Swit, McLean
   Stevenson, Harry Morgan, Larry Linville, Gary Burghoff, Jamie Farr,
   William Christopher, David Ogden Stiers
DVD: Twentieth Century Fox

Same plot as Altman's movie version, with more of an emphasis on character, especially Hawkeye's. The long-running series won fourteen Emmys and
a Peabody award.
   Film's treatment of femininity: Women are much more complex than in
the motion picture version. Virtually all kinds of women in war are found in
the series' 251 episodes.

MAN'S FAVORITE SPORT? (1964)

Director: Howard Hawks
Screenplay: Pat Frank and John Fenton Murray
Cast: Rock Hudson, Paula Prentiss, Maria Perschy, John McGiver, Ros-
   coe Karns, Norman Alden, Regis Toomey
Oscars: None
DVD: Universal Home Video

Cute comedy having nothing to do with war, but having everything to do
with a prototypical Hawksian woman. A best-selling author of a book on
fishing, who in reality is a fraud who's never been fishing in his life, is
coerced into entering a fishing competition by his overbearing boss, the
owner of the department store where the author sells fishing tackle. Many
comic gags ensue as the romance between the Hawksian woman and the
author proceeds.
   Film's treatment of femininity: As the typical Hawksian woman, Abigail
is quite comfortable in the company of men, and, in this case, is also an
accomplished camper, water sports enthusiast, and fisherwoman. She falls
instantly for Roger, the author, who finds her irritating at first, since she is
becoming a major distraction to his manly task—catching fish to save his
job. Needless to say, every time she tries to help him, things go from bad to
worse, being chased by a bear, losing his fiancée, and then the competition
(when he tells the truth about how he caught the winning fish in his waders

when he fell into the lake) and finally his job. But in the end, he gets his job back and Abigail to boot.

MATA HARI (1931)

Director: George Fitzmaurice (uncredited)
Screenplay: Benjamin Glazer and Leo Birinsky
Cast: Greta Garbo, Ramon Novarro, Lionel Barrymore, Lewis Stone, C. Henry Gordon
Oscars: None
DVD: MGM

In this tragic romance version of the life of infamous World War I spy Mata Hari, Mata carries on affairs with military men to obtain secret information that she passes on to the Germans. Eventually, she falls in love with a young officer and wants to give up the spy game, but before she can she is arrested and executed by the French.

Film's treatment of femininity: This film demonstrates that one of the ways a female spy can serve her handlers is by using her body to attract men, but that she cannot afford to act unprofessionally and fall in love with one of her victims. If she does, she will find that the spy game is too unforgiving.

MATA HARI (1985)

Director: Curtis Harrington
Screenplay: Joel Ziskin
Cast: Sylvia Kristel, Christopher Cazenove, Oliver Tobias, John Gottfried, Michael Anthony
Oscars: None
DVD: MGM

This version of the Mata Hari story was done for the R-rating. As with the Garbo version, Mata carries on affairs with military men to obtain secret information that she passes on to the Germans. In this version, she also spies for the French. But she falls in love with a German officer, which eventually leads to her undoing. Despite her service to the French, she is arrested and executed.

Film's treatment of femininity: This film demonstrates even more than in the Garbo version that one of the ways a female spy can serve her handlers is by using her body to attract men. Again, the theme holds true that she cannot afford to act unprofessionally and fall in love either with one of her victims or with anyone involved in the spy game.

MEMPHIS BELLE (1990)

Director: Michael Caton-Jones
Screenplay: Monte Merrick
Cast: Matthew Modine, Eric Stoltz, Tate Donovan, D. B. Sweeney, Billy
    Zane, Sean Astin, Harry Connick Jr., David Strathairn, John Lithgow
Oscars: None
DVD: Warner Home Video

Highly fictionalized World War II story of the last bombing mission of the B-17 bomber, named the *Memphis Belle*. The crew of this bomber will be the first to complete their twenty-five missions and rotate home, but first they must complete a mission to bomb Bremen, a target full of danger due to its defenses, which include heavy antiaircraft fire and German fighters.

Film's treatment of femininity: Women pictured in this film are all of the chattel variety, girls attending a big dance in the bomb group's hangar. Most appear to be sexually experienced, one even tenderly providing a young bomber crewmember with his first sexual experience—in the cabin of the bomber!

MRS. MINIVER (1942)

Director: William Wyler
Screenplay: Arthur Wimperis, George Froeschel, James Hilton, and Clau-
    dine West from the book by Jan Struther
Cast: Greer Garson, Walter Pidgeon, Teresa Wright, Dame May Whitty,
    Henry Travers, and Richard Ney
Oscars: Nominations for Best Actor, Supporting Actor, Supporting Ac-
    tress, Film Editing, Special Effects, and Sound Recording; Oscars for
    Best Picture, Actress, Supporting Actress, Director, Adapted Screen-
    play, and Black-and-White Cinematography
DVD: Warner Home Video

Story of an upper-middle-class English family in the days surrounding the evacuation of Dunkirk in 1940. Kay Miniver maintains the home as a haven of quiet contentment, challenged by the war, which even affects husband Clem, when he volunteers himself and the family's cabin cruiser to assist British efforts at Dunkirk. A wounded German pilot is shot down, and for a short time terrorizes Kay, who still manages to be polite, serve him food, and confiscate his Luger when he passes out. Her eldest son, Vin, home from Oxford, romances and marries Lady Beldon's granddaughter, and shortly thereafter becomes an RAF pilot. The family spends time in their bomb shelter when the German raids are at their worst. Their town is also bombed, and some residents killed, including Kay's new daughter-in-law. But in their bombed-out church the next Sunday, everyone maintains a stiff upper lip and carries on.

Film's treatment of femininity: Kay is a Madonna prototype, as close to perfection as possible. Carol, whom Vin falls for, is, like the two young women mentioned above in *The Best Years of Our Lives*, a Madonna in training, whose life ends too soon. Even the somewhat distant and at times belligerent Lady Beldon softens due to her relationship with Kay.

MISS V FROM MOSCOW (1942)

Director: Albert Herman
Screenplay: Arthur St. Claire and Sherman Lowe
Cast: Lola Lane, Noel Madison, John Vosper, Howard Banks, Paul Wei-
    gel, Wilhelm von Brincken
Oscars: None
DVD: Alpha Video

A female Russian spy impersonates a deceased German spy whom she resembles, fooling the Germans, and one colonel in particular, into believing that she works for them. Then she obtains valuable information on German submarine operations that will make Allied convoys to Russia safer. The spy disappears, leaving the German colonel to be blamed and executed for the breach in security.

Film's treatment of femininity: Shows how some males' egos can be manipulated by a clever woman spy.

THE MOON IS DOWN (1943)

Director: Irving Pichel
Screenplay: Nunnally Johnson, John Steinbeck from his novel
Cast: Cedric Hardwicke, Henry Travers, Lee J. Cobb, Peter van Eyk,
    Dorris Bowdon, Margaret Wycherly
Oscars: None
DVD: Warner Home Video

One of the stories of the heroic resistance of the Norwegian people during the German occupation. In this town, the mayor does everything he can to maintain civil relations between his people and the Germans, represented by the commandant, but he knows it won't last long. The German Army tries to mobilize the townspeople to work for them, but the Norwegians respond with sabotage. Some soldiers are killed as well. Finally, the Germans decide to use reprisals to terrorize the people into submission. They arrest and hang the leaders of the town, and, in the climax of the film, as the hangings begin, major explosions are seen and heard in German installations around the town and in the town's coal mine, making a clear statement to the Germans that if they kill one leader, others will rise to take his place.

Film's treatment of femininity: The most interesting case is Molly Morden, young widow of a man who refused to work in the coal mine and killed a German officer. For this offense, Morden is taken out and shot. Later, a rather stupid German officer tries to romance Molly. Furious, she manages to hold her temper and even lead the officer on. Later, when he meets secretly with her, she is prepared and kills him. Also, Annie, who is the mayor's cook, works for the resistance. She is so young—and, of course, female—so she is not suspected.

THE NAKED AND THE DEAD (1958)

Director: Raoul Walsh
Screenplay: Denis Sanders, Terry Sanders, based on the novel by Norman
     Mailer
Cast: Aldo Ray, Cliff Robertson, Raymond Massey, William Campbell,
     Richard Jaeckel, Joey Bishop
Oscars: None
VHS: Amazon.com

On an island in the Pacific during World War II, a selfish, elitist general's campaign to overcome Japanese resistance bogs down. The general sees to it that he and his officers have the best quarters, food, and conditions, but he ignores the needs of the enlisted men under his command. To him, such men are pawns to sacrifice for his success. His aide, a young officer, protests, standing up for the men, which gets him fired from his safe and cushy job as general's aide and shoved back into the front lines. There he comes into conflict with a sergeant whose attitude, although different, is every bit as cynical and cruel as the general.

Film's treatment of femininity: A number of different kinds of women, mostly chattel, appear in flashback.

NAVY SEALS (1990)

Director: Lewis Teague
Screenplay: Chuck Pfarrer, Gary Goldman
Cast: Michael Biehn, Charlie Sheen, Rick Rossovich, Bill Paxton, Dennis Haysbert, Joanne Whalley
Oscars: None
DVD: MGM

Elite Navy commandos conduct combat and rescue operations in the Middle East. Plot centers on recovering or destroying a cache of Stinger missiles that have come into the possession of a group of terrorists. Along the way, SEAL culture is shown to be one part skill, bravery, and sacrifice, and an equal part fraternity hijinks.

Film's treatment of femininity: Women are of two varieties, companions or Madonnas the SEALs return to after missions, and a female Middle East journalist who provides the Americans with important information.

NIGHT OF THE GENERALS (1967)

Director: Anatole Litvak
Screenplay: Joseph Kessel and Paul Dehn from the novel by Hans Hall-mut Kirst
Cast: Peter O'Toole, Omar Sharif, Tom Courtenay, Donald Pleasence, Philippe Noiret
Oscars: None
DVD: Columbia

A German military policeman pursues a serial killer of prostitutes, who happens to be a German general, throughout most of World War II. In the end, the killer kills the policeman. But a friend, an Interpol Inspector, takes up the case and two decades after the war is over, apprehends the killer.

Film's treatment of femininity: The murder of prostitutes is thought by German generals to be the simple disposal of chattel not worth investigating. Only two policemen consider the women to be human beings who deserve justice.

OPERATION CROSSBOW (1965)

Director: Michael Anderson

Screenplay: Emric Pressburger (as Richard Imrie), Derry Quinn, and Ray Rigby

Cast: George Peppard, Sophia Loren, Trevor Howard, John Mills, Tom Courtenay, Jeremy Kemp, Lilli Palmer, Anthony Quayle

Oscars: None

DVD: Warner Home Video

A fictional story adapted from actual accounts of the real Operation Crossbow, which was actually a great many espionage missions by Allied countries aimed at countering German secret weapons during the latter portion of World War II in Europe. This film centers on efforts to destroy sites for testing of the V-1 and V-2 rockets, followed by the infiltration of Allied spies into a top-secret German factory for the construction of a rocket with the range to the reach the United States.

Film's treatment of femininity: It features two women of note. The first is an outstanding officer in London whose work in analyzing aerial reconnaissance photos uncovers the location of the German "flying bomb" launch site in northern France. The second woman is a member of the German Resistance, an innkeeper who provides safe, temporary shelter for Allied spies. In this case, she courageously assists a spy by killing a woman who could reveal his identity.

OPERATION PACIFIC (1951)

Director: George Waggner

Screenplay: George Waggner

Cast: John Wayne, Patricia Neal, Ward Bond, Scott Forbes, Philip Carey, Martin Milner

Oscars: None

DVD: Warner Home Video

All too pat World War II story about "Duke," a submarine executive officer who assumes command after his captain is killed in combat. While in port, Duke discovers and pursues his ex-wife, a nurse, who coincidentally is dating a Navy flyer who just happens to be the younger brother of the late sub's captain. All things sort themselves out when back in the Pacific—again coincidentally—Duke's sub is assigned to rescue this same Navy flyer when he is shot down in combat.

Film's treatment of femininity: This nurse does her duty while trying to decide between a younger suitor or her ex-husband, both of whom pursue her with enthusiasm.

PATTON (1970)

Director: Franklin J. Schaffner
Screenplay: Edmund H. North, Francis Ford Coppola, based on the books
Patton: Ordeal and Triumph by Ladislas Farago and *A Soldier's Story*
by Omar Bradley
Cast: George C. Scott, Karl Malden, Stephen Young, Michael Strong,
Frank Latimore, James Edwards, Lawrence Dobkin, Karl Michael Vo-
gler, Tim Considine
Oscars: Nominations for Best Original Score, Cinematography, and Spe-
cial Visual Effects; Oscars for Best Picture, Actor, Director, Original
Screenplay, Film Editing, Art Direction, and Sound
DVD: Twentieth Century Fox

Patton chronicles the exploits of the famous/infamous World War II Army
commander. Defeating Rommel's Africa Corps, Patton's leadership turns the
tide of the war in North Africa. Commanding American forces in the Allies'
invasion of Sicily, he selfishly competes with British Field Marshall Montgomery to lead the first Allied army into Messina. Later, Patton's public
statements and harsh treatment of a shell-shocked soldier get him relieved of
his command. However, after D-Day, Gen. Omar Bradley gives Patton another chance, and he and the Third Army strike out boldly and successfully
against the Germans, including relieving American forces during the Battle
of the Bulge. Later, at war's end, Patton's intemperate remarks and distrust
of Russian allies cannot survive the peace, and as the film ends, so, effectively, does Patton's career. The film does not depict the fact that soon after, the
general died in a car accident.

Film's treatment of femininity: The general has a double standard where
women are concerned. While inspecting a barracks, he comes upon the picture of a comely pinup. He gives it a good, slow look before casting it to the
ground, growling, "This is a barracks, not a bordello."

PEARL HARBOR (2001)

Director: Michael Bay
Screenplay: Randall Wallace
Cast: Ben Affleck, Josh Hartnett, Kate Beckinsale, Cuba Gooding Jr.,
Alec Baldwin, Jon Voight, Tom Sizemore, Jennifer Garner
Oscars: Nominations for Best Music, Visual Effects, and Sound; Oscar
for Sound Editing
DVD: Touchstone

Set against the backdrop of the Japanese attack on Pearl Harbor, this story-line creates a fierce love triangle among two fighter pilots and an Army nurse. The two pilots distinguish themselves by getting their fighter planes airborne and shooting down a half dozen Japanese. Throwing history to the four winds (since only volunteer pilots from the 17th Bomb Group flew the raid), the plot next places these two fighter pilots in the cockpits of two of the 16 B-25 bombers launched from the carrier USS *Hornet* in the Doolittle Raid to strike back against the Japanese homeland. One of the two is killed, and the surviving pilot marries the nurse.

Film's treatment of femininity: The women depicted are all young nurses, out for adventure, love, and service during World War II. While all are dedicated professionally, their main collective goal seems to be a competition over who will marry first, thereby ending their nursing careers.

PLATOON (1986)

Director: Oliver Stone
Screenplay: Oliver Stone
Cast: Charlie Sheen, Willem Dafoe, Tom Berenger, Forest Whitaker,
John C. McGinley, Kevin Dillon
Oscars: Two nominations for Best Supporting Actor, Original Screen-play, and Cinematography; Oscars for Best Picture, Director, Film Editing, and Sound
DVD: MGM

Nominated for eight Academy Awards, and winner of four Oscars including Best Picture and Best Director, *Platoon* proves the adage that in Vietnam, one wouldn't believe what a nineteen-year-old American boy is capable of. Chris, a young, naive infantry replacement, joins a platoon fighting the enemy in the jungles of Vietnam, trying to stay alive long enough to learn how to survive. He gets no help from one brutal sergeant, Barnes, but is befriended and assisted by another veteran sergeant, Elias, and later by some of the troops. After a My Lai–type incident involving the murders of Vietnamese villagers, the two sergeants' feud divides the platoon's loyalties. Later, Barnes murders Elias, and Chris discovers the crime. During a climactic battle, Barnes attempts to kill Chris to silence him, but an air attack foils his plans. Chris later shoots Barnes and—because he has been wounded in two battles—Chris is airlifted to safety and a trip home.

Film's treatment of femininity: Young girls are attempted rape victims in the same manner as *Casualties of War*.

PURPLE HEARTS (1984)

Director: Sidney J. Furie
Screenplay: Sidney J. Furie, Rick Natkin
Cast: Ken Wahl, Cheryl Ladd, Stephen Lee, Annie McEnroe, R. Lee
   Ermey, James Whitmore Jr.
Oscars: None
DVD: Warner Home Video

Dr. Don Jardian is a U.S. Navy surgeon stationed in Vietnam. He could have avoided service, but he thought it was the best place to get twenty years of surgical experience in a twelve-month tour, a good way to serve both his future as a doctor and his country. What he didn't expect to find was a nurse so attractive in so many ways that he falls in love, a problem for a man engaged to a rich surgeon's daughter back in the states, a surgeon who was going to bankroll Jardian's practice. But fall he does, and becomes much more human in the process. Nurse Deborah cares so deeply about the wounded boys in her care that her enthusiasm rubs off on Jardian. This plus his own experiences patching up the boys in an aid station cause him to turn into the kind of doctor who calls off his engagement and ends up following Deborah to a low-paying civilian job at a veterans' hospital after the war.

Film's treatment of femininity: If there are two major kinds of stereotypical nurses, this film has them. Deborah is totally professional, compassionate, and dedicated to caregiving, not interested in snagging a doctor or a casual dalliance. Hallaway, on the other hand, may have some of Deborah's positive attributes, too, but she's a wild child, ready for fun, always flirting, and not shy about parading naked in front of a man. One senses that Hallaway would love to party alongside Hawkeye Pierce on *M*A*S*H*.

RED RIVER (1948)

Director: Howard Hawks
Screenplay: Borden Chase, Charles Schnee
Cast: John Wayne, Montgomery Clift, Joanne Dru, Walter Brennan, John
   Ireland, Noah Beery Jr.
Oscars: Nominated for Best Original Story and Film Editing.
DVD: MGM Video

Not a war film, but a prototypical Western featuring a prototypical Hawksian woman, played by Joanne Dru. In a historic cattle drive, a conflict arises between tougher-than-nails Dunson and his adopted son, Matt. In the middle of their conflict, acting as a love interest for Matt (although Dunson is somewhat interested in her, too) is Tess Millay. Separated from her besieged wagon train, Tess attaches herself to the cattle drive and the two quarreling men.

Film's treatment of femininity: As the Hawksian woman, Tess provides food for thought for both protagonists, as they ponder what life would be like with a rugged young woman at their side.

RESISTANCE (2003)

Director: Todd Komarnicki
Screenplay: Todd Komarnicki from the Anita Shreve novel
Cast: Julia Ormand, Bill Paxton, Phillipe Volter, Sandrine Bonnaire, Antoine Van Lierde
Oscars: None
DVD: First Floor Features

The story of an illicit affair between a downed American flyer and the wife of a member of the French Resistance. The flyer, injured in a crash landing, is hidden in a farmhouse from the Germans. While the flyer recovers, he falls in love with the wife. The husband finds out and betrays him to the Germans, who kill the husband, and capture and torture both the flyer and the wife. Eventually, the flyer gives the Germans false information in return for the wife being turned over to the Red Cross.

Film's treatment of femininity: This is another scenario in which a woman in an occupied country is initially not involved in Resistance efforts, but as circumstances change, she becomes involved.

THE RIGHT STUFF (1983)

Director: Philip Kaufman
Screenplay: Philip Kaufman from the Tom Wolfe book
Cast: Sam Shepard, Scott Glenn, Ed Harris, Dennis Quaid, Fred Ward, Barbara Hershey, Kim Stanley, Veronica Cartwright
Oscars: Nominations for Best Picture, Supporting Actor, Cinematography, and Art Direction; Oscars for Best Original Score, Film Editing, Sound, and Sound Effects Editing

From the best-selling Tom Wolfe book, *The Right Stuff* is the story of NASA's seven Mercury astronauts and their amazing early space race with the Soviets. Their story parallels the tale of "greatest pilot of them all," the exploits of ace war hero and test pilot Chuck Yeager, the first pilot to break the sound barrier.

Film's treatment of femininity: There are two Hawksian women in this film, Yeager's wife, Glennis, and the salty owner of Edwards AFB's "Pancho's Happy Bottom Riding Club," Pancho Barnes. These dynamic women contrast greatly with the more conventional and long-suffering astronaut wives, who try desperately to raise families amid the chaotic early days of the space race. Relentlessly under media scrutiny, these women try to conduct themselves as much like Madonnas as they can while their husbands risk their lives on the under-tested rockets rushed into service to try to beat the Soviets into outer space.

RIO BRAVO (1959)

Director: Howard Hawks
Screenplay: Jules Furthman, Leigh Brackett
Cast: John Wayne, Dean Martin, Angie Dickinson, Ricky Nelson, Walter Brennan, Ward Bond, John Russell
Oscars: None
DVD: Warner Home Video.

Not a war film, but another prototypical Western featuring a prototypical Hawksian woman, played this time by Angie Dickinson, who goes by the nickname Feathers. Sheriff John T. Chance arrests the younger brother of a powerful cattleman, and then must hold onto his prisoner with the help of a drunk, an old man, a young gunfighter, and a saloon gal. As in *Red River,* Feathers gives lifelong bachelor Chance all he can handle as he begins to imagine her in his life, if he has a life at all after dealing with this crisis. Not used to dealing with female feelings and emotions, Chance is constantly distracted from the manly job at hand to deal with this newly formed relationship with Feathers.

Film's treatment of femininity: As the Hawksian woman, Feathers also provides food for thought for Chance, as he ponders what life would be like with a world-weary but vital woman at his side.

RIO GRANDE (1950)

Director: John Ford
Screenplay: James Kevin McGuinness from the story by James Warner Bellah

    Cast: John Wayne, Maureen O'Hara, Ben Johnson, Claude Jarman Jr., Harry Carey Jr., Victor McLaglen, Chill Wills, J. Carrol Naish
    Oscars: None
    DVD: Lions Gate Home Entertainment

The first of Ford's legendary cavalry trilogy and an example of the Hawksian woman as interpreted by Ford, the B plot centers around the U.S. Cavalry's war against the Apaches. However, this conflict doesn't get in the way of the A plot: the surprise return of estranged wife Kathleen to the world of Lt. Col. Kirby Yorke. This is because their son appears as a new recruit for the cavalry, whose life and privations Kathleen rejected many years ago in favor of a soft, East Coast existence. Ostensibly a tug-of-war between the two parents over their son's future, it turns into a reconciliation between the two.

    Film's treatment of femininity: At first, the audience does not see what Kirby saw in Kathleen in the first place, but as time goes on, we see that Kathleen, not at heart a citified dandy from Philadelphia, fits right in with the men, providing the same Hawksian counterpart as Feathers did for Chance or Tess for Dunson.

THE SAND PEBBLES (1966)

    Director: Robert Wise
    Screenplay: Robert Anderson from the Richard McKenna novel
    Cast: Steve McQueen, Richard Attenborough, Candice Bergen, Richard Crenna, Mako, Gavin MacLeod
    Oscars: Nominated for Best Picture, Actor, Supporting Actor, Color Art/ Set Decoration, Cinematography, Film Editing, Music, and Sound.
    DVD: Fox

Story centers on a sailor, Jake Holman, chief engineer on board an American gunboat patrolling the Yangtze River in China in 1926 supporting U.S. political and economic interests in that country. The Chinese are in open revolt against the "foreign devils" occupying their country, and the gunboat is ordered into the middle of this conflict to rescue American missionaries cut off up river.

    Film's treatment of femininity: Besides female Chinese extras, the woman character we get to know is an American missionary, a Madonna with whom Holman is infatuated, who stubbornly refuses to abandon her mission and colleagues when the conflict begins.

SANDS OF IWO JIMA (1949)

Director: Alan Dwan
Screenplay: Harry Brown, James Edward Grant
Cast: John Wayne, John Agar, Forrest Tucker, James Brown, Wally Cassell, Richard Webb, Arthur Franz
Oscars: Nominations for Best Actor, Original Story, Film Editing, and Sound Recording
DVD: Republic Pictures

There is no fiercer squad leader in the World War II–era Marines than John Stryker, as the men he browbeats and trains incessantly will attest, especially Pvt. Conway. Conway, a humanist, is at first against everything Stryker stands for, and conflicts with him often. But the value of Stryker's brand of soldiering pays off for the men when he leads them into combat first at Tarawa, and later up the slopes of Mt. Suribachi on Iwo Jima. There, in the shadow of the men who raised that famous flag, a sniper shoots and kills Stryker. Inspired by Stryker's leadership, Conway begins channeling his sergeant and leads the squad up to the top. The film received four Academy Award nominations, including one for Wayne as Best Actor and Original Story.

Film's treatment of femininity: There are two women: One is Stryker's ex-wife, who divorced the sergeant for failing to be an adequate husband. Stryker implies that he always favored the Marine Corps over his marriage. The other is a Madonna with whom Conway falls in love.

SAVING PRIVATE RYAN (1998)

Director: Steven Spielberg
Screenplay: Robert Rodat
Cast: Tom Hanks, Tom Sizemore, Jeremy Davies, Edward Burns, Barry Pepper, Adam Goldberg, Giovanni Ribisi, Vin Diesel, Matt Damon, Paul Giamatti, Ted Danson
Oscars: Nominations for Best Picture, Actor, Original Screenplay, Dramatic Score, Art Direction, and Makeup; Oscars for Best Director, Film Editing, Cinematography, Sound, and Sound Effects Editing
DVD: Dreamworks Video

Nominated for eleven Academy Awards, including Best Picture, Best Actor (Hanks), and Best Original Screenplay, the film received five Oscars, most notably Best Director for Spielberg. This story describes the trek taken by a squad of survivors of D-Day, led by Capt. Miller, to find and remove a single soldier, Pvt. Ryan, from harm's way. Ryan's three brothers had just been killed in action, and their mother received word of their deaths on the same day. Gen. George C. Marshall wishes to spare Mrs. Ryan another death notice. This idea doesn't sit well with Capt. Miller's men, who have just waded through their comrades' blood on Omaha Beach, and consider "this entire mission [to be] a serious misallocation of valuable military resources." When the squad finally finds Ryan, the young private won't leave his buddies shorthanded, because they must stay and defend a bridge against the Germans. Miller's squad ends up joining Ryan.

Film's treatment of femininity: At the beginning, there is an unnamed but conscientious female clerical worker who discovers that Mrs. Ryan has lost three sons, and then there is Mrs. Ryan herself, a housewife Madonna faced with great tragedy when she learns about the deaths of her sons.

SERENITY (2005)

Director: Joss Whedon
Screenplay: Joss Whedon
Cast: Nathan Fillion, Gina Torres, Summer Glau, Adam Baldwin, Alad Tudyk, Chiwetel Ejiofor
Oscars: None
DVD: Universal Studios.

Continuation of the short-lived but excellent TV series into a feature film, a group of space war veterans, intent on merely some intergalactic smuggling, ends up in the middle of the Alliance hunt for a teenager who knows too much. Captain Mal Reynolds refuses to hand the girl over to a fascist Alliance he hates anyway (he and a few other crew were on the losing side of the war that put the Alliance in power). Trying to avoid both savage mutants known as the Reavers and an Alliance hit man out to kill them and all their friends as well, Mal decides to "misbehave," and manages to broadcast the girl's terrible secret to the entire galaxy.

Film's treatment of femininity: Two women are featured: One is a professional soldier who fought alongside Mal in the war and the other is a girl who has been the subject of horrible experiments by the Alliance, who now suffers from mental illness.

SEVEN BEAUTIES (1975)

Director: Lina Wertmuller

Screenplay: Lina Wertmuller

Cast: Giancarlo Giannini, Fernando Rey, Shirley Stoler, Elena Fiore, Piero Di Iorio, Enzo Vitale

Oscars: Nominated for Best Foreign Language Film, Best Actor, Best Director, and Best Original Screenplay

Pasqualino Settebellezze (of the Seven Beauties) is the street name of a petty crook in Naples who has seven, charitably speaking, very plain-looking sisters. Convicted of the honor murder of a pimp who seduces one of his sisters into prostitution, he gets the chance for "freedom" if he joins the Italian Army during World War II. In the war, Pasqualino has many harrowing adventures, including a time in which he ends up a prisoner in a Nazi death camp. To save his life, he tries to seduce a sadistic female commander. Finally, having survived the war, Pasqualino returns home to his family to find that now all of his sisters, his virginal teenage girlfriend, and even his mother have become prostitutes. Sadly, we see that Pasqualino, not the brightest bulb in the box, has learned nothing from all of his wartime experiences.

Film's treatment of femininity: The situation for Pasqualino's sisters, his girlfriend, and his mother demonstrates that in wartime, otherwise virtuous Madonnas must stoop to do whatever they can to avoid starvation and survive. The case of the female death camp commander is another story: She is both a soldier and a true Nazi, and except for keeping Pasqualino alive for sport, is a sadistic murderess, who, if she were not fictional, would have been tried, convicted, and hanged at Nuremberg after the war.

SHE WORE A YELLOW RIBBON (1949)

Director: John Ford

Screenplay: Frank S. Nugent, Laurence Stallings (Story: James Warner Bellah)

Cast: John Wayne, John Agar, Ben Johnson, Harry Carey Jr., Victor McLaglen, Joanne Dru, Mildred Natwick

Oscar: Best Color Cinematography

DVD: Warner Home Video

This is the second installment in director Ford's famous Cavalry Trilogy, about U.S. Cavalry Capt. Nathan Brittles, as he leads one last patrol to avoid war between whites and the allied Cheyennes and Arapahos, who break out from the reservation after the defeat of George Armstrong Custer. Meanwhile, Brittles must assure that the two young lieutenants who will soon replace him are properly seasoned. This becomes problematical as these two young men fall over themselves competing for the hand of a beautiful young lady, the niece of the fort's commanding officer. Using his experience and his relationship with one of the Indian chiefs, Brittles tries a parlay to stop the war, but young, ambitious warriors prevail at the council fires. Finally, Brittles returns with his men to raid the village, and chase off all the horses. Without mounts, the Indians cannot win, so they have no choice but to walk back to the reservation in disgrace. Promoted to lieutenant colonel and given a new assignment as Chief of Scouts, Brittles postpones his retirement indefinitely.

Film's treatment of femininity: There are two women: One is a Madonna married to a cavalry officer, full of wisdom and affection. The other is a flirtatious young woman, courted enthusiastically by bachelor junior officers, who enjoys the chase and the attention.

SHINING THROUGH (1992)

Director: David Seltzer
Screenplay: David Seltzer from the Susan Isaacs book
Cast: Michael Douglas, Melanie Griffith, Liam Neeson, Joely Richardson, John Gielgud
Oscars: None. Plenty of Razzie awards, though, including Worst Picture
DVD: Fox

A legal secretary who speaks fluent German volunteers to serve as a spy in Germany, hoping to get jobs as a domestic for important Nazis. Working for one general, she manages to photograph secret plans, and then must get the film out of Germany and to the Allies.

Film's treatment of femininity: *Shining Through* features two women working as spies. One is the aforementioned American secretary, an amateur who volunteers and trains to become a spy, and the other is a sophisticated double agent working for the Nazis who is engaged in counter-espionage.

THE SIEGE OF FIREBASE GLORIA (1989)

Director: Brian Trenchard-Smith
Screenplay: William L. Nagle, Tony Johnston
Cast: Wings Hauser, R. Lee Ermey, Robert Arevalo, Mark Neely, Gary Hershberger, Margi Gerard, Richard Kuhlman
Oscars: None
VHS: Delta Library

A Marine long-range reconnaissance patrol in Vietnam, let by tough, wily Sgt. Maj. Hafner, discovers signs of a huge enemy mobilization that will shortly become the Tet Offensive, but can't convince anyone in Saigon to believe him. Hafner and his patrol come upon a firebase desperately in need of reorganization, led by an officer called "the Ghost" who lies naked in his bunker getting high all day long. Soon "the Ghost" has an "accident," and Hafner is in operational command, just in time, as the Viet Cong are about to attack in force. Hafner and his troops, with the help of attack helicopters and air strikes from above, hold back the superior force of Viet Cong.

Film's treatment of femininity: A female doctor running the aid station at this firebase tries to act humanely to both wounded American and enemy soldiers, but finds that when war is at her door, she must pick up a rifle and defend herself.

SINCE YOU WENT AWAY (1944)

Director: John Cromwell
Screenplay: Margaret Buell Wilder (from her book) and David O. Selznick
Cast: Claudette Colbert, Jennifer Jones, Joseph Cotton, Shirley Temple, Robert Walker, Monty Woolley, Agnes Moorehead
Oscars: Nominations for Best Picture, Supporting Actor, Actress, Supporting Actress, Film Editing, Black-and-White Cinematography and Art Direction, and Special Effects; Oscar for Best Music
DVD: MGM Video

Chronicles the life and times of a family whose father, Tim, is serving in the U.S. Army during World War II. A saga of the home front, the film demonstrates how the mother, Anne, takes over the finances and other logistics formerly done for her by her traditional husband. Later, following her daughter's example, Anne joins the war effort by going to work as a defense plant worker. Tim is listed as missing in action, but at the end of the story, the family learns he's alive and on his way home.

Film's treatment of femininity: As in so many of Selznick's films, the women protagonists are all Madonnas, or Madonnas-in training. There is one antagonist woman, Emily, who provides contrast to all the Madonnas. Emily, a divorcee whom we get the feeling is constantly trolling for men and is not very picky, considers the war one large inconvenience for her social life. She refuses to sacrifice anything for the war effort and maintains her selfish lifestyle by obtaining all her little delicacies on the black market. Emily is hypocritically disdainful when Anne's daughter Jane volunteers as a nurse's aide, because the young woman may come into contact with soldiers' bodies. Emily is a truly odious woman whom Anne finally dismisses as a friend. We get the feeling that Anne would have done so many years earlier but was not assertive enough before she became head of the family.

SINK THE BISMARCK! (1960)

Director: Lewis Gilbert
Screenplay: Edmund H. North, based on the book by C. S. Forester
Cast: Kenneth More, Dana Wynter, Carl Möhner, Laurence Naismith, Geoffrey Keen, Karel Stepanek, Michael Hordern
Oscars: None
DVD: Twentieth Century Fox

Based on the true World War II story of the British Navy's all-out campaign to sink the most powerful battleship afloat in the Atlantic, the *Bismarck*. Much of this story is told from the point of view of officers at British Naval Headquarters in London, especially Capt. Shepherd, the Director of Operations. After the *Bismarck* sinks the HMS *Hood*, the best ship in the British fleet, Shepherd convinces the admirals to bring in air power. They summon the aircraft carrier the *Arc Royal*, whose air attacks cripple the *Bismarck*, damaging the huge battleship's ability to steer. Then the rest of Britain's surface fleet closes in and sinks her.

Film's treatment of femininity: One female speaking character represents a number of WREN officers serving in the Admiralty's operations headquarters, deep underground in London. She's a Madonna with a big heart and a good head for strategy who serves as a professional and, eventually, an emotional helpmate to Capt. Shepherd.

SO PROUDLY WE HAIL (1943)

Director: Mark Sandrich
Screenplay: Allan Scott
Stars: Claudette Colbert, Paulette Goddard, Veronica Lake, George Reeves, Sonny Tufts
Oscars: Nominated for Best Supporting Actress, Black-and-White Cinematography, Special Effects, and Original Screenplay
DVD: Universal

Told in flashbacks, the film is the story of a group of nurses supporting the fighters on Bataan and Corregidor as the Japanese slowly decimate the

American and Philippine forces fighting against them. It centers on the romances between a few nurses and soldiers.

Film's treatment of femininity: Most of these nurses are Madonnas, although a few have rough edges. But all pitch in to do their jobs, and some die doing them.

THE SPY WHO LOVED ME (1977)

Director: Lewis Gilbert

Screenplay: Christopher Wood and Richard Maibaum from the Ian Fleming novel

Cast: Roger Moore, Barbara Bach, Curt Jurgens, Richard Kiel, Walter Cotell, Bernard Lee, Desmond Llewelyn

Oscars: Nominated for Best Art Direction, Best Original Score, and Best Song

DVD: MGM

Not a war film, this is the tenth picture in the James Bond spy series, and the third starring Roger Moore as superspy 007. In this iteration, Bond teams with a beautiful Russian secret agent, Maj. Amasova, to foil the insane plans of the latest megalomaniac, a billionaire named Stromberg, who has snatched British and Russian nuclear submarines and hopes to use them to destroy all human life above the sea. Making matters more difficult, in a past mission, Bond has killed Amasova's lover, another Russian secret agent.

Film's treatment of femininity: This film tries awfully hard, for 1977, to demonstrate Maj. Amasova's talent and abilities as equal to Bond's. Certainly she's a formidable intellectual comparison, but as she prances around the Egyptian desert in a low-cut evening gown for a half hour of the movie, Wood's and Maibaum's script constantly reminds that she is first and foremost a "Bond girl," not the hero. More than once, Bond must step in and rescue Amasova from trouble, such as "Jaws" the assassin and from Stromberg himself. Ultimately, Amasova becomes Bond's second banana in terms of spy shenanigans.

STALAG 17 (1953)

Director: Billy Wilder

Screenplay: Billy Wilder, Edwin Blum, based on the play by Donald Bevan and Edmund Trzcinski

Cast: William Holden, Otto Preminger, Peter Graves, Sig Ruman, Don Taylor, Robert Strauss, Harvey Lembeck, Neville Brand

Oscars: Nominations for Best Supporting Actor and Director; Oscar for Best Actor
DVD: Paramount

In every POW camp, there's a "scrounger," a black marketeering soldier who can get you anything you want, usually for a price. Sgt. Sefton is the scrounger of Stalag 17. Not popular with the men because he's all business and no charity, Sefton is barely tolerated. But all goes well for Sefton until men from their barracks are shot while trying to escape. The prisoners assume that since Sefton trades with the Germans as well as the prisoners, he's the traitor. After the men put him out of business and beat him badly, Sefton discovers who the true traitor is: another prisoner, a spy planted in the barracks by the Germans. Appropriately, the men arrange for this spy to be "shot while trying to escape." Nominated for three Academy Awards, including Best Director and Best Supporting Actor (Strauss), the sole Oscar went to Holden for Best Actor.

Film's treatment of femininity: Again, as in *Patton*, there is really only one female character, a chattel pinup of Betty Grable who is the fantasy girl of one of the POWs. There are female prisoners housed in another enclosed area of the camp, but only Sefton, through bribery, gets to visit them. They are, by definition, chattel to be bargained for.

STAR TREK: VOYAGER (TV SERIES, 1995–2001)

Directors: Various. Creators/show runners were Rick Berman, Michael Piller, and Jeri Taylor
Screenplays: Various
Cast: Kate Mulgrew, Robert Beltran, Roxann Dawson, Robert Duncan McNeill, Ethan Phillips, Robert Picardo, Jeri Ryan, Garrett Wang, Tim Russ
DVD: Paramount

A spinoff from the original *Star Trek* franchise, this series tells the stories of starship *Voyager*, which was pulled by an alien force to the far side of the galaxy. Now the captain and crew of *Voyager* must work together to find a quicker way home, or the trip will take them seventy-five years.

Film's treatment of femininity: Although some of *Star Trek*'s theatrical motion pictures featured women in command of starships, this was the first and only of the three spinoff TV series to put a woman permanently in the captain's chair. Occasionally issues pertaining to her femininity arise during an episode, including the married captain's "more than friends" attraction to first officer Chakotay. But for the most part, the captain behaves the same as any male captain and earns her crew's respect. However, rather than being called the Star Fleet regulation "sir," she prefers being called "Ma'am" or "Captain."

STARSHIP TROOPERS (1997)

Director: Paul Verhoeven
Screenplay: Edward Neumeier from the Robert A. Heinlein book
Cast: Casper Van Dien, Denise Richards, Dina Meyer, Jake Busey, Neil Patrick Harris, Michael Ironside
Oscars: Nominated for Best Visual Effects
DVD: Sony Home Entertainment

In a future following "the failure of democracy" on planet Earth, a fascist federation of humans finds itself at war with the bug-like inhabitants of another planet. Akin to the Roman Empire, to obtain citizenship in this new world order, people must serve in a branch of the military. Protagonists Johnny, Carmen, Dizzy, and Carl graduate from high school, join up and fight to defeat the bugs.

Film's treatment of femininity: One positive attribute of this fascist society is what appears to be total female equality with men. In the military, women train with men, sleep in the same barracks, even take showers together! There appears to be no glass ceiling preventing women from leadership roles.

STARSHIP TROOPERS 2 (2004)

Director: Phil Tippett
Screenplay: Edward Neumeier
Cast: Richard Burgi, Ed Lauter, Billy Brown, Kelly Carlson, Colleen Porch, Sandrine Holt
Oscars: None
DVD: Sony Home Entertainment

A low-budget video sequel to the original, featuring terrible low-key lighting to accompany terrible acting. In this story, another species of bug, unknown to the Federation, possesses humans by crawling down their throats. This story concerns an officer and a soldier who discovers this new threat and successfully attempt to prevent this infestation from getting back to Earth.

Film's treatment of femininity: The soldier mentioned above, a woman, is every bit as professional and hardcore as the colonel, and the two work together to uncover and stifle this new threat.

STARSHIP TROOPERS 3: MARAUDER (2008)

Director: Edward Neumeier
Screenplay: Edward Neumeier
Cast: Casper Van Dien, Jolene Blalock, Stephen Hogan, Boris Kodjoe, Amanda Donohoe, Marnette Patterson
Oscars: None
DVD: Sony Home Entertainment

Bringing back the popular Johnny Rico character, this film returns Casper Van Dien as an older and tougher Rico, who has risen to the rank of colonel in the Federation's Mobile Infantry. In this film, the sky marshal of the Federation has been brainwashed by the "brain bug" captured at the end of the first film. This causes problems for Rico and threatens to destabilize the Federation. But Rico leads a team of soldiers inserted into robotic bodies to defeat and destroy the super brain bug, the enemy's leader.

Film's treatment of femininity: Two female characters stand out: The first is tough soldier/starship pilot Captain Lola Black, who leads crash survivors through a bug-infested wilderness. The other is Admiral Enolo Phid, the second in command of Federation forces, who eventually angles her way to the top spot. This is a role usually cast for a male, but Admiral Phid's "dragon lady" personality is easily up to the task of being sneaky and mendacious. At one point, she even sees an advantage in reconsidering the banned role of religion in their fascist society, so she arranges for a "reconsideration" of the Federation's ban, returning religion to earthly society. Why? Because she realizes that the promise of eternal salvation can be used to motivate the people to more readily sacrifice their lives. "They might be on to something," she remarks.

THE STEEL CLAW (1961)

Director: George Montgomery
Screenplay: Ferde Grofe Jr., George Montgomery, Malvin Wald
Cast: George Montgomery, Charito Luna, Mario Barri, Paul Sorensen, Carmen Austin
Oscars: None
DVD: Alpha Video

In this poorly written and directed B movie, a one-armed American officer, Capt. Larsen, leads a mission to rescue an American general held prisoner by the Japanese. He recruits and leads two bands of Filipino partisans to assault a Japanese railroad depot to achieve the rescue, only to discover that the real general is dead and the man held by the Japanese is a sergeant masquerading as the general to get better treatment from his captors.

Film's Treatment of Femininity: Two principal characters, Lolita and Rosa, create two very different female roles. Lolita is a prostitute and pretty much of a ninny, seemingly incapable of taking care of herself, but quite capable of complicating the captain's mission. Rosa, on the other hand, is a leader of a Filipino guerilla band fighting the Japanese, but these two groups of partisans appear more like roving gangs of bandits. She constantly feuds with Santana, the leader of the other gang, although it is obvious that she is attracted to him. Working together under Capt. Larsen, Rosa distinguishes herself in leadership and in battle. At the end, the audience senses that in the future, there is romance brewing between Rosa and Santana.

THE TERMINATOR (1984)

Director: James Cameron
Screenplay: James Cameron, Gale Anne Hurd
Cast: Arnold Schwarzenegger, Linda Hamilton, Michael Biehn, Paul
    Winfield, Lance Henriksen
DVD: MGM Video

A cyborg called a terminator is sent back in time to kill the mother of the human resistance leader whose heroic actions and leadership in the future may defeat the machines who have taken control of the Earth. The leader sends his right-hand man, Kyle Reese, back through time to protect her from the terminator, also realizing that Kyle will become his father.

Film's treatment of femininity: The Sarah Conner character begins as anything but a GI Jane. At the start of this picture, she's a frivolous young woman more concerned with her hair and outfit for tonight's partying. Soon she's running for her life from a creature beyond belief, beginning to realize that her life—thanks to the coming apocalypse—is over, and a new, survivalist future for her has begun. Amazing character arc.

TERMINATOR 2: JUDGMENT DAY (1991)

Director: James Cameron

Screenplay: James Cameron, William Wisher Jr.
Cast: Arnold Schwarzenegger, Linda Hamilton, Edward Furlong, Robert
   Patrick, Joe Morton
DVD: Lions Gate

In this sequel to *The Terminator*, Sarah Connor has been deemed insane and
committed to a mental hospital because she sticks to her story about terminator cyborgs from the future and the apocalypse to come. Her son, John, is a
restless adolescent bouncing from one foster home to another. An even more
advanced terminator, a T 1000 model, is sent from the future by Skynet, the
machine network, this time to kill John. But John in the future reprograms a
captured T 101 terminator and sends him back in time to protect himself. The
T 101 breaks Sarah out of the mental hospital and protects them both from
the T 1000. Sarah, now lean and mean after years of living among survivalists and outcasts, wants to do a little prevention of her own, and sets out to
kill the scientist who used salvaged T 101 parts from the first movie to create
Skynet in the first place. The scientist, Sarah, the T 101, and John work
together to try to reverse the future, but fail.

Film's treatment of femininity: The character arc that began in the first
Terminator film has had its effect on Sarah, now a prototype GI Jane. Too
much of her femininity has disappeared, but being around her son again
brings some of her ability to feel and love back to the surface.

TERMINATOR 3: RISE OF THE MACHINES (2003)

Director: Jonathan Mostow
Screenplay: James Cameron, Gale Anne Hurd, John D. Brancato, Michael
   Ferris
Cast: Arnold Schwarzenegger, Nick Stahl, Claire Danes, Kristanna Lok-
   en, David Andrews
Oscars: None
DVD: Warner Home Video

In this third installment of the *Terminator* saga, John Connor is a twenty-
year-old drifter, living "off the grid" of society to make it hard for new
terminators to track him. But once again, Skynet sends an even more powerful terminator, called the T-X, who tracks John and once again tries to kill
him. Also, John in the future once again sends another T 101 terminator to
help protect himself. John meets his future wife, Kate, and finds out that her
father, a general, is responsible for hooking up Skynet to the country's defense computer grid in the first place. The two, with the T 101's assistance,

try to avoid the T-X and reach her father to stop the inevitable Skynet take-over. They fail, but end up in an old government nuclear bomb shelter and communications bunker where they get into contact with others who survived the initial atomic holocaust. John begins what will be a lifelong mission to organize human resistance against the machines.

Film's treatment of femininity: Sarah Connor is deceased, having died of cancer, but she still manages to play a small part in *Terminator 3*. John finds that what he thought was Sarah's coffin was actually an arms cache she had left for John. Other women in *T-3* include Kate, who, like Sarah, goes through an arc of unbelief, evolving into her commitment to defeating Skynet. There is also a nonspeaking superwoman character, since the T-X is designed to look like a beautiful female.

THEY WERE EXPENDABLE (1945)

Director: John Ford
Screenplay: Frank Wead, based on the book by William L. White
Cast: Robert Montgomery, John Wayne, Donna Reed, Ward Bond, Marshall Thompson, Leon Ames
Oscars: Nominations for Best Special Effects and Sound Recording
DVD: Warner Home Video

Based on a true story, at the outset of World War II, PT boats had not yet been used in combat. And at first, the Navy, barely holding onto the Philippines, had no use for them either. But Lts. Brickley and Ryan continued to hope that they will get their chance, and finally they do. Sinking an amazing amount of enemy tonnage, the small, fast, and effective PTs helped delay the Japanese takeover of the islands. Finally Brickley, Ryan, and a few other PT officers are ordered to Australia and then back to the United States to teach PT boat tactics.

Film's treatment of femininity: If there was ever a prototype nurse/Madonna character, it's the Donna Reed character, Sandy. She's even able to tame the "savage beast" that John Wayne plays in this film.

THE THIN RED LINE (1998)

Director: Terrence Malick
Screenplay: Terrence Malick, based on the novel by James Jones
Cast: James Caviezel, Sean Penn, Adrien Brody, Ben Chaplin, Nick Nolte, Elias Koteas, John Cusack, Woody Harrelson, George Clooney

Oscars: Nominations for Best Picture, Director, Adapted Screenplay, Dramatic Score, Film Editing, Cinematography, and Sound
DVD: Criterion

Nominated for seven Oscars including Best Picture, Malick's artful, highly visual adaptation of the James Jones novel begins following one soldier in particular, Pvt. Witt, as his U.S. Army company takes over for the Marines to clear Japanese off the island of Guadalcanal during World War II. Eventually Malick explores other soldiers' stories, but at first we learn that Witt is not really a fighter, and he sometimes gets in the mood to go AWOL just to smell the roses. His company commander is in conflict with their ambitious battalion CO, more concerned with taking the high ground than conserving the lives of his men. Finally, they take the Japanese position, but Witt ends up in the wrong place at the wrong time, and is killed.

Film's treatment of femininity: As a beautiful daydream, a fantasy to look forward to, Pvt. Bell's wife appears to be a prototype sensual Madonna. But near the end, we learn that she fell off her pedestal, defeated by the enemy loneliness, and she throws over Bell for another man. Her "Dear John" letter also becomes a stereotype, as she still hopes they can be friends.

THIRTY SECONDS OVER TOKYO (1944)

Director: Mervyn LeRoy
Screenplay: Dalton Trumbo, based on the book by Ted W. Lawson and Robert Considine
Cast: Van Johnson, Phyllis Thaxter, Robert Walker, Tim Murdock, Don DeFore, Herbert Gunn, Robert Mitchum, Spencer Tracy
Oscars: Nomination for Best Black-and-White Cinematography; Oscar for Best Special Effects
DVD: Warner Home Video

From pilot Ted Lawson's book, this is the factual story of the Doolittle Raid, the daring bombing mission on the Japanese mainland in retaliation for Pearl Harbor. Told through the eyes of Lawson, who commanded the B-25 "*The Ruptured Duck*," the story follows these flyers as they train for the mission, conduct the raid, crash land in China, and are rescued by brave Chinese allies who prevent them from falling into the hands of the Japanese.

Film's treatment of femininity: Lawson's wife is another prototypical wartime Madonna, with no flaws at all: an angel.

THIS LAND IS MINE (1943)

Director: Jean Renoir
Screenplay: Dudley Nichols
Cast: Charles Laughton, Maureen O'Hara, George Sanders, Walter Slezak, Una O'Connor
Oscars: Best Sound
DVD: Warner

A World War II occupied-country picture in which a cowardly mama's boy schoolteacher witnesses Nazi violent suppression of dissent and even the murder of his own mentor and father figure. This causes him to grow up, become courageous and bear witness to the resistance by reading France's Declaration of the Rights of Men to his students. Before he is finished reading, he is arrested by the Nazis and is taken away to be executed. Made bold by his example, a female teacher then takes up the cause of freedom and of the resistance, concluding his reading of the Declaration, demonstrating that even if the Nazis murder one dissenter, another will rise up to take his place.

Film's treatment of femininity: Aside from Una O'Connor's stereotypical "smothering mother" role, O'Hara's schoolteacher is another example of circumstances dictating that an otherwise uninvolved woman becomes a part of the resistance.

THREE CAME HOME (1950)

Director: Jean Negulesco
Screenplay: Nunnally Johnson from the book by Agnes Newton Keith
Cast: Claudette Colbert, Patric Knowles, Sessue Hayakawa, Mark Keuning, Howard Chuman
Oscars: None
DVD: Twentieth Century Fox

True story of Agnes Newton Keith, her husband, and son's detention in a Japanese prisoner of war camp during World War II. Based on Keith's 1947 best-selling book.

Film's treatment of femininity: Agnes is a Madonna, but not a home-front type. Instead, this is the story of a Madonna imprisoned by a cruel and heartless enemy.

TOMORROW NEVER DIES (1997)

Director: Roger Spottiswoode
Screenplay: Bruce Feirstein
Cast: Pierce Brosnan, Jonathan Pryce, Michelle Yeoh, Teri Hatcher, Gotz
    Otto, Judi Dench, Desmond Llewelyn
Oscars: None
DVD: MGM

Not a war film, this is the eighteenth iteration in the James Bond spy film series. This time, a crazed media mogul (a veiled caricature of Rupert Murdock) attempts to incite a war between the UK and China so that he can establish global media coverage.

Film's treatment of femininity: Teri Hatcher plays an old girlfriend, Paris Carver, now wife of villain Elliot Carver, with whom Bond reignites a relationship. But Carver (Jonathan Pryce) has her murdered. Bond then teams with Chinese superspy Wai Lin to defeat Carver's plans. While Hatcher, typical chattel, suffers the usual deadly penalty in these films for betraying the villain and sleeping with Bond, Wai Lin matches Bond nearly stunt for stunt in superspy antics. Michelle Yeoh's athletic performance greatly exceeds what the script allowed superspy Barbara Bach to do in *The Spy Who Loved Me* back in 1977.

TONIGHT WE RAID CALAIS (1943)

Director: John Brahm
Screenplay: Waldo Salt
Cast: Annabella, John Sutton, Lee J. Cobb, Beulah Bondi, Howard Da
    Silva
Oscars: None
DVD: Fox

French farmers, both men and women, assist a British commando in identifying a German munitions plant in occupied France. A woman named Odette, initially prejudiced against the British, witnesses Nazi treachery firsthand and joins in the resistance. Together with a group of French women, they set on fire their own wheat fields surrounding the munitions plant to light the way for an Allied bombing mission.

Film's treatment of femininity: Typical of many pictures set in occupied countries made during World War II, this shows women who are just trying to survive difficult circumstances giving up neutrality and sacrificing everything to achieve the final victory. These character arcs turn Madonnas into guerilla resistance fighters.

TOP GUN (1986)

Director: Tony Scott
Screenplay: Jim Cash, Jack Epps Jr.
Cast: Tom Cruise, Kelly McGillis, Val Kilmer, Anthony Edwards, Tom Skerritt, Meg Ryan
Oscars: Nominations for Film Editing, Sound, and Sound Effects Editing; Oscar for Best Song
DVD: Paramount

Suffering from an advanced case of testosterone poisoning, a group of Navy aviators train and compete at Miramar Naval Air Station at the Top Gun Naval Flying School. The best pilot in his class, nicknamed "Maverick," whose pilot father crashed in Vietnam under suspicious circumstances, has more to prove than the rest. Maverick's erratic but excellent flying record at the school and his chance to win the Top Gun trophy suffer a setback when "Goose," his "rear" (electronic warfare officer who sits in the seat behind the pilot) is killed in an accident. After graduation, once again flying off an aircraft carrier in the Indian Ocean, Maverick manages to put aside his grief over Goose's loss, distinguishing himself in actual aerial combat.

Film's treatment of femininity: Two women stand out in *Top Gun*. The first is a wife and mother who doubles as the life of the party who must suddenly deal with the death of her beloved husband, and a female aerial combat instructor who must fight for the respect of the flyers she teaches. She remains a frosty and committed GI Jane until she falls in love with Maverick. Then she gives up a promotion that goes with a new job in Washington to become a camp follower, staying with Maverick, who's been assigned instructor pilot duty at Miramar.

TO THE SHORES OF TRIPOLI (1942)

Director: H. Bruce Humberstone
Screenplay: Lamar Trotti
Cast: John Payne, Maureen O'Hara, Randolph Scott, Nancy Kelly, William Tracy
Oscars: Nominated for Best Color Cinematography
DVD: Fox

A new Marine recruit develops a crush on a U.S. Navy nurse, Mary. During the course of his training, the Marine tries a number of harebrained tactics in hopes of winning Mary over, but although she likes him, Mary is all Navy and all professional dedication and will not give in. The recruit has the chance to take a civilian job in Washington, but Mary's urging and good example coupled with the news that the Japanese have attacked Pearl Harbor convince him to remain in the Marines.

Film's treatment of femininity: Besides a stereotypical rich woman with too much time on her hands, the important female role is that of Mary, not only a Madonna nurse tottering precariously on the edge of her pedestal, but a woman whose example changes a man into a dedicated Marine.

TUNNEL RATS (2008)

Director: Uwe Boll
Screenplay: Uwe Boll from a Dan Clarke story
Cast: Michael Pare, Wilson Bethel, Adrian Collins, Scott Cooper, Mitch Eakins, Jane Le
Oscars: None
DVD: Vivendi Entertainment

Story of a platoon mostly assigned to ferret out Viet Cong in a maze of tunnels near their camp. Many claustrophobic scenes of men hunting other men in dark tunnels, trying to avoid booby traps and the possibility of the enemy waiting around every corner to attack.

Film's treatment of femininity: Shows that although the VC woman is a skilled and savage GI Jane, she is also a mother who will defend her children to the death.

VIETNAM WAR STORY EPISODE "THE PASS" (1987)

Director: Kevin Hooks
Screenplay: Patrick Sheane Duncan, Ronald Rubin
Cast: Tony Becker, Merritt Butrick, Hetty Edwards, Bill Nunn, Wendell Pierce
Oscars: None
DVD: HBO Home Video

This is an HBO miniseries episode that takes place in a sleazy bar/brothel in Vietnam. An REMF ("rear echelon motherfucker") misrepresents himself as a combat soldier as he and two combat soldiers spend an evening getting drunk, fighting, making up, and eventually singing songs. Unfortunately, this bar is frequented by Americans during the day and the Viet Cong at night. The soldiers don't obey the curfew and have to lie low when the VC arrive. Later, while trying to sneak out, they awaken the drunken enemy, and the REMF is killed.

Film's treatment of femininity: A "mama san," a tough businesswoman runs the bar and keeps the peace as best she can.

WARBIRDS (2008) MADE FOR TV

Director: Kevin Gendreau
Screenplay: Kevin Gendreau
Cast: Jamie Elle Mann, Brian Krause, Shauna Rappold, Lucy Faust, Caleb Michaelson
Oscars: None
DVD: Anchor Bay Entertainment

A World War II fantasy film in which a B-29 loaded with an A-bomb crash-lands on a Pacific island inhabited by thousands of flying dragons. The B-29 crew is made up of Women's Airforce Service Pilots (WASPs) commanded by an OSS colonel. Ordered to keep radio silence, they can expect no help as they fight off these savage dragons in their attempts to lift off from the island and deliver the bomb to Tinian, the base used by American airmen for their raids on Japan.

Film's treatment of femininity: The colonel in charge of the mission is a male chauvinist who initially resents having been assigned a female aircrew for such an important job. As the film goes on, however, he becomes more impressed with these tough, skilled GI Jane pilots.

THE WAR LOVER (1961)

Director: Philip Leacock
Screenplay: Howard Koch, based on the novel by John Hersey
Cast: Steve McQueen, Robert Wagner, Shirley Anne Field, Gary Cockrell, Michael Crawford
Oscars: None
DVD: Sony Pictures

Buzz Rickson is a great pilot who, despite taking chances while on World War II bombing missions over Germany, always brings his plane—and his admiring aircrew—back alive. But his exceptional flying ability is all Buzz has going for him. His egotism and abrasive personality assure that his only friends are the loose women he relentlessly pursues when he's off duty. He even tries to seduce his own copilot's girlfriend. Eventually, Buzz's luck runs out, and, returning from a mission, his bomber is too badly shot up to return to base. He orders all the crew to bail out and then tries his luck once more, but this time he goes down with his ship.

Film's treatment of femininity: There are a few barmaids who are insulted by Buzz, but the main chattel in Buzz's crosshairs is Daphne, whom Buzz considers an objective to conquer.

WE WERE SOLDIERS (2002)

Director: Randall Wallace
Screenplay: Randall Wallace, based on the book *We Were Soldiers Once . . . and Young* by Harold G. Moore and Joseph L. Galloway
Cast: Mel Gibson, Barry Pepper, Sam Elliott, Madeleine Stowe, Greg Kinnear, Chris Klein
Oscars: None
DVD: Paramount

Vietnam War story based on a book by Harold G. Moore and Joseph L. Galloway tells the story of the first major engagement between the North Vietnamese Army and the newly formed U.S. Army Air Cavalry. From time to time, the film cuts away to the home front, as the commander's wife and other officer's wives deal with comforting those whose husbands have been killed. Outnumbered five to one in a sector that became known as "the valley of death," the forces of the Air Cavalry—thanks to their cerebral commander's strategy and tactics and the great spirit of his men—overcome the enemy.

Film's treatment of femininity: While their men are in the middle of a bloody battle, Madonna wives are fighting the battle of the home front: dealing with running households without their men and in constant worry as the "death telegrams" from an unfeeling Department of the Air Force begin to arrive by taxi.

WHERE EAGLES DARE (1968)

Director: Brian Hutton
Screenplay: Alistair MacLean from his novel
Cast: Richard Burton, Clint Eastwood, Mary Ure, Patrick Wymark, Anton Diffring, Darren Nesbitt

Oscars: None
DVD: MGM

Story of a team of allied agents ostensibly trying to rescue an American general from a nearly impregnable German castle deep in enemy territory. Plenty of twists and turns in the plot, since some of the team and even the general are not who they appear to be.

Film's treatment of femininity: The two main female roles are shown to be seasoned intelligence professionals who infiltrate the castle, distract the enemy, and assist the team in completing the mission. These women do all the tasks required of the male intelligence operatives, proving their ability.

THE WIND AND THE LION (1975)

Director: John Milius
Screenplay: John Milius
Cast: Sean Connery, Candice Bergen, Brian Keith, John Huston, Steve Kanaly, Simon Harrison, Polly Gottesman
Oscars: Nominated for Best Original Music and Best Sound
DVD: Warners

An American woman, Eden Pedecaris, and her children are abducted from their home in Tangier, Morocco, by a Berber sheik who uses them as hostages in his political revolt against his uncle, the bashaw of Tangier. As in the plot of O. Henry's short story, "The Ransom of Red Chief," the sheik has no idea the kind of spunky woman he has kidnapped. She and the children cause him considerable trouble, but during their captivity, the Stockholm Syndrome develops, and both become attracted to and respectful of the other.

Film's treatment of femininity: Although born into an era in which women typically were chattel and knew their subordinate place, Eden Pedecaris is a true Hawksian woman. She becomes a handful for her abductor and, as Hawksian women do, complicates his plans considerably.

WINDTALKERS (2002)

Director: John Woo
Screenplay: John Rice, Joe Batteer
Cast: Nicolas Cage, Adam Beach, Peter Stormare, Roger Willie, Noah Emmerich, Mark Ruffalo, Christian Slater
Oscars: None
DVD: MGM

Decorated Marine Joe Enders suffers from hearing loss as well as posttraumatic shock after his stubborn refusal to disobey orders causes the death of his entire squad in the Allied campaign to take Guadalcanal during World War II. He fakes a hearing test so he can return to duty, presumably to atone for surviving. Enders's next assignment is to protect another Marine, a Native American "windtalker," who uses a coded version of the Navajo language to communicate during combat via radio to avoid the Japanese intercepting their messages. Still in pain over the orders that caused his men to die the last time, Enders is conflicted by his new orders, which include killing his Marine windtalker, rather than let him be captured and tortured for the code. This time, although at the cost of his life, Enders refuses to do his duty, sparing his windtalker's life when it looks like the Japanese are closing in.

Film's treatment of femininity: As in *Cross of Iron*, a nurse is in love with her patient, and is willing to do something illegal to help him. In *Cross*, it was to get him away from the war, but in this film, a nurse helps fake her man's medical test so he can get back to the war.

WING COMMANDER (1999)

Director: Chris Roberts
Screenplay: Kevin Droney
Cast: Freddie Prinze Jr., Saffron Burrows, Matthew Lillard, Jurgen Prochnow, Ginny Holder
Oscars: None
DVD: Fox

New fighter pilots full of bravado but no experience join the interstellar equivalent of an aircraft carrier, fighting on humanity's behalf against an aggressive race bent on their destruction. It's up to a female wing commander to harness the pilots' energy, testosterone, and daring to create a smoothly working fighting machine.

Film's treatment of femininity: As both fighter pilots and as a commander, women have equality, but fighting is clearly defined in macho male terms. To fit in and to earn respect, these GI Janes must set aside their femininity and act and talk like the men.

WINGS (1927)

Director: William Wellman
Screenplay: Hope Loring, Louis D. Lighton (Story: John Monk Saunders)

Cast: Buddy Rogers, Richard Arlen, Clara Bow, Jobyna Ralston, Gary Cooper, Roscoe Karns

Oscars: Oscars for Best Picture, Engineering Effects

DVD: None. VHS: Paramount

Winner of two Oscars, including Best Picture, *Wings* tells the story of two young Americans who leave their love lives behind in pursuit of glory in the skies as World War I fighter pilots. Unwilling to let her beau run away to war without her, Mary (Bow) signs up to be a nurse and follows her man to the front. The melodramatic story confirms that war is hell, air battles are final, and that in spite of goodness, not every hero comes home.

Film's treatment of femininity: A wealthy woman of loose morals out for adventure volunteers for canteen duty not far from the front. Although she goes where the men are, she's not the typical camp follower, trailing one man from post to post. She is more like a "vamp" (or "tramp") from this period in the movies; she refuses to settle for one man: she wants them all.

ZERO DARK THIRTY (2012)

Director: Kathryn Bigelow

Screenplay: Mark Boal

Cast: Jessica Chastain, Joel Edgerton, Chris Pratt, Jennifer Ehle, Kyle Chandler

Oscars: Nominations for Best Picture, Actress, Original Screenplay, and Film Editing; Oscar for Best Sound Editing

The story of a decade-long hunt to bring Osama bin Laden to justice, told through the experiences of a real-life, still-in-the-field CIA agent given the screen name of Maya. Butting heads with male section chiefs and top CIA and White House officials, Maya uses her amazing intellect to persuade her superiors that she's located the elusive al-Qaeda leader, and that if they don't act quickly, history will not treat them well for their caution.

Film's treatment of femininity: For all of their training, female CIA agents, no matter how qualified, are treated differently and with less respect by the male establishment. Female agents must adopt macho attitudes and vocabulary to hold their own against their own colleagues.

References

Basinger, Jeanine. 2007. *The Star Machine.* New York: Random House.
———. 1986. *The World War II Combat Film: Anatomy of a Genre.* New York: Columbia University Press.
———. 1993. *A Woman's View: How Hollywood Spoke to Women, 1930 – 1960.* Middletown, CT: Wesleyan University Press.
Benshoff, Harry, and Sean Griffin. 2009. *America on Film: Representing Race, Class, Gender and Sexuality in the Movies.* Malden, MA: Wiley Blackwell Publishers.
Bernstein, Barbara. 1977. "That's Not Brave, That's Just Stupid." In *Women and the Cinema: A Critical Anthology*, edited by Karen Kay and Gerald Peary. New York: E.P. Dutton.
Bourdeau, Annette. 2013. "The Best Lady Spies of Movies and TV." *Moviephone*, January 11, 2013. http://news.moviefone.ca/annette-bourdeau/best-female-spies-movies-tv_b_2457763.html.
Boxwell, David. 2002. "Howard Hawks." *Senses of Cinema.* http://sensesofcinema.com/2002/great-directors/hawks/.
Brackett, Leigh. 1977. "Working with Hawks." In *Women and the Cinema: A Critical Anthology*, edited by Karen Kay and Gerald Peary. New York: E.P. Dutton.
Chandler, Daniel. n.d. "Television and Gender Roles." Aberystwyth University MCS site: www.aber.ac.uk/media/Modules/MAinTV/gendertv.html.
Chayefsky, Paddy. 2000. *The Collected Works of Paddy Chayefsky, Vol. 1.* New York: Applause Books.
Cohen, J., and Weimann, G. 2000. "Cultivation Revisited: Some Genres Have Some Effects on Some Viewers." *Communication Reports*, 13 (2): 99.
Doherty, Thomas. 1993. *Projections of War: Hollywood, American Culture and World War II.* New York: Columbia University Press.
Donald, Ralph R., and Karen A. MacDonald, 2011. *Reel Men at War: Masculinity and the American War Film.* Lanham, MD: Scarecrow Press.
Farrell, William. 1976. "Women's Liberation as Men's Liberation." In *The Forty-Nine Percent Majority: The Male Sex Role*, edited by D. S. David and R. Brannon. Boston: Addison-Wesley.
Flamethrower Magazine. 2013. Unsigned article describing the Hawksian Woman. January 4. www.flamethrowermagazine.com/ " the-hawksian-woman"/.
Freeman, Jo, and Nancy Henley. 1994. "The Sexual Politics of Interpersonal Behavior." www.jofreeman.com/womensociety/personal.htm.
Grealis, Tom. 2003. Movie review, *Charlotte Gray. RTE ten.* www.rte.ie/ten/2002/0221/charlottegray.html.

Greer, Germaine. 2006. "Siren Song," *Guardian*, December 29. www.guardian.co.uk/film/2006/dec/30/film.

Hanson, R., and R. Mendius. 2009. *Buddha's Brain*. Oakland, CA: New Harbinger Publications.

Haskell, Molly. 1973. *From Reverence to Rape: The Treatment of Women in the Movies*. Chicago: University of Chicago Press.

———. 1997. *Holding My Own in No Man's Land: Women and Men and Film and Feminists*. New York and London: Oxford University Press.

Heath, Roderick. 2012. Review of the film *M*A*S*H*. *Wondersinthedark*, October 16. http://wondersinthedark.wordpress.com/212/10/16/49-mash/.

Henry, Monica. "Stand by Your Man." *Peace and Conflict Monitor*, April 2006. www.monitor.upeace.org/innerpg.cfm?id_article=359.

Homaday, Ann. 2010. "Action Figure: Angelina Jolie Is Out to Prove She's an Actress Worth Her 'Salt.'" *Washington Post*, July 22.

Jeffords, Susan. 1989. *The Remasculinization of America: Gender and the Vietnam War*. Bloomington: Indiana University Press.

———. 1990 "Reproducing Fathers: Gender and the Vietnam War in U.S Culture." In *From Hanoi to Hollywood: The Vietnam War in American Film*, edited by Linda Dittman and Gene Michaud. New Brunswick, NJ: Rutgers University Press.

———. 1995. "Friendly Civilians: Images of Women and the Feminization of the Audience in Vietnam War Films." In *Film Genre Reader IV*, edited by Barry Grant. Austin: University of Texas Press.

Kimmel, Michael S. 1987. "Rethinking Masculinity." Chap 1 in *Changing Men*. Newbury Park, CA: Sage.

Komisar, Lucy. 1976. "Violence and the Masculine Mystique." In *The Forty-Nine Percent Majority: The Male Sex Role*, edited by D. S. David and R. Brannon. Boston: Addison-Wesley.

Kreisman, Jerold, and Hal Straus. 1989. *I Hate You- Don't Leave Me*. New York: Avon Books.

Kuhn, Annette. 1982. *Women's Pictures: Feminism and Cinema*. London: Routledge and Kegan Paul.

Leed, Eric J. 1989. "Violence, Death and Masculinity." *Vietnam Generation* 1 (3–4): 168–89.

Levy, Emanuel. 2010. "*M.A.S.H.* (1970): Altman's Hit." *Emanuel Levy Cinema 24/7*. www.emanuellevy.com/review/mash-1970-40-years-ago-1/.

MacNab, Geoffrey. 1997. "Just Like a Man," *Independent*, January 15. www.independent.co.uk/arts-entertainment/just-like-a-man-1283227.html.

McBride, Joseph. 1982. *Hawks on Hawks*. Berkeley: University of California Press.

Miller, Andrew. 2007. "The Representation of Femininity in Contemporary Vietnam War Films." B.A. dissertation abstract, University of Portsmouth. http://eprints.port.ac.uk/302/.

Montalvan, Louis C. 2011. *Until Tuesday: A Wounded Warrior and the Golden Retriever Who Saved Him*. New York: Hyperion Press.

Sarup, Kamala. 2004. "War Increases Prostitution." Posted on *Strategy Page*. www.strategypage.com/militaryforums/93-5288.aspx#startofcomments.

Schickel, Richard. 1986. "Cinema: Help! They're Back!" *Time*, July 28.

Sotomayor, Sonia. 2013. TV interview on *Katie*. February 11. Video at http://katiecouric.com/videos/sonia-sotomayor-from-bronx-housing-projects-to-the-u-s-supreme-court/.

Spicuzza, Mary. 2001. "Butt-Kicking Babes." *Alternet*, March 26. www.alternet.org/story/10630/butt-kicking_babes.

Starlet, Charlotte. 2007. "Women in Action Movies: Empowered Role Models or Chicks with Guns?" *Helium*, May 9. www.helium.com/items/125634-women-in-action-movies-empowered-role-models-or-chicks-with-guns.

Stiehm, Judith Hicks. 1981. *Bring Me Men and Women: Mandated Change at the U.S. Air Force Academy*. Berkeley: University of California Press.

Summers, Harry D. 2003. "*M*A*S*H* (1970)." *The Truth About Nursing*. www.truthaboutnursing.org/media/films/mash.html.

Sussman, Herbert. 2012. *Masculine Identities: The History and Meanings of Manliness*. Santa Barbara, CA: Praeger Books.

Swofford, Anthony. 2003. *Jarhead: A Marine's Chronicle of the Gulf War and Other Battles.* New York: Scribners.

Tasker, Yvonne. 2011. *Soldiers' Stories: Military Women in Cinema and Television since World War II.* Durham, NC: Duke University Press.

Weatherford, Doris. n.d. "The Evolution of Nursing." Posted on the blogs section of the National Women's History Museum's website. www.nwhm.org/blog/the-evolution-of-nursing/

Whereeaglesdare.com. 2008. Interview with Ingrid Pitt. www.whereeaglesdare.com/movie/index.php?page=articles&id=12.

Wise, Naomi. 1996. "The Hawksian Woman." In *Howard Hawks: American Artist*, edited by Jim Hillier and Peter Wollen, 111–19. London: British Film Institute.

Zeisler, Andi. 2008. *Feminism and Pop Culture.* Berkeley, CA: Seal Press, 2008.

Index

About the Authors

Dr. Ralph Donald is a professor of mass communications at Southern Illinois University–Edwardsville. He has taught broadcasting, journalism, and film at the college level for forty years. Professional credits include jobs as a newspaper reporter and copy editor, a radio and television news producer, TV station production manager, and a writer-producer-director of commercials and documentaries on film and video. Dr. Donald's research and publications include gender-related research in film and television, film and television propaganda, motion picture history, American studies, and pedagogical and curriculum issues in mass communications.

Dr. Karen MacDonald, a clinical psychologist, has been in private practice for the better part of twenty-five years. Besides counseling returning veterans suffering from posttraumatic stress disorder, she provides clinical psychological services and conducts family therapy and group psychotherapy. Much of her focus has been in the areas of attention deficit disorder with hyperactivity, marital and conflict resolution, sexual trauma issues, and depression in children and adults. She has performed psychological evaluations for Missouri's Division of Family Services, attorneys, Head Start and school systems, Social Security Disability, and County Medical Assessment eligibility.

Dr. MacDonald and Dr. Donald, who are married, reside in Edwardsville, Illinois.